THE GREAT

75 YEARS

BRITISH RALLY

RAC TO RALLY GB – THE COMPLETE STORY

Rally Giants Series
Audi Quattro (Robson)
Austin Healey 100-6 & 3000 (Robson)
Fiat 131 Abarth (Robson)
Ford Escort MkI (Robson)
Ford Escort RS Cosworth & World Rally Car (Robson)
Ford Escort RS1800 (Robson)
Lancia Delta 4WD/Integrale (Robson)
Lancia Stratos (Robson)
Mini Cooper/Mini Cooper S (Robson)
Peugeot 205 T16 (Robson)
Saab 96 & V4 (Robson)
Subaru Impreza (Robson)
Toyota Celica GT4 (Robson)

WSC Giants
Audi R8 (Wagstaff)
Ferrari 312P & 312PB (Collins & McDonough)
Gulf-Mirage 1967 to 1982 (McDonough)
Matra Sports Cars – MS620, 630, 650, 660 & 670 – 1966 to 1974 (McDonough)

General
1½-litre GP Racing 1961-1965 (Whitelock)
AC Two-litre Saloons & Buckland Sportscars (Archibald)
Alfa Romeo 155/156/147 Competition Touring Cars (Collins)
Alfa Romeo Giulia Coupé GT & GTA (Tipler)
Alfa Romeo Montreal – The dream car that came true (Taylor)
Alfa Romeo Montreal – The Essential Companion (Classic Reprint of 500 copies) (Taylor)
Alfa Tipo 33 (McDonough & Collins)
Alpine & Renault – The Development of the Revolutionary Turbo F1 Car 1968 to 1979 (Smith)
Alpine & Renault – The Sports Prototypes 1963 to 1969 (Smith)
Alpine & Renault – The Sports Prototypes 1973 to 1978 (Smith)
An Austin Anthology (Stringer)
An Incredible Journey (Falls & Reisch)
Anatomy of the Classic Mini (Huthert & Ely)
Anatomy of the Works Minis (Moylan)
Armstrong-Siddeley (Smith)
Austin Cars 1948 to 1990 – A Pictorial History (Rowe)
Autodrome (Collins & Ireland)
Automotive A-Z, Lane's Dictionary of Automotive Terms (Lane)
Bahamas Speed Weeks, The (O'Neil)
Bentley Continental, Corniche and Azure (Bennett)
Bentley MkVI, Rolls-Royce Silver Wraith, Dawn & Cloud/Bentley R & S-Series (Nutland)
Bluebird CN7 (Stevens)
BMC Competitions Department Secrets (Turner, Chambers & Browning)
BMW 5-Series (Cranswick)
BMW Z-Cars (Taylor)
BMW Classic 5 Series 1972 to 2003 (Cranswick)
British at Indianapolis, The (Wagstaff)
British Cars, The Complete Catalogue of, 1895-1975 (Culshaw & Horrobin)
BRM – A Mechanic's Tale (Salmon)
BRM V16 (Ludvigsen)
Bugatti – The 8-cylinder Touring Cars 1920-34 (Price & Arbey)
Bugatti Type 40 (Price)
Bugatti 46/50 Updated Edition (Price & Arbey)
Bugatti T44 & T49 (Price & Arbey)
Bugatti 57 2nd Edition (Price)
Bugatti Type 57 Grand Prix – A Celebration (Tomlinson)
Carrera Panamericana, La (Tipler)
Chevrolet Corvette (Starkey)
Chrysler 300 – America's Most Powerful Car 2nd Edition (Ackerson)
Chrysler PT Cruiser (Ackerson)
Citroën DS (Bobbitt)
Classic British Car Electrical Systems (Astley)
Cobra – The Real Thing! (Legate)
Competition Car Aerodynamics 3rd Edition (McBeath)
Concept Cars, How to illustrate and design – New 2nd Edition (Dewey)
Cortina – Ford's Bestseller (Robson)
Cosworth – The Search for Power (6th edition) (Robson)
Coventry Climax Racing Engines (Hammill)
Daily Mirror 1970 World Cup Rally 40, The (Robson)
Daimler SP250 New Edition (Long)
Datsun Fairlady Roadster to 280ZX – The Z-Car Story (Long)
Dino – The V6 Ferrari (Long)
Dodge Challenger & Plymouth Barracuda (Grist)
Dodge Charger – Enduring Thunder (Ackerson)
Dodge Dynamite! (Grist)
Drive on the Wild Side, A – 20 Extreme Driving Adventures From Around the World (Weaver)
Dune Buggy Files (Hale)
Dune Buggy Handbook (Hale)
East German Motor Vehicles in Pictures (Suhr/Weinreich)
Essential Guide to Driving in Europe, The (Parish)
Fast Ladies – Female Racing Drivers 1888 to 1970 (Bouzanquet)
Fate of the Sleeping Beauties, The (op de Weegh/Hottendorff/op de Weegh)
Ferrari 288 GTO, The Book of the (Sackey)
Ferrari 333 SP (O'Neil)
Fiat & Abarth 124 Spider & Coupé (Tipler)
Fiat & Abarth 500 & 600 – 2nd Edition (Bobbitt)
Fiats, Great Small (Ward)
Ford Cleveland 335-Series V8 engine 1970 to 1982 – The Essential Source Book (Hammill)
Ford F100/F150 Pick-up 1948-1996 (Ackerson)
Ford F150 Pick-up 1997-2005 (Ackerson)
Ford Focus WRC (Robson)
Ford GT – Then, and Now (Streather)
Ford GT40 (Legate)
Ford Midsize Muscle – Fairlane, Torino & Ranchero (Cranswick)
Ford Model Y (Roberts)
Ford Mustang II & Pinto 1970 to 80 (Cranswick)
Ford Small Block V8 Racing Engines 1962-1970 – The Essential Source Book (Hammill)
Ford Thunderbird From 1954, The Book of the (Long)
Formula 1 - The Knowledge 2nd Edition (Hayhoe)
Formula One – The Real Score? (Harvey)
Formula 5000 Motor Racing, Back then ... and back now (Lawson)
Forza Minardi! (Vigar)
The Good, the Mad and the Ugly ... not to mention Jeremy Clarkson (Dron)
Grand Prix Ferrari – The Years of Enzo Ferrari's Power, 1948-1980 (Pritchard)
Grand Prix Ford – DFV-powered Formula 1 Cars (Robson)
GT – The World's Best GT Cars 1953-73 (Dawson)
Hillclimbing & Sprinting – The Essential Manual (Short & Wilkinson)
Honda NSX (Long)
Immortal Austin Seven (Morgan)
India - The Shimmering Dream (Reisch/ Falls (translator))
Intermeccanica – The Story of the Prancing Bull (McCredie & Reisner)
Jaguar - All the Cars (4th Edition) (Thorley)
Jaguar from the shop floor (Martin)
Jaguar E-type Factory and Private Competition Cars (Griffiths)
Jaguar, The Rise of (Price)
Jaguar XJ 220 – The Inside Story (Moreton)
Jaguar XJ-S, The Book of the (Long)
Jeep CJ (Ackerson)
Jeep Wrangler (Ackerson)
The Jowett Jupiter – The car that leaped to fame (Nankivell)
Karmann-Ghia Coupé & Convertible (Bobbitt)
Kris Meeke – Intercontinental Rally Challenge Champion (McBride)
Lamborghini Miura Bible, The (Sackey)
Lamborghini Murciélago, The book of the (Pathmanathan)
Lamborghini Urraco, The Book of the (Landsem)
Lambretta Bible, The (Davies)
Lancia 037 (Collins)
Lancia Delta HF Integrale (Blaettel & Wagner)
Lancia Delta Integrale (Collins)
Land Rover Design - 70 years of success (Hull)
Land Rover Emergency Vehicles (Taylor)
Land Rover Series III Reborn (Porter)
Land Rover, The Half-ton Military (Cook)
Land Rovers in British Military Service – coil sprung models 1970 to 2007 (Taylor)
Laverda Twins & Triples Bible 1968-1986 (Falloon)
Lea-Francis Story, The (Price)
Le Mans Panoramic (Ireland)
Lexus Story, The (Long)
Lola – The Illustrated History (1957-1977) (Starkey)
Lola – All the Sports Racing & Single-seater Racing Cars 1978-1997 (Starkey)
Lola T70 – The Racing History & Individual Chassis Record – 4th Edition (Starkey)
Lotus 18 Colin Chapman's U-turn (Whitelock)
Lotus 49 (Oliver)
Making a Morgan (Hensing)
Maserati 250F In Focus (Pritchard)
Mazda MX-5/Miata 1.6 Enthusiast's Workshop Manual (Grainger & Shoemark)
Mazda MX-5/Miata 1.8 Enthusiast's Workshop Manual (Grainger & Shoemark)
Mazda MX-5 Miata, The book of the – The 'Mk1' NA-series 1988 to 1997 (Long)
Mazda MX-5 Miata, The book of the – The 'Mk2' NB-series 1997 to 2004 (Long)
Mazda MX-5 Miata Roadster (Long)
Mazda Rotary-engined Cars (Cranswick)
Maximum Mini (Booij)
Mercedes-Benz SL – R230 series 2001 to 2011 (Long)
Mercedes-Benz SL – W113-series 1963-1971 (Long)
Mercedes-Benz SL & SLC – 107-series 1971-1989 (Long)
Mercedes-Benz SLK – R170 series 1996-2004 (Long)
Mercedes-Benz SLK – R171 series 2004-2011 (Long)
Mercedes-Benz W123-series – All models 1976 to 1986 (Long)
Mercedes G-Wagen (Long)
MG, Made in Abingdon (Frampton)
MGA (Price Williams)
MGB & MGB GT– Expert Guide (Auto-doc Series) (Williams)
MGB Electrical Systems Updated & Revised Edition (Astley)
MGB – The Illustrated History, Updated Fourth Edition (Wood & Burrell)
Mini Cooper – The Real Thing! (Tipler)
Mini Minor to Asia Minor (West)
Mitsubishi Lancer Evo, The Road Car & WRC Story (Long)
MOPAR Muscle – Barracuda, Dart & Valiant 1960-1980 (Cranswick)
Morgan Maverick (Lawrence)
Morgan 3 Wheeler – back to the future!, The (Dron)
Morris Minor, 70 Years on the Road (Newell)
Motor Racing – Reflections of a Lost Era (Carter)
Motor Racing – The Pursuit of Victory 1930-1962 (Carter)
Motor Racing – The Pursuit of Victory 1963-1972 (Wyatt/Sears)
Motor Racing Heroes – The Stories of 100 Greats (Newman)
MV Agusta Fours, The book of the classic (Falloon)
Nissan 300ZX & 350Z – The Z-Car Story (Long)
Nissan GT-R Supercar: Born to race (Gorodji)]
Nissan – The GTP & Group C Racecars 1984-1993 (Starkey)
Norton Commando Bible – All models 1968 to 1978 (Henshaw)
Nothing Runs – Misadventures in the Classic, Collectable & Exotic Car Biz (Slutsky)
Off-Road Giants! (Volume 1) – Heroes of 1960s Motorcycle Sport (Westlake)
Off-Road Giants! (Volume 2) – Heroes of 1960s Motorcycle Sport (Westlake)
Off-Road Giants! (Volume 3) – Heroes of 1960s Motorcycle Sport (Westlake)
Patina Volkswagens (Walker)
Peking to Paris 2007 (Young)
Pontiac Firebird – New 3rd Edition (Cranswick)
Porsche 356 (2nd Edition) (Long)
Porsche 908 (Födisch, Neßhöver, Roßbach, Schwarz & Roßbach)
Porsche 911 Carrera – The Last of the Evolution (Corlett)
Porsche 911R, RS & RSR, 4th Edition (Starkey)
Porsche 911, The Book of the (Long)
Porsche 911 – The Definitive History 2004-2012 (Long)
Porsche – The Racing 914s (Smith)
Porsche 911SC 'Super Carrera' – The Essential Companion (Streather)
Porsche 914 & 914-6: The Definitive History of the Road & Competition Cars (Long)
Porsche 924 (Long)
The Porsche 924 Carreras – evolution to excellence (Smith)
Porsche 928 (Long)
Porsche 930 to 935: The Turbo Porsches (Starkey)
Porsche 944 (Long)
Porsche 964, 993 & 996 Data Plate Code Breaker (Streather)
Porsche 993 'King Of Porsche' – The Essential Companion (Streather)
Porsche 996 'Supreme Porsche' – The Essential Companion (Streather)
Porsche 997 2004-2012 – Porsche Excellence (Streather)
Porsche Boxster – The 986 series 1996-2004 (Long)
Porsche Boxster & Cayman – The 987 series (2004-2013) (Long)
Porsche Racing Cars – 1953 to 1975 (Long)
Porsche Racing Cars – 1976 to 2005 (Long)
Porsche – The Rally Story (Meredith)
Porsche: Three Generations of Genius (Meredith)
Powered by Porsche (Smith)
Preston Tucker & Others (Linde)
RAC Rally Action! (Gardiner)
Rallye Sport Fords: The Inside Story (Moreton)
Roads with a View – England's greatest views and how to find them by road (Corfield)
Rolls-Royce Silver Shadow/Bentley T Series Corniche & Camargue – Revised & Enlarged Edition (Bobbitt)
Rolls-Royce Silver Spirit, Silver Spur & Bentley Mulsanne 2nd Edition (Bobbitt)
Rootes Cars of the 50s, 60s & 70s – Hillman, Humber, Singer, Sunbeam & Talbot, A Pictorial History (Rowe)
Rover Cars 1945 to 2005, A Pictorial History
Rover P4 (Bobbitt)
Runways & Racers (O'Neil)
Russian Motor Vehicles – Soviet Limousines 1930-2003 (Kelly)
Russian Motor Vehicles – The Czarist Period 1784 to 1917 (Kelly)
RX-7 – Mazda's Rotary Engine Sportscar (Updated & Revised New Edition) (Long)
Sauber-Mercedes – The Group C Racecars 1985-1991 (Starkey)
Schlumpf – The intrigue behind the most beautiful car collection in the world (Op de Weegh & Op de Weegh)
Singer Story: Cars, Commercial Vehicles, Bicycles & Motorcycle (Atkinson)
Sleeping Beauties USA – abandoned classic cars & trucks (Marek)
SM – Citroën's Maserati-engined Supercar (Long & Claverol)
Speedway – Auto racing's ghost tracks (Collins & Ireland)
Standard Motor Company, The Book of the (Robson)
Subaru Impreza: The Road Car And WRC Story (Long)
Supercar, How to Build your own (Thompson)
Tales from the Toolbox (Oliver)
Taxi! The Story of the 'London' Taxicab (Bobbitt)
This Day in Automotive History (Corey)
Toleman Story, The (Hilton)
Toyota Celica & Supra, The Book of Toyota's Sports Coupés (Long)
Toyota MR2 Coupés & Spyders (Long)
Triumph & Standard Cars 1945 to 1984 (Warrington)
Triumph Bonneville Bible (59-83) (Henshaw)
Triumph Bonneville!, Save the – The inside story of the Meriden Workers' Co-op (Rosamond)
Triumph Cars – The Complete Story (new 3rd edition) (Robson)
Triumph Motorcycles & the Meriden Factory (Hancox)
Triumph Speed Twin & Thunderbird Bible (Woolridge)
Triumph Tiger Cub Bible (Estall)
Triumph Trophy Bible (Woolridge)
Triumph TR6 (Kimberley)
Two Summers – The Mercedes-Benz W196R Racing Car (Ackerson)
TWR Story, The – Group A (Hughes & Scott)
Unraced (Collins)
Volkswagen Bus Book, The (Bobbitt)
Volkswagen Bus or Van to Camper, How to Convert (Porter)
Volkswagens of the World (Glen)
VW Beetle Cabriolet – The full story of the convertible Beetle (Bobbitt)
VW Beetle – The Car of the 20th Century (Copping)
VW Bus – 40 Years of Splitties, Bays & Wedges (Copping)
VW Bus Book, The (Bobbitt)
VW Golf: Five Generations of Fun (Copping & Cservenka)
VW – The Air-cooled Era (Copping)
VW T5 Camper Conversion Manual (Porter)
VW Campers (Copping)
Volkswagen Type 3, The book of the – Concept, Design, International Production Models & Development (Glen)
Volvo Estate, The (Hollebone)
You & Your Jaguar XK8/XKR – Buying, Enjoying, Maintaining, Modifying – New Edition (Thorley)
Wolseley Cars 1948 to 1975 (Rowe)
Works MGs, The (Allison & Browning)
Works Minis, The Last (Purves & Brenchley)
Works Rally Mechanic (Moylan)

WWW.VELOCE.CO.UK

First published in October 2019, this paperback edition published October 2020 by Veloce Publishing Limited, Veloce House, Parkway Farm Business Park, Middle Farm Way, Poundbury, Dorchester DT1 3AR, England.
Tel +44 (0)1305 260068 / Fax 01305 250479 / e-mail info@veloce.co.uk / web www.veloce.co.uk or www.velocebooks.com.
ISBN: 978-1-787117-36-5; UPC: 6-36847-01736-1.
 British Library Cataloguing in Publication Data – A catalogue record for this book is available from the British Library. Typesetting, design and page make-up all by Veloce Publishing Ltd on Apple Mac. Printed and bound by CPI Group (UK) Ltd, Croydon, CR0 4YY.

THE GREAT BRITISH RALLY

75 YEARS

RAC TO RALLY GB – THE COMPLETE STORY

VELOCE PUBLISHING
THE PUBLISHER OF FINE AUTOMOTIVE BOOKS

CONTENTS

DEDICATION

BY DAVID RICHARDS, CBE

The first time I ever saw a rally car was in the 1960s. I was a schoolboy standing at the side of a forest road with my three younger brothers, near our home in North Wales, watching the RAC Rally pass by. We stayed until the very last car, and, even though the cars looked grubby and their crews exhausted, it captured my imagination, and I've been an enthusiast ever since.

But how much has rallying – and myself, for that matter – changed since then? In the years which have passed, I have progressed from being an enthusiastic schoolboy spectator to a World Championship winning co-driver, and then manager of the Subaru World Rally Team.

Over a 20-year period we won numerous world titles with Colin McRae, Richard Burns and Petter Solberg.

Today I not only oversee on my own Prodrive business interests, which have expanded way beyond their original roots in motorsport, but I also have the honour of being the Chairman of Motorsport UK.

Rallying in Great Britain is a sport that has changed dramatically since the very first RAC Rally of 1932, and I am delighted to see that two of the sport's most diligent historians – Graham Robson and Martin Holmes – have finally got together to tell the complete story. It is important to recognise that neither has been just an observer of our

sport, as both have been active co-drivers at all levels ('works' teams and Championships all over the world), and both have been involved with Rally GB (as we must now call it) since the early 1960s. In fact they were probably competing in that first RAC Rally I remember as a schoolboy!

To my joy, I find that this is not just a book that shows exciting images of events in years gone by, along with the bald statement of the winners and their achievements, but it also digs deeply into the sporting trends, the changes in regulations, and the individual highlights which have kept us all enthralled with every year that passes.

I have enjoyed delving into the year-on-year stories, to remind myself of the events in which I competed in cars as varied as a Group 1 Triumph Dolomite Sprint and a Rothmans-sponsored Ford Escort. Reminding myself of the thrills (and spills!) of rallying with Ari Vatanen, and how my original Prodrive operation coped with the tempestuous period when Group B was banned, and we went on to develop World Rally Cars which still form the basis of the current technical regulations.

It's wonderful to re-live the years when I saw 'my' sport progress from Ford Escort domination to the age of the Audi Quattro, to the time when Lancia ruled the roost, and when my own Subaru team were winning in the 1990s. It's also good to remember so many old friends, Roger Clark, Hannu Mikkola, Colin McRae, Richard Burns, Carlos Sainz and Markku Alén, who all regularly took part in Britain's top event. Throughout these years Rally GB has gone from strength to strength, and has now become recognised as one the most professional and well organised rallies in the World Championship.

This book is due to be published immediately before the 75th running of this iconic event, which I'm sure will be just as exciting and competitive as when I was first attracted to the sport, as a young schoolboy stood by the side of the road all those years ago.

Like so many others I'll be at Rally GB again this year, watching from the side lines and wishing I was still taking part. However it's good to know that I can still re-live all my old exploits on the event as I read this wonderful book.

DAVID RICHARDS, CBE
CHAIRMAN OF MOTORSPORT UK

www.veloce.co.uk / www.velocebooks.com
All current books • New book news • Special offers • Gift vouchers

FOREWORD

The rally which every motoring enthusiast came to know as 'The RAC …' was founded in 1932, and rapidly became one of the most important events in the calendar. Not only did it move seamlessly from being 'National' to 'International', but it then joined the European scene, has been a World Rally Championship qualifier since 1973, and has changed its name several times along the way.

Both the authors – Martin Holmes and myself – have been closely involved in the event for many years, and have now taken this opportunity to write what – we hope – will be the full story of the event's development over the first 75 times it has been run. The difference between 'then' and 'now', of course, is vast, but the object of the exercise has always been the same. Quite simply, the challenge of the event is that brave young drivers, usually in cars bearing some relation to those which are being sold in the showrooms of the world, have set their skills against the roads, tracks and weather conditions of the United Kingdom, and against the time schedules and even the route-finding problems thrown at them by the organisers.

For many years the accent was not only on performance and driver skills, but on endurance, for until recent years, every event embraced roads, manoeuvring tests and other challenges in England, Wales and Scotland, often covering up to five days, and totally more than 2000 miles. Nor was this a leisurely tour of the nation, for it was only rarely that there was more than one mid-rally overnight rest halt, and on several occasions there was none at all.

Although I have been involved in the rally in so many ways – as spectator, competitor, reporter, researcher, press liaison man (for the organisers), sponsor's adviser, or even as a special stage commentator, radio or TV pundit – every year I am excited enough to want to be out there, watching the high-speed heroics of the superstars, and sometimes marvelling at the way they continue to drag battered and bruised cars around an event which had already tried to eliminate them completely.

For me, it all started when, as a schoolboy, I stood at a roadside in my native Yorkshire market town, marvelling at the way the rally cars

could look so dirty and careworn, though also being enthralled by the glamour they exuded as they swept past. It was not long before I got involved in the sport myself, soon found that I was far more competent as a co-driver than a driver, and finally reached the pinnacle of being enlisted in various 'works' team cars. It was in those years that I fell hopelessly in love with rallying, finding it much more appealing than trying to break into motor racing, for which my funds were certainly not sufficient.

It was in those years (not, admittedly, in the 1930s, when I was not yet around to see the fun …) that I saw how the event moved seamlessly from a social event with a few driving tests involved (the 1930s) to one where 'The Rally of the Tests' lived up to its name (1950s), to one where the event joined rallying's European mainstream by embracing the use of many special stages (1960s and thereafter).

The cars themselves progressed from being strictly 'showroom' (and there was a Concours side of the competition during the1930s) to being much modified, to being 'homologation specials' (1960s), then onwards to being specially developed FIA Groups 2, 3 and 4 of the 1970s. Not only that, but the modest 'works' teams of the 1930s and 1950s rapidly grew to be bigger, more professional, more enterprising, and more likely to inspire their bosses to develop increasingly more specialised products. Their progress was often only limited by the FIA's regulations, and by the need to have minimum numbers of cars built to satisfy them.

By 1980, therefore, 'The RAC' – which had become the 'Lombard-RAC' by this time – was about to change considerably. Not only was four-wheel-drive finally to be authorised, but a brand new set of regulations – embracing Groups N, A, and B – was to be imposed.

This, therefore, is the ideal point at which my co-author, Martin Holmes, should take up the story.

GRAHAM ROBSON

Rallying for me started on my first day at University. I was there to study Law, but before I opened my first textbook I met someone who changed my life. A fellow student arrived looking very scruffy, apologising for his appearance by saying he had come straight from competing in an all-night motor rally the other side of Britain. Suddenly in the late 1950s my world opened up much more than expected. Rallying gradually became a more integral part of my life. The RAC Rally – as the Rally GB used to be called – became a cherished annual pilgrimage, followed by me as a spectator, journalist and photographer.

It was only a matter of weeks before I became immersed in the world of time controls and the art of concentrating during sleepless nights, courtesy of the University's motor club. As soon as I started participating as a navigator and co-driver, I found rallying was a splendid chance to go to many new places increasingly at other people's expense! It was the activity where my love of cars and maps merged in most agreeable harmony. When I finally stopped regularly competing, the World Rally Championship had recently got off the ground, and I concentrated on following these events. I became the first person to have personally attended 500 WRC events.

The chance to work with Graham on his book was a wonderful opportunity, not only to learn a lot about rallying from the days before I became professionally involved, but also to dive into my double-storey garage to search through the files which I had kept from every event. And, maybe even more attractive for our publishing masters at Veloce, the opportunity to select suitable Rally GB pictures from among the hundreds of thousands of pictures at my home as part of the deal! Choosing suitable images for the book was not straightforward. Only in recent years has British rallying become a photogenic activity. In the early days it was largely run at night, when the cars were already muddy and competition numbers obscured. And taking pictures of cars in the forests is challenging in itself. One corner in a forest stage looks much like any other and most are very difficult to access.

From 1987 many of the selected images were taken by Maurice Selden, and I also had a lot of help from freelance photographers who worked with Martin Holmes Rallying on events. Digital photography provided rallying's burgeoning PR industry with the chance to provide copyright-free images to the media. With the move by Rally GB organisers to run daylight stages this has greatly elevated the pictorial opportunities, which we hope readers will enjoy. When selecting images for the book, I have been keen to show the ever-changing types of cars on our country's major rally as well as capturing the activities of the sport's top stars when they came to Britain.

The main thrust of my written work has been to help tell the story of the RAC Rally and Rally GB from 1981 to 2018, bringing us up to the 75th event in 2019. I still retain copies of all my original contemporary reports, which have unearthed situations long since lost in time. So many dramatic events had for me been forgotten – and many only became noteworthy many years later. During this period of time the pace of development in the sport has dramatically escalated. What is especially noticeable is that with every change in the sport, the style of reporting the events also kept developing and changing, as new reporting opportunities emerged. For example even as late as the early 1980s, the organisers did not publish the times of every competitor, or publish the overall positions after every stage. The digital results service provided immensely new opportunities, and at the same time many new aspects of the sport became important. Spurred on by the media, especially the TV media, the relevance of every event in the evolution of each season's championship chase became almost as important as the chase for victory at each event. In the current millennium, there has been a new emphasis on the emergence of the various support championships. I hope we have covered these changes in a way which explains how Rally GB, call it what you will, is a worthy bearer of the title of "The Great British Rally."

MARTIN HOLMES

WHERE IT ALL BEGAN

For all but a wealthy few, Britain was a miserable place to be at the end of 1931. In the previous two years the western world, triggered by the sudden and catastrophic economic crash in North America, had suffered a traumatic collapse in business confidence, international trade contracted sharply, there was general recession, and economic near disaster.

Britain's motor industry had suffered badly, with annual sales of new cars down to only 159,000 in the year, and only about a million cars on our roads. Not even the most jingoistic British publications –

such as *The Times* and *The Daily Telegraph* could lift the public mood. Motoring for sport and for competition, therefore, was at a very low ebb, with Brooklands as the only permanent British race circuit, while rallying was a very rare occupation, a rather gentle hobby with entries really restricted only to the prosperous. The only bright spot on the horizon, it seemed, was that the country's much-hated 20mph overall speed limit had recently been abandoned.

Suddenly, it seemed, influential enthusiasts like 'Sammy' Davis of Britain's most prominent motoring magazine, *The Autocar*, set out

In 1900, many years before the RAC Rally was first promoted, the Automobile Club of Great Britain and Ireland organised the 1000 Miles trial, which was a competitive tour of the nation. 65 cars started, but only 23 finished.

to change the public mood. Backed behind the scenes by the Royal Automobile Club, on 20 November 1931 the magazine published this Editorial:

By the late 1920s, rallies in Britain were mainly gentle road tours with driving tests to enliven the finish, and there was no attempt to impose high speeds, or arduous conditions, on the competitors. This was F F Austin's Morris Cowley, which won the Southport rally in 1928.

A RALLY AT HOME?
Combining Sport with National Economy

FOR many years past one of the most popular of the annual international motoring fixtures has been the Monte Carlo Rally. Quite a number of British competitors have taken part, with no little credit to themselves and to their cars, and the whole affair has provided good British propaganda on the Continent. In the present economic emergency, however, we have to consider whether or not the results, from the point of view of increasing the demand for our productions abroad, justify the very considerable sums of money that British participants spend in France and Monaco.

Frankly, we think that, however sporting a trip the great rally may have been, it was only worthy of support so long as the pound sterling was valued in France at about 124 francs. Recent events have put a very different complexion on the subject. A request not to spend money abroad has been issued to the nation, and the appeal applies to motorists just as much as to other travellers. Is there, then, no way in which the fun of the Monte Carlo Rally can be enjoyed without doing anything which is deprecated by the Government?

The Value of a Rally The answer, we think, is in the affirmative. A rally is good for trade, and a rally should be held and widely supported; but why not keep the course within the boundaries of our own country? This subject was discussed at the Scottish Motor Show last week, and it was considered that a very attractive rally at home could be organised. Several of our South Coast resorts would be suitable as rallying points—Torquay was one which was favoured—and the starting points could be any towns in England, Scotland, Wales, or Northern Ireland, marks being given for distance covered, just as is the case in the Monte Carlo Rally.

If, in addition to the rally proper, there were to be a *concours d'élégance*, the appeal of the event would be widened, and it might be decided that the cars should be sent over a supplementary reliability course on Dartmoor. The idea is well worthy of serious debate.

… and sat back to await reaction.

This column, that insisted "The idea is well worthy of serious debate" was well received, and letters and phone calls began to pour in, both to the magazine, and to the RAC itself. Only a week later, in *The Autocar*'s 'Disconnected Jottings,' the gossip columnist had this to say:

"The idea of holding a rally in England on the lines of the popular Monte Carlo affair is quite a good one … At the moment a wave of

patriotism is sweeping the country, and people in all classes are making sacrifices to the country's good, so it is quite possible that an English rally may be regarded as a gesture on the part of those who would go to Monte Carlo were conditions happier …

"An English Rally, for its first year at all events, could not aspire to be more than a jolly all-British affair, and I am sure there are few Englishmen who will be so insular as to imagine that it can leap into instant fame as a rival to the Monaco rally. Britain cannot afford to keep out of International events …"

A two page feature, entitled 'A British Rally,' immediately followed this, with many telling extracts of messages from the motoring public, and – significantly – from F P Armstrong, who was the secretary of the RAC organisation itself:

"I write to confirm the opinion … that the RAC would gladly give its support to the scheme and undertake the organisation of the competition …"

Even at this point, it was clear that if the Monte Carlo Rally habitually ended up on the French Riviera, then a British event should aim to conclude on the 'English Riviera', which explains why, on the nod, wink, and nudging shoulder process, the town of Torquay was soon mentioned. Within days, it seems, an *Autocar* staff member (probably H S Linfield, who was known to be a West Country addict) had visited the local Council, put the growing consensus to local officials, led by the Mayor, Councillor Callard, and found that: "All these gentlemen expressed the warmest appreciation of the proposal, and promised the utmost assistance that they could offer."

Things then progressed so rapidly that it was only two weeks later, in its issue of 4 December 1931, that *The Autocar*'s main Editorial confirmed that a national rally, backed by the Royal Automobile Club, would indeed be held early in 1932:

THE RALLY APPROVED
Concerning the Route, Regulations, and Date

WHEN we suggested, in *The Autocar* of November 20th, the organisation in this country of a big motor rally, more or less on the lines of the famous Monte Carlo event, we scarcely ventured to hope that the idea would receive in so many quarters so warm a welcome as has, in fact, been accorded it. Not only has the proposal appealed to keen competition drivers of both sexes, but it has aroused great interest among car owners who, while they enjoy a spice of competitive flavour in their motoring, as a rule abstain from participation in the bigger events on the ground that their experience is insufficient to justify them in pitting themselves against drivers of international repute.

The general character of the appeal made by a rally at home makes it all the more imperative that this British event should not be "above the head" of the normal motoring family man. This point will, we are sure, not escape the attention of the R.A.C.'s sub-committee which has been set up to draft the rules and regulations. If it is to prove the success that we all hope, the ordinary private car owner must be catered for. This need not mean that the event is designed as a mere gentle amble to the final rallying point, but it does presuppose that the route and the time schedule will not be so exacting that only the hardiest and most experienced competition drivers will have a reasonable chance of coming through with success.

Big Entry Essential for Success — We emphasise this aspect of the affair because already there are signs that some, at least, of the "international trial brigade" are anxious to see the rally develop into a very grim struggle indeed. They must bear in mind that a really big entry is necessary if this venture, which may well become an annual event, is to be launched to the best advantage, and that, on this occasion at any rate, we shall, in all probability, not receive many entries from overseas. Hence the need that the rally shall appeal to the motorist of average skill and physical endurance.

We wish to make it quite clear that the British Rally is in no way intended as an "attack" on the Monte Carlo event. British prestige abroad owes much to the sweeping successes of British competitors in that great trial, and we hope, most sincerely, that British cars and drivers will participate in it as successfully in 1932 as they have done in years gone by. In determining the date of the British Rally we are confident that due regard will be paid to the needs of those who desire to take part in both events.

At that time, the choice of Torquay as the rallying point was not yet confirmed, nor was the overall mileage of the event finalised, but it was clear that there would be a big entry for this pioneering British rally. Even so, the flag dropped on the start a mere three months after the running of this major enterprise was first suggested.

And that was all of 88 years ago …

DRIVING TESTS AND CONCOURS

It was almost inevitable that once the decision had been taken to run an RAC Rally in 1932, it should evolve in a totally traditional and familiar way, as Great Britain, and almost every aspect of the lives of its inhabitants, was a very smug place to be in the 1930s. Almost everything in people's lives was arranged in the same way that it had always been, and evolved very slowly. Accordingly, this meant that the layout of the new RAC Rally would rely on what was already familiar in British motorsport as it was perceived at the time.

A small group of sporting enthusiasts (usually financially secure, and often quite interested in the world outside the UK) knew about events like the Monte Carlo Rally, and, to some degree, the Austrian and French Alpine events, but by British standards these were altogether more demanding, were often run off in winter or hot-and-high summer conditions. Not only that (and this was difficult to accept for most UK drivers) they involved a great deal of fast driving!

So, the RAC club organisers decided to go ahead on a familiar basis which, they thought, would attract a large (and lucrative!) entry, where many of the drivers wouldn't seriously expect to win anything, but might enjoy a bit of adventure, a long drive around parts of the UK they might not know well, would be happy to tackle just a few manoeuvring tests to sort out a result, and would also look forward with great pleasure to some socialising and a smart white-tie dinner and party afterwards.

Perhaps the RAC might have chosen a different time of the year to run its event in the 1930s, but the choice of spring-like jaunts was made not only to give rallyists an alternative to tackling the Monte Carlo Rally (January), but also to find a suitable seaside resort, with many hotels, and desire for out-of-season business, which could welcome more than a thousand people all at once! It was this sort of reasoning that led to the RAC merely granting the event a national permit throughout the 1930s, which meant that overseas licence holders and rally enthusiasts would not be allowed to enter. Not that this seemed to deter any of the bigger European 'names,' who could recognise a rather milk-and-water event when they saw one …

There was also the decision to include a major, important, and prestigious concours d' elegance competition at the close of the event: the important regulation in this case being that no matter how elegant, rare, and even exotic a car might be, to take part in the concours it would first have to complete the road section *and* the driving tests of the event itself. After arrival at the close of the road sections and the manoeuvring tests, every competitor would have up to 24 hours to re-prepare the cars for judging – with some of them bringing a team of staff and helpers to do that for them.

Even though this generation of concours was always seen to be a rather unrelated 'add-on' to what, after all, was a long-distance driving event, it would be retained for every RAC Rally held in the 1930s, and always attracted a good, sometimes outstanding, selection of elegant motor cars. It was those cars which tended to be entered and driven by ambitious or high-end motor traders, social climbers, or even the occasional member of the aristocracy and nobility, though they rarely figured in the overall results of the rally itself.

Almost without exception, the road sections of the rallies proved to be long, tedious, and event free, the principal hazard being for the crew to get enough (mobile) rest while one of them kept flogging on from remote RAC hotel to remote RAC hotel. The open-road target average speeds were set so low as to make lateness penalties unlikely, and many entrants often managed to get a few hours sleep in the furthest flung hotels along the way.

Assuming that they would reach the rallying point without penalty, and with a still-healthy car, the competitors would then have to face up to a tiny handful of manoeuvring tests, where the object was in precision – stopping, starting, into and out of boxes, and braking tests after crossing a line were all familiar to the devotees – and there was often just one sprint, to allow the truly fast cars to exercise their acceleration.

As to the awards- one is reminded of the *Alice's Adventures in Wonderland* situation, where "Everybody has won, and all must have prizes" seemed to apply, through a multitude of classes and sub-divisions. It was for this reason, no doubt, why individuals were certainly allowed to win their classes, but under no circumstances was an outright winner ever announced. This tradition, indeed, would be continued for two years after World War Two, where the RAC Rally victors were still pronounced 'unofficial' at first!

If all this sounds rather pusillanimous, then that was indeed so, for the RAC seemed determined to make sure every competitor had a good time, and as many as possible should go away with a happy memory. In addition, this allowed many manufacturers to trumpet their cars' successes in post-event advertising. All in all, it seems, at this time the formula was extremely popular, for entries of between 250 and 350 were regularly achieved, so that drivers could enjoy their two-day trundle to (they hoped) some winter sunshine in an out-of-season resort.

It would all be very different in postwar years.

Rallying in the 1930s – leisure motoring, gentle competition

Looking back so many years, it is still difficult to understand quite why the RAC Rally caused such a stir on the motoring scene when it was first promoted in the 1930s. Until, that is, one realises how restricted the hobby was at that time. At that time there was some motor racing – mostly held at the Brooklands circuit in South West London (the UK's only permanent circuit) – a smattering of long-distance trials (such as the Exeter and Lands End), and a series of strictly local sprints, hill-climbs, and driving test meetings – but virtually no rallying of any kind.

The records show that in the UK in 1931, the 'man in the street' – or rather, the well-to-do man in the street – was very ill-served by road events of any sort, and if he was really insistent on competing in that sort of event he had to travel across the Channel, to tackle the Monte Carlo Rally, or one of a tiny handful of similar events.

As has already been made clear in the introductory section, it was the state of the British economy which had an influence on the birth of the event. One therefore should recall that it was still only 12 years after the end of the First World War, that most of the developing world had been hit hard by the onset of the Great Depression, which originally struck – in the USA – in 1929, and that a massive slump in trade, in business confidence, and in jobs had swept across Europe.

Britain's motor industry, which had expanded so mightily during the 1920s, had fallen away dramatically in 1930 and 1931, and although the first signs of a recovery were just becoming evident, there simply did not seem to be the money for motorists to throw around to indulge in overseas escapades like the Monte Carlo Rally.

At this time there were still only about one million cars on British roads, and the majority of working people just could not afford to buy a motor car of any description. Although tiny models such as the Austin Seven and the Morris Minor were already on the market (they were about to be joined by the original Ford Eight Model Y),

it was cars in what we might describe as the RAC 'Ten' and 'Twelve' horsepower market which appealed to the middle-classes, while the more prosperous classes (doctors, solicitors, bank managers, company owners, etc) tended to buy Rileys, Rovers, Armstrong-Siddeleys and the like.

Those of more substantial and independent means often bought sporting cars, or glossy machines in the Bentley, Daimler and Rolls-Royce category. Even so, the sports car sector (mainly covered by MG, Riley and Singer) was only a tiny part of the overall scene. Private motoring, in other words, was still very much of a middle-class and upper-class occupation, which was nevertheless well covered by the motor trade, and it is surely no coincidence that many of the well-known characters involved in British motorsport at the time were also in the motor trade as garage owners.

H J Gould's Lagonda and Miss Caulfield's AC passing the finish banner at the end of the Torquay road section in 1932.

It was for them that the original layout of RAC Rallies was developed – one in which privately-owned cars could be dusted down, equipped with a modicum of winter equipment, and subjected to a long road run, which was not likely to do them any harm unless unreliability struck. The challenge, therefore, was first of all to complete about 1000 non-stop miles, but since there ought to be some semblance of competition at the end of the event to sort out 'winners' from 'losers,' some additional tests were arranged. Such a format was rather like that of the Monte Carlo Rally, but on a more modest and less glamorous scale.

In March 1932 there were to be no time controls between the chosen starting point, and arrival in Torquay, and with a required overall average speed of only 22mph (for cars with engines of up to 1100cc), and 25mph for larger-engined cars, the actual open-road motoring could seem interminable.

Consider, for instance, that in that year the first car left the London start control (the Rootes Service Station in St John's Wood) at 12:30pm on 1 March, and that his arrival in Torquay was timed for 10:05am on 3 March. Along the way, however, he had to report at Passage Controls at the Majestic Hotel in Harrogate, then carry on to the North British Hotel in Edinburgh, then return south via the Palace Hotel in Buxton and the University Arms in Cambridge, before making for the West Country and the 'English Riviera.'

Although there was no specific route laid down for those cars to follow, there were, of course, no motorways or dual carriageways to ease the pain. A detailed study of the times suggested that the crews might get a short night's rest in Edinburgh, and then in Cambridge – but along the way there was always going to be the problem of getting comfortable in the rally car itself (cars were both smaller, and less well sprung in those days), and coming to terms with the fact that no production car was yet on the market with a built-in heater!

This, therefore, was the driving format of the original 1932 event, and one which would not be changed, except in detail, throughout the 1930s. The other, and more controversial, factor was that the RAC refused to nominate an outright winner of the event in this period, and was never really willing to say why this should be so. The only obvious reason, it seems, is that it gave every opportunity for many different cars, in different classes, to win something, and to be able to advertise their successes afterwards. For them, and in many cases for the trade that was supporting them, this was important.

Would this all have been about to change in the 1940s? We would have to wait until 1951 to find out.

1932: The first-ever RAC Rally

Organised at extremely short notice, the very first RAC Rally was run in March 1932, with a massive contingent of cars arriving in Torquay, from no fewer than nine widely-scattered starting points around England. Each and every competitor had completed more than 1000 miles, without any scheduled rest, without any stops at compulsory time controls – and with no competitive motoring along the way.

The format, which was to persist throughout the 1930s, was that there would be no competition, as such, for the entrants until after they had reached the rallying point, had a good night's rest there, and be ready for a series of tests on the promenade of the chosen resort. Purely as an example, therefore, a competitor who chose to start from London would have to find his own way to visit Passage Controls at major hotels in Harrogate, Edinburgh, Buxton and Cambridge, before making his weary way across country to reach Torquay. From Newcastle-on-Tyne, on the other hand, he would have to visit Cambridge, then Chester, Eastbourne and Droitwich.

Until he reached Torquay, no times of reporting at those controls were recorded. There was no provision for anyone to arrive hours early at Torquay (there would be penalties, even).

A quick calculation shows that a team in – say – a Riley 9 would have to be en route for more than 45 hours, though if they bustled along on England's mainly empty roads of the period, they might average – say – 30mph, and only need to be on the move for 33 hours. Many professional crews did just that, and arranged to have a series of cat-naps, in hotels or at check points, along the way! By the health-and-safety obsessed standards of today, this may now sound like a criminally insane way of arranging an open-road, long-distance event, but as the Monte Carlo Rally was already making similar demands on rally drivers, usually in worse weather conditions, there was no resistance.

All this, of course, was merely a preliminary, a warm-up as it were, to the driving tests which were laid out on the Torbay Road Promenade, immediately next to the harbour. In 1932, a mere three tests were laid out, end to end, to sort out a result – this being an arrangement which would be repeated for other events later in the 1930s. In 1932, the opening test was the one which caused so much controversy that it was hastily abandoned for future events, for a competing car had to be driven as *slowly* as possible (but always non-stop) for 100 yards, followed immediately by a 100 yard acceleration test, followed by a brake test. The wrinkle here, of course, was that the longer it took for a car to complete the 'slow-driving' test, the higher the marks it would gain …

There had been so much interest in this pioneering event that there were no fewer than 367 entries, of which 342 cars actually started, and many of those drivers were either in works prepared cars, or were given substantial support by their makers. Many of Britain's most notable racing drivers, rally drivers, and motor traders were all involved, together with a smattering of those from the aristocracy. Prominent among all these were Donald Healey, Sir Henry ('Tim') Birkin, Lord Howe, the Earl of March, various members of the Riley (car-manufacturing) family, several Siddeleys, and George Lanchester.

As far as the motor traders (and even some of the manufacturers) were concerned, the running of a concours/coachwork competition on the day *after* the sporting side was over, was thought to be very important, and this aspect of the 'competition' survived until 1939 – but was not revived in the more seriously competitive events which commenced once again in 1951.

Kathleen, Countess of Drogheda in her SS1 on the brake test in Torquay in 1932.

The Hon Cyril Siddeley, one of the family which controlled the Armstrong-Siddeley marque, entered one of his own products in the 1932 rally, used it very competently, and finished ninth overall.

Although it was not made plain or obvious, at the time, neither in the press reports, nor around the event itself while it was in progress, some of the 'personality' entrants did not tackle the special tests themselves, but had 'drivers' to do it for them. Although the winner's 'man' has not been recorded for posterity, it is known that the second-placed Daimler entered by J Mercer was actually driven by a mechanic/fitter called 'Lofty' England, who would go on to become one of Jaguar's most revered personalities in later years.

The road sections themselves could be best described as 'long' or 'tedious,' the crews then spent most of their time in bed, rather than attending the various functions laid on by the Torbay local authority, before the sporting activities got under way on the promenade on the Friday morning. Well beforehand, it had become clear that the slow-driving part of the test would probably sort the sheep from the goats, and the truly 'dedicated' competitors made haste to prepare cars which had extremely flexible engines, backed by transmissions of the fluid flywheel variety (at this point in history, no fully automatic transmissions had yet been marketed), which would allow the machinery to truly crawl over the 100 yards: to make sure that there was no cheating as to how this was to be achieved (and all manner of enterprising details were proposed), the RAC put a neutral observer into each car as it went through its paces.

As it unfolded, all the forecasts regarding the slow-driving test were justified, for the marks gained by going slowly far exceeded those gained by sprinting over the next 100 yards or braking hard to a stop thereafter. The fact that Donald Healey's Invicta (the type of sports

The very first RAC of 1932 featured a slow-driving test on the seafront at Torquay, which was won by Col A H Loughborough's 15/18hp Lanchester. Fluid-drive transmission was a feature!

car in which he had won the Monte Carlo Rally only a year earlier) was significantly faster than anyone else, was of no avail, if only because his car was more than two minutes 'faster' (yes, faster) than the eventual winner on the slow-driving sector.

There was, it seems, no answer to the performance of the fluid transmission brigade. As was once written, after the event: "Best, by quite a margin, was Col A H Loughborough [though – as already suggested, the driving was actually being done for him …], in a large and ponderous Lanchester 15/18, who loitered over the 100 yards for no less than 5min 7.8sec – 40 seconds longer than his nearest rival, J Mercer, who was in a Daimler Double Six 30/40 Limousine. The Colonel's performance was quite sensational – it represented an average speed of 1170 yards an hour, or 0.66mph – and led one wag to suggest that it was going to take so long to complete that Torquay might as well make it an Easter attraction, several weeks hence."

The fact that the staid and upright Lanchester then took only 8.6 seconds for the 100 yard sprint (a mere second slower than Healey's Invicta) must surely have meant that it was a rather specially-tuned example.

Loughborough's and Mercer's performances were so outstanding, incidentally, because only six more competitors took more than three minutes, with a further seven cars recording more than two minutes. Healey's Invicta, incidentally, recorded 2min 59.4 seconds …

And so it was that the RAC's first attempt to run a nationwide rally, conceived, organised and run in a mere three months, was acclaimed as a success – but that significant changes could be made to improve on it for 1933.

RESULTS

Event held: 1 March to 4 March. Nine starting points: Bath, Buxton, Edinburgh, Harrogate, Leamington, Liverpool, London, Newcastle-on-Tyne and Norwich. Finishing/rallying point at Torquay.

341 starters, 311 finishers.
Four driving tests.

There was no outright winner, but awards were made in two different capacity classes:

Class		Total marks (all tests)
Class 1: Cars over 1100cc		
1 Col A H Loughborough	Lanchester 15/18	315.00
2 J Mercer	Daimler Double Six 30/40	303.37
3 G F Dennison	Riley 14hp.	301.47
Class 2: Cars up to 1100cc		
1 V E Leverett	Riley 9	291.31
2 R St G Riley	Riley 9	288.17
3 G H Strong	Standard 9	285.29

Team Prize: MCC D-Team (Col A H Loughborough, D Healey and R Way).
Ladies Prize: Class 1 Lagonda (Lady de Clifford), Class 2 Riley (Mrs M M Riley).

SPEED LIMITS

Throughout the life of the rally of Great Britain, the oft-differing question of obeying public-highway speed limits, has coloured the layout, and severity, of the event.

From 1903 until the end of 1930, public roads were subject to an overall speed limit of 20mph – whether in the centre of busy towns and cities, or in the most remote parts of the countryside. This limit was much criticised, and virtually ignored by the general public. In due course, when the maximum speed of current road cars, such as the Bentleys of the day, had risen to around 100mph, the limit was abolished.

Before this abolishment, it would have been impossible for the law-abiding Royal Automobile Club to set reasonably demanding average speeds for the long road sections of its rally. However, from 1932 it was legally acceptable for a 25mph average to be imposed – and, of course, rally cars could go through any built-up area at any speed they considered to be safe and proper.

The next change to the law came in March 1935 – just before the running of the RAC Rally of that year – when a speed limit of 30mph was imposed in built-up areas, though there was still no out-of-town limit to be obeyed.

(No further imposition of open-road speed limits was made until December 1965, when a 70mph limit was imposed, originally for an 'experimental period,' but soon made permanent. This occurred, therefore, after the running of the 1965 RAC Rally, but no changes to future events were ever thought necessary.)

1933: Growing pains, but fewer gimmicks

Although the original event of 1932 had been hailed a great success, no-one suggested that it been perfect, and many suggestions (some of them unworkable) were suggested for the future. Even so, major features such as the big choice of 1000-mile road runs to the rallying point, and the use of an out-of-season seaside resort to host the final driving tests, had been well liked, and were retained for 1933.

It was probably no more than a case of 'Buggins' Turn' which saw Hastings chosen as the rallying point (the event would return to Torquay in 1936), and no fewer than nine starting points were available, one of them a long way north, in Glasgow.

As far as the competition was concerned, the major change was that the entry was now to be split into three classes – up to 10hp, 10hp to 16hp, and over 16hp (all these ratings being calculated by the much-disliked RAC/taxation calculation) – and the overall set average speeds were to be 22mph, 24mph, and 26mph, respectively.

At the close of the event, to be held on the seafront of this town,

or on a steep hill within the town itself, there were to be three tests – a slow-running test (but not as severe as in 1932), an acceleration/braking test on the flat, and a final acceleration/braking test up a 1-in-6 road between houses in the town itself.

As in 1932, the road runs, which were mainly afflicted by wet weather, were tedious, but necessary to make this even a mild facsimile of the famous Monte Carlo Rally. London starters, for instance, had to reach Hastings via Liverpool, Edinburgh, Scarborough and Gloucester, while those starting from Leamington had to drive by way of Harrogate, Edinburgh, Chester and Torquay! On this (and future) occasions, cars had to clock in at those four intermediate points at particular times, but it was still a very relaxed schedule. Even so, no fewer than 340 crews set out, with almost all of them reaching Hastings without penalty.

The controversy which followed the 1932 event, where Col Loughborough's fluid-flywheel-equipped Lanchester had spent more than five minutes crawling along a 100-yard 'slow-driving' test had certainly borne fruit, for although there was still a 'slow-driving' test in the latest event, it was a much less demanding proposition. All crews had to present their cars in top gear (there were RAC observers aboard to ensure that no cheating took place …), and were challenged to complete a 50 yard test on the seafront, from a rolling start, in not less than 25 seconds.

In round figures, this meant that each car was challenged to chug along *in top gear* at less than 5mph, without the aid of a slipping clutch. To quote *The Autocar*, who followed this pantomime with great interest:

Conditions on the seafront at Hastings for the 1933 RAC Rally were persistently wet, and the road surface could best be described as slippery. This was T D W Weston's Rover Speed 20 tackling one of the manoeuvring tests.

"Healey's Invicta succeeded by fine handing, Anthony's Aston-Martin also. To the fluid-flywheel Daimlers and Lanchesters this was child's play, the big cars gliding along with not a sound save the definite, regular, slow beat of their engines. On the other hand, havoc was wrought among the majority ... The list of those losing marks is immensely long ...and in all 118 competitors were penalised, including the ultimate winner [T D W Weston] of the big class."

Some sanity was then restored by the immediate need to complete a 'start, accelerate, stop astride a line, accelerate again ...' test – one made especially challenging because the road surface was wet, though not slippery. Predictably the largest-engined cars (harried by Rover technical chief Maurice Wilks' Rover) were fastest of all, setting times in the 19-second bracket, but no-one else could match these six experts. Weston, incidentally, was the manager of Rover's London Service Station, which gives us an idea of the way that the motor trade was embracing this event.

The final challenge, one which brought out the best in the very best, but humiliated many others, was for them to tackle a go-stop-go test up a steep street in the town, one which: "officials said was 1-in-6, and the competitors alleged to be anything between 1-in-2 and 1-in-4..." It was

here that only Donald Healey and Weston set times better than eight seconds, with almost everyone else significantly behind, but there was one exceptional performance in Class 2 where Kitty Brunell urged her AC Ace tourer up the hill in 8.4 seconds.

Although there was no official General Classification, it was clear that all three class winners had put up tremendous performances, particularly in the way that Weston had defeated that ultimate professional, Donald Healey, and Kitty Brunell had not only beaten all the men, but won her class too. If the way of correlating test marks had been amalgamated, Ms Brunell would have emerged as the outright winner – thus preceding Pat Moss as a superstar by a full generation.

RESULTS
Event held: 14 March to 17 March. Nine starting points: Bath, Buxton, Glasgow, Harrogate, Leamington Spa, Liverpool, London, Newcastle-on-Tyne and Norwich. Finishing/rallying point at Hastings.

340 starters, 308 finishers.
Three driving tests.

There was no outright winner, but awards were made in three different capacity classes:

In 1933, Spencer Wilks, CEO of Rover at the time, won his class in the coachwork section of the rally in this two-door Rover Sports saloon.

Class		Total marks (all tests)
Class 1: Cars over 16HP (RAC Rating)		
1 T D W Weston	Rover Speed Twenty	244
Class 2: Cars of 10hp to 16hp		
1 Miss Kitty Brunell	AC Ace	253
Class 3: Cars up to 10hp		
1 G Dennison	Riley 9	251

Team Prize: Riley Motor Club (V E Leverett, G Dennison and R St G Riley).
Ladies Prizes: Class 1 Ford V8 (The Hon Mrs Chetwynd), Class 2 AC Ace (Miss Kitty Brunell, Class 3 Riley 9 (Miss D C N Champney).

1934: As you were

The reaction to the running of the 1933 event had been so positive that the RAC saw no need to make major changes for 1934. Once again the event would be run in March, once again there would be nine starting points, and once again the sporting and social activities would be run at an out-of-season resort.

With the prize of hosting the business of at least a thousand well-to-do rally drivers and their families, several holiday towns had been pitching for that prize, and in 1934 it was Bournemouth that took the honours. Even though Britain's rally drivers had rediscovered the Monte Carlo Rally by that time (the nation's economy was on the mend, and there seemed to be a more up-beat atmosphere in the

country) there was even more interest in this event, for well over 400 enquiries were received, and in fact 384 cars took the start.

For 1934 the sporting side of what had become a great social occasion was no more intense than before: the road section was still 1000 miles long, there would be no more than four waypoints on each of the nine routes, and only a handful of driving tests on the seaside road, Undercliff Drive, would be organised to produce a result.

On this occasion, incidentally, the number and type of special driving tests was not disclosed in advance, which led to the more serious competitors going out of their way to practice all kind of manoeuvres at home – 'just in case' – and to many being seriously relieved when they discovered what was actually going to be asked of them on Undercliff Drive. To almost everyone's undisguised relief, there was to be no slow-driving test of any type, though quite a few people had practiced their skills in advance. Such a ridiculous 'circus act' would never again be a part of this important event.

In the end, just three tests were set, two on the Drive itself (which, on the day, was somewhat spattered by the spray as the winds were quite high, and the tide boisterous), and one short hill-climb test.

For the first time in three years, the runs in from nine scattered start points was more demanding than expected, as there was some road-side evidence of previous snows, and some flurries as the cars were passing, but no-one seems to have become stuck, and their 'end-to-end' stories were certainly taller than the drifts they actually encountered at the time.

As for the tests, that laid out on the drive was of the familiar 'start, stop, reverse, divert, start, sprint, stop' variety, which, because of the

These were the days when industry tycoons took part in the rally, even if they got test drivers to do all the hard work for them. Here, in March 1934, a trio of works Standard models is led by Captain John Black (far left), with his Technical Director, Ted Grinham, to his immediate left.

In 1934, Singer always backed a works team of its sports cars in the RAC Rally. In 1934 this trio of Singers – driven by (left to right) the Barnes brothers, the Langley brothers, and W J B Richardson, won the prestigious Team Prize. The event finished in Bournemouth.

rather restricted width of the road itself, seemed to favour the smaller sports cars over the larger, and more powerful variety. The hillclimb was up a 1-in-7 gradient, and very restricted in length, such that the fastest 'Big Car' climb was by T B W Weston in just 13.4 seconds, although Stanley Barnes' Singer Le Mans and Jack Harrop's MG PA Midget each took a mere 12.2 secs.

As usual, there was no General Classification, so each of three class/category winners basked in their own more limited glory. This, however, was just one of the minor grumbles which were beginning to circulate – the road sections were too boring, and too easy, there was too little competitive motoring at the end, the concours was given too much attention, and more, and more. It would be interesting to see how the RAC would react, and what changes they would make for 1935.

RESULTS

Event held: 13 March to 16 March. Nine starting points: Bath, Buxton, Glasgow, Harrogate, Leamington, Liverpool, London, Newcastle-on-Tyne and Norwich. Finishing/rallying point at Bournemouth.

384 starters, 351 finishers.
Two driving tests.

There was no outright winner, but awards were made in three different capacity classes:

Class		Total marks (all tests)
Class 1: Cars over 16HP (RAC Rating)		
1 T D W Weston	Rover Speed Twenty	160
Class 2: Cars of 10hp to 16hp		
1 S B Wilks	Rover 12hp	159.6
Class 3: Cars up to 10hp		
1 F R G Spikins	Singer 9 Le Mans	161.6

Team Prize: Singer B-Team (W J Richardson, A H Langley and J D Barnes).
Ladies Prizes: Class 1 Sunbeam (Mrs R M Harker), Class 2 Rover (Mrs K E Wilks) and Class 3 Singer 9 (Miss J Astbury).

1935: Competition? What competition?

Looking back, it seems that in 1935 the Rally organisers had decided to take a step backwards, by retaining all the elements of a developing competition, but by electing to run an event where there were no losers – only winners. Instead of categorising the cars by their RAC horsepower rating, and awarding 1-2-3 class results, they reverted to the well-proven First Class, Second Class and Third Class awards system instead.

The result was an altogether unexciting event, which finished in Eastbourne, no fewer than 107 of the 241 finishers gained First Class Awards, and none of them were pronounced outright winners of anything. This was neither satisfactory nor popular, and would not be repeated in the future.

Although nine starting points were available (the farthest flung being in Edinburgh), and the overall length of each itinerary was about 1000 miles, there would only be four widely-separated intermediate check points along the way, and each entrant was required to average 26mph – which occupied about 41 hours and 45 minutes on the road, there being no scheduled rest halts along the way. Although this was by no means arduous, it should be noted that the 30mph speed limit had recently been applied to towns and villages – and that the police were avid in enforcing this, with speed traps.

These were the days when there was no rush to get from stage to stage, this being C M Foss' Rover 12hp on the 1935 rally. The Standard, parked up on the verge, is presumably the photographer's transport.

Fun and games at the end of the 1935 event, with Colonel Rippon's Rippon-bodied Rolls-Royce having its wheel alignment checked at the end of the event in Eastbourne.

Nevertheless, the motoring press, ever-kind to the motor industry as it was in those days, pronounced it a great success, pointing out that it was 'fairer' to all competitors, but wondering if a stiffer element of competition ought to be reintroduced for 1936. After all, in 1935 the true elements of 'competition' were merely a cold-start test for the cars after they had spent a night in the open in Eastbourne, followed by two wiggle-woggle type driving tests, one of which was on Greville Hill (and a 1-in-6 gradient) in the town, the other being on the seafront Parade.

Not an event to be remembered with much nostalgia, however …

RESULTS

Event held: 26 March to 29 March.
Nine starting points: Buxton, Edinburgh, Great Yarmouth, Harrogate, Leamington, Liverpool, Llandrindod Wells, London and Torquay.
Finishing/rallying point at Eastbourne.

281 starters, 241 finishers.
Two driving tests, one overnight cold-start test.

There was no outright winner, nor even class winners, but the following Finishers' awards were made:

First Class awards	107
Second Class awards	81
Third Class awards	50
No Award, but finished	3

There was no Team Prize, nor a Ladies Prize.

1936: Real competition again – but no outright winner

After the flaccid conclusion of the 1935, the RAC Rally organisers clearly had a rethink, reinstated the more popular class-winning theme for 1936, and chose to return to Torquay as its finishing point. There was still much complication, of course, for now there were to be eight classes, delineating closed from open cars, in four different 'RAC Horsepower' groups.

With this in mind, the two manoeuvring tests were more ambitious than before, although thankfully there was no sign of the 'slow-running' test which had marred the running of the original 'Torquay' event of 1932, and the running average on the 1000-mile road sections from the nine starting points was reduced to 24mph.

Of the special tests, a classic type of 'wiggle-woggle' was located on the Torbay Road seafront carriageway (as in 1932), while a short and rather fierce hillclimb test was held on St Marks Road, just a few hundred yards inland of the Imperial Hotel. Students of history will wish to know that the fastest time of all on the hillclimb test was set by Mrs Aileen Moss, who was Stirling and Pat Moss' mother.

If an outright winner had been announced, that award would

Godfrey Imhof drove this Singer Le Mans sports car in the 1936 rally, which ended in Torquay – this was one of the driving tests on a steep hill in the suburbs of this seaside town.

For some, the coachwork competition was always more enjoyable than the real rallying. Here, at the end of the event, in Torquay in 1936, J L Sears' 3½-litre Alvis Speed Twenty, complete with its bespoke Vanden Plas DHC coupé body, showed off its class-winning form.

certainly have gone to A H Langley's Singer Le Mans, while the Singer works team, with the two Barnes brothers driving the other Le Mans model entries, deservedly won the Manufacturers' team prize.

So … real competition again. Were things finally looking up for the RAC Rally?

RESULTS

Event held: 24 March to 27 March. Nine starting points: Blackpool, Bristol, Buxton, Glasgow, Harrogate, Leamington, London, Newcastle-on-Tyne and Yarmouth. Finishing/rallying point at Torquay.

274 starters, 252 finishers.
Two driving tests.

There was no outright winner, but awards were made in eight different capacity classes:

Class		Total marks (all tests)
Group 1: Open cars up to 8HP (RAC Rating)		
1 N E Bracey	MG Midget	74.2
Group 2: Closed cars up to 8HP		
1 C E A Westcott	Austin	129
Group 3: Open cars 8HP to 14HP		
1 A H Langley	Singer	66.8
Group 4: Closed cars 8HP to 14HP		
1 A G Imhof	Singer	72.2
Group 5: Open cars 14HP to 20HP		
1 C G Fitt	Frazer-Nash-BMW	72.2
Group 6: Closed cars 14HP to 20HP		
1 J L Finigan	Frazer-Nash-BMW	75.8
Group 7: Open cars over 20HP		
1 F R G Spikins	Spikins Hudson Special	67
Group 8: Closed cars over 20HP		
1 S E Sears	Bentley	73.2

Manufacturers' Team Prize: Singer (F S Barnes, A H Langley and J D Barnes).
Ladies Prizes: Open Cars: Triumph (Miss J Richmond. Closed cars: Armstrong-Siddeley (Miss M Wilby).

1937: Toughest so far

It was almost as if the tide had turned. After years of providing a milk-and-water event with very little tough going, the 1937 rally turned out to be more demanding than before. Although the overall driving distance was reduced to only 900 miles, and a mere 24mph average was demanded, several more 'sporting' sections were included, and there were three driving tests at the rallying town – Hastings – to help provide a result, though one had to be cancelled after arrival.

Because the event was held two weeks earlier in the year than usual, the remains of wintry weather could be expected to play a part,

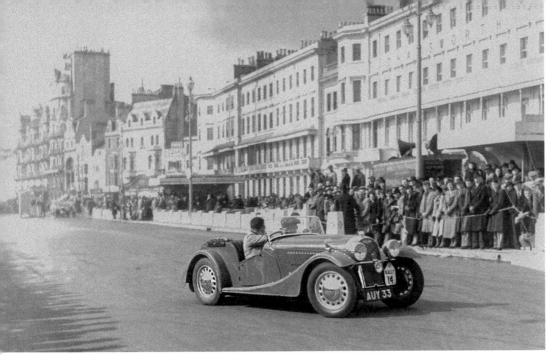

Although Morgan had only recently announced the new 4/4 model (the company's first-ever four-wheeler), company director George Goodall put up a fine performance, especially in the driving tests in Hastings.

In 1937, the well-known journalist Tommy Wisdom borrowed this SS100 to compete in the rally, which ended in Hastings. His wife, Elsie (always known as 'Bill'), looks cold in this study.

which it duly did, and on this occasion there were only six different classes to be contested. Was this, then, the reason why the entry was way down – for only 192 crews started?

By chance, a considerable amount of snow, ice and fog was encountered along the way, but at least the planned passage of the Bwlch-y-Groes was rendered unnecessary by the flexible nature of the route in Wales. There was snow at one of the start points (Buxton), and across the Pennines in the north, with ice to be found on many main roads, yet all but eight starters actually made it through from the six starting points to the seaside resort.

The driving tests were conventional enough – or would have been if one of the seaside manoeuvring tests had not had to be cancelled due to sea spray and debris being blown on to the road from the nearby beach! The most significant detail was that the tests were dominated by sporting cars that were to become truly famous – these including George Goodall's Morgan 4/4, J F A Clough's smart two-seater Riley Sprite, Lew Pearce's 2-litre Triumph Gloria Vitesse, and Jack Harrop's two-seater SS100, not to mention the team of SS100s which won the Manufacturers' Team Prize, and the smart trio of 1½-litre Singer Sports cars (all factory prepared) which won the 'club' team prize.

Although there was no suggestion of an outright winner, a study of special test marks show that Jack Harrop's SS100 would have been a worthy winner (he was much faster in the tests than anyone else …), with Tommy Wisdom (also in an SS100) second overall.

RESULTS
Event held: 9 March to 12 March.
Six starting points: Bristol, Buxton, Harrogate, Leamington, London and Stirling. Finishing/rallying point at Hastings.

192 starters, 184 finishers.
Three driving tests.
There was no outright winner, but awards were made in six different capacity classes:

Class		Total marks (all tests)
Group 1: Open cars up to 10HP (RAC Rating)		
1 G Goodall	Morgan4+4	930.2
Group 2: Closed cars up to 10HP		
1 B W Fursdon	Wolseley	928.0
Group 3: Open cars 10HP to 15HP		
1 J F A Clough)	Riley Sprite	937.4
Group 4: Closed cars 10HP to 15HP		
1 L Pearce	Triumph Vitesse	934.8
Group 5: Open cars over 15HP		
1 J Harrop	SS100 – 2½-litre	943.0
Group 6: Closed cars over 15HP		
1 D Impanni	Frazer-Nash-BMW	935.4

Manufacturers' Team Prize: SS (T H Wisdom, Hon B Lewis and E W Rankin).

Ladies Prizes: Open Cars: Ford V8 (The Viscountess Chetwynd).
Closed cars: Triumph (Miss S Bradley).

1938: Harrop's second triumph

In more ways than one, this was 'the mixture as before,' albeit with better weather and a more spring-like date to enjoy. As before, Jack Harrop's SS100 dominated proceedings, other brands such as Morgan and Triumph were prominent, and the gentle road run culminated in a gathering at an out-of-season seaside resort.

For 1938, however, the organisers decided to balance the use of more predictable weather (and, therefore, road conditions), with a more demanding time schedule, for this year the 1000 miles had to be completed at 26mph – which meant running for only 38 hours and 30 minutes, instead of loafing along in 41 hours and 40 minutes! On the other hand, along the way there were to be two compulsory night rest halts – at Largs (south of Greenock, in Scotland) for half of the field, or at Tenby (in West Wales) for the other half.

Not only that, but the prescribed route took in a climb and descent of Bwlch-y-Groes for certain routes, balanced by a drive over the Honister Pass (in the Lake District) for the others. Not that these were too demanding, as *The Autocar* made clear in its after-rally report for they were dismissive about the Bwlch, and said: "… Honister was no better. It was amusing, it was worth climbing, but it had no effect at all on the rally."

So typical of the RAC Rally in the 1930s, this shows Lord Waleran unleashing the power of his V12-engined Lagonda along the promenade in Blackpool, for one of the special tests of the 1938 event.

Here, therefore, was something beginning to approach what we would see as a 'real' rally, even though the only competitive action would take place in Blackpool. Even so, only six of the 237 starters failed to reach Blackpool after their scenic tour of Great Britain, to find an out-of-season resort which was sunnily awaiting them. Once again, however, there were to be only three special tests, this year with the accent more on performance rather than on manoeuvrability – and it was really no surprise that Jack Harrop (now with a 3½-litre engine in his SS100) once again set up fastest overall times, and should undoubtedly have been proclaimed the definite winner.

One of those tests was an outright sprint along the promenade close to the Imperial Hotel (it was to figure again in postwar RACs …), of a standing start quarter-mile, followed by a compulsory halt within 80 yards of the flying finish. Two more tests were tackled on the next morning (after crews had had a night's rest), where the SS100s, the Frazer-Nash-BMWs, and the V8-engined Fords all showed why they were such formidable competitors of their time.

With this RAC Rally turning the corner from a mere tour, to something of a real challenge of man and machine against their rivals, the portents for 1939 were strong.

RESULTS
Event held: 26 to 29 April. Five starting points: Glasgow, Harrogate, Leamington, London and Torquay. Finishing/rallying point at Blackpool.

237 starters, 231 finishers.
Three driving tests.

There was no outright winner, but awards were made in six different capacity classes:

Class		Total marks (all tests)
Group 1: Open cars up to 10HP (RAC Rating)		
1 G Goodall	Morgan 4/4	914.4
Group 2: Closed cars up to 10HP		
1 B W Fursdon	Wolseley	908.4
Group 3: Open cars 10HP to 15HP		
1 C M Anthony	Aston Martin	921.4
Group 4: Closed cars 10HP to 15HP		
1 L Pearce	Triumph Dolomite	910.6
Group 5: Open cars over 15HP		
1 J Harrop	SS100 – 3½-litre	923.4
Group 6: Closed cars over 15HP		
1 D Loader	Ford V8	916.4

Manufacturers' Team Prize: Riley (J F A Clough, G H Beetson and Mrs K M Hague).

In the 1937 and 1938 events, Jack Harrop set best performance overall in this SS100. Here he is seen in typical driving-test action on another event.

Ladies Prizes: Open Cars: Riley Sprite (Mrs K Hague). Closed cars: Rover (Miss O Bailey).

1939: Tougher, but not tough enough
For the first time since 1932, this RAC Rally looked as if it might have more challenging routes than ever before – but in the end the rather unseasonal weather put a stop to all that. All of which left the long-established format to be used again – several starting points, a rather leisurely road section, and only three driving tests to be held at the close of the event. As ever, there was no attempt to delineate an outright winner, and the concours held after the finish was seen as an important conclusion to any open road event.

It had all looked so promising at the planning stage. Only four starting points were made available, all the routes starting from those places would converge on Scarborough, there would be a compulsory five-hour rest at that point, after which competitors could choose between routes to Buxton, one of which would be demanding, sometimes described as 'colonial.' (Although no records of the route are known to survive, this 'colonial' section is thought to have involved a lengthy journey through the forestry 'roads,' which – more than 20 years later – would form one of the special stages seen on more modern rallies in the Yorkshire forests.)

Because there was also to be an overnight rest halt in Buxton, the open road section was limited to 800 miles. Not only that, but the target averages were 26mph to Scarborough, 24 mph from there to Buxton, and what appeared to be a rather dashing 30mph from Buxton to the finish.

Unhappily, when competitors turned up for the start – from London, Torquay, Blackpool and Stratford-on-Avon – they were notified that the so-called 'colonial' section from Scarborough to Buxton had been cancelled, reputedly because of road conditions which had deteriorated due to stormy weather. No less than 138 miles

Cowdale, near Buxton, was on the road section of the 1939 rally, where the loose surface of the track brought several cars to a standstill.

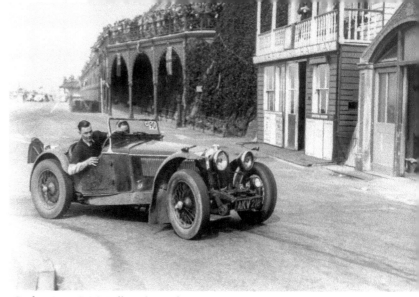

In the 1930s, RAC Rallies always finished at an out-of-season seaside town. It 1939 it was the turn of Brighton to welcome the field, with a special test situated on the Madeira Drive. This works-entered Riley Sprite was typical of the entry.

of demanding motoring, therefore, was abandoned, and was replaced by a more leisurely potter on main roads to Buxton.

On this occasion the entry was enlivened by the premier appearance of the new Raymond Mays sports car, and by the inclusion of aviatrix Amy Johnson as one of the drivers. Serious competitors, however, were trying to weigh up the relative chances of two sports cars – the fleet of Frazer-Nash-BMWs (really these were no more than rebadged BMW 328s), pitted against the sleek and wickedly powerful SS100s.

After the halt at Scarborough, the route covered the hilly sections through Hackness (this being the first time that rally cars had tackled routes in what became more familiarly known as the North Yorkshire forests in the 1960s), before making for Whitby, and eventually returning south to Pickering. It was in this area that the 'colonial' section had been abandoned, and, except for a touch of interesting motoring in the Peak District south of Buxton, the need for enterprising driving seemed to be missing.

On arrival in Brighton, all crews had to tackle a wiggle-woggle test situated on a 1-in-4½ hill in the town, but it wasn't until after they had all had a night's rest that they tackled a further two tests on Madeira Drive.

If only the organisers could have brought themselves to announce an outright winner, then it would certainly have been A F P Fane, driving one of the works Frazer-Nash-BMWs – though Coventry motor trader Sammy Newsome (SS100) ran him very close.

Because of the outbreak of war in September 1939, this was therefore the last of the original 'gentlemanly' RAC Rallies, and it would be another 12 years before a radically different type of event could be announced.

RESULTS

Event held: 25 April to 27 April. Four starting points: Blackpool, London, Stratford-on-Avon and Torquay. Finishing/rallying point at Brighton. A common route from Scarborough to the finish.
200 starters, 192 finishers.
Three driving tests.

There was no outright winner, but awards were made in six different capacity classes:

Class		Total marks (all tests)
Group 1: Open cars up to 10HP (RAC Rating)		
1 G Goodall	Morgan 4/4	901.2
Group 2: Closed cars up to 10HP		
1 H F S Morgan	Morgan 4/4	894.6
Group 3: Open cars 10HP to 15HP		
1 M H Lawson	HRG	909.6
Group 4: Closed cars 10HP to 15HP		
1 G A Davison	Triumph Dolomite Roadster	890.2
Group 5: Open cars over 15HP		
1 A F P Fane	Frazer-Nash-BMW	916.4
Group 6: Closed cars over 15HP		
1 H J Aldington	Frazer-Nash-BMW	908.2

Manufacturers' Team Prize: Frazer-Nash-BMW (A F P Fane, L G Johnson and D H Murray).
Ladies Prizes: Open Cars: Riley Sprite (Mrs K Hague). Closed cars: Ford V8 (Viscountess Chetwynd).

AN INTERNATIONAL 'RALLY OF THE TESTS'

Although the Second World War had ended in August 1945, it took ages for anything like normal life to be re-established throughout the world. For the vanquished nations – Germany, Italy, Japan and their erstwhile supporters – the problem was not only to rebuild their countries' shattered infrastructure, but to get their economies back on a sensible, peaceful, basis – and to pay off many debts. There was utterly no way that normal motor sporting activities could be resumed at first.

For the winners – notably the United States, the Soviet Union, and Great Britain – the first priority was to wind down the huge military activity and financial expense which had dominated the previous six years, then to look after the rehabilitation of the 'loser' nations, while trying to rebuild their own peacetime economies. In the case of Britain, huge and persisting debts had to be paid off, or financed, normal peacetime activities had to be resumed, and adequate new long-term supplies of staples such as food and fuel had to be ensured.

This process was going to take years, especially as the United States' 'Lend Lease' programme was abruptly disbanded in 1945/1946. Great Britain, for sure, was hugely in debt to the rest of the world, its industries were instructed to 'Export or Die,' and some aspects of rationing would persist until the early 1950s.

As far as British motorsport (and rallying in particular) was concerned, the major problem was fuel supply. Strict rationing was in force from 1945, private motoring was banned for a time in 1948, and it was not until 1950 that rationing was completely abandoned. The Motor Cycling Club (MCC) then jumped the gun by organising a long-distance national rally later in that year, but it was not until 1951 that the RAC could arrange to revive the RAC Rally.

With 12 years in which to mull over the record of the original events, and after considering all the lobbying which had taken place since then, the club actually raised its eyes and watched what was happening overseas. Not only had European rallying re-started before they could even consider it (the first postwar Monte Carlo Rally was held in 1949, for instance), but there had been a big demand for starting places, not only in the Monte 'classic,' but in events like the Dutch Tulip, and the Lisbon events too. Although there were still signs of special stages being invented, and refined, it was clear that the trend was to set more challenges all along a lengthy and sometimes arduous route.

Accordingly, for the revival of the RAC Rally, it was decided to make it an 'International' event – which would allow competitors from other countries to visit the UK to compete – and although the established format of offering multiple starting points would be retained, there would also be a multiplicity of different driving challenges at many places on the common route. These would sometimes be sprints or time trials on racing circuits, speed hillclimbs on established venues, manoeuvring tests, often at remote locations, or

NUB 120, a Jaguar XK120 which went on to become a legendary rally machine, was driven to victory in the first postwar RAC Rally by Ian Appleyard.

even 'regularity tests,' where two or more road sections would have to be completed in the same elapsed time.

Thus, what became known as the 'Rally of the Tests' was born. The challenge was to become even more complex by the introduction of lengthy night-navigation tests, often in the depths of Wales, or in the Peak District, where a navigator's skills were more important than the performance of the car, for the ability to read large-scale Ordnance Survey maps, and – even more critical – to be able to decipher the six-figure map references which the RAC organisers sometimes used to pin-point the position of controls and special tests.

Such maps had matured, expanded and included much more detail in recent years, and at their most popular scale of 1 inch to 1 mile, they were able to include every main road, minor road, and unmetalled track in the country. The ability to read such maps was an invaluable skill for a British navigator, as, in the past, European co-drivers had never had anything better than smaller-scale Michelin maps to use.

It was this quirk of British rally thinking, along with a reluctance to include much high-speed motoring in the mix of Britain's only International rally, which made it made it very difficult to attract high-profile entries from overseas. Nevertheless, demand from British entrants held up remarkably well, especially as this was also the period when a small number of prestigious British works rally teams were also set up (and which added some glamour to the competition).

By the end of the 1950s, however, European rallies had continued to evolve – adding higher-speed open-road sections to their events, and (in the case of Scandinavian rallies) adding newfangled high-speed sections called 'Special Stages' into the format, that the 'Rally of the Tests' began to look out-moded.

Starting in 1959, therefore, the rally was subjected to a radical shake-up, which would come to full maturity in the early 1960s.

1951: More tests, no concours

After 12 years without rallying, the organisers of the RAC Rally were finally able to get their show on the road. Six years of total war, followed by six more years of spirit-numbing austerity in the country, and a great deal of navel-gazing, had led to major changes being made to the event. Compared to 1939, therefore, the 1951 'RAC' was a very different event from the cosy round-Britain trundles which had been seen every year in the 1930s.

For the first time, the RAC Rally would have an International permit, which meant that overseas drivers could compete. In many ways the 'social' aspect of the event had been downgraded, for a concours was no long included (it would never reappear), the number of separate starting points was progressively cut, there would be a common route for much of the event (starting from Silverstone on this occasion), and for those who thought that rallying should be mostly about endurance, the overall route mileage was considerably extended. The organisers, on the other hand, were not about to take any chances with unpredictable, possibly wintry, weather, so the 1951 event was moved to June instead of March or April.

Except that no high-speed sections (later called Special Stages) were included, many more special tests – driving tests, sprints, high-speed time trials on circuits, and some navigation – would feature, these being situated all around the route, some of them in geographically remote locations. Almost immediately this was christened the 'Rally of the Tests,' which it would remain for the whole of the 1950s.

Because the accent was now to be more on speed and sporty driving, rather than an event in which all the hard work was concentrated into three tests and a matter of minutes, the line-up of drivers and entrants was rather different. No longer were large, sumptuously trimmed and carefully prepared limousines entered (so that they could compete in the concours that they once graced), nor were the social butterflies, the aristocracy and the landed gentry at all prominent. In their place came a flood of younger, battle-hardened crews (this was literally true, for many had served throughout the recent conflict), many of them from the motor trade, many of them already with experience of tough continental rallies.

No sooner had they got the details of the forthcoming rally, than entrants saw how much the theme of the event had changed. After a gentle run to Silverstone, they faced a circuit test on that circuit, a long drive (at a target average of 30mph) via Scarborough to Grantown-on-Spey, and a speed hillclimb at Rest and be Thankful in Scotland (the famous hillclimb near Arrochar and Loch Lomond would become very familiar to all rally enthusiasts in the future), and on to an overnight rest halt at Dunoon. The following day, the route led south, over the famed (and feared!) Hardknott and Wrynose passes in the Lake District, before making for a driving test on the promenade in

Variety at Bournemouth in 1951: the first 'international' RAC Rally, with a Leeds-registered Healey Silverstone leading the queue.

Blackpool, and another rest halt in that seaside town. Details of these tests were not published in advance.

On the next day, the route led through the centre of Liverpool (and through the tunnel) before tackling a 1.9-mile speed test on what were then unfamiliar roads on the Eppynt ranges, before making for a third night halt, this time at Weston-Super-Mare. The final day's motoring took them through, and back from, the most picturesque parts of Devon and Cornwall (the route finally turned east again at Launceston) before finding their way back through Exeter and Dorchester to reach Bournemouth and the end of the event.

In an event run in perfect early-summer weather, using tests which were all on sealed surfaces, it was inevitable that the fastest sports cars should be expected to dominate the event – and so it proved. No saloon, of any type, could approach the performance of the sports cars. In the rather 'unofficial' general classification (which would somehow became 'official' some years later) the best performance by a saloon put it way down, in 23rd place, behind a phalanx of Jaguars, Morgans, HRGs and Jowett Jupiters; not only that, but in the 'unlimited' Open Cars category, no fewer than 13 of the top 15 best performances were put up by Jaguar's sensational new XK120s. If it had not been for scintillating performances by two of the works Vanguard-engined Morgan Plus 4s (one driven by driven by Peter Morgan himself), there would have been a Jaguar clean sheet in that category.

Ian Appleyard, whose family controlled the Jaguar distributorship in Leeds, and who had already made himself famous in his works XK120 – NUB 120 – dominated the event, and duly won the event by a convincing margin. Co-driven by his wife, Pat, who was Jaguar founder William Lyons' daughter, this team set the standard that no other competitor could match – and would repeat the trick again in 1953.

On the first speed test, at Silverstone, crews had to complete a set number of laps on the club circuit – no more and no less – in 30 minutes. Several cars suffered from suspension or wheel failures, but almost all survived, then made the long – very long – trek north via Scarborough, Jedburgh, Braemar, and Grantown-on-Spey, before turning south and making for Rest and be Thankful. Appleyard's XK120 set fastest time of the day (in 70.5 seconds), and it was surely significant that the fastest saloon of all (Mike Coupér's Mk VI Bentley in 83.1 seconds), was all of 12.6 seconds slower than that.

The entire Hardknott and Wrynose section of six-miles was set as a special test (minimum-and-maximum times being specified) for everyone, as was a timed section on the Eppynt ranges in South Wales: this latter, of course, was to become more familiar in future years. Apart from the imposition of a wiggle-woggle test on the promenade at Blackpool, the final days were little more than scenic days' drives through Wales and the West Country, before the route led to the finish in Bournemouth.

The following morning there was a final manoeuvring test (the usual wiggle-woggle/chicanes/sandbags variety), tackled only by the leading 25 cars in each class where, once again, the XK120s dominated.

For 1952, it seemed, there were lessons to be learned, though everyone seemed to agree that this event had been more satisfactory than anything promoted in the 1930s. Would the organisers take heed of all the comments?

RESULTS
Event held: 4-9 June 1951. Four starting points: Brighton, Cheltenham, Harrogate, and Skegness. Common route from Silverstone, through Grantown-on-Spey and Launceston. Finish at Bournemouth.

229 starters, 185 finishers.
Sprints, time trials and driving tests.

General classification		Penalties
1 I Appleyard/Mrs P Appleyard	Jaguar XK120	109.61
2 P Morgan/--	Morgan Plus 4	112.99
3 G Goodall/--	Morgan Plus 4	114.55
4 D Bennett/--	Jaguar XK120	116.30
5 B Bradnack/--	Jaguar XK120	117.30
6 E Wadsworth/--	Jaguar XK120	117.37
7 H Sutcliffe/--	Jaguar XK120	120.12
8 Brown/--	HRG 1500	120.47
9 Ms M Newton/Ms A Newton	Jaguar XK120	120.51
10 Ms N Mitchell/--	HRG 1500	120.61

Note: In 1951, co-drivers' names were not quoted in the official results lists.

Team Prize: Morgan (P H G Morgan, W A G Goodall, and W D Steel). Ladies Prizes: Open Cars: Jaguar XK120 (Miss M Newton). Closed cars under 1500cc: Hillman Minx (Ms S Van Damm). Closed cars over 1500cc: Daimler (Miss D Corbishley).

1952: 1800 miles and ten tests
Although they stuck faithfully to the title 'Rally of the Tests,' every year the RAC organisation made the competitors roam further and further afield, and set the tests far and wide. Accordingly, in 1952, not only was there a start from Hastings (the other being from Scarborough), but the southernmost test was at Castle Combe circuit, near Bath, with the northernmost at the Rest and be Thankful hillclimb north of Glasgow, and the route visited every demanding road in between.

The fact that in March 1952 the weather was not promising – many competitors had difficulty in reaching the first time control (Silverstone and a speed test) on schedule because of snow drifts on main roads, and because of the timidity of some 'ordinary' drivers along the way – it made a leisurely-looking start more arduous. Even so, in areas where snow might have been expected to halt even the brave (South Wales, North Wales, the Lake District and Scotland) there seemed to be no hold-ups!

After 20 years of the RAC Rally, though, little effort was still being made to attract hard-bitten entrants from overseas to take part (it was now a fully-fledged 'International' after all). A few notable 'names' however – Maurice Gatsonides and Marcel Becquart among them – turned up, though they cannot have been impressed by the hour after hour of seemingly-pointless 'sight-seeing' which was broken up only occasionally by short bursts of competitive action.

All in all, there was nothing new to inspire the regulars – for Silverstone, Eppynt, Bwlch-y-Groes, Hardknott and Wrynose passes and Rest and be Thankful were all used once again. Even so, on this occasion, only two starting points – Hastings and Scarborough – were made available, and although this was the first RAC to impose such a big mileage, there were to be two overnight rest halts – at Blackpool and Edinburgh – along the way.

The effects of snowy weather caused the planned Silverstone test to be cancelled, so after the route meandered south to the coastal town of Bridport, it was a full 15 hours before the first cars tackled a manoeuvring test on the Castle Combe race circuit. Eight hours after that, crews finally got to tackle a short speed test over the Eppynt ranges, but this was only two miles in length, was followed by breakfast at Llandrindod Wells, and then there was another meander around North Wales to tackle a non-stop but untimed (why?) climb of Bwlch-y-Groes. Just 30 hours after setting out, the column finally reached Blackpool, another wiggle-woggle test on the Promenade – and an overnight sleep. This was not a tough event, for sure – which explains why so few foreign entrants were attracted to compete in this period.

With more than half of the event still to come, the leading positions had all settled down, with stalwarts like 'Goff' Imhof (Cadillac-engined Allard J2X), Ian Appleyard (Jaguar XK120), and George Goodall (Morgan Plus 4), all prominent in the standings. On the following day, much of the mileage was a rather meaningless ramble through the Lake District and the Border counties before reaching Edinburgh for another rest – the oddity being that this included routeing the cars over

the same stretches as would form the timed 'regularity test' in two days' time. On the fourth day – Edinburgh to Carlisle by way of Pitlochry, all of it in Scotland – there was only one competitive section, this being the famous Rest and be Thankful hillclimb, tackled in broad daylight, where the fastest times were set by a quartet of XK120s (Ian Appleyard, Leslie Johnson, Syd Henson and T B D Christie), with Imhof's ferociously competitive Allard close behind.

On Day Five came the complex regularity test in the Lake District, when, after starting from a time control at Ulpha (a tiny village north of Broughton-in-Furness), cars had to tackle three back-to-back sections, which were challenged to be completed in the same time – these sections including the passage of the formidable Hardknott and Wrynose Passes, and ending at the summit of Kirkstone Pass, north of Windermere.

It was here that the seasoned professionals such as Ian Appleyard, Peter Morgan (Morgan Plus 4) and Ken Bancroft (Morgan Plus 4) began to stretch clear of their rivals, but there was then a long run across country to Scarborough, where no fewer than 199 cars actually clocked in, another night's rest, and a final blast around the Oliver's Mount circuit the following morning. It was here that the massive torque of the Allard's Cadillac proved conclusive, for Imhof headed no fewer than seven XK120s and five Morgan Plus 4s to dominate the sports cars which set all the fastest times.

RESULTS

Event held: 31 March to 5 April 1952. Two starting points: Hastings and Scarborough. Common route from Silverstone, via Pitlochry (Scotland). Overnight halts in Blackpool and Edinburgh. Finish at Scarborough.

242 starters, 199 finishers.
Sprints, time trials' regularity sections, and driving tests.

General classification		Penalties
1 G Imhof/Ms B Frayling	Allard J2X	183.8
2 Broadhead/--	Jaguar XK120	185.0
3 Appleyard/Ms P Appleyard	Jaguar XK120	186.6
4 Christie/--	Jaguar XK120	190.8
5 Reece/--	Morgan Plus 4	198.2
6 Morgan/--	Morgan Plus 4	199.4
7 Rollings/--	Healey	200.4
8 Bradnack/--	Jaguar XK120	200.8
9 Ms M Newton/Ms A Newton	Jaguar XK120	202.4
10 Bancroft/--	Morgan Plus 4	202.6

Note: in 1952, co-drivers' names were not quoted in the official results lists.

Team Prize: Morgan (P H G Morgan, W A G Goodall, and W D Steel).

Godfrey Imhof won the 1952 rally in his Cadillac-powered Allard J2X.

Ladies Prizes: (Open cars) Jaguar XK120 (Miss M Newton), (Closed cars) Rover (Miss C Sadler).

1953: The olde order changeth not …

For 1953 the RAC had a bright idea. Because its International rally was clearly very important, and this year was to be that in which the new Queen was to be crowned, it would be called the 'Coronation RAC' rally.

Not that there was much more that would change, and there were few novelties – for as usual it was held in March, there was very little competitive motoring in a long event, and the regulations and timing targets made it almost certain that the winner would once again be a sports car.

Even more frustrating for the RAC was that they could still not attract any of the 'heavy hitters' of European rallying, and there were only seven entrants from overseas. Even so, one of those (financially supported, no doubt, by the factory) was Maurice Gatsonides, who had recently won the Monte Carlo Rally in a Ford Zephyr. From Britain, however, there was evidence that car makers themselves were now taking an interest, for there were teams from Ford, BMC (MG Y-Type saloons) and the Rootes Group (Sunbeam-Talbot 90s).

Although there was little more competitive motoring than in

previous years, the event struck a little deeper into unfamiliar territory, for on the first night the cars had to pass through Haverford West, on the western tip of Wales, while two days later they visited Stranraer in Scotland. Even so, the 1500-mile road route included only seven driving or manoeuvring tests, along with regularity sections in the Lake District and in Yorkshire.

As ever, the event started in a leisurely manner, with two long columns leaving Blackpool and Hastings to converge on Silverstone, there to tackle a half-sprint. After that they trekked unwillingly to Ringwood in Hampshire, then turning north to reach the Castle Combe race circuit (formerly an airfield until 1950) for a manoeuvring test. This was followed by a moonlight spring up the Prescott hillclimb, a long and rather pointless meander around south-west Wales, and then across to Llandrindod Wells for a driving test alongside the lake, after which the route led to Blackpool, a driving test on the Promenade, and a night's rest!

By then the leaders had laid down markers, which were not likely to be upset in the days that followed – and all was remarkably similar

The Y-Type MG saloon – here driven by Geoff Holt in 1953 – was agile and reliable, but not quite fast enough to challenge the leaders.

Col O'Hara-Moore and John Gott tackle the Park Rash hillclimb test in the 1953 rally, in their Frazer-Nash Le Mans Replica.

In 1953 the 'Rally of the Tests' featured a special wiggle-woggle test in the outskirts of Llandrindod Wells.

Having won the Monte Carlo Rally, the Gatsonides/Zephyr/VHK 194 combination was entered for the 1953 rally, which ended at Hastings. No success here, though.

By 1953 NUB 120 and Ian Appleyard had become the most famous and successful rallying duo in Europe, XK120 winning its second RAC Rally.

Ronnie Adams finished second overall in this Sunbeam-Talbot 90 in the 1953 event.

to 1952. Ian Appleyard (still in his famous Jaguar XK120, NUB 120), 'Goff' Imhof in his 1952-winning Allard J2X, and Peter Morgan (Morgan Plus 4) were all on the leaderboard, though a notable new name (in second place, overnight) was Ronnie Adams of Northern Ireland, in a works Sunbeam-Talbot 90.

After the overnight halt, the field was faced with the same three back-to-back 'regularity' tests in the Lake District, where consistency was more important than total performance. These hit hard at 'names' like Marcel Becquart (whose Jowett Javelin suffered from fuel starvation, Gatsonides' works Zephyr, which seemed to be over-geared when tackling an uphill start, and even Peter Harper (driving J S Smith's Allard) who suffered a damaged transmission.

By the time the route turned about at the Turnberry hotel, Adams' Sunbeam-Talbot 90 had taken the lead, but there were only three more linked 'regularity' tests in Yorkshire (one of them being up Park Rash hillclimb), before crews were faced with a 300-mile drag south to Hastings, a night's rest in Hastings, a short run to the Goodwood race track, a return to Hastings, another night in bed, and two final driving tests in Hastings itself.

It was in these tests that Ian Appleyard showed that he was the complete master of the XK120, which he handled precisely and fast, so that Ronnie Adams was pushed back into second place, purely because his saloon was by no means as rapid as the massed ranks of high-performance sports cars.

The specialist press, as one might expect, praised this 'Coronation' event to the skies, but the fact is that there was too much mileage and too little purposeful motoring involved for the experienced crews. The RAC, however, was not yet ready to embrace too much fast motoring on its event – and promised much the same mixture for 1954.

RESULTS
Event held: 23-28 March 1953. Two starting points: Blackpool and Hastings. Common route from Silverstone, via Turnberry and Haverford West. Overnight halts at Blackpool, and Hastings. Finish in Hastings.

194 starters, 154 finishers.
Sprints, time trials, regularity tests, and driving tests.

General classification		Penalties
1 Appleyard/Mrs P Appleyard	Jaguar XK120	29.37
2 Adams/Pearman	Sunbeam-Talbot 90	22.77
3 Imhof/Mrs B Frayling	Allard J2X	19.51
4 Broadhead/Lilley	Jaguar XK120	16.97
5 Bennett/Mrs E Bennett	Jaguar XK120	16.31
6 Shaw/Finnemore	MG Y-Type	12.45
7 Turnbull/Dean	Vauxhall Velox	8.39
8 Grounds/Hay	Jaguar XK120	6.05
9 Hartwell/Scott	Sunbeam Talbot 90	-0.49
10 Scott/ --	Jaguar Mk VII	-2.07

Team Prize: Jaguar (I Appleyard, W Grant-Norton, F Grounds).
Ladies Prize: Sunbeam-Talbot 90 (Ms Sheila van Damm – Mrs F Clarke).

1954: Domination by the Triumph TR2
For 1954, it seemed, there would be significant changes to Britain's premier rally. Not only would the route become more compact (the forecast was for only 1200 of road mileage), and the event would venture no further north than Blackpool, but there would be two night navigation sections, and the type of cars would be different too. In retrospect, in fact, this was the event where the new Triumph TR2 signalled its arrival as *the* new sports car for the driver to buy, and there were no fewer than 15 such cars in the list.

Although a total of 229 cars took the starters' flag, it was fascinating to see how widely spread the favourite competitors were placed, for the organisers clearly did not yet believe in 'seeding'. The route, too, was certainly widespread (rather like the 1930s 'touring' events had been) for Blackpool starters faced a trek to Thetford in East Anglia, while Hastings starters had to visit Llanwrda in West Wales. It was an event where the same special tests had to be tackled in the first half of the event, though in an entirely different order for

either starting place convoy, and it was only after the overnight halt in Blackpool that there was to be a simultaneously common route – from Blackpool, through hilly Yorkshire, into southern Scotland, and back to Blackpool by way of the usual tortuous passes of the Lake District. A tough schedule, and a great deal of overnight fog, meant that only 21 crews completed the road section without lateness penalties.

Although the organisers had certainly not deliberately intended it to be that way, the layout and sequence of events, allied to the navigation sections, no longer favoured big fast cars like the XK120s, as right from the start it was one of the many TR2s, the TR-engined Morgan Plus 4s, and the fleetest of rather more compact saloons which filled up the leaderboard. Not only that, but well-organised factory teams such as those from Ford and Sunbeam-Talbot added real expertise to what was an increasingly professional-looking event. Maybe it was because the RAC was now labelling its event as the 'Rally of the Tests' that there were still very few overseas entrants – and only one of them (Walter Schlüter in a front-wheel-drive DKW) who finished in the Top 50.

The night navigation sections – the Welsh one using many tiny roads close to Welshpool, and the Peak District one based in Macclesfield – tended to be over 150 miles long (which meant more than five hours of hard graft for drivers *and* co-drivers), and were dubbed 'special stages' by the RAC, but were not the sort of speed sections with which we would eventually be familiar. Instead, there wasreally a microcosm of British club rallying events which were developing fast at this time.

Because those were the days pre-computers, pre-internet, and pre-rolling results service, no one really knew who was leading the event before the cavalcade set out on the final, northern, loop from Blackpool. The RAC's now-familiar three-in-one regularity tests then sorted out the dedicated from the dilettantes – the first was over three

In March 1954, Johnny Wallwork took a brand-new Triumph TR2 to victory in the RAC. Other TR2s took second, fifth and the Ladies Prizes in the same event.

hills in Lancashire and Yorkshire (Catshaw, Darnbrook and Park Rash), the second being a Lake District combination of Hardknott, Wrynose and Kilnbank – and there was a final figure-of-eight test on the Promenade in Blackpool, before the event was completely over.

The RAC then published a mind-bogglingly detailed list of car-by-car, test-by-test results – there being no fewer than 13 of them – which proved that the most successful entrants were those (like Johnny Wallwork, Peter Cooper and 'Cuth' Harrison) who not only had a great deal of experience of the most demanding British roads, but had vastly experienced co-drivers alongside them.

TR2s – in order, Wallwork, Cooper, and Bill Bleakley – dominated the top of the results, with the Harrisons (father and son) in a works Ford Zephyr, and Peter Harper in a Sunbeam-Talbot 90 close behind. A detailed study showed that Harper might have been third instead of fourth if he had been just one second faster over the long high-speed test around the Goodwood circuit, and that Ronnie Adams (driving an outwardly unsuitable Alvis TC21/100 saloon) was probably driving that car up to, and maybe even above, its theoretical limits at all times.

But was this enough for what was still growing as a major International rally? The self-congratulatory RAC club thought it was, but the fact that there were only eight overseas drivers in the huge entry told another story.

RESULTS

Event held: 9-12 March 1954. Two starting points: Blackpool and Hastings. Blackpool route via Eppynt, Oulton Park, Hastings, Macclesfield. Hastings route via Macclesfield, Goodwood, Eppynt, Prescott, Oulton Park. One overnight rest halt in Blackpool (for Hastings starters) or Blackpool (for Hastings starters). Finish at Blackpool.

229 starters, 164 finishers.
Sprints, time trials and driving tests.

General classification		Penalties
1 Wallwork/Brooks	Triumph TR2	416.67
2 Cooper/Leighton	Triumph TR2	436.05
3 T C Harrison/E Harrison	Ford Zephyr	440.50
4 Harper/Humphrey	Sunbeam-Talbot 90	441.00
5 Bleakley/Glaister	Triumph TR2	445.85
6 Adams/Rawlinson	Alvis TC21/100	449.70
7 Ray/Mrs K Ray	Morgan Plus 4	457.35
8 Newsham/Beaumont	Morgan Plus 4	458.05
9 Hartwell/Scott	Sunbeam-Talbot 90	462.60
10 Ashworth/Wesley	Jaguar Mk VII	469.40

Team Prize: Ford (T C Harrison, J Reece, Mrs Nancy Mitchell).
Ladies Prize: Triumph TR2 (Ms Mary Walker).

MISSING HERO?

He had won the RAC Rally in 1951, finished third in 1952, and won again in 1953, so why did Ian Appleyard not even start the 1954 event? It seems that his famous white Jaguar XK120 – registered NUB 120 – had built up such as colossal competition mileage in four years that Appleyard decided to retire it after the 1953 season, after which it was put on show in Jaguar's premises in Coventry. For the next year or so, he was so busy running, and expanding, his Jaguar dealership in Leeds, Yorkshire, that he had no time to have a replacement constructed for him, so opted out, and did not return until 1955 when he ran an MG TF sports car instead.

NIGHT NAVIGATION IN THE 1950s

In the 1950s, when the RAC Rally took on its 'International' role, the co-driver/navigators in each competing car found themselves with a difficult and vital role to play. Not only did they get virtually no notice of where the rally was to lead – which meant that route-plotting often had to be done on the evening before the start – but they had to get used to using Ordnance Survey maps to chart their progress, and to use six-figure map references to pin-point control locations.

The use of map references in motorsport was a postwar phenomenon, and was purely a British art because of the excellent maps that were available. The maps, and the skills surrounding their use, had been developed massively during the Second World War, and it was no coincidence that top rallying crews of the 1950s often had military experience to back them.

Overseas crews, however, had none of these advantages and, if they had not rallied in the UK beforehand, found the whole idea of map references and large-scale maps alien to what they were used to. That, and the use of a multiplicity of short, tight, road sections in poor visibility at night, made it no coincidence, therefore, that overseas crews did not fancy tackling the RAC Rally in any numbers until the navigational side of the event was simplified. This also explains why most of the pioneers from overseas employed British co-drivers to help them find their way.

As a perfect example, Erik Carlsson's early RAC Rally co-drivers were John Sprinzel (1959), Stuart Turner (1960), John Brown (1961) and David Stone (1962), while Rauno Aaltonen's co-driver in 1965 was Tony Ambrose, who had already occupied the winning car of Lyndon Sims in 1956.

1955: A saloon car victory at last

If the Triumph TR2 had caused such an upheaval in the 1954 RAC Rally, it was its humble little stablemate, the Standard Ten, which upset every possible applecart in 1955. Not only did Jimmy Ray's much-modified works Standard win the event outright, but his team boss, Ken Richardson, took third place, and (along with Bobby Dickson) the works Standards won the Team Prize too.

Although the organisers seemed determined to make the routeing, the special tests, and the navigation sections as complex as possible, they still called this event the 'Rally of the Tests,' subjected the crew to a 2000-mile route around England and Wales (but nowhere further north than the Lake District), and allowed only a single overnight rest halt mid-event. All this was daunting enough – but in March 1955 the weather was extremely wintry, with lashings of snow and ice, and a huge build-up of delays, jams and mishaps, to make it a truly difficult challenge.

All in all, this continued to deter all but a handful of overseas entrants, but there was now much interest from works teams – from BMC, Ford, Standard-Triumph, Rootes (Sunbeam-Talbot), and DKW from Germany, along with individual covert assistance to certain individuals, including Ronnie Adams' Alvis TC21/100.

Before the start, two names who made the headlines were Ian Appleyard, who had abandoned his love affair with Jaguars in favour of a works-supported MG TF, and Pat Moss, also using an MG TF, who was making her breakthrough into a factory team. For Appleyard it was one of his increasingly rare forays into International rallying, while for Pat Moss it was just the start of what would be a glittering career.

The testing schedule was at once old-fashioned, but intensive, for there were to be 11 special tests, mainly of the manoeuvring variety, interspersed with UK-style navigational sectors in South Wales, Yorkshire, the Lake District and in the far West Country. Total performance was rarely required on many of these tests, though accurate route finding and timekeeping (on the navigational sectors) most certainly were. The weather, frankly, was awful on many tests. How many, even of the competitors who had raced in certain areas before this event, had ever tackled Cadwell Park with snow on the track, and how many relished tackling the worst of the Yorkshire roads, and especially sections such as Hardknott Pass in the Lake District, where the challenge was not merely to keep accurate time, but even to keep going at all!

Progress reports of the standings in mid-event were non-existent, but it soon became clear that certain cars were dominating certain classes – two-stroke DKWs, Ford Anglia 100Es, Sunbeam-Talbots, Standard Tens, Ford Zephyrs, MG TFs and Triumph TR2s – being the most prominent. In the end, it was clear that accurate navigation (and luck with weather conditions) was going to count for more than flashing acceleration. Jimmy Ray, already a celebrated club rallyist and BTRDA Champion, had a nimble modified Standard to give him a good start, while Harold Rumsey and Peter Roberts (already well known in club circles) ran him close throughout.

This RAC Rally, like its predecessors however, emphasised why it was never likely to be accepted as truly 'International' in its existing format. As *The Autocar*'s sports editor, J A Cooper, wrote the following week:

Jimmy Ray won the 1955 event outright, not only by having a much-modified Standard Ten, but by having an expert co-driver for the navigational sections.

In her very first international rally, Pat Moss drove this MG TF1500 in the 1955 RAC Rally, finishing third in the Ladies Prize competition.

"The complicated layout of the rally was perhaps over-ambitious, comprising as it did four special road stages of different types, and 11 equally variant special tests… Is it fair, in an International rally counting towards the European touring championship, to include the use of map references on the peculiarly British grid system – especially when none of the regulations or instructions are printed in any other language than English? …"

The behind-the-scenes mutterings about the basic layout of what was supposed to be Britain's premier rally were, in other words, already becoming persistent, but it would be another four years before anything was done about it.

RESULTS

8-12 March 1955. Two starting points: Blackpool and Hastings. Complex 'common' route, with variations, from Whitney-on-Wye. One overnight rest halt at Blackpool. Finish at Hastings.

229 starters, 164 finishers.
Sprints, time trials and driving tests.

General classification		Penalties
1 Ray/Harrocks	Standard Ten	258.1
2 Rumsey/Roberts	Triumph TR2	462.3
3 Richardson/Heathcote	Standard Ten	559.5
4 Adams/Wilkins	Alvis TC21/100	583.4
5 Imhof/Mackenzie	Allard J2X	615.4
6 Grieg/Pigott	Triumph TR2	829.4
7 Appleyard/Mansbridge	MG TF1250	904.4
8 Baker/Stark	Ford Anglia 100E	921.7
9 Done/Storrar	Fiat 1100	937.5
10 Richards/Nott	Ford Anglia 100E	1105.4

Team Prize: Standard (J Ray, K Richardson, B Dickson).
Ladies Prize: Sunbeam Mk III 90 (Ms Sheila Van Damm/Mrs A Hall).

GIANT-KILLING STANDARD TEN

Although this was years before the phrase 'homologation special' had even been invented, the works Standard Tens would certainly have qualified for that description. If entered in the unmodified touring car category, even drivers like Jimmy Ray would have struggled to win their class. In 'showroom' cars. As it was, Standard had developed a twin-SU version of the 948cc engine, which boosted the peak power output from 33bhp to more than 45bhp, and used those power units to enter the team cars in the 'GT and Modified Touring' category. Similar engine kits were eventually put on sale to private owners, and were delivered in reasonable quantities. On the works cars, Pennants were so-equipped in the 1958 RAC Rally, when they almost won the event outright.

1956: Tougher then ever, with more tests

One year on from the heavily-criticised 1955 event, for 1956 the RAC Rally organisers listened, did nothing to mend their ways, and except for simplifying the route, came up with more of the same. This time no fewer than 16 special tests were promised in 2100 miles, a visit to the southern counties of Scotland was scheduled, and there were to be only three tough navigational tests – one in the West Country, another in Yorkshire, and the final one in the Lake District.

British rally enthusiasts seemed to be content with this well-established format, which meant that 205 cars started. This time, happily, the weather was positively spring-like, so crashes and other excursions were less prevalent than in 1955, and no fewer than 165 of them made it to the finish in Blackpool.

The novelties, such as they were, were mainly concentrated on the cars one was seeing for the first time, with Pat Moss' MG MGA making its rally debut, Bill Bleakley performing capably in his Jaguar 2.4-saloon, and Ian Appleyard making a welcome return to Jaguars, this time in an XK140. The biggest novelty of all, however, was that Lyndon Sims appeared in his well-used Aston Martin DB2) a model which had already dropped out of production) – and beat everyone, works teams included.

It was also an event where several names, later to be even more important in British rallying, figured in the results – Tony Ambrose (winning co-driver), Ian Hall (fourth place co-driver), Ann Wisdom

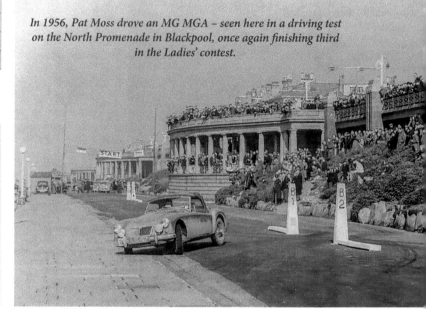

In 1956, Pat Moss drove an MG MGA – seen here in a driving test on the North Promenade in Blackpool, once again finishing third in the Ladies' contest.

In a rally that was won and lost by a driver's prowess in special tests, Lyndon Sims surprised everyone by winning the 1956 event in a three-year-old Aston Martin DB2.

Jack Sears used this Austin A50 to take third in his class, and was a member of the winning BMC team in the 1956 event. Goodwood, the 'wrong way round' was used as a speed trial.

(co-driving Pat Moss), Stuart Turner (second in class, co-driver), Peter Harper (second in class) and Willy Cave (class winner, co-driver) among them.

Since this was probably the best of the 'Rally of the Tests' (the format would change dramatically in 1960), it is worth recalling the nature of most tests which were held. The manoeuvring test at Hastings (or Blackpool, depending on where one started) was first, the hillclimb sprint at Prescott was next, a long night navigation section on Exmoor followed, then a driving test at Castle Combe circuit, and there were more tests at Matchams Park, Goodwood and Brands hatch, before an overnight rest halt in Hastings. The second leg included a test at Silverstone, two more at Cadwell Park and Gamston, then into the horrors of night navigation in Yorkshire (23 time controls in 350 miles!). To follow that, tests at Otterburn, then Charterhall, led to more navigation and special sections in the Lake District (including Hardknott Pass, and 13 controls in 112 miles), a downhill braking test at Tow Top, and three final driving tests all on the Promenade in Blackpool.

Because those were the days before electronic transmission of results was possible, there were few indications of those who looked likely to win, and of those who were lagging, but it was always clear that the seasoned driving test experts were most comfortable with the format of the event. Welshman Lyndon Sims, however, who had no other outstanding successes in his CV, could not possibly have won the event without the undoubted navigational skills of his navigator Tony Ambrose, or of the performance of his Aston Martin DB2, nor could Ian Appleyard have possibly finished second in his bulky Jaguar XK140 if he didn't already have a mountain of experience in many European events.

RESULTS

Event held: 6-11 March 1956. Two starting points: Blackpool and Hastings, common route from Prescott. One overnight halt in Hastings. Finish at Blackpool.

213 starters, 165 finishers.
Sprints, time trials and driving tests.

General classification		Penalties
1 Sims/Ambrose/Jones	Aston Martin DB2	29.2
2 Appleyard/Mrs P Appleyard	Jaguar XK140	50.0
3 Spare/Meredith	Morgan Plus 4	54.8
4 Bleakley/Hall	Jaguar 2.4	65.1
5 Cooper/Holland	Standard Ten	81.6
6 D Johns/Mrs J Johns	Austin A90 Westminster	82.9
7 Senior/Hall	Austin A540 Cambridge	90.0
8 O'Leary/Canty	VW Beetle	91.9
9 Wallwork/Cave	Standard Ten	112.6
10 Harper/Humphrey	Sunbeam Mk III	114.5

Team Prize: BMC Austins A50 and A90 (G Burgess, Mrs J Johns and J Sears).
Ladies Prize: Austin A40 Sports (Ms Angela Palfrey and Miss A Jervis).

THREE INTO TWO *WILL GO* ...

After Lyndon Sims had won the 1956 rally in his Aston Martin DB2, he proudly posed for a picture which showed that the car had carried a three-man crew throughout – Sims himself, Roger Jones and Tony Ambrose. Yet the DB2 was only a two-seater coupé, so how on earth had this been possible?

Classic car watchers have been worrying about this one for years. It was only recently that the full story emerged. Roger Jones, apparently, had been the front seat passenger for much of the time (driving at times, and acting as a 'gate opener' at others ....), while Tony Ambrose (a specialist navigator who went on to become an established co-driver in the BMC rally team of the 1960s) somehow survived behind those seats, on wooden boarding specially installed for the event, with a few cushions to make it marginally comfortable....

This was not a tactic carried out by any other serious entrants ....

NUMBER 16 — R.A.C. INTERNATIONAL RALLY

The works-entered Austin team, killing line on the section up into Scotland, following the Yorkshire night navigation section.

A Personal Story of an Enjoyable Outing   By PETER GARNIER

The second of Jack Sears solo turns: climbing Prescott Hill while the crew stands and waits at the foot. The substantial tread of the Dunlop Weathermasters can be seen clearly on the left-side front wheel.

In the 1956 RAC Rally, Autocar's then Sports Editor, Peter Garnier, competed, as Jack Sears' co-driver in a "works" BMC A55 saloon, no. 16, and helped win the manufacturer's team prize.

Competitors started simultaneously from Hastings and Blackpool at 8 am on Tuesday 6 March and finished on 11 March at Blackpool. Altogether, the route covered 2,100 miles throughout the length and breadth of Britain and included 16 driving tests.

DURING the opening stages of the Monte Carlo Rally, the A.C. Aceca, in which I was competing, proceeded in company with a works Austin A.50 driven in turn by Jack Sears. Archie Scott-Brown (both of whose racing exploits in Lister-Bristols are well known) and Kenneth Best, competition manager of National Benzole. The remarkable thing about this expert crew, whenever we met them in controls from beginning to end, was their overflow of good spirits—an unusual state of affairs among tired people. Boxed in a car on a long rally, there was no hesitation, therefore, and my "Good heavens, yes," when Ken asked me if I would like to join Jack and himself on the R.A.C. Rally. Archie

having had to drop out because of Sebring and the opening of his new business near Cambridge.

The car was a "modified" Austin A.50: that is, basically A.50 but with certain modifications permitted by the F.I.A. in Appendix J of the International Sporting Code under the heading "Special Series Production Touring Cars". The rules concerning permitted modifications are fairly undemanding, the basic requirement being that these cars shall be directly derived from their untuned Normal Series Production stablemates. In fact, provided you do not replace the conventional rear axle and half-elliptic springs by a de Dion layout, or substitute the four-cylinder engine with a six, you have a pretty free hand so far as improving the performance and road holding is concerned.

The only snag about all this is that, instead of running against the everyday production cars, the modified car moves up a class and finds itself matched with Gran Turismo cars which means an increase in the average speed required of it.

Briefly, the modifications to which the car had been subjected included fitting a B-series B.M.C. engine brought up to M.G.A. specification, and a close ratio gear box with central change; the rear axle was standard. The brakes had been modified to Le Mans M.G. specification and the suspension had been lowered. The car handled extremely well, despite Dunlop Weathermaster tyres which, though excellent for

their purpose, do not generally improve the high speed handling of a car. The performance, of course, was a considerable improvement over that of a normal A.50 and the car gave the impression of being extremely robust—which was proved by the outcome of the rally.

The car has had considerable competition experience, being used by John Gott in the Liège-Rome-Liège Rally last year (when he, Burgess, Poynter and Strose, running as the R.A.C. team, won the Inter-club Team Trophy) and by Joan and Douglas Johns in several National events in the most recent of which—the 'Cats' Eyes—it scored a class win.

In the official B.M.C. Austin team there were the following cars: Douglas and Joan Johns' modified A.90, running in class 7 (Grand Touring Series Production and Special Series Production cars of 2,600 c.c. and over); Gerry Burgess and Sam Croft-Pearson's unmodified A.90 in class 4, for Normal Series Production Touring—the largest class of all; and our A.50 in class 6 (G.T. Series Production and Special Series Production cars of 1,301—2,600 c.c.). This class included such formidable opposition as John Patten's Porsche 1,500, Reg Phillips' Ford Zephyr, Ken Wharton's Riley Pathfinder and three 2.6-litre Aston Martins.

The Hastings starting point was chosen—largely for convenience—and, after Jack had performed the first driving test, we set out for Prescott. The main road schedule was undemanding; we reached Cheltenham at an average of around 37 m.p.h.—3 m.p.h. below the 40 to exceed which might mean exclusion from the Rally. The minimum average from control to control was 30 m.p.h. and the time we had in hand was to prove a blessing. Turning out of Cheltenham, we found the Bishops Cleeve road a frustrating, crawling queue bound for Cheltenham Racecourse and the Hunt Cup. We reached Prescott with little time in hand and Jack performed the second of his obbligatos—in 66.3 sec., which was fair enough; the high first gear of the Austin's box, which allowed a maximum of 30-plus m.p.h., was ideal for special tests, but did not help a quick getaway.

No fewer than 14 of the 16 driving tests were carried out with only the driver in the car—which meant that the journey was punctuated by these solo performances of Jack's, while Ken and I stood on the touchline and watched. With characteristic thoroughness, Jack had laid out at Snetterton, and practised all the tests except those which were kept secret or did not demand it. This proved to be invaluable as there was often insufficient time to look up and memorise details before embarking on the test.

On a long rally of this sort it is of utmost importance to keep fit and adequately fed—in Gatsonides' words, "Eat as much as possible; drive as little as possible." So, when it was available, we eat steak at meal stops, backed up by vitamin pills which Jack unearthed from the turmoil on the floor of the car whenever we went off to a restaurant. Even at this early stage one of us was usually fast asleep. At the start we had been issued with the route card for the first night's special navigation section. As soon as this had been marked up on Ken's and my maps, we took it in turn to drive, letting Jack sleep and build up strength—we hoped—for the night's drive.

Bridgwater provided the first of a long line of snags, and we set out as it grew dark for Exeter and southwards to Peanore, the stepping-off point for the night's excitements. The plan was that we should both navigate simultaneously, each with a separate set of maps, while Jack did the driving; whoever was sitting in front gave the instructions while the navigator travelling steerage kept a careful check. We joined up with the other team cars at Peanore, stamped the route card when our turn came, in the Printogines time recorder, and set off.

The first control came up in the right place and a few minutes early—as did the second. The third, unfortunately, did not. What had started as a metalled lane degenerated into mud. We hurried on, both trying to convince Jack that we were right, but both extremely doubtful. After all, we knew

Cadwell Park, bleak and deserted in its winter guise. The A.50, Jack Sears up, takes one of the acute bends in the thin sunshine.

that the route would take us into small lanes, even cart tracks or worse; it could still be right. Jack's farming knowledge told him that it was disused—even to us it had become quite clear that no rally cars had sped through in front of us. So we turned round and stormed the muddy hill leading back to civilisation.

Three attempts were terminated by wheelspin, though the considerably abashed and subdued navigators tried to make amends by pushing like mad. Finally, B.M.C.'s pride and joy slid into a ditch. We tried pushing, lifting, bouncing and even snow grips before it came out and, navigators still pushing, struggled to the summit. Had we not been using Dunlop Weathermasters I doubt if, even then, we would have got the car out.

We set out as fast as we could go, found the right road and, by the next control, had made up five of the 14 minutes our mistake had cost us. By the following control we had made up our deficiency, but we had lost 9 minutes, or 90 points; we decided not to make any more navigational errors.

At Hunters Inn, the end of the first loop, we foregathered with the other crews in the team, found that they were through clean and apologised humbly for our having let them down. We adjusted brakes—already showing signs of wear after considerable abuse. There was no steak at Hunters Inn, so we ate hot Cornish pasties and completed the second, less difficult loop

Final tests at Blackpool, the finish of the Rally. The car did not, in fact, touch the wall on this occasion. In a subsequent test it did, but not seriously.

Prize-giving at Blackpool: the crews of the three Austins. Left to right: Douglas Johns, Kenneth Best, Joan Johns, Gerry Burgess, P.G., Sam Croft-Pearson and Jack Sears.

without loss of points, returning through Bridgwater and Bath to Castle Coombe where we arrived for the third of Jack's obbligatos at around 6.45 a.m. on the Wednesday.

Main roads led back through Matchams Park, near Ringwood, Goodwood and Brands Hatch to Hastings; driving tests at each of these three circuits punctuated our journey. After the brakes had been adjusted by the Girling representatives at Brands Hatch we reached Hastings, and yet another driving test, at around 6 p.m. There we had baths and, to ensure that we did not go short of vitamins, two steaks each.

The somewhat unruly crew members, Best and Garnier, were convinced that it would do them no harm to repair to the bar for a pint after dinner, but the less easily swayed Sears decided otherwise; we were in bed and asleep by 9 p.m.

So far as we could see, we were well placed in our class and were in the lead for the team award; John Patten's Porsche, which had been doing splendidly in the tests and had lost no marks on the road, was leading in the general classification. But there was an awful lot of rally left, we decided; the position could alter considerably.

The next stage started at 4.16 a.m. on the Thursday morning. We were called with a cup of tea at 3.15 a.m. and when I grumbled to the maid that it was a frightful hour to be getting up she replied, "Well, it's your hobby; nobody makes you do it"—which was true enough.

We called in at Jack's home at Bolney and let ourselves into the garage to borrow some petrol, and hurried to join Silverstone as fast as possible to gain time to drink some coffee and plot the second night navigation section Yorkshire, this time—on our maps.

Our average from Bolney to Silverstone was just over 30 m.p.h. during which journey I slept. I was awakened at the circuit by Ken and looked at the time, remarking, "Blimey, we must have hurried." Ken, the humorist who kept us in fits of laughter more or less from start to finish, said, "Yes, we've been giving it the full treatment; four-wheel drifts, valve bounce in built-up areas, full use of pavements—the lot."

Sleeping in the back of the car was pleasant. There was a flexible pipe which led hot air from the heater into the rear compartment and by poking this up a trouser leg one obtained efficient central heating.

After Silverstone and its driving test we hurried northwards to Stamford where we joined A1, forgetting temporarily the 40 m.p.h. average. Just before Stamford we passed an ominous looking black XK Jaguar with "Official" on its windscreen: it could, all too easily, have been a secret check, as the distance from Silverstone was, according to the route card, 46.25 miles. When the distance between controls was less than 40 miles there was no risk of secret checks. Where distances of over 40 were involved there was a distinct chance of them, as warned in the regulations.

We stopped in Stamford and set about some calculations; 46.25 miles in 74 minutes gave an average of around 37.5 m.p.h.—we seemed to be safe. During this time we were joined by Ronnie Adams and Godfrey Imhof who, too, were worried—with more justification than ourselves as their cars bore higher numbers than ours and had started later. We decided that we were all just about within the limit and set off for the tests at Cadwell Park and Gamston.

The Gamston test was one of the most complicated and difficult. There had been no previous instructions for it, so drivers had to learn it from instructions issued on the airfield itself. It also imposed considerable strain on the transmissions of the cars due to the frequent reversals of loading as they drove backwards and forwards into the "garages".

Competitors on the Yorkshire night navigation section started simultan-

D. J. Farquharson's Volkswagen passing through Lincoln on the Thursday afternoon.

eously from York and Harrogate, the A.50 starting from York as it bore an even number. Odd numbers went to Harrogate, then drove northwards, broadly speaking, on the western section before cutting across south-east to the start of the eastern section; the York contingent covered the same broad pattern, but starting on the western section.

By the start of the second full night on the road the A.50 had completed something over 1,600 miles. Apart from the need to adjust brakes on several occasions there were no signs of trouble, existing or to come, and the car continued to run and handle beautifully.

We left York and became, once more, the slaves of the Printogines clocks. The Yorkshire section covered some 350 miles and included 23 time controls—each, as with the West Country and final Lake District sections, indicated by six-figure map references on one-inch Ordnance Survey maps; this gave an average of nearly 20 miles between controls.

This time we made no navigational errors, which was just as well; the scheduled average speed was far harder to maintain on the Yorkshire lanes than it had been in the West Country. The undulating switchbacks which seem to be characteristic of this part of the world gave the suspension an appalling time, the springs alternately at full rebound, wheels pawing the air, and crashing against the bump stops. Any thoughts we had of saving the suspension from punishment had to be forgotten in the interests of maintaining our average. The brakes, too, had more than their share of work.

Between us we kept the driver warned of any particularly bad corners or precipitous descents so that he could adjust speed accordingly. But, inevitably, there were those corners whose severity was not fully indicated on the maps—or which we failed to spot—with the resultant violent use of the brakes.

Apart from a delay to tighten wheel nuts, which cost us two minutes (20 marks), we covered the Yorkshire section without incident. It became a prolonged dash through the narrow lanes, punctuated by the briefest of halts at controls while Jack ran and stamped the card and we studied the maps before dashing away again.

The various vitamins with which we had been stuffing ourselves seemed to be doing us good. We all felt comparatively wide awake and, though we carried them, never felt the need for "keep awake" pills. Though these work well with many people, they can produce side affects and we decided to avoid them. We emerged from the section at Scotch Corner—and more steak. We quickly adjusted the brakes, checked oil and water levels, and heard that

Uopkirk's little Standard had retired with big end trouble. Our lead in the team award seemed assured unless the navigation went badly awry.

It was gathered that, at Harrogate, Imhof's Cadillac-Allard had retired with gearbox trouble. His tender car, a Ford Anglia in which his and Ian Mac-Kenzie's luggage was carried, had, by arrangement, met them in Harrogate. Goff had quickly transferred the luggage to the Ford and pressed on, without competition numbers. There was no intention of carrying on this deceit—the final scrutineering would have put paid to any such idea—but it worked throughout the Yorkshire section, the marshals usually remarking, "Got an Anglia this time, Goff?" The absence of numbers at the front of the car was simply accounted for by the fact that they had fallen off; their absence at the rear went unnoticed in the darkness.

The final route card was issued at Scotch Corner and was comparatively easily followed up through Ottterburn and Charterhall, with their driving tests, and back to Penrith. The only difficulty on this section was that certain of the controls could be approached from one direction only; no map references were given, the route being outlined in much the same way that route instructions are given by the R.A.C. or A.A. for a normal journey—though far less detailed.

At Penrith we again went through the routine of adjusting brakes, checking oil and water and tightening wheel nuts. With the high first gear on the car, we were worried about the climb of Hard Knott Pass. Park Rash, in the Yorkshire section, had slowed the car to a walking pace and Hard Knott was considerably steeper.

The Lake District section covered 112 miles before the final, less exacting 54-mile stretch down from Spark Bridge to Blackpool.

Pulling out of Penrith as it grew dark on the Friday night, we wedged

A new Ford Zephyr was the control headquarters at Woodland station as Burgess' Austin A.50 checks in on the Friday night.

This is how The Autocar's Sports Editor, Peter Garnier, reflected on his experiences in a works Austin A50 in the 1956 event.
(Courtesy The Autocar)

*Anglo-German: J. P. Boardman's
Borgward, on Friday, the last day of
the long event, passes through Stainfordham on his way down to the Lake
District special section.*

ourselves in, maps spread out in front of us, and Jack set about the final and most difficult section. There were 13 controls in the 112 miles—an average of only some nine miles between controls. All went well as far as Hard Knott: we reached the controls with a minute or two in hand.

We stormed the Pass, swinging as fast as possible round the hairpins in the hope that the inside rear wheel would run off the road and we had to stop and let him sort out his troubles. The restart was too much for the A.50 and Ken and I set about pushing the car up. As there was no hope of building up speed between hairpins, our services were needed right up to the summit; we pushed for all we were worth round the hairpins and ran after the car on the short straights.

All this set us back about ten minutes. The section that included Hard Knott was known to be very, very tight in normal circumstances. It seemed that we had no alternative but to being ten minutes late at the next control and losing 100 penalty marks. We collapsed, exhausted, in the car while Jack set about regaining lost time.

For the next few miles we were alternately pressed hard into the seats or up against the roof—mostly Jack tore down the other side and along the winding lanes. We caught the Jaguars of Ronnie Adams and Pat Appleyard, and an Aston Martin—and edged our way past them.

The contents of the back of the car slopped from side to side like water in a rocked dinghy, until the interior of the car was a sweeping mass of maps, clothes, Thermos flasks and all the impedimenta of rallying. It was a truly fantastic ride, the car leaping about through the narrow lanes.

At one point where a short straight appeared, the speedometer registered 75 m.p.h. The extraordinary thing was that neither Ken nor I was worried.

First competition appearance of the new 2.4-litre Jaguar, and a successful one, too. W. D. Bleakly swings the car round the pylons at Blackpool on his way to fourth position.

Throughout the event the three team cars had kept together, running into the controls one after the other. Unfortunately, Gerry Burgess had been delayed when, in a fit of enthusiasm after Hardknott, he left the road. The indomitable Jean Johns had completed all three special sections without loss of marks—a magnificent effort. We kept company with the Johns' car down to the finish at Blackpool, having lost Gerry Burgess on the way and collected Pat and Ian Appleyard instead.

A final adjustment of brakes in the early hours of the Saturday morning, and the final checking-in at the finishing control completed Ken's and my rally; Jack had yet three driving tests to do on the Saturday morning. So far as we could see, apart from the somewhat tired dampers the car had not suffered. As an indication of the severe use to which the brakes had been put, the front wheels of the car were covered with a thick layer of dust from the linings; as yet we have not heard from Marcus Chambers, B.M.C. competition manager, of the state of the linings, but there cannot have been much left.

So our rally ended, with a share of the team prize and third place in our class. It had been incredibly good fun with so far as I can remember, never a cross word; the three green Austins stood travel stained outside, undamaged except for a minor dent in the front of ours, caused when we slid gently into a wall in the Lake District.

1957: No rally. Suez stopped play

In summer 1956, Egypt's dictator, Colonel Nasser, nationalised the Suez canal, and in November the UK got together with France to invade the country, and set out to restore the canal to its rightful shareholders. Chaos followed, the USA made it clear that they did not support the military action, the USSR threatened rocket attacks – and within days a fuel supply crisis developed in the Middle East. Petrol rationing was imposed in several countries (including the UK), and all hope of promoting an RAC International Rally for 1957 were abandoned.

Strict petrol rationing was imposed on 17 December 1956, but

later, as something approaching normality was resumed in the Suez canal area (where tankers could therefore make a ready passage), rationing was abandoned on 14 May 1957. By then, of course, the RAC Rally would normally have taken place, and no suitable gap could be found in the crowded European calendar for it to be organised later in the year.

1958: The last traditional 'Tests' event

Because they had not been able to run an RAC Rally in 1957, the organising team had plenty of time to make changes, and improvements for 1958. Although this showed through, in certain features, they elected to run the event in its traditional March 'slot' in the International calendar and still relied on a multitude of tests to ensure a result.

Compared with 1956, however, the routeing was much simplified, for although the 'two starting points' layout was still used, the two streams met up at Prescott hillclimb, and stayed together throughout the remainder of the event. Even so, from that point the action seemed to be intense, for as usual there were driving tests, sprints and two intense navigational nights (in Wales and the Lake District/Scottish borders) to keep the crews busy.

In many ways, though, it was 'the mixture as before,' with 20 special tests (in 1850 miles) scheduled for Prescott, Chateau Impney, Eppynt, Lydstep, Oulton Park, Aintree, Blackpool, Lake District (two tests), Charterhall, Otterburn, Croft, Sherburn-in-Elmet, Chapel-en-le-Frith, Snetterton, Mallory Park, Silverstone, Brands Hatch, and finally at the finish in Hastings. The fact that the navigation sections no longer required a knowledge of the British Ordnance Survey maps system was no attraction to foreign competitors, there being a single overseas private entrant (in a Saab), and Annie Soisbault in a Standard Ten.

All this sounded demanding enough, but the fact that the UK was gripped by near-blizzard conditions made following the complete route, without being time-barred for lateness, virtually impossible, and many crews were obliged to miss out certain time controls and tests in the middle of Wales and the Lake District. Things were so extreme that in the end only 15 cars managed to storm the Hardknott Pass in the Lake District, and only 82 visited the special test on Charterhall racing circuit in the Scottish borders.

It was for this reason that penalties were so high, and in some cases the results were bizarre. As *The Autocar*'s sport editor, Peter Garnier, wrote a week after the event: "One or two people, disillusioned by the hardships of the Welsh section, decided to spend the night at Blackpool, and rejoin the route the following morning, cutting out the Lake District and northern sections. They qualified for their finishers' awards just as much as those who plodded round the whole course …"

There was still no 'seeding,' so the works cars were grouped, according to their class, and to the tidy-minded whim of the organisers, many minutes back along the column, and had to wait

Although the 1958 rally was almost obliterated by blizzard-like conditions, Peter Harper and his works Sunbeam Rapier Mk II kept going, managed to visit every snow-bound control, and won the event outright.

Tom Gold and Willy Cave drove this modified Standard Pennant into third place overall in the 1958 rally, which ended with this driving test in Hastings.

(patiently or otherwise) in the inevitable traffic jams which built up on the ice and snow-covered roads. Some of the professionals, whether they started near the front of the queue, or towards the end, suffered more than most, for Peter Harper (who won outright, and was one of

the 'Heroes of Hardknott') started at No 173, while Pat Moss followed at No 201, while the two valiant works Standard Pennants of Tom Gold and Ron Gouldbourn started at Nos 35 and 34 respectively.

The snow began to intrude soon after the cars reached Chateau Impney, but the blockages (due to impassable surfaces, or crashes which impeded the narrow roads) became endemic in the darkness of the Welsh section. Cars, incidentally, were routed over the notorious Bwlch-y-Groes, but there was no passage control on top of the hill to enforce that, and many cars could not reach the summit anyway!

By the time the cavalcade reached Blackpool, many had fallen by the wayside, but the foremost runners – the Gold and Gouldbourn Pennants (which had both failed to reach Hardknott) were leading, Peter Harper's Rapier was close behind, and the redoubtable Pat Moss in her Morris Minor 1000 was already well-placed. The second half of the event was even more chaotic than the first, for the Lake District roads were much more demanding than those in Wales had been, so by the time the depleted line of cars turned south from Scotland, to trek all the way down to a driving test at the Ferodo factory in Chapel-en-le-Frith, they still had 20 more hours of boring (now snow-free) driving to reach the end of the event at Hastings.

And there it all ended, in great controversy, and huge dissatisfaction. This shambles, it was suggested, must never be allowed to happen again – and for 1959 it was not. A new era in British rallying was about to begin.

RESULTS
Event held: 11-15 March 1958. Two starting points: Blackpool and Hastings. Common route from Prescott hillclimb. One overnight rest halt in Blackpool. Finish at Hastings.

196 starters, 135 finishers.
Sprints, time trials and driving tests.

General classification		Penalties
1 Harper/Deane	Sunbeam Rapier	652.8
2 Gouldbourn/Turner	Standard Pennant	1179.3
3 Gold/Cave	Standard Pennant	1231.4
4 Ms Moss/Ms Wisdom	Morris Minor 1000	1474.5
5 Wadham/Wadham	Morris Minor 1000	1789.4
6 Corbishley/Simister	Standard Ten	1919.5
7 Brinkman/ -	Jaguar 3.4	2084.7
8 Clark/Johns	Riley 1.5	2180..3
9 Smits/Tymon	Fiat 1100	2242.2
10 Lee/Sinclair	Riley 1.5	2407.5

Team Prize: Standard (R Gouldbourn, T Gold and P Hopkirk)
Ladies Prize: Morris Minor 1000 (Ms P Moss and Ms A Wisdom)

CAN I BUY A COMPLETE AXLE, PLEASE? FOR FITMENT RIGHT NOW? THE FACTORY WILL PAY

Due to the awful weather, and the bizarre marking system on the event, when Paddy Hopkirk found his works Standard Pennant needing a rear axle change, he was so far adrift of the time schedule that he decided to call in on a Standard dealership at Kelso, bargained with the proprietor for an on-the-spot repair, and bought (and had fitted) the complete rear axle of a Standard Ten that he saw in the showroom. Although running late, he then resumed the event, and was one of the Standard team that won the Team Prize.

Erik Carlsson's first drive in the RAC Rally came in 1959, in this Saab 93, but he crashed out on a Welsh road section. Things would unfold rather better a year later.

1959: The Tomintoul debacle

The story of the 1959 rally has often been told, but the rancour, the arguments, and the long-lasting cries of 'We Wuz Robbed' live on. The fact is that one part of the route in Scotland, completely blocked by snow, caused many fancied crews to fall by the wayside, and those who took a pragmatic decision to avoid the blockage ended up taking all the awards.

The blockage meant that crews wishing to survive the carnage had to take colossal diversions, on roads otherwise not on the official route, even to reach the Braemar control. Delays of 30 minutes and more were inevitable, and those who elected to miss out this control, which they were sure would be cancelled from the results, were irretrievably penalised.

Jack Kemsley was brought in as the rally organiser for 1959 and beyond. It was his team which quite transformed the event in the decade that followed.

Compared with the 1958 event, which had been shambolic in many ways, the 1959 event was the first to be devised and organised by the experienced and well-liked competitor Jack Kemsley. Although a series of special tests were retained, not only did he make sure that there was more 'real rallying' than ever before, there was to be no overnight rest halt of any type, there would be only one starting point (Blackpool was chosen), and the date was moved from March to mid-November, at the very end of the 'International season.'

Not only that, but the entry was 'seeded' for the first time – with many of the fancied runners (or those in high-powered machinery) starting near the front of the queue. The professionals loved it, and this must have explained he presence of entries from Erik Carlsson (Saab), Annie Soisbault (Triumph TR3A), several works Citroën DS19s from France – and Wolfgang Levy's Auto-Union 1000 from Germany.

Tiny Lewis and his Triumph Herald Coupé tackle the Prescott Hill test in the 1959 RAC Rally.

The penalty marking system, too, was fresh, for it separated road penalties from all those in the many special tests – manoeuvring tests, sprints, hillclimbs, and short circuit races – and meant that a competitor 'cleaning' the road sections (which were very tough in 1959), but faring badly on the tests would automatically finish above all those who were penalised at time controls along the way. This, as will become clear, became vitally important as the event evolved.

Naturally, all the usual British works teams turned out in force – and the scores of British clubmen who savoured the atmosphere of the RAC also liked what they saw. This was the first of the truly 'all-Britain' events, for the 2000-mile route included tests, sprints or circuit tests at Blackpool, Charterhall, Rest and be Thankful, Aintree, Oulton Park, Eppynt, Prescott, Harleyford Manor, Brands Hatch and Crystal Palace, and stretched all the way north to Gairloch in north-west Scotland, and Carmarthen in south-west Wales.

Works cars (this being Burgess' winning Ford of 1959) did not need high-tech equipment to go rallying in the 1950s.

On the first night, navigation tests in Yorkshire and the Lake District were difficult (there was fog and slippery roads), so that only 32 cars were still unpenalised at the Brough control. That number had dropped to 20 at the Peebles breakfast halt, where it seemed that the works Austin-Healeys, and Rapiers were all well placed. It soon became clear that Wolfgang Levy's Auto-Union, John Wallwork's Volvo and Jimmy Ray's works Sunbeam Alpine were all performing impeccably on the tests, and were clearly close to the top of the lists – though the results service was so slow that no-one really knew what was happening until at least 24 hours after the event had passed on to its next phase!

The next 24 hours' motoring on Scottish roads were scenic, but (apart from the brief sprint up Rest and be Thankful) were dull and free of excitement. Jack Sears' works Austin-Healey 3000 was fastest up 'The Rest,' but there were no major changes in the order before the rally arrived at the control at Nairn, where the first car was due to leave at 10.42pm on a wet and gloomy Scottish November night.

It was soon after this that the unexpected drama began to unfold. Although the theoretical schedule of the next road section was a 68-mile, 2 hr 16 minute run up and over the Lecht Road (the A939 south of Tomintoul) to a control at Braemar, and looked easy enough, this took no account of the possibility of inclement winter weather. However, the summit of the 2000ft Lecht road had already become impassable with deep snowdrifts, and no one seemed to have notified

Snow blocking roads in the mountains of Scotland decimated the RAC Rally field in November 1959, but Gerry Burgess somehow raced around the impasse in his Ford Zephyr II to claim outright victory. Here he is seen on the final hairpin of the Rest and be Thankful hillclimb in Scotland, before that drama unfolded ...

... and here, near the end of the event at Prescott hillclimb in Gloucestershire.

the officials at the Nairn controls (no mobile phones, no mobile 'pilot' cars, and no internet in those days of course), and the rally cars were dispatched in blissful ignorance of what was to follow.

All went well until the first group of cars had passed through Grantown-on-Spey and Tomintoul before they found impassable snow drifts, rally cars stuck, crews digging, and no obvious way through. The only way that the later numbers even got a sense of this was when they began to meet rally cars retracing their steps to Grantown, many miles back along the route. Those determined to reach Braemar somehow, within 60 minutes of being inflicted with a maximum 300 mark penalty, set off around the Cairngorms – but alternative routes were scarce, and the only two sensible diversions (one via the A9 through Pitlochry, the other through Dufftown and the A941) each added 40 miles to the section.

In the end, only 15 of the 131 starters clocked into Braemar within their 60 minute penalty, and at a stroke the leaderboard (complete with Braemar penalties) looked like this:

Ford Zephyr II (G Burgess, running No 66)	29 minutes penalty
Sunbeam Rapier (E Malkin, running No 98)	36 minutes
Singer Gazelle (Dr J T Spare, running No 87)	40 minutes
Austin-Healey Sprite (T Gold, running No 51)	41 minutes
Riley 1.5 (M Sutcliffe, running No 103)	43 minutes
Austin-Healey 3000 (D Morley running No 9)	44 minutes

What is interesting here is that almost none of those running early in the field figured here, as they were marooned on the mountain. It is a lasting miracle that the Morley Twins had somehow managed not to have become embroiled in the digging and pushing, had turned back at an early stage, and used the immense performance of their Big Healey to race round the mountain, and to help them retrieve something.

Half the field was eliminated in that wintry Scottish night, and the rest were exhausted, wet and disgruntled, which made the long drag down through southern Scotland, a hectic night scrabbling around the lanes of Wales, and a final trek across country from Carmarthen, to Prescott, to Brands Hatch, then to London's Crystal Palace race circuit, seem like a tedious irrelevance. The final 'road' section of all was a sprint (at a 30mph set average speed!) from Brands Hatch to Crystal Palace, through London's outer suburbs on a mid-Friday evening!

The drama was not yet over, even then, for no sooner had the 53 survivors clocked in at Crystal Palace, and had their cars impounded for the night in Parc Ferme, than Wolfgang Levy and his co-driver, Stuart Turner, entered an official protest, demanding the abandonment of the Braemar control. But who was Levy, and why did he protest?

The answer was not only that he was in a works front-wheel-drive two-stroke Auto-Union, but his performance on all the special tests had been quite impeccable, so, although his co-driver had directed him around the chaos ahead (he was running at Number 139, very close to the end of the cavalcade), he had still incurred 50 minutes of lateness before reaching Braemar.

The last test in the 1959 rally was a short circuit race at Crystal Palace – here John La Trobe's Volvo Amazon leads an unidentified Volvo, and two of the works Rapiers – Peter Harper in No 79 and Peter Jopp in No 93.

All in all, this was a most unsatisfactory way to bring an otherwise well-organised and freshened event to a close. But with Kemsley promising an eventual end to fiddly special tests, and even some highly-secret special stages for the 1960 RAC, he was speedily forgiven.

RESULTS

Event held: 17-21 November 1959. One starting point: Blackpool. No mid-event overnight halt. Finish at Crystal Place, London.

131 starters, 53 finishers.
Sprints, time trials and driving tests.

General classification		Penalties (minutes of road penalties)
1 Burgess/Croft-Pearson	Ford Zephyr Mk II	32
2 Gold/Hughes	Austin-Healey Sprite	42
3 Sutcliffe/Astle	Riley 1.5	43
4 Morley/Morley	Austin-Healey 3000	44
5 Malkin/Robson	Sunbeam Rapier	46
6 Morgan/Thompson	Morgan Plus 4	48
7 Spare/Barley	Singer Gazelle	50
8 Levy/Turner	Auto Union 1000 Coupé	50
9 Jopp/Leston	Sunbeam Rapier	50
10 Hodson/Collinson	Triumph TR3A	52

Team Prize: Triumph TR3As (D Seigle-Morris, E Hodson, and Mlle A Soisbault)
Ladies Prize: Ford Anglia 105E (Mrs A Hall and Ms Patsy Burt)

IF THE PROTEST HAD BEEN UPHELD

If Wolfgang Levy's protest about the legality of retaining the Braemar control had finally been upheld, not only would he have won the rally outright, but this would have lifted him to second overall in the 1959 European Rally Championship. Not only that, but cancellation of the penalties incurred at the Braemar control would have caused a sweeping change in the other leading positions. According to the unofficial 'new' classification later computed by *Autosport* magazine, only nine competitors had completed the balance of the road section without penalty, so the general classification would have looked like this:

		Test penalties
1	Auto-Union 1000 (W Levy and S Turner)	3
2	Volvo (J Wallwork/M Wood)	11
3	Sunbeam Alpine (J Ray/P Crabtree)	15
4	Sunbeam Rapier III (P Harper/P Procter)	18
5	Triumph Herald Coupé (I D L Lewis/R Porter)	23
6	Austin-Healey 3000 (D Morley/E Morley)	35
7=	Morris Minor 1000 (Ms P Moss/Ms A Wisdom)	38
	Ford Anglia 105E (D Scott/M Armstrong)	38
9	Aston Martin DB2 (L Sims/R Jones)	41
10	Austin-Healey 3000 (J Sears/W Cave)	6 (plus 1 road penalty)

On the other hand, because he incurred four road penalties away from his heroic drive to the Braemar control, Gerry Burgess would have been demoted to 17th spot, and Tom Gold (Sprite, with two other penalties) would have dropped to 14th.

This was the combination that celebrated the major change in the rally's format – Erik Carlsson, Stuart Turner and their Saab 96. In 1960 they were the only crew to beat the target times on all four of the event's special stages.

1960: The first 'special stages' event

It was in the RAC Rally of November 1960, that there were four – just a modest four – Special Stages included in the event for the very first time. These were the very first stages, indeed, which were included in any British event, their use having been inspired by what was happening at the time in Scandinavia. Previous RAC Rallies had occasionally used special tests that (in the language of the day) were identified as 'special stages,' but racing against the clock had not been involved, and the 'special' side of those sections had meant to show that they were different in tone from the remainder of the competitive sections of those events.

Up to 1958 the RAC had been the 'Rally of Tests,' then for 1959 Jack Kemsley had taken over the organisation, when it became a more demanding long-distance event, still with night navigation and special tests, but with more endurance (there had not been an overnight rest halt …), and quite gruelling sections in Wales. For 1960, however, Jack Kemsley promised even more hard driving, and even fewer special tests ('circus acts' as some cynics called them).

Superficially, therefore, it looked rather like the 'mixture as before,' for there would be anything between speed climbs of the Rest and be Thankful hill in Scotland, to a circuit race at Mallory Park, and a driving test on a greasy skid pan near Coventry – but now there was to be the added challenge of four genuine high-speed special stages – all of those stages being located in Scotland. In theory the route was kept secret until the day before the start, so it was quite amazing that Erik Carlsson and Stuart Turner found time to put in a lot of 'route survey' work in Scotland, an enterprise which at one point led to the Swede's car colliding with a local car on a narrow road, and with Erik breaking two ribs!

Even so, this still seemed to be too 'British' a rally for most European works heroes, who generally stayed away. However, as the results of the European Championship were still at stake, Mercedes-Benz and Citroën both entered cars, but no sooner had René Trautmann crashed out of the event in his DS19 (which eliminated Citroën from the reckoning of Championship points) than Mercedes-Benz withdrew its own cars, and high-tailed it back to Germany.

Starting from Blackpool on 21 November, stopping overnight

In 1960, the RAC held the Prize Giving at the Talk of the Town theatre in central London. The winning Saab, and its crew, were displayed on the stage at the time.

John Sprinzel put up a remarkable performance in 1960 in his famous Austin-Healey Sprite, taking second place.

Beryl Neate about to tackle the RAC's first-ever special stage – Monument Hill, in Scotland, in 1960.

on Tuesday/Wednesday 22/23 November in Inverness, and ending at Brands Hatch on Friday, 25 November, it was to be another marathon. The first night involved tight road sections in Yorkshire and Cumbria which were fog-bound, the result being that only six crews – the Morley Twins, John Sprinzel, Geoff Crabtree, Erik Carlsson, David Seigle-Morris and Johnny Wallwork – were still unpenalised on the road section by the time they reached the first breakfast halt at Peebles. There was more of the same in Yorkshire on the last night, but apart from speed hillclimbs, sprints and circuit tests, much of the mileage was, well, just mileage.

All the stages were in Scotland, three of them in the north-west, but of course it was the very first of them, over Monument Hill,

near Dalmally (which is 20 miles east of Oban) which caused a stir. Somehow Bob Tennant-Reid, the secretary of the Royal Scottish Automobile Club, had persuaded the forestry commission to let him use a remote track which was rocky and gravel-strewn, and had set a two-mile stage in a target time of three minutes. That was a target of just 40mph, but as everyone now knows, only one car – Erik Carlsson's two-stroke Saab – could beat that.

The marking system was byzantine, and class-based, but it seems that Ian Walker's car, four seconds late, was the fastest runner-up, being docked one point. According to *Autosport*'s report, Peter Riley (Healey 3000), Ronnie Adams (Healey 3000) and Pat Moss (Sprite) lost one point, everyone else losing two or more. The mass of private owners had never seen, or experienced, anything like this before, and were terrified of damaging their cars. In future years, though, they would be forewarned.

After the overnight halt, there were three more special stages on the next day, all of them on tiny Scottish roads closed specially for the occasion, and set at a 30mph average. One, on the coast north of Lochinver (next stop, the Atlantic Ocean), was the 'Scottish Safari,' roughish but possible. There was another stage close to Inverness, and the final stages (dubbed 'Auf Wiedersehen') followed a climb of the famous corkscrew road and the Inverfarigaig hairpins to the east of Loch Ness. Because of the 30mph target averages, these were just about cleanable, which meant that the first stage – over Monument Hill – was always going to be the clincher.

Looking back over 50 years, the miracle is that the stages could be included at all, because the Royal Scottish Automobile Club must surely have bent all manner of laws to close sections of what were public highways. When a historian once asked Bob Tennant-Reid how it could be done, he merely smiled secretively and replied: "Oh, no problem. This is Scotland, Laddie ..." No doubt he would have liked to set higher target averages, but simply dare not, so three of the four stages were set at just 30mph, and rendered rather pointless.

A service car park in the 1960 event, and not a sponsor's display in sight. The array of cars included Sunbeam Rapiers, Morris Minor 1000s, Austin-Healey Sebring Sprites, Minis, and Ford Anglia 105Es. Author Robson was co-driving Julian Easten's car No 117.

It may not be necessary to point this out, but even without the special stages, this rally would have ended up with the same worthy winner. Even though he started at No 178 – just seven from the back of the 184-car field – Carlsson was consistently class-fastest on all the other special tests. However, for the entire field, the sting came in the tail, for as the rally approached London on the Friday late afternoon, normal (heavy) traffic became a problem, and the organisers had not reduced the target averages to suit.

First of all the cars had to call at a time control near Maidenhead, then visit another check at a road house on the old A25 near Dorking, after which they had to fight their way through Redhill on that infamous road (this was decades before the M25 was even planned) to reach Brands Hatch circuit itself, all at an unforgiving 30mph average speed. Wily British navigators already had one-inch maps with them to work out diversions, and people like Stuart Turner admitted that they had used very odd routeings at times to keep up with the average. One of the authors of this book, co-driving in Julian Easten's Rapier, had to resort to similar tactics, and had nothing in hand at the end of the session!

Lessons to be drawn? Special stages were a great success, traditional old-style tests were despised more than ever before, and for 1961 the demand for more stages would have to be met. Indeed it was, for that was the year in which high-speed averages would be set on Forestry Commission land spaced all around the country.

RESULTS
Event held: 21-26 November 1960. One starting point, from Blackpool. Finish at Brands Hatch Circuit. One overnight rest halt in Inverness.

172 starters, 138 finishers.
Sprints, time trials, driving tests – and four special stages.

General classification		Minutes/penalties
1 Carlsson/Turner	Saab 96	0/0
2 Sprinzel/Bensted-Smith	Austin-Healey Sprite	2/23
3 D Morley/E Morley	Austin-Healey 3000	2/25
4 Berry/Sears/Cave	Jaguar 3.8	3/8
Detailed results have not survived. However, the balance of the Top Ten, shown by minutes of road penalties, was:		
5 Wallwork/Brooks	Volvo	3
6 Seigle-Morris/Elford	BMC Mini-Minor	3
7 Lewis/Sheppard	Triumph Herald Coupé	3
8 Crabtree/Woolley	Ford Anglia 105E	4
9 Mrs A Hall/Ms V Domleo	Ford Anglia 105E	5
10 Riley/Ambrose	Austin-Healey 3000	7

Manufacturers' Team Prize: BMC/Austin-Healey (D Morley, P Riley, and R Adams).
Ladies Prize: Ford Anglia 105E (Mrs A Hall and Ms V Domleo).

RAC RALLY 1960 – THE PIONEERING SPECIAL STAGES
Stage 1: Monument Hill, near Dalmally, 20 miles from Oban, Scotland. Private road, 40mph target average: only Erik Carlsson (Saab 96) achieved that target. Now a very well-known route, but no longer used for motorsport.

Stage 2: Between Drumbeg and Lochinver (a public highway now listed as B869). Along Scotland's west (Atlantic) coast, the stage being taken North to South. Night-time. 5.8 miles, set in 11min 36sec (30mph average). Rough in places and very twisty – dubbed the 'Scottish Safari' by the organisers. Lochinver is NW of Inverness, Scotland.

Stage 3: Inverfarigaig, NE of Fort Augustus, a minor but still public highway, approx 20 miles south of Inverness, starting from the eastern shores of Loch Ness, and ending at the junction with the B862 near the tiny village of Torness. 1.5 miles, 3 minutes allowed. A 'traditional' rally section, well-known to all regular competitors.

Stage 4: Dubbed 'Auf Weidershen' by the organisers, this one was a five miler (10 minutes allowed), starting at a junction with A862 (about 15 miles from Inverness), striking south-east past Loch Duntelchaig, then Loch Ruthven, and ending at a tiny hamlet called East Croarchy (on the B851).

Chapter 3

1960-1971

SPECIAL STAGES AND SCANDINAVIANS

It was after the 1958 RAC Rally had almost vanished under the controversy caused by the heavy snows, the disruption to the route, and the organisational confusion this caused during the event, that the demands for major changes surfaced. The time had come, it was suggested, that the 'old guard' organising team's emphasis on special tests but not on speeds, and its insistence on using club-level navigational sections, should be swept away.

More than that, it was clear that major changes were needed if the event was ever likely to attract some of the big names, and the most prestigious factory teams, from overseas. To their credit, the 'Great and the Good' at the RAC took all this on board, cast around, and invited Jack Kemsley, a man who already had a great deal of experience of competition in the Monte Carlo and Tulip rallies, to develop his own theme. They hoped that he would transform the rally's reputation, and make it more 'modern' in every way.

Jack accepted, apparently without hesitation, and set about a root-and-branch change in the way that Britain's premier rally should be run in future years. It is to his eternal credit that the changes he wrought in the early and mid-1960s can still be seen in the modern versions of this long-standing event.

Not that it could all be done at once. First, the world of rallying had to take on board what was proposed, secondly a new format would have to evolve over time, and thirdly a startling new concept of settling the event according to the performance and durability of the cars, rather than their drivers' dexterity, would have to take over.

A fourth factor – that Kemsley wanted to be more sure that 'his' new event would not be disrupted by the weather – meant making a major change to the season in which it should be held. He was either lucky with his choice, or even more knowledgeable about the world of rallying than most of us had ever thought, when he persuaded the RAC to run its event in future years in November (rather than March), which just happened to be towards the very end of the year, and could often mean that the RAC Rally would become a vital 'must-do' event

for serious contenders in the European Rally Championship, of which it was already a qualifying round.

Looking back, it is now fascinating to see how the old style of RAC Rallying was transformed into the new 'Kemsley-style' of rallying in just five years, in some ways so gradually that the upheaval was not really noticed, or criticised. In 1959 (the first which author Robson ever contested), there was to be only one starting point, more endurance and more hard motoring – no overnight rest halt, for instance – but still a big variety of tests, speed hill climbs, and short circuit tests. A year later, in 1960, came the major innovation, the inclusion of four so-called 'Special Stages' to add to the tests, but in 1961 there were 24 scheduled Special Stages, the very first to be used on Forestry Commission roads and tracks – and a higher-speed driving test along Madeira Drive in Brighton to bring this groundbreaking event to a close.

In 1962 the march towards making this a pure speed + endurance + car strength event continued, for in that year there were no fewer than 38 special stages (almost all of them on Forestry Commission land), in 1963 there were 43 scheduled stages, and in 1964 that figure had risen to no fewer than 56 stages. It was no surprise, therefore, to note that as the emphasis on special stages became more and more obvious, the number of European entries (particularly from Scandinavia) continued to rise.

Credit for this breakthrough, of course, was due to the event's ability to run Special Stages from 1960 onwards. In 1960, as already described in the previous Chapter, only four such 'stages' had been held, all of them in Scotland, of which one (Monument Hill) was on private land, while the other three were all on public roads which had been specially closed for the occasion. Those three stages, incidentally, were timed at a mere 30mph, and were 'cleanable' by many determined crews, but they were, at least, a taster for what Kemsley had in mind for the event's future.

For 1961, however, he somehow managed to persuade high

officials in the Forestry Commission (a government-owned body which owns and controls many thousands of acres of forests, complete with many miles of gravel surfaced tracks through them) that the RAC Rally should be routed through a number of these, where against-the-clock stages could be set at higher average speeds. At first it was suggested that some tests could carry 'Target Times' of up to 50mph, but after just one year it became clear that all would be timed at that level. (In later years, incidentally, some were timed at even higher speeds, but how this was done without offending the RAC's motorsport law-makers is not known ...)

No sooner had such stages become available for use on the RAC Rally (for a significant fee, it must be emphasised) than they were adopted by other British Championship events too, so it was not long before venues such as Dovey (Central Wales), Keilder (the English/Scottish borders), and Dalby (North Yorkshire) became well-known to tens of thousands of competitors, spectators, and media outlets.

For most of the 1960s, therefore, the rally settled happily, successfully, and, it seems, popularly, into a stable format – originally by starting at one out-of-season resort, finishing at another, enjoying one overnight rest halt, and tackling an ever-growing number of mainly Forestry Commission stages. From the mid-1960s, that rigid format was changed to make the event more easily accessible to the media – particularly to the TV companies, who planned to cover the start, the finish, and perhaps one or two stages closer to the capital – by basing the event around London.

In all this time there were two major hiccups for the promoters. One of them came in 1967, when Great Britain was suddenly afflicted by a massive and wide-ranging epidemic of bovine foot & mouth disease, which caused huge areas of the UK to be unavailable to wheeled traffic, and led to the last-minute cancellation of the event. Only a year after that, and surely in circumstances where the RAC could have insisted on a change of dates, the RAC faced up to the attraction of the original London-Sydney Marathon, which was not only due to start from London at the same time as the RAC, but which also attracted all the major rally teams to compete. That one clash saw entries for the RAC fall from 160 to 96, and they were hard-pressed to recover in future years.

Even so, by the end of the 1960s, the RAC Rally had established itself as one of the handful of 'must-do' events, which every professional driver and team really wanted to tackle at every opportunity. Those events – RAC, Monte Carlo, East African Safari, and French Alpine – were undoubtedly the best, the most demanding, and the most characteristic, so it was interesting to speculate on how rallying would change and develop in the decade that followed.

1961: Full-blooded special stages – at last
This was the year in which the RAC Rally was dragged, kicking and screaming, into the modern era, when flat-out special stages, some very long, and almost all of them on Forestry Commission tracks, made up the competitive part of the event. Here was the type of event which Jack

Kemsley had always envisaged when he took control in 1959, and here was a format which finally attracted serious entries from European factory teams.

To use the language of the real, dyed-in-the-wool rally enthusiasts, here was a 'real' rally' – at last. From Blackpool, to Brighton, by way of a night halt at Inverness, there was to be a 2123 mile road section, and no fewer than 24 flat-out special stages, plus a modicum of familiar visits to race circuits around the country, for there were still one or two simple speed tests or circuit/sprints (including a now-traditional visit to Rest and be Thankful, and a manoeuvring test on the seafront at Brighton), but almost all the high-speed/open-road/navigation scheduling had been abandoned. The only irritant was that there was still to be a severe penalty (equivalent to a 'maximum' on a special stage) for arriving at the finish with a body-damaged car. Championship contender Hans Walter, co-driven by John Sprinzel, evaded this rule by arriving at the start with 'damaged' front wings, declared them, and was thus immune for the rest of the event!

This was, on the whole, an extremely popular formula, so it was no wonder that the event had attracted full-blooded factory team entries from BMC, Ford, Sunbeam, Saab and Volvo, with factory support also behind cars like the Porsche 356 Carrera of Hans Walter and Raymond Baxter's Humber Super Snipe.

Ford developed the Anglia 105E into a capable little rally car. This was Anne Hall, in a driving test, at the close of the 1961 RAC Rally in Brighton.

Carrying No 1 (because he had won the event in 1960) Erik Carlsson also won the 1961 RAC Rally in his Saab 96. Here he is seen on the time trial at Mallory Park ...

Although the format of the special stages – individual against-the-clock racing to meet near-impossible target times (these sections were mostly set at a 50mph average) – were familiar to those who had previously tackled events in Scandinavia. To the majority of drivers, even the professionals, they were a British novelty. When first encountered, the stage surfaces were invariably of well-graded loose gravel (although these gradually got cut up, became rougher and more rock-strewn, as more and more cars passed over them), and the route through complex forests was well signposted at every junction. Pre-event practising, of course, was totally forbidden, a ban which seems to have been totally absorbed.

Would the Scandinavians prove to be significantly faster than the other Europeans? After a 6.00pm start from Blackpool, the leading cars had to wait until midnight, when they lined up at the start of the very first stage, north-west of Hexham. This stage was known as Keilder, and it would become legendary in future years. Seven drivers beat the target time on this stage – Erik Carlsson, Pat Moss, Donald Morley, David Seigle-Morris, Hans Walter, Peter Harper and Rauno Aaltonen (driving Eugen Böhringer's works Mercedes-Benz saloon), but mechanical breakdowns, damage, excursions, and sheer inexperience began to nibble away at those close behind them. Even so, seven stages (including three in Northumberland, and four in and around Loch Ness in Scotland) confirmed the early forecasts that Erik Carlsson would outstrip everyone, even though his front-wheel-drive two-stroke Saab only had an 0.85-litre engine. Of the Brits, the Big Healeys were both formidable and tough, with the works Sunbeam Rapiers not far behind them – yet an early

... and here on the final driving test on Madeira drive in Brighton at the end of the event.

BMC entered a team of MG Midgets for the 1961 event, where Derrick Astle won his class, and finished eighth in this car.

The perils of driving on stages with punctured tyres. Peter Procter and author Robson show off the remains of two wheels on their works Rapier. They were determined to finish ... and did.

upset came in Scotland when the Aaltonen/Böhringer Mercedes-Benz found itself irretrievably ditched at one point.

After the welcome overnight rest halt in Inverness, the route led direct to another forest which was to be come familiar in the future – Culbin (near Forres), a fast 13-miler – where Carlsson was as dominant as before, but where Walter's Porsche went off for ten minutes, Gunnar Andersson's Volvo punctured, and Ewy Rosqvist was forced to abandon her Volvo P1800 with a broken fuel tank. The route then led via the infamous Lecht Road (no signs of snow, unlike 1959), and into the Newcastleton and Kershope forests on the England/Scotland border.

In the next few hours, where the event first encountered a special stage in the North Yorkshire complex, at Staindale (a 21-miler, set in 25 minutes, which was quite impossible for everyone to meet) the Morley Twins' Austin-Healey 3000 retired with a broken rear axle, but the leaderboard was beginning to settle down. Carlsson was ahead of everyone else, with Pat Moss struggling to keep up in second place, Peter Harper's Rapier in third place, and Paddy Hopkirk's sister car close behind.

The last 30 hours of the event then settled back into an amalgam of 'old-style' RAC Rallying, interspersed with yet more special stages. Accordingly, there were tarmac sprints, tarmac stages (including 11.5-miles on Eppynt), or circuit tests on Oliver's Mount

(Scarborough), Mallory Park, Oulton Park, and Prescott, while newfangled stages were held in Selby, Sherwood Forest, Cannock Chase, Dovey, Radnor and Speech House Walk.

To give a feel for the fact that the rally was still changing its format, and learning for the future, the all-gravel Dovey stage measured 17.4 miles, for which the target time was 23 minutes – a 45mph set average. No-one approached parity here, with Carlsson's Saab 2min 50sec adrift, and Pat Moss' Austin-Healey a further 40 seconds behind. The problem was clearly not connected with driver bravery, but with the way in which no cars were using anything approaching winter-tread tyres (the use of radial-ply types would not follow until 1964) and that – frankly – they were not yet as fleet as they would become in the future.

The drag from Prescott to Brighton was tedious, being set at only 25mph on main roads, but free of heavy traffic (the organisers had learnt from their 1960 faux pas), so there were no further changes in the standings. Before arrival in Brighton, most factory teams had found time to freshen up their cars, to make sure that damage penalties would not be incurred, and it was reported that only four cars were penalised when scrutinised after the event. Peter Procter's Rapier, for instance, which had careered off the track in the Monaughty stage, carried on for another two days, and eventually arrived at Mallory Park to find a complete, glazed, painted-up driver's door with competition number sticker-applied, ready to be exchanged – which was done in a matter of minutes.

The final day, at Brighton, involved no more than a high-speed mile-long driving test along Madeira Drive (better known for its use in the city's speed trials) where, predictably enough, the day's fastest time was put up by Hans Walter's Porsche, though Pat Moss' Austin-Healey ran him close. Carlsson's Saab, with nothing to lose, screamed its way from one end to the other, emphasising his complete mastery of this first 'modern' RAC Rally.

Erik, by the way, had cleaned no fewer than 15 of the 24 stages without penalty, which encouraged Jack Kemsley's team to considering raising the set averages to 50mph as soon as possible. He also left every other team manager to wonder if front-wheel-drive, and Scandinavian drivers would be needed to ensure success. They were right – but it would take a few years for this to be emphasised.

RESULTS
From 1961, the RAC Rally's emphasis changed from driving tests to special stages. It is with this in mind that from 1961 onwards we change the way in which the results are presented.

Event held: 13-17 November 1961. One starting point, from Blackpool.

Finish at Brighton. One overnight rest halt in Inverness.

150 starters, 81 finishers.
Sprints, driving tests – and 24 special stages.

General classification		Group	Penalties
1 Carlsson/Brown	Saab 96	1/2	89
2 Ms P Moss/Ms A Wisdom	Austin-Healey 3000	3	129
3 Harper/Hall	Sunbeam Rapier	1/2	150
4 Hopkirk/Scott	Sunbeam Rapier	1/2	166
5 Seigle-Morris/Ambrose	Austin-Healey 3000	3	170
6 Andersson/Johns	Volvo PV544	1/2	184
7 Ray/Hopwood	BMC Mini 850	1/2	204
8 Ms A Hall/Ms V Domleo	Ford Anglia 105E	1/2	204
9 Astle/Roberts	MG Midget	3	217
10 Sutcliffe/Fidler	MG Midget	3	239

Team Prize: Sunbeam Rapiers (P Harper, P Hopkirk and P Procter).
Ladies Prize: Austin-Healey 3000 (Ms P Moss and Ms A Wisdom).

FORBIDDEN PRACTICING

No sooner had the first Special Stages been included in the format of the RAC Rally, than the organisers made it clear that pre-event practicing (and, for that matter, the making of Pace Notes on sections which would clearly be used again) was strictly forbidden.

The less scrupulous of competitors (and, to be frank, there were many of them), tried to get around this, by infiltrating forestry commission areas and cruising around some sections 'on holiday,' and it was not long before some of the more obvious routes through the forests became known, even famous (and in some cases infamous). It did not help the RAC organisers' case, of course, that some forests – like those in Central Wales, North Yorkshire, and the Keilder complex in the Scottish borders – soon came to be used on fewer events, and well-versed co-drivers became adept at adding such visits to their memory banks.

In some cases, too, there would be several stages in one complex – the North Yorkshire area was a good example – where one stage ended, and the next one began at a junction on private land. Even so, those service crews with experience could often penetrate to such points, and provide emergency assistance if needed. This was totally 'sporting illegal,' of course, but became common. Neither of the authors of this book would admit to having been involved in guiding team managers to certain places, to arrive smugly at those points,

only to find that other rival teams had also achieved the same cloak-and-dagger exploits too!

As the years passed, in this cramped little island there were few totally 'secret' stages that could be used, which explains why the average speeds achieved continued to rise, and why large groups of spectators could often be found some miles from so-called civilisation.

Even so, it was many years before the smug assumption that the stages would still be 'secret' was dropped.

1962: A hat-trick for Erik Carlsson

The 1961 event had been a great success, but for 1962 the RAC Rally set out to be bigger, more competitive, more demanding – and more popular than ever before. Not only were 38 special stages listed, but no fewer than the six front-running 'seeded' drivers were from overseas. A newcomer to this event, running way down at No 38 in a BMC Mini-Cooper, was from Finland – his name being Timo Mäkinen.

The entry list was oversubscribed, the fastest and most experienced crews were all listed at the front of the field, BMC, Ford, Reliant, Rover, Sunbeam, and Triumph had all entered factory teams, to be met by Mercedes-Benz, Saab and Volvo from overseas, and the competition looked set to be the most intense so far encountered. Ford entered a single Group 3 Cortina (its debut in rallying), while the big and luxuriously trimmed Rover P5 saloons were a novelty.

In 1962, Erik Carlsson, this time with David Stone as his co-driver, used this two-stroke Saab 96 to win his third consecutive RAC Rally.

Wisely, arch-organiser Jack Kemsley had asked competitors and team managers to tell him what had been right about the 1961 event so that further improvements could be made, and the response had been almost entirely positive – except that all made it clear that the traditional old tests and sprints must surely be abandoned?

And so it was, for apart from the now traditional visits to Oulton Park (a five-lap sprint), and a stage over the tarmac-surfaced (military controlled) Eppynt ranges, each and every one of the competitive sections was now to be on loose-surfaced tracks, mainly in Forestry Commission territory: each and every one of the 300 miles of stages was now set at 50mph, which usually meant that 'clean' sheets would no longer exist.

The basic route took in five days of motoring, in which there was to be only one overnight rest halt (back in Blackpool), with stages mainly concentrated in North Yorkshire, Keilder, the far north of Scotland, the Lake District, and a final 12-stage flourish in Wales. The high-speed action began in the Cropton, Pickering and Staindale forests, where Eugen Böhringer's works Mercedes-Benz 220SE became the first high-profile casualty (it hit a tree, which was even more sturdy than the big German car), and the Morley Twins' Austin-Healey 3000 rolled, and injured its driver. Erik Carlsson's Saab 96, on the other hand, was as fast, as exuberantly noisy, and as effective as ever, and led as the field reached the first breakfast halt at Peebles.

By the time the event reached its most northern control, at Inverness, the leaderboard was already settling down. Carlsson led, the two Austin-Healey 3000s of Paddy Hopkirk and Pat Moss were struggling to keep up, and the rest, frankly, were struggling to get on terms. David Seigle-Morris' works MG1100 blew its engine, Anne Hall inverted her Ford Anglia 105E, though Tom Trana and Bengt Söderström (both of them in Mini-Coopers) were in and around the 'Top Six.' So, too, was the wild man from Finland – Timo Mäkinen – who was proving to be much faster than anyone had ever expected.

Many competitors, new to this sort of rough-road rallying at high-speed, found the underside of their cars suffering from rocks and flying debris, along with the challenge of varying surfaces and unforgiving verges. The Scandinavians, on the other hand, treated it all as normal, which explains why they would eventually occupy six of the top ten places.

If the Welsh section had been run at the start of the event, rather than in the last 36 hours, no doubt it would have created even more carnage than it did, but, as it transpired, no fewer than 120 cars were still running when the event set off again from Blackpool, and the order had virtually settled down. Oulton Park changed nothing – only four drivers, in the two Austin-Healey 3000s, Gunnar Anderson's Volvo 544, and Alan Fraser's Sunbeam Rapier reaching the target time for the five laps of the circuit – but it was the cluster of stages in North Wales

Pat Moss' last-ever drive in an Austin-Healey 3000 – 3rd in the 1962 RAC.

By 1962, BMC had developed the Big Healey's 3-litre engine into a ferocious 210bhp machine – a true 'homologation special.'

Pat Moss always said she was frightened by the Austin-Healey 3000 – but she excelled in the RAC Rally.

RESULTS

Event held: 12-16 November 1962. One starting point, from Blackpool. Finish at Bournemouth. One overnight rest halt at Blackpool.

157 starters, 102 finishers.
38 special stages.

General classification		Group	Penalties
1 Carlsson/Stone	Saab 96	G1/ 2	204
2 Hopkirk/Scott	Austin-Healey 3000	G3	264
3 Ms P Moss/ Mrs P Mayman	Austin-Healey 3000	G3	314
4 Lewis/Mabbs	Sunbeam Rapier	G1/ 2	349
5 Aaltonen/Ambrose	BMC Mini-Cooper	G3	352
6 Taylor/Melia	Ford Anglia 105E	G3	354
7 Mäkinen/Steadman	BMC Mini-Cooper	G1/ 2	394
8 Andersson/Johns	Volvo Amazon	G1/ 2	397
9 Thuner/Gretener	Triumph TR4	G3	430
10 Ms S Österberg/ Ms C Pattison	Volvo Amazon	G1/ 2	442

Team Prize: BMC Mini-Cooper (R Aaltonen, T Mäkinen, L Morrison). Ladies Prize: Austin-Healey 3000 (Ms P Moss and Mrs P Mayman).

(in Clocaenog, Gwydyr and Coed-y-Brenin forests) which began to weed out the wounded and limping private entrants. Both Söderström and Trana's Mini-Coopers disappeared, Rosemary Smith ditched her works Sunbeam Alpine, and Tom Gold's Midget slid off the road, to be irretrievable ditched.

With the last Welsh stage held on Eppynt, there remained only a 12-hour drag across country, through Gloucester (the Severn Bridge was still not completed, of course), Bristol, Glastonbury, and Bridport, before arriving at Ministry of Defence land near the Bovington Tank Museum for two final stages.

The damage penalty still applied, to every works team's disgust, but fortunately, the organisers had allowed a great deal of time for the cars to get into Bournemouth and reach the final control, which allowed the teams to patch up any damage which remained. This year, for the first time ever, however, there was no 'show-business' final driving test to waste everyone's time on the final day, so the transition to a 'real' European-standard event had been achieved. Even so, out in the wide world, there were people who did not understand how specialised modern rallying had become, for one letter published in the press asked why no one had bothered to enter a Jaguar: "which would surely have performed better than a front-wheel-drive Saab …"

Erik Carlsson completed his RAC Rally hat-trick with great aplomb, and with an undamaged car (though at one point his Saab 96 had suffered a rear axle failure, and a spare part had to be 'borrowed' from a spectator's Saab which just happened to be nearby. Three wins with three co-drivers – Stuart Turner, John Brown and David Stone – was a unique achievement.

1963: Trana and Volvo – old car, new star

Four years on from the big change in tone (1960 being the first of a new generation of RAC Rallies …), the transformation of Britain's biggest rally was now complete. This year the route was to be 2200 miles long with 400 miles of special stages; the difference, limited but significant, was that a total of 43 special stages were listed, of which only four – Oulton Park and the Porlock toll road in Devon, and two on MoD land in Dorset – were on tarmac.

Clearly this is what the world of 'professional' rallying wanted, for apart from the British works teams from BMC, Ford, Triumph, Rootes, Reliant, and Rover, the European factory entries came from Ford-USA, Saab, Volvo and VW (Sweden). Not only that, but among the newcomers to this event was the full team of old-fashioned but sturdy 1.8-litre Volvo PV544s, the first of the still-fragile Ford Lotus-Cortinas, the first of the Mini-Cooper S types (for Paddy Hopkirk to drive), and two of the 4.2-litre Ford Falcons, which had surprised so many by their first appearances in European events during the season.

The event was held in the already-established fashion, with a start from Blackpool, a single overnight rest halt back in that Lancashire resort, and the finish in Bournemouth. This year there was to be no visit to North Yorkshire, but special stages were encountered as far apart as Culbin Sands near Inverness, the Keilder complex on the Scottish border close to Newcastle and Hexham, several stages in the

Two works Rover P5s on the 1963 RAC rally – with Ken James' car nearest the camera.

Tom Trana on his way to an unexpected victory in the 1963 Rally, in this sturdy 1.8-litre Volvo PV544.

Timo Mäkinen flat out in his works Austin-Healey 3000 in the 1963 rally, taking 5th.

Lake District, and no fewer than 11 stages during the final night in Central Wales.

Before the event got under way, much of the talk had been about 'the Carlsson conundrum.' Even though Erik's Saab 96 only had an 841cc two-stroke engine, he had already won the previous three RAC Rallies, but this year he was to be faced by the works BMC Mini-Cooper and Mini-Cooper S cars, the formidable Austin-Healey 3000s (with Timo Mäkinen, Rauno Aaltonen and Donald Morley behind their wheels), and especially with native opposition from Tom Trana,

Carl-Magnus Skogh, and Gunnar Andersson in their well-development PV544s. Not only that, but this would be the first year in which Erik had not carried a British co-driver – would that make a difference, to the good or the bad?

What followed was one of the most arduous RACs yet held, for there seemed to be endless rain, persistently disappearing traction, and awful track conditions in many places. It was no wonder that retirements came thick and fast, with only 91 survivors creaking across the finish line after five chassis-breaking days. After only eight stages, the rally arrived at the Turnberry Hotel on the Ayrshire coast, where several significant retirements were already noted ('Tiny' Lewis, David Seigle-Morris, and Raymond Baxter among them …), and where a fresh-faced young Swede by the name of Tom Trana was already in the lead, with Mäkinen and Gunnar Andersson behind him. Carlsson, for his part, was in seventh place, and most of the British elite drivers seemed to be struggling.

It was soon after this that Mäkinen's Healey began a series of adventures which eventually limited him to fifth place, for he actually slid off the Tulloch stage just before the end of the 5.4-mile stage, and lost four minutes before brute force (and spectator assistance) got him going again. Soon after this, the Morleys' Healey stopped with water in the ignition, which did nothing for their temper or position in the event.

It was rapidly becoming clear than the Scandinavians were not only driving the best-prepared cars, but were relishing the awful conditions, so by the time the cars had completed their long Scottish loop, Trana's Volvo was still firmly in the lead, though Harry Källström (who would win the event in a Lancia in years to come) was up to second in an under-powered VW 1500, Erik Carlsson's Saab 96 was up to third – and Paddy Hopkirk's Mini-Cooper S was equal with him. Rootes and Triumph teams, however, were in trouble: Roy Fidler (TR4)

Team boss and ex-European Rally Champion Gunnar Andersson drove this Volvo PV544 into eighth place in the 1963 event – here he is seen rounding a hairpin on the ascent of the Porlock special stage.

By 1963, low-slung sports cars like Triumph's TR4s were struggling to cope with the loose surfaces of the RAC Rally stages – this is Roy Fidler's car in the Lake District.

having rolled his car, which had been rebuilt following a French Alpine accident earlier in the year, while Bo Ljungfeldt's massive Ford Falcon had plunged off the road before he could really show the pace of this surprising car.

No fewer than 112 cars were still running when the event restarted after its Blackpool rest halt, but the leaderboard had already seemed set in stone. Just behind the leaders, however, not only was Pat Moss' works Ford Cortina GT up in sixth place, but she was enjoying a cheerful inter-team battle with Henry Taylor, who was in an original-specification 'coil spring' Lotus-Cortina. For the specialist press, following the fortunes of this twin-cam-engined car made for a fascinating week, as it seemed to have to be regularly rebuilt by Boreham's mechanics (especially the troublesome rear suspension), and it only just made it to the finish. (It is interesting to recall, however, that a developed version later won the 1966 RAC Rally at a canter …)

Even so, and just when everything seemed to be settled, the leading Volvo developed a serious rear (beam) axle problem, and the entire unit had to be changed in a garage at Cross Gates (just north of Llandrindod Wells). It took an hour to do this, behind closed doors on the premises, but was completed in time for Trana to carry on, unpenalized on the road section. Little now remained to excite tired and befuddled minds – except that two of the last three stages (all in Dorset, near the coast at Lulworth Cove) were on MoD land, where there was some tarmac surface, all very slippery indeed.

But then it was all over, the Carlsson-dominance had been broken, and the merits of a bravely driven front-engined/rear-drive car (the PV544) had been re-emphasised. Clearly the Scandinavians had enjoyed what they soon came to consider as 'their' type of event – there would be many more of them in future years.

RESULTS

Event held: 11-15 November 1963. One starting point, from Blackpool. Finish at Bournemouth. One overnight halt in Blackpool.

163 starters, 91 finishers.
43 special stages.

General classification		Group	Penalties
1 Trana/Lindström	Volvo PV544	G1/2	246
2 Källström/Häggbom	VW1500	G1/2	293
3 Carlsson/Palm	Saab 96	G1/2	293
4 Hopkirk/Liddon	BMC Cooper S	G1/2	306
5 Mäkinen/Wood	Austin-Healey 3000	G3	311
6 Taylor/Melia	Ford Lotus-Cortina	G1/2	347
7 Ms P Moss-Carlsson /Ms J Nadin	Ford Cortina GT	G1/2	356
8 Andersson/Johns	Volvo PV544	G1/2	358
9 Morley/Morley	Austin-Healey 3000	G3	363
10 Orrenius/Donigren	BMC Mini Cooper S	G1/2	376

Team Prize: Ford (H Taylor, Ms P Moss-Carlsson and P Riley).
Ladies Prize: Ford Cortina GT (Ms P Moss-Carlsson/Ms J Nadin).

A miscellany of cars in the 1964 event – Tom Trana's winning Volvo PV544, a Ford Cortina GT, a VW Beetle, a Sunbeam Rapier, and a Triumph 2000 among them.

After this Austin-Healey 3000 had won the Spa-Sofia-Liege Marathon in 1964, BMC allocated it to the Morleys for the 1964 RAC Rally, where it finished down in 21st place.

1964: A 'nearly' for Mäkinen

Although the 1963 event had been a great success, the organisers made sweeping changes when planning the layout of the 1964. Not only would the route be arranged to visit almost every corner of England, Wales and Central Scotland, but the start and finish were both to be located at the Duke of York's Barracks in Central London. One reason for this was to keep the 'mass media' interested, whether in London or in almost every other part of the nation. There would be no fewer than 56 special stages, and only a single overnight rest halt (at Perth in Scotland).

Not only did every serious British works team turn up with fleets of their latest rally cars, but since the Swedes had now won the previous four RAC Rallies, more and yet more entrants came flooding in from Scandinavia. Four works Saabs (including the formidable duo of Erik Carlsson and Pat Moss – who was now Mrs Carlsson), three Volvos and three VW1500s all took the start, along with others likely to be competitive, including Bengt Söderström in a Swedish-prepared Ford Cortina GT and Bo Ljungfeldt in a 4.7-litre Ford Falcon GT.

'Britain's best' included eight cars from BMC (with four Mini-Cooper 1275S and two Austin-Healey 3000s), three Ford Cortina GTs, four Triumph 2000s, three Rover 2000s – and a positive tidal wave of privately-owned Mini-Cooper S types (the entry list showed 53 such cars in the field of 180 runners!).

The basic route was a complete, if rather sinuous, clockwise circuit of Great Britain, by way of the West Country, Wales, the Lake District, the south and central parts of Scotland, followed by the Keidler Complex, North Yorkshire, and a final flourish in Norfolk, where the last stage of all was to be set on the motor racing circuit of Snetterton.

Straight away, following the start, it became clear that British works

teams had learned a lot from their Scandinavian rivals, for their pace was rapid, their expertise more obvious than ever before, and it soon developed into a battle between the works Minis and Timo Mäkinen's Austin-Healey 3000, both against the fast-developing Ford Cortina GTs (where Vic Elford had joined the team, and was determined to show that he was the best of the Boreham bunch …). On the contrary, the two-stroke Saabs, it seemed, had finally reached the end of their development road, and even Tom Trana's rugged Volvo was struggling to keep up with the leaders.

By the middle of the first night's rallying, at Llandrindod Wells, there were three works Mini-Coopers in the top six, with Trana, Erik Carlsson and Bengt Söderström all fighting to stay on terms. Elford had had the first of his 'off-and-on' moments, Mäkinen likewise, and it was not long before the Morleys ditched their Austin-Healey 3000, their car needing a big rebuild before they could continue.

By the time the 100 survivors arrived in Perth, several of the stars had hot big trouble. Carl-Magnus Skogh's Volvo had hit a tree, Erik Carlsson's Saab had strayed three miles off course in the maze of roads on Eppynt, Simo Lampinen had rolled his works Saab, and Vic Elford had been off the track – again. One of the major problems was that weather and road conditions had proved to be demanding, where every possible combination of thick fog, ice, snow, standing water and the enforced absence of pace notes meant that many excursions were inevitable.

By this time, too, three of the fleet of works Mini-Cooper 1275S types were already out of the running – Paddy Hopkirk having hit a tree, Aaltonen and Pauline Mayman both out with mechanical problems, and Harry Källström (second in 1963 in a VW, don't forget) had begun to experience transmission problems. The new star of the

Ford's works team of Cortina GTs was strong enough to win the Manufacturers' Team Prize in 1964. Here are the three cars in 'squadron formation' at Snetterton just before the end of the event.

Timo Mäkinen took a new co-driver – Don Barrow – with him to contest the 1964 rally, in which he finished second.

Triumph team, Terry Hunter, lost all chance of a very high finish by over-sleeping at a breakfast halt, though Roy Fidler began to show well by climbing into the top six.

As the event continued to unfold, through the unforgiving wastes of Keilder, and the long, fast, Yorkshire stages, Tom Trana's Volvo PV544 moved into a secure lead, but at the same time Timo Mäkinen's Austin-Healey 3000 (co-driven on this occasion by British map-reading expert Don Barrow) had rocketed up into second place, seemed to treat every corner as if it were his last, but had no chance of making up his penalties from two off-stage excursions.

Unhappily, on this particular event there was to be no sting in the tail, for after the rally cars had all trailed dismally south from Yorkshire to a much-needed breakfast halt at the Olde Bell Hotel in Barnby Moor, through Kings Lynn and on to the Snetterton area, they found that all three scheduled special stages had been cancelled at the last minute. All that was left, therefore, was a chance to complete a six-lap special stage around the Snetterton racing circuit, before tackling another long, and equally dreary, trip down the main road to the Duke of York's Barracks in London.

This gave some highly-organised service crews time to patch up battered and travel-sore machines – but there was one repair which could not be made good, one which almost affected the leaderboard. At the end of the Snetterton test, it was discovered that Mäkinen's Austin-Healey was leaking copious amounts of oil from its gearbox/overdrive transmission, a replacement was not available, and with their hearts in their boots the BMC team sent Timo and the bedraggled car off towards London, re-filling filling the gearbox was cans of oil at very opportunity. This succeeded – just – but if they had failed this would have elevated Roy Fidler's Triumph 2000 (running as a Group 3 car) into a class lead in its very first RAC Rally.

Triumph developed very non-standard 2000s for the mid-1960s RAC Rallies – this being Jean-Jacques Thuner's car in the 1964 event.

There were several morals to be drawn from this ultra-demanding event – two of the principal ones being that BMC still had much to learn about the reliability of its Mini-Coopers, Ford could look forward avidly to being able to run Lotus-Cortinas instead of GTs in 1965, while British teams such as Rover and Rootes came to realise that they were losing out in the power race.

Even so, with more than 30 entries from overseas, and with Scandinavian drivers figuring in four of the top six finishing positions, the organisers could sure look forward to an even more 'International' flavour in future years.

RESULTS
Event held: 8-12 November 1964. One starting point, from London. Finish in London. One overnight rest halt, in Perth, Scotland.

158 starters, 89 finishers.
56 special stages.

General classification		Group	Penalties (seconds)
1 Trana/Thermanius	Volvo PV544	G1/2	3528
2 Mäkinen/Barrow	Austin-Healey 3000	G3	3860
3 Elford/Stone	Ford Cortina GT	G3	4758
4 Ms Moss-Carlsson/ Ms Nyström	Saab 96	G3	5066
5 Söderström/Ohlsson	Ford Cortina GT	G1/2	5096
6 Fidler/Grimshaw	Triumph 2000	G3	5364
7 Carlsson/Palm	Saab 96	G1/2	5399
8 Jansson/Pettersson	VW1500	G1/ 2	5414
9 Seigle-Morris/Nash	Ford Cortina GT	G3	5473
10 Ms Österberg/Ms Sadel	Volvo PV544	G1/2	5549

Team Prize: Ford (H Taylor, V Elford and D Seigle-Morris).
Ladies' Prize: Saab 96 (Ms P Moss-Carlsson – Ms E Nyström).

HOMOLOGATION SPECIALS
Until the late 1950s, almost every rally – and especially the RAC Rally- was run for cars which were very closely related to what we might call 'showroom' models. In the 1950s, for instance, the event (and the special tests which were included) tended to favour high-performance sports cars, and it was only the inclusion of much navigation and manoeouvring tests that brought some balance back to the competition.

In the 1960s, however, first it was cars like the works Austin-Healey 3000s, then the Mini-Cooper S types that followed, and Ford's Lotus-Cortinas, which suddenly heralded the arrival of machines specifically intended for motorsport.

It was this author, I claim, who invented the phrase 'Homologation Special', to describe a new model which was designed, developed, and put on sale for the principal purpose of making it ideal for rallying or saloon car racing. In the UK, the RAC Rally, and the British Saloon Car Championship, were soon dominated by such machines. So, how did it happen, and who were the pioneers?

So what does 'Homologation' specify? Here is what the Oxford Dictionary has to say on the matter:

Homologate: 1 acknowledge, admit. 2 confirm, accept. 3 approve (a car, boat, engine, etc) for use in a particular class of racing.

In motorsport, therefore, homologation describes the approval of a new car, or component, for use in the sport, and it also means that the authorities are satisfied that a certain minimum number of identical cars, or components, have been produced.

The full test of the FIA's International Sporting Code in something called Appendix J, originally came into force in February 1955, but it was some time before the process of homologation followed – along with the use of detailed forms full of facts, figures, dimensions, weights and photographs. The further tightening of Appendix J was necessary because then, as later, some drivers and teams were happy to cheat if they could get away with it. In fact, Appendix J was further revised for 1957, and again for 1958, this being the first year in which Homologation Forms were issued. From then, until they were superseded by a radically revised set of rules in 1982, these were the regulations which governed International motorsport, and of course the RAC Rally:

Group 1: Production saloon cars of which 1000 had to be built. Virtually no modifications were allowed.

Group 2: Production saloons cars of which 1000 had to be built. If manufacturers could prove that an equal number of parts or kits had been sold, many other modifications could be made.

Group 3: Production sports cars of which 500 had to be built: saloon cars modified outside and beyond the limits of Group 2 could also run as Group 3 cars.

There were other Groups – 4, 5, 6, and more – which usually did not apply to rallying. Four-wheel-drive, incidentally, was totally banned, and would not become allowable until 1979.

Now for the most important requirement, which was that to 'prove' that the minimum numbers had been built, the authorised required a solemn written statement with every application from a senior executive of the company concerned that this was so. Even if the circumstances were questionable, such statements always seem to have been accepted. In those original days there was no question of production quantities being inspected, either by the authorities, or by a company's rivals. Except that they often tried to hurry a car through the system, most manufacturers played the game, although cars like the BMC Mini-Cooper S, the Alfa Romeo Guilia GTA, the Ford Lotus-Cortina, the Ford Falcon Sprint, and the Lancia Fulvia HFs were all homologated well before the minimum quantities had been produced.

Until the end of 1965, Group 3 cars could use optional components of which the company had sworn that 100 examples had been made. This encouraged companies like BMC and Standard-Triumph to produce optional aluminium cylinder heads, different exhaust manifolds, four-wheel disc brakes and alternative transmission equipment. Also until the end of 1965, Group 3 cars could use different bodyshell skin materials (usually aluminium instead of steel pressings) to reduce weight, and alternative fittings such as lengthened noses, and drag-reducing hardtops.

However, from the end of 1965, a major recasting of Appendix J led to the immediate banning of alternative cylinder heads, optional carburation, different body shapes, and different body skin materials. The biggest change, however was that henceforth, for 1966 and beyond, a saloon car could not be homologated into Group 1 unless a certified 5000 identical cars had been built in a 12-month period.

This was the point at which some manufacturers began to massage the truth of their claims considerably, a process which brought more and more of what we might call 'Homologation Specials' into existence. Somehow or other, both the BMC Mini-Cooper S 1275 and the Ford Lotus-Cortina became 'Group 1' cars, even when it rapidly became clear that nothing like the minimum of 5000 cars had ever been built in a preceding year. Lancia were no more honest than this. In addition, when it became necessary for Ford to claim that more than 1000 Escort Twin-Cams, and (later) RS1600s, they did so without the slightest intention of allowing themselves a blush ...

1965: A Mini win at last

It was perhaps in this year that the RAC Rally finally came close to having 'show-business' status. Although the route, and the challenge of the special stages, was as demanding as ever, the organisers made sure that the start and finish were in London. They also made it certain that the finish would take place in time for TV evening programmes to be arranged to feature the arrival – and they even arranged for F1 World Champion Graham Hill to ceremonially wave off the leading cars when they started the event.

As expected, there was a total capacity entry for this established 'forest road race', with works teams from BMC, Ford, Lancia, Triumph,

Two of Britain's most powerful rally team bosses of the mid-1960s were Stuart Turner of BMC (left) and Alan Platt of Ford, whose Austin-Healeys, Minis, and Cortinas enlivened year after year of the RAC Rallies of the period.

Roger Clark at the wheel of the Rover P6 which he drove in the 1964 RAC Rally.

Saab, Rootes (Sunbeam and Hillman), and Rover, and with a team of two-stroke Wartburgs entered for the very first time. Volvo had also

Rauno Aaltonen on his way to victory in the 1965 rally.

David Seigle-Morris drove this 'leaf-spring' Ford Lotus-Cortina in the 1965 rally.

entered a full team, but withdrew at the last moment before the start, due to legal complications concerning a crash which Trana's car had suffered earlier in the year in another British event. Before the event the Austin-Healeys of Timo Mäkinen and the Morley Twins had been significantly modified, with high-mounted exhaust systems, and were about to tackle their very last event as works machines.

However, even before the event started from Forte's Airport Hotel near Heathrow, Abingdon's fleet of works Mini-Cooper S cars had emerged as firm favourites. Although this was the year that Ford had finally produced a robust version of the Lotus-Cortina, which looked as if it might be able to beat the Minis, the 1275S was approaching the peak of its formidable performance and capabilities. However, although Timo Mäkinen had won the Monte Carlo and 1000 Lakes rallies, it was Rauno Aaltonen, with four outright victories, and a commanding lead in the 1965 European Rally Championship, who looked likely to set the pace in the early stages.

With the Minis about to start their sixth RAC Rally, and with a complete failure even to get cars to the finish in 1964, BMC's team boss, Stuart Turner, was taking no chances, for he entered no fewer than five Minis, and two of the Austin-Healey 3000s for this 2000-mile event. The rally included no fewer than 57 Special Stages in a route which started and finished in London, but encompassed the West Country, Wales, North Yorkshire, Keilder, South and Central Scotland, the Lake District, and finally a second passage through Wales. There would be only a single overnight rest halt (in Perth, after 37 stages), and the weather forecast included ice, fog, and snow (lots of it …).

Seeded at No 5, Rauno had Timo Mäkinen's Austin-Healey and Vic Elford's Lotus-Cortina ahead of him, with Simo Lampinen (a 150bhp Triumph 2000), Erik Carlsson (Saab 96 Sport) and Paddy Hopkirk all close behind, so, as the event unfolded, he was always likely to know how well he was doing. F1 driver Graham Hill waved the flag at the hotel start to get the first of the 162 runners on their way, but there was

very little competitive motoring before the cars entered Wales by way of Gloucester. As expected, several Minis were already battling with Mäkinen's Austin-Healey (no team orders there!), Lampinen's Triumph 2000, and Elford's Lotus-Cortina, though Vic soon crashed his Ford, which eliminated one competitor at a stroke.

During the first night in Wales, the cars encountered snow for the first time, and this looked like getting worse – wetter, and deeper – as the route turned across England into North Yorkshire. It was at this time, with the snow getting deeper and deeper, that the organisers re-confirmed that studded tyres could not be used. The story, confirmed by BMC's Bill Price, is that the BMC service crews resorted to calling at pet shops along the route, buying up dog leads and similar kit, to make up temporary 'snow chains' to give an aid to traction!

At this point, Timo Mäkinen's Austin-Healey was leading the event, well ahead of Rauno Aaltonen and Erik Carlsson's Saab 96, though Lampinen's Group 3 Triumph 2000 was also proving to be amazingly competitive before it blew a cylinder head gasket, and was forced to retire. Well before the survivors reached Perth, Mäkinen got his Healey stuck on one slippery climb, and needed much help to get him started again. It was this affliction (which did not delay Aaltonen's Mini as it had much better traction) that caused the lead to change not once, but several times, in the next 48 hours. As to the other works Minis, they kept on going, and although most were not at their absolute peak, Jorma Lusenius (co-driven by Britain's Mike Wood) was going remarkably well in his Group 3 1275S, and holding down sixth place overall.

At a cold and wintry Perth, Mäkinen led the event with what was beginning to look like a rather battered Austin-Healey, Rauno Aaltonen was 4 min 27 seconds behind him, and Erik Carlsson was handily placed in third. Harry Källström's Mini was fourth, Lusenius was eighth, and Lars Ytterbring (in a privately-entered car) was ninth. Just 68 cars were still running, the remainder having found conditions

Simo Lampinen's Triumph 2000 led the rally briefly in 1965 before the engine failed.

The 'Big Healey' on its very last RAC Rally – this being the Morley twins in the 1965 event.

too difficult. Källström's car broke its transmission a few hours later, while Paddy Hopkirk and Tony Fall were still struggling on in their works Minis – Fall needing the replacement of a front driveshaft coupling which snapped just after the start of a Lake District stage.

The climax – gloomy for some, frustrating for others, and totally exhilarating for Aaltonen, followed during the final night of flat-out motoring – eight special stages between Mold on the Cheshire/Welsh border, and Rhayader in Central Wales. The weather continued to be awful, with a great deal of ice and snow on all the stages. By this time almost everyone, including the crews, the service mechanics, the travelling press and most of the spectators were cold, wet and miserable – but there was no letting up of the battle for the lead in the event itself.

Although it began to look as if the amazing Mäkinen, in his monstrously powerful Austin-Healey, was finally going to win an RAC Rally, there was drama still to come. As my *Autocar* colleague Martin Lewis wrote in his notes about that final night:

"It was in these muddy, greasy, sections that Mäkinen and Big Healey lost the rally. Time and again the car slithered to a halt, the driver unable to get the 200-odd bhp onto the road. There was more water inside the car than out, and one stage was finished by [co-driver] Paul Easter standing on what remained of the back bumper, hanging on to the petrol filler cap, and bouncing in trials fashion."

Bill Price also recalls that there was one particular stage where Rauno's Mini actually passed the Healey in mid-stage, the sports car being almost unable to move at all – and once he had taken that lead it was never to be lost. All that now remained was for an exhausted, but elated Aaltonen to guide the Mini through Hereford, Newbury and Reading, before arriving at Fortes London Airport Hotel at 6.00pm, just in time for the finish, to be placarded all over the main TV evening news bulletins. With that victory, not only had the Mini chalked up its first triumph in the RAC (it would not be able to repeat that …), but Rauno had been confirmed as European Rally Champion.

Even in those days, BMC's publicity machine was well-greased, with all the appropriate contacts. No sooner had the car been released by the scrutineers, than it was whisked off to appear on TV's *Sunday Night at the London Palladium*, a quick camshaft change was then made to the highly-tuned engine, and Rauno drove it with every due caution to pass his British driving test!

It was an ideal way to prove just what a versatile car the Mini-Cooper S had become, whether standard, nearly-standard or fully-prepared …

RESULTS
Event held: 21-25 November 1965. One starting point, from London. Finish in London. One overnight rest halt in Perth, Scotland.

163 starters, 62 finishers.
57 special stages.

General classification		Penalties (min:sec)
1 Aaltonen/Ambrose	BMC Mini-Cooper S	531:23
2 Mäkinen/Easter	Austin-Healey 3000	534:31
3 Larsson/Lundblatt	Saab 96 Sport	537:18
4 Carlsson/Aman	Saab 96 Sport	540:33
5 Fidler/Taylor	Triumph 2000	554:16
6 Lusenius/Wood	BMC Mini-Cooper S	560:28
7 Ytterbring/Haakansson	BMC Mini-Cooper S	561:04
8 Lundin/Lindberg	VW 1600TL	576:53
9 Karlsson/Ericsson	VW 1600TL	577:06
10 Ms P Moss-Carlsson/ Ms E Nyström	Saab 96 Sport	577:27

Team Prize: Rootes Group Imps (IDL Lewis, Ms R Smith, A Cowan).
Ladies Prize: Saab 96 Sport (Ms P Moss-Carlsson/Ms E Nyström).

THE MINI – JUST ONE SUCCESS: AN EIGHT-YEAR SAGA
It took a long time, and the effort involved was phenomenal, but Britain's then-dominant works team, BMC, finally won the RAC Rally six years after its first faltering efforts.

Complete books have been written about the exploits of the amazingly nimble little front-wheel-drive Minis, Mini-Coopers, and Mini-Cooper Ss, all of them concentrating on the way that the breed eventually improved from using a 34bhp/848cc engine to a race-proved 100bhp/1293cc version of the same power unit. In the first half of the 1960s, the works team, based at Abingdon, concentrated on the development of three models – the BMC Minis (sometimes badged as Austins, sometimes as Morrises …), the MG MGBs, and the formidable Austin-Healey 3000s.

Although the works Minis had phenomenal handling, traction, and surprising performance, they were always hampered by having tiny 10in road wheels, and limited ground clearance. Underbody damage, therefore, and transmission failures were almost inevitable on the longer, rougher, events – a type for which the ever-toughening RAC Rally certainly qualified.

This, therefore, is a short summary of the way in which that particular breed of rally car changed, and finally succeeded, in the RAC Rallies of the period:

1959: Four Mini 850s started, but none of them finished.
1960: Three 850s (which produced perhaps 50bhp) started, and two of them finished creditably – sixth overall (David Seigle-Morris driving) and eighth overall (Mike Sutcliffe).
1961: No works Minis started.
1962: Three works 997cc-engined Mini-Coopers (with 65/70bhp?) started, and all completed the event, with Rauno Aaltonen fifth, Timo Mäkinen seventh, and Logan Morrison 13th.
1963: Three works cars started – one a 997cc-engined Mini-Cooper (Logan Morrison, 19th overall), and two new-type Mini-Cooper 1071S types with perhaps 80bhp, for Paddy Hopkirk, who took fourth overall, and Pauline Mayman (30th overall).
1964: Four works Mini-Cooper 1275S cars started, but not a single car finished.
1965: Five works Mini-Cooper 1275S cars, with perhaps 90bhp, started, with four of them reaching the finish. Rauno Aaltonen's car (registered DJB 93B) was the outright victor, while Jorma Lusenius (DJB 92B) won his class, running as a modified 'Group 3' car.
1966: No fewer than eight works Mini-Cooper 1275S cars took the start, of which four cars reached the finish – with Harry Källström (second), Rauno Altonen (fourth), and Tony Fall (fifth) at their head.
1967: This event was, of course, cancelled before the start, at a mere 12 hours notice. In fact BMC had prepared four 1275S cars for this event, one of them (to be driven by Timo Mäkinen) set to run in the 'Group 6' (ie 'non-homologated' class, complete with a fuel-injected eight port cylinder head. As it happened, that car then took part in the hastily-arranged TV 'spectacular,' which ran on a forestry stage close to London, on the day that the real RAC Rally should have started.

1966: Ford's 'twin-cam' year
Although Ford's Zephyr had most unexpectedly won the 1959 RAC Rally, after that the team had struggled to repeat the trick. Despite the fact that its Cortinas had grown faster and stronger as the 1960s progressed, somehow Ford could not quite match the flamboyant and nimble front-wheel-drive cars from Saab and BMC, or the rugged worth of the old-fashioned Volvos. Now, though, in 1966, it was time for the tide to turn, and with the amiable Swedish driver, Bengt

Bengt Söderström won the 1966 event outright by a huge margin in this Lotus-Cortina.

Söderström, at the wheel, one of its twin-cam engine Lotus-Cortinas finally dominated the world's opposition.

As far as the national press was concerned, however, the headlines were mainly made by double F1 World Champion Jim Clark, who was persuaded (easily, it seems) to compete in another works Lotus-Cortina, would set up a series of amazingly competitive stage times, and would finally crash out (without personal injury) towards the end of the event. As to Ford's other Clark – Roger – he was little to be seen, and Söderström's winning margin was a colossal 13min 35sec!

Although the basic layout of the 1966 event was similar to that of the previous year – the start and finish were both at the Forte's Excelsior Hotel near Heathrow Airport in London, and the night halt was in Scotland – the big change was in the publicity build-up, which had to be credited by the event's new sponsor, the *Sun* national newspaper.

F1 World Champion Jim Clark spent a lot of time testing for the 1966 rally beforehand. Here he was discussing his experiences with Boreham personnel …

… and he was very fast on the rally itself.

*During the 1960s, Saab supported the RAC Rally on every occasion.
This was the 1966 team, ready for the start.*

*Lancia began its assault on the RAC Rally in 1966, originally with
simple-looking 1.2-litre cars like this. The cars became faster and more
successful only three years later.*

It was the financial muscle of the sponsor which persuaded not only
Jim Clark to compete, in a works Lotus-Cortina, but also his friend
and rival Graham Hill turned out, this time in a works BMC Mini-
Cooper S. In addition, to add glamour to the occasion, the first cars
were flagged away from the starting ramp by three-times world F1
Champion Jack Brabham ...

By this time, indeed, the RAC Rally had become so important
in world motorsport, that there were serious works team assaults
from BMC, Ford, Rootes/Hillman, Triumph, Lancia, Opel-Sweden,
Renault, Saab, Volvo, with a large proportion of entrants coming from
Scandinavia, where the special stages had similar characters to those
now familiarly located in the UK. On this occasion there were to be
63 special stages, covering 2400 miles in five days, spanning Dorset
and central Scotland, Keilder and Wales, Yorkshire and Wales. By this
time every stage had target times set at 50mph, which might have
been possible for some expert drivers, but which sometimes seemed
to be rather longer than advertised in the programme! The total stage
mileage now exceeded 400 miles, and apart from the traditional visit to
Silverstone, each and everyone of these used the loose gravel surfaces
of the Forestry Commission.

After an early meandering visit to the West Country – there were
stages in Dorset and Devon, and a time control at Bristol Airport – the
order was already settling down, with Timo Mäkinen's Mini-Cooper
S providing most of the fire and fury. By this stage, however, Roger
Clark had already crashed out (very rare for him ...), while Jim Clark,
who was learning stage-craft very rapidly indeed, had had his first brief
meeting with the side of a stage!

Behind Timo, however, the leaderboard was beginning to settle
into place, with Söderström's Lotus-Cortina well placed, along with
Paddy Hopkirk and Rauno Aaltonen in their Minis, and Erik Carlsson,
Pat Moss-Carlsson and Åke Andersson, all in Saab 96s, and Tom
Trana's Volvo 132 all being closely bunched.

At Bristol, the crews had tackled only ten stages totalling 41.7
miles, but once they swept over the new Severn Bridge, and were
faced with the forests of Wales, the endurance challenges mounted
up. Between Bristol and the mid-afternoon control at Oulton Park, 14
more special stages had to be tackled, among them the twinned (and
geographically close) monster stages near Machynlleth, of Pantperthog
(10 miles long) and Dovey (23 miles long).

The result was that only 92 of the original 144 starters reached
the rest halt at the newly-developing ski resort of Coylumbridge, near
Aviemore, in Scotland, where some of the surviving machines looked
very bedraggled indeed after completing more than 30 forestry stages,
with Mäkinen's Mini still leading Bengt Söderström's Lotus-Cortina
by four minutes, and with Håkan Lindberg's rear-engined Renault
R8 Gordini third, and Tony Fall in fourth place in his works Mini.
Jim Clark, on the other hand, had now had another serious shunt,
which left the Lotus-Cortina in ninth place, nine minutes behind
Mäkinen (he had beaten the Finn three times before ...), but he
was as enthusiastic as ever, much-liked by all his rivals, and seemed
determined to make it to the finish.

It was on the daylight run south from the night halt which saw
the first of several major retirements. Jim Clark flew off the road on
one high-speed jump in the Glengap stage, finding that "rally cars
don't steer very well when the front wheels are off the ground ..." and
destroying his machine in the process. Andrew Cowan's works Rally

Simo Lampinen made a mistake on the 1966 event, rolled his Mini-Cooper S, but continued in this 'air-conditioned' state until forced to retire.

Imp also failed when its transaxle collapsed, and the pretty but not-yet-robust Lancia Fulvia Coupés began to look more and more fragile. Not long afterwards, Erik Carlsson's and Åke Andersson's works Saabs both blew-up their two-stroke engines, as did the Lotus twin-cam engine on Vic Elford's Lotus-Cortina. It was that sort of rally …

Unhappily, there was more to come. Suddenly, in the evening, and in the cruelly unforgiving high-speed stages of the Keilder and North Yorkshire forest complexes, everything started to go wrong for BMC. Not only did Paddy Hopkirk's car boil its engine almost to destruction after the fan belt broke, then suffer ultimate retirement when a transmission driveshaft broke, but Mäkinen's leading car had to retire when his engine, too, gave up under the strain. Quite suddenly, therefore, the lead passed over to Bengt Söderström's amazingly fast and reliable Lotus-Cortina (these twin-cam engined machines had improved rapidly in the two previous seasons …), who was well over ten minutes clear of Harry Källström's works Mini by then, and stretching that gap all the time.

Söderström, the placid and frankly rotund ex-lorry-driver, had never looked like leading this event until Mäkinen's Mini-Cooper S gave up the struggle of fighting against all the punishment the charismatic Finn could throw at it, but he had always been on the pace, always in control, and never appeared to have a single moment when his Lotus-Cortina left the track. His co-driver, Gunnar Palm, serious, intense, but extremely organised, had much to do with all this.

Even so, with Mäkinen out (he spent the last night of the event, on the way back to London, in a journalist's car, happily communing the remainder of the event with a whisky bottle …), and with only two special stages (in Sherwood Forest), and a six-lap time trial at Silverstone remaining after the morning breakfast halt at Barnby Moor, all the tension drained away. From Silverstone to London, there was only the M1 on a November afternoon left to keep the 63 surviving crews awake, but nothing disturbed Söderström's gentle progress in his

Lotus-Cortina, and Ford's faith in that 'homologation special' design was rewarded at last.

RESULTS

Event held: 19-23 November 1966. One starting point, from London. Finish in London. One overnight rest halt at Coylumbridge (near Grantown-on-Spey), Scotland.

144 starters, 63 finishers.
63 special stages.

General classification		Penalties (min:sec)
1 Söderström/Palm	Ford Lotus-Cortina	475:15
2 Källström/Haakanson	BMC Mini-Cooper S	488:50
3 Trana/Andreasson	Volvo 122	489:50
4 Aaltonen/Liddon	BMC Mini-Cooper S	490:22
5 Fall/Wood	BMC Mini-Cooper S	495:17
6 Damberg/Riggare	Renault Gordini 1300	496:34
7 Andersson/Davenport	Lancia Fulvia HF	498:14
8 Gullberg/Palm	Opel Record	502:34
9 Ms P Moss-Carlsson/ Ms Nyström	Saab Monte Carlo 850	503:12
10 Mrs S Österberg/ Ms Edenring	Renault Gordini 1300	504:04

Manufacturers' Team Prize: Not awarded (no finishers).
Ladies Prize: Saab Monte Carlo (Ms P Moss-Carlsson/Ms E Nyström).

1967: Cancelled at the 11th hour

The most startling fact about the 1967 RAC Rally is that it did not take place. The even more startling fact is that everything for this event was prepared, the competing cars had all gathered at the Start HQ near London's Heathrow Airport, and pre-rally scrutineering was complete – when during the Friday evening before the scheduled start, the event was abruptly cancelled. To keep the TV companies happy (as time had been allocated for live coverage of an early special stage on MoD land in Surrey), an informal one-event special stage extravaganza was run off – after which everyone went home, and wondered what they would now do with their expensively prepared rally cars.

The situation was even worse for the considerable band of overseas entrants, as during the same weekend Prime Minister Harold Wilson announced the immediate devaluation of the Pound Sterling (from $2.80 to $2.40 to the Pound), which meant that the overseas teams who had already prepared all their spending on the event were now obliged to turn devalued British money back into their own currency before they went home!

If the 1967 event had not been cancelled because of an outbreak of Foot-and-Mouth disease which rendered many stages unusable, Rauno Aaltonen was anxious to prove a point in this very special Austin-Healey 3000.

The closest World F1 Champion Denny Hulme got to tackling the RAC Rally of 1967 was when he tested a 'hack' Triumph 2000 beforehand.

All in all, this was an enormous disappointment, but so much planning had taken place, and many novelties arranged, that is worth summarising what 'might have been'. A complex 2500-mile route was originally to have included 69 special stages, the most westerly being on the Porlock toll road, the most northerly near Peebles in Scotland, the most concentrated in the Keilder and North Yorkshire forests, and a final and concentrated night in Wales before the exhausted crews would make their way back to London. Except for the ritual visits to Silverstone, Mallory Park and Oulton Park, almost all the flat-out motoring was to be in the forests.

In and around all this, only a single overnight rest halt (in Blackpool) was scheduled, but a capacity field of 160 cars were entered. All the usual works teams were entered, including groups of Lancias, Saabs, Renaults – and several factory-supported Porsche 911s, including that of Vic Elford. Every single one of the European 'Big Names' was entered, these including F1 World Champions Graham Hill (Ford Lotus-Cortina) and Denny Hulme (Triumph 2.5 prototype.

From the UK, BMC had not only included a fleet of its latest Mini-Cooper 1275S types (including a fuel-injected type for Timo Mäkinen), but there was also the last and definitive works Austin-Healey 3000 for Rauno Aaltonen. Ford produced three Lotus-Cortinas with fuel-injected engines, while Sunbeam had several Sunbeam Rallye Imps.

All this, of course, came to nought, for although every car passed through scrutineering on the Friday afternoon, the neat paperwork now included a hastily produced list of amendments as to which stages in South Wales had already been cancelled, and which in the Midlands had been added to compensate. Then came the hastily arranged press conference at the start hotel, which was attended by high-ranking government officials, and by approximately 8pm that evening the event was abruptly cancelled.

Event scheduled to be held: 18-22 November 1967. One starting point, from London. One overnight rest halt in Blackpool. Finish in London.

160 entrants.
69 proposed special stages.

This was the 'RAC that never was.' 12 hours before the scheduled start of the event, the bovine foot-and-mouth epidemic that was then raging in the British countryside caused the enforced cancellation of many stages, and a complete re-routeing of the first 24 hours, which had originally been scheduled for the West Country and the Midlands.

On the evening before the scheduled start, from the London HQ hotel, a government edict that the event should be cancelled, was accepted.

1968: A clash with the London-Sydney Marathon

When the mighty *Daily Express* decided to back the concept of a transcontinental marathon rally from London to Sydney in Australia – by way of Bombay and a long sea voyage to Fremantle in Western Australia – the RAC Rally organisers were dismayed to realise that its chosen dates would clash with the long-established RAC Rally. Not only that, but it soon became clear that the major British works teams – BMC/British Leyland, Ford and Rootes/Chrysler – could not afford to commit time, facilities and, most importantly, money to tackling both events.

Although the idea of the Marathon was launched in January 1968, with a start from London pencilled in for two days after the 1968 RAC Rally would end in November, no amount of lobbying from the RAC could persuade the organisers to move their Marathon forward in the calendar. Their principal reason, with which the opposition could not argue, was that their schedule all revolved around the availability of a big ocean liner to take the cars from Bombay to Australia.

For the RAC this was a shattering blow, for early in 1968 they were still trying to recover from the abrupt cancellation of the 1967 event, and now they would have to compete for entries, and for media interest, with this massive (and, as it transpired) one-off marathon event. But there was no short-term solution, and although an extra special effort was made, by way of introducing a new section called the

'European Club Rally – for non-homologated Group 6 cars – the entry plummeted, and only 113 cars took the start: a mere 35 of those would finish. To their credit, *The Sun* newspaper, and Lombank, continued their excellent and enthusiastic sponsorship.

With all the British works teams absent, the major competition was going to be between Lancia (with brand-new 1.6-litre Fulvia HF Coupés, along with the familiar 1.3-litre variety), Porsche with three 911s for Vic Elford, Tony Fall and Björn Waldegård, and three Saab V4s from Sweden. Britain's Ford Escort Twin-Cam was still finding its feet in world rallying, but Boreham had loaned one car to David Sutton, for Timo Mäkinen to drive – and he was certainly the 'dark horse' that everyone wanted to watch. It was good, incidentally, to see that Wartburg of East Germany entered an entire team of four two-stroke, front-wheel-drive cars – not fast, for sure, but well-prepared and determined to win their capacity class.

Although the entry was well down, and some of the gilt had been rubbed away (for 1968, at least), Jack Kemsley's team had worked hard to present the toughest route yet devised. Not only did the route start and finish at London Airport, as was becoming usual, but it would take in a trip to the West Country, then Wales, then the Lake District, then south and central Scotland, Keilder, and North Yorkshire, before returning to base, with only one night halt – in Edinburgh – to ease the pain. A monumental total of 87 special stages were originally scheduled, the first being at Hawley Common near Bagshot, the very last being in the grounds of the Culham laboratories south of Oxford. The longest stage of all would be the 15-miler of Dalby South (near Scarborough), the shortest being the 1.2-mile sprint up Rest and be Thankful in Scotland.

Although many of the world's top rally-driving stars were present, little did we know that this was an event where almost all of them would be forced out, either by mechanical problems, or by accidents. Two of the works Saabs – those of Simo Lampinen and Calle Orrenius – would finish first and second, but each and every one of the other cars on the leaderboard were amateurs. No Porsches, no Lancias, and no other Saab – they all failed to finish. If this was an event where bookmakers had been present, they would have made a fortune.

When the rally began to settle down at the end of the short and hurried visit to the West Country, Waldegård's Porsche 911 was leading, the Saab V4s were close behind him, and the various Lancias were not only looking, but sounding and going spectacularly fast too. Tony Fall's 91, however, had destroyed its transmission, Elford's 911 was also in trouble, and Timo

Lancia entered Group 6 'prototype' Fulvia HF1600s in the 1968 RAC Rally, this being Sandro Munari's car, which was forced to retire.

Simo Lampinen and John Davenport were emphatic winners in 1968 in this works Saab V4.

Timo Mäkinen used his works-loaned Escort Twin-Cam to lead the 1968 event for many hours, before an engine failure forced him to retire.

Mäkinen's Ford Escort Twin-Cam destroyed its rear differential on the Thruxton race track time trial.

And that was before the classic Welsh stages began to take their usual toll – with Tom Trana's Saab breaking its transmission, Håkan Lindberg's Saab blowing its engine, Waldegård's 911 losing the lead (and having to retire) with another broken transmission, Pat Moss-Carlsson rolling her Lancia out of contention, and Harry Källström suffering a 15-minute delay when his Lancia suffered an electrical failure.

Things looked black, too, for Simo Lampinen's Saab, which needed a complete gearbox change (to get rid of a troublesome limited-slip differential) – but the ever-resourceful Swedish mechanics found an hour in a very relaxed time schedule which led up the M6 into Blackpool. Not only did they change the gearbox, but they took the entire engine/front-wheel-drive transmission out of the car to do it, and completed the job in just one hour, without Lampinen needing to incur any road penalties. In the meantime, the 1.6-litre Lancias were still going mighty fast in the 'Club rally' section, while Timo Mäkinen's so-called 'private' Escort was back in the lead of the rally itself.

All the way up to Scotland, and to the welcome overnight rest halt in Edinburgh, it was Lampinen's Saab and Mäkinen's Ford that scrapped for the lead (if only we had realised that this brand-battle would be repeated during the RAC Rally many times in the next decade). Along the way, Mikkola's prototype Lancia went off the road and got stuck, most of the other Lancias needed much work to keep them going at all, and Vic Elford's Porsche 911 kept going, but only in fourth place overall.

When the rally turned south after the halt at Edinburgh, Mäkinen's Escort was just ahead of Lampinen's Saab, with Orrenius' Saab just nine minutes behind. In the Group 6 'Club' rally, Rauno Aaltonen's and Sandro Munari's 1.6-litre Lancias were leading – and that was just about a complete roll-call of the very few top-level drivers who were still running.

What happened next is best summed up by requoting my own words from the *Autocar* report of the event, in 1968: "As ever, it was the South Scotland and Northumberland stages which settled the whole event. Effectively, the order was decided by the time Chollerford was reached …"

In fact, it was only hours after the restart that Mäkinen's Escort fell out, when an engine cooling fault led to the Twin-Cam engine blowing a cylinder head gasket. This left Lampinen in the lead by nine minutes from Orrenius' sister car, and in spite of both cars having minor bothers in the next 24 hours, that gap only reduced by three minutes.

It was in the forestry wastes of the Keilder complex that Lancia finally killed off its own triumphal procession in the 'Club' rally. Not only did Sandro Munari go off the road and leave his Fulvia leaning on a tree, but Aaltonen repeated the trick a little later and Källström's 1.3-litre car suffered a cracked sump, and the loss of all his engine oil. Finally, these superstars were joined by Vic Elford, whose Porsche had been in trouble for hours, when the front suspension collapsed in mid-stage and catapulted him off the road into a friendly fire-break!

All of a sudden, and with 24 relatively relaxed hours still to go, privateer Jimmy Bullough found himself in third place in his privately-prepared Escort Twin-Cam (he would eventually finish there, no fewer than 24 minutes (yes, minutes …) behind Lampinen, while Rod Cooper's private Ford Lotus-Cortina Mk I (a three-year-old car, with a 1.65-litre version of the engine) inherited the lead of the 'Club' Rally. He would have 35 minutes more stage penalties than Lampinen …

For them, the run down to London, from the lengthy forests of North Yorkshire, must then have seemed endless, but there was still time for visits to two stages in the Sherwood Forest, to Mallory Park,

and to Silverstone, before making it back to the bright lights of TV and film-crew coverage at the end of a very long afternoon.

But what an unexpected outcome, in so many ways! Before the start, who could possibly have expected John Barnes to bring his humble Peugeot 204 into sixth place, and for one of the East German Wartburgs not only to win its class, but to take seventh (in spite of being 111 minutes off the lead)?

We would have to wait another year to see if anything like RAC Rally 'normality' would return.

RESULTS

Event held: 16-20 November 1968. One starting point, from London. Finish in London. One overnight rest halt, in Edinburgh.

113 starters, 35 finishers (of which three were in the European Club Rally section).
87 special stages.

General classification		Penalties (min:sec)
1 Lampinen/Davenport)	Saab V4	650:34
2 Orrenius/Schröderheim	Saab V4	666:04
3 Bullough/Barrow	Ford Escort Twin-Cam	715:08
4 Cooper/Bennett	BMC Mini-Cooper S	731:45
5 Wilkinson/Billett	Ford Escort Twin-Cam	747:29
6 Barnes/Pettie	Peugeot 204	759:33
7 Ruttinger/Bork	Wartburg Knight	761:19
8 John/Harwood	Ford Lotus-Cortina	764:13
9 Jago/Spence	Ford Cortina GT	786:40
10 Mossop/Johnstone	Ford Lotus-Cortina	788:13

Team Prize: Not awarded (no finishers).
Ladies Prize: Not awarded (no finishers).

European Club rally (FIA Group 6)

1 R Cooper/I Cooper	Ford Lotus-Cortina	685:23
2 Bean/Drury	Ford Lotus-Cortina	702:41
3 Cook/Brundle	Ford Anglia GT	848:41

1969: Lancia wins, but the Escort is coming

If only we had known it, this was the year – 1969 – when the Escort's decade-dominance of the RAC Rally truly began. They might not have won until 1972, but until then there was never an occasion when they were not one of the most competitive models.

Happily, the 1969 event recovered completely from the difficulties

G Ruttinger took an amazing seventh place in 1968 in his two-stroke Wartburg Knight, though he was 110 minutes behind the winner!

Datsun's first appearance in the RAC Rally came in 1969. Roy Fidler and John Sprinzel drove this SSS Coupé.

1969 winner Harry Källström looks exhausted after steering the Lancia Fulvia HF1600 to victory.

it had suffered in 1968, when a clash with the London-Sydney Marathon had persuaded the works teams to stay away. This time, they were all back with a vengeance, in an event which attracted no fewer than 153 starters. Although enthusiastic material and financial support continued to come from *The Sun* newspaper, and Lombank, no amount of persuasion could attract any famous F1 driver to take part, so the halcyon days of Jim Clark versus Graham Hill were permanently ended.

Rallying enthusiasts, however, had much to excite them, for on this occasion there were fully-fledged works or supported teams from Ford (three Escort Twin-Cams), British Leyland (three Triumph 2.5PI saloons, Lancia (four 1.6-litre Fulvia HF Coupés), Saab (six V4s), Datsun (three 1600SSSs), and Porsche (a single 911 for Björn Waldegård). On this occasion, however, there were to be no East German Wartburgs, and they were affectionately missed. The mass of the entry, however, was made up by positive fleets of privately-entered, and prepared, Ford Escort Twin-Cams and BMC Mini-Cooper Ss.

At first the promised route looked familiar, but a closer study revealed what was effectively a 'mirror-image' of the 1968 event, and still at least 2400 miles long. We use the phrase 'mirror image' advisedly, for the overall geographical profile of 1968 appeared again – but totally the other way around! In 1969, therefore, the rally started with a long, and mainly boring, trundle north from the London starting point to the North Yorkshire stages, and ended with another pointless return from the West Country, having visited Wales on the previous night. On this occasion, therefore, the overnight rest halt, after the cars had tackled 44 stages, was to be in Blackpool. The other big difference, but of course no-one realised this at the pre-rally planning stage, was that the weather would be extremely wintry, with heavy snow on the stages in Scotland and Wales. At a stroke, when encountered, this gave an advantage to Lancia's and Saab's front-wheel-drive machines, and made the heroes in their powerful Escorts have to work even harder to stay competitive.

As was becoming conventional on this event, the accent was on including many relatively short stages – for, according to the pre-event information, the shortest would have target times of only two minutes, while the longest was Dalby South, for which 21 minutes was allowed. Cynics noted that the length of the stages was no longer quoted, as the performance of the cars had recently increased considerably, it would have been pointless to set the target times at a mere 50mph average any more!

With the start set for 11.00am from the Centre Hotel at London Airport on Saturday, 15 November, the long trek north to Yorkshire meant that the floods of spectators had very little real rallying to see until darkness, for the group of six Yorkshire stages did not begin until about 9.00pm. The incidents, and the high-pressure retirements, came in those early hours – Timo Mäkinen's Lancia Fulvia hit a dog on the route between two of the Yorkshire stages, which wrecked his car's radiator, boiled the engine, and immediately wrecked it. Hannu Mikkola crashed his Escort on Dalby North, close to many spectators, and the car was wrecked – the result being that this event immediately entered rallying folklore as 'Mikkola's Corner'. Not only that, but a rising star from Sweden, Stig Blomqvist, in his Saab V4, went off at the same place, and also had to retire on the spot. Only hours later, Sandro Munari's works Lancia broke a driveshaft in the unreachable depths of

the Keilder complex, while Simo Lampinen's Saab V4 (he had won the event in 1968, don't forget) blew a cylinder head gasket and joined him.

By the time the survivors reached Moffat for their first breakfast halt, no fewer than 53 cars had already dropped out – which left just 100 still running – and it was really no surprise to learn that the leader at this point was Björn Waldegård's Porsche 911 (for Björn had won the Monte Carlo Rally earlier in the year in a similar model), by more than four minutes, while Harry Källström's Lancia Fulvia (afflicted by successive punctures) was in second place.

By the time the cars reached Dumfries on the second morning, the consequence of snow and ice was clear from the listings – for Waldegård's Porsche, two front-wheel-drive Lancias (Källström and Tony Fall), and two front-wheel-drive Saabs (Calle Orrenius and Tom Trana) held the first five positions, with an ever-spectacular Ove Andersson sixth in his Escort, already 17 minutes adrift of the Porsche. Hours later, as the 81 survivors trickled their way into Blackpool for a night's rest, there was no change at the top, but Roger Clark's Escort needed a complete gearbox change, which Boreham's mechanics achieved in 58 minutes. That time, incidentally, would be much reduced in future years – probably because the team got so much practice!

The following day conditions were worse, not better, than before,

Roger Clark found 200bhp of works Escort difficult to control on the snows of the 1970 event, but took sixth place overall.

The works Triumph 2.5PIs struggled for traction in the very wintry RAC of 1969. This was Andrew Cowan on his way to a class win, and a member of the winning team.

and it was clear that several stages were so snow-bound that they would have to be cancelled, and that a number of cars would flounder and simply run out of time. Among those personalities suffering incidents were Jack Simonian (Datsun) who rolled his Japanese car, Andrew Cowan, whose Triumph 2.5PI crashed in front of TV cameras, and Jerry Larsson, whose Swedish-entered Porsche also rolled. Tony Fall's works Lancia suffered a major shunt, which the hard-working mechanics somehow repaired, while Colin Malkin's 'Jolly Club' Lancia suffered from broken suspension and a damaged gearbox.

In Machynlleth, at the end of what had been a chaotic day, Waldegård's Porsche still led Källström's Lancia, but by only two-and-a-half minutes. Still, it was a case of 'engine-over-driving wheels' cars in the lead, the rest nowhere – and 'nowhere' was now led by Rauno Aaltonen in his Datsun, 19 minutes behind the Porsche.

The big change then followed, for between Machynlleth and the final breakfast halt at the M4 Severn Bridge, Björn Waldegård put his Porsche 911 off the road in one of the Hafren stages, languishing there for more than 20 minutes, and dropped right out of the running. Other cars, in what had seemed to be a settled line-up, then moved up by a place, and to everyone's astonishment (for forecasts had been that the Lancias were not yet tough enough to withstand an RAC Rally) Harry Källström then took the lead. At this time he was five minutes ahead of Orrenius' Saab V4, and 'first conventional car', was the ever-persistent Ove Andersson.

With only five stages remaining to be tackled – all of them in daylight, including the Porlock Toll road, it seemed to be all over, and after the last stage – King Alfred's Tower, near Wincanton, the crews faced only a cruise back up the A303 and the A30 to London Airport. And so it was, for the only significant change was that Anderson's Escort forged ahead of Trana's Saab to take a rousing fourth place, Roger Clark finally shrugged off all his mechanical troubles to finish sixth, and Datsun took the Manufacturers' Team Prize, in a very close-run-thing with the Triumph 2.5PIs. Waldegård, poor Waldegård, got going again after his long 'rest' in Hafren, and finally finished 12th overall, and won his capacity class.

The morals of this story – and there were several lessons to be learned – included the fact that Ford might win any number of events if only it could persuade its Escorts to transmit their rear-wheel-drive power to the road, that Lancia had now well-and-truly proved that its Fulvia HF could (and often did) win in almost any conditions, while it was clear to the media that if Porsche decided to concentrate on rallying as opposed to motor racing, then the rest of the rallying circus might just as well go home!

RESULTS

Event held: 15-19 November 1969. One starting point, from London. Finish in London. One overnight rest halt at Blackpool.

153 starters, 69 finishers.
73 special stages.

General classification		Penalties (min:sec)
1 Källström/Häggbom	Lancia Fulvia HF	479:17
2 Orrenius/Stone	Saab V4	483:32
3 Fall/Liddon	Lancia Fulvia HF	494:36
4 Andersson/Palm	Ford Escort Twin-Cam	494:46
5 Lindberg/Reinicke	Saab V4	495:32
6 Clark/Porter	Ford Escort Twin-Cam	497:04
7 Trana/Andreasson	Saab V4	497:34
8 Aaltonen/Ambrose	Datsun 1600SSS	498:28
9 Larsson/Lundblad	Porsche 911S	498:57
10 Jonsson/Eliasson	Saab V4	501:21

Team Prize: Datsun 1600SSS (R Aaltonen, J Simonian, J Sprinzel).
Ladies Prize: BMW 2002 (Ms J Robinson/Ms A Scott).

1970: Lancia repeats the trick

As the 1970s opened, the RAC Rally was going from strength to strength. For 1970, not only were 82 special stages totalling 425 miles promised (three stages were to be cancelled just before the start), but there were no fewer than 213 entries listed– and a new major sponsor, the *Daily Mirror* newspaper.

The basic routeing, and the basic layout, of the 2300 milk event, was much as before, with a start and finish from the 'traditional' hotel close to Heathrow Airport, as usual the late autumn weather threatened to provide a lot of snow in the stages themselves, and the pre-rally forecasts were that one or other of the engine-over-driving wheels works cars – either front-engined machines such as the Lancias, or rear-engined cars like Porsche – would dominate.

Although this year's gimmick was to have all-female crews running at the front of the field (none of them was likely to figure strongly in the final results …), they were followed by a positive flood of the competitive works crews. This year there were no fewer than ten fully-fledged teams from Ford, Fiat, Lancia, Porsche, Saab, Datsun, Alpine-Renault, Opel, Škoda and Wartburg – of which Alpine-Renault's tiny but powerful A110s were not thought to be strong enough to withstand the battering that the Forestry Commission stages would certainly hand out. Ford, incidentally, became one of the pioneering rally teams to plaster its cars with sponsors' colour schemes – the *Daily Express*, the *Daily Telegraph*, and the *Evening Standard* on their three works Escorts. All this, please note, on an event sponsored by a rival to those national newspapers!

Accordingly, ex-BMC/British Leyland team boss Peter Browning, by this time working on rally matters for *Autocar*, was quite justified when, before the event started, he wrote: "I cannot recall any rally with such an array of talent – 10 manufacturers' teams representing eight countries, and the entry list of 190 drivers with 30 reserves reads like

On-car advertising had arrived with a flourish in 1970. Here were two brand-new Ford Escort Twin-Cams for The Telegraph magazine (KHK 599J) and The Evening Standard (KHK598J). Neither would finish that event.

a 'who's who' of the rally world. Never has an event been so open and, ignoring any luck stories, there must be at least 16 drivers who could win …"

Above all, this was a year in which the 'ifs' and 'maybes' were even more significant than ever before. Ford might just have won the 16,000 mile World Cup Rally, but would its cars do the same job in the UK? And, if so, would it be Roger Clark's brand-new 16-valve Escort RS1600 which proved its potential? Against such formidable opposition, would Lancia be able to repeat its great triumph of 1969? Would Porsche (this time with four works 911S types, including Monte victor Björn Waldegård) stick together at last? And would the new Datsun 240Zs be as fast as forecast? Oh – and would Saab have found more power from its old-fashioned V4 engines to help match the car's rugged chassis?

Although this turned out to be a wet, rather than a wintry, RAC Rally, it proved to be extremely taxing on the competitive cars, for members of virtually every works team had to retire because of broken transmissions. Even so, the first day started gently, with a long passage of main roads from London towards darkness in the awesome forests of North Yorkshire where, incidentally, Dalby South was the longest stage of all (with an unreachable target time of 19min 30sec). That first, pulsating, night visited stages in Yorkshire, and of the course the dreaded Keilder complex, and by time daylight returned, and the first snow had been encountered in the Glendevon section, several important retirements had been recorded.

Timo Mäkinen's Escort Twin-Cam matched fastest times with Björn Waldegård's Porsche 911S at first, while Orrenius' fuel-injected

Saab V4 broke its transmission differential, Ove Andersson's Alpine-Renault also expired, and Tony Fall's Datsun 240Z also struck transmission problems. Two other 240Zs, driven by John Bloxham and Rauno Aaltonen, also broke their transmissions., though the Finn managed to continue.

In the meantime, Blomqvist's and Lindberg's Saab V4s moved rapidly up to challenge Mäkinen and Waldegård, while Hannu Mikkola's Escort also began to figure in the fast times. Trana's Saab V4, on the other hand, retired when the engine suffered a broken crankshaft. All this drama intensified in the 250-mile Scottish loop, where the leading Porsche retired with a broken gearbox, Clark's BDA-engined Escort needed a new gearbox, Safari-winner Edgar Hermann's Datsun broke its transmission, as did Mikkola's Escort.

All this saw two of the amazing Lancia Fulvias (which, don't forget, had once been dismissed as pretty but fragile) of 1969-winner Harry Källström and 1968-winner Simo Lampinen, move up into leading positions, though the lead was still being fought between Mäkinen's Escort and Blomqvist's Saab V4. Amazingly, at this point, Jean-Luc Thérier's rear-engined Alpine-Renault was third, and all three of the humble works 1.9-litre Opel Kadetts were close behind.

There was more drama to unfold in South Scotland, and in the Lake District, before the 97 survivors finally reached the haven of Blackpool on the Monday afternoon, and a very welcome overnight rest halt. All three of Ford's Escorts had retired, all of them with broken transmissions (team boss Stuart Turner once said that 'half shafts' would be engraved on his heart …), Stig Blomqvist went off-route in Kirroughtree, while the Lancias and the Opels consolidated their places at the top. Before the restart came from Blackpool, it was clear that Lancia was looking very strong, the fleet of Opels was looking ominously reliable, and even the Alpine-Renault challenge (Andrew Cowan was in fifth place) was well-placed. Gerard Larrrouse (in reality, a French tarmac and winter-rally expert) was the only survivor of the Porshe 911S team by this time.

A day's rallying in North Wales, which included 11 special stages, saw the field reshuffled once again, with near-sensational developments along the way. First of all, Simo Lampinen's second-placed Lancia

Although Björn Waldegård was fast enough to lead the rally in 1970, his Porsche 911S let him down with mechanical problems in the middle of the event.

Lancia succeeded in making their front-wheel-drive Fulvia HF 1600 a very successful rally car, with Harry Källström winning the event in 1969 and (here) in 1970.

dropped back, and finally retired with – guess what – a broken transmission, while Blomqvist's Saab followed on with the same problem just hours later.

It was then that Källström's Lancia, although leading, struck trouble – not once, but twice. In the first place, the highly-stressed V4 engine sprung a leak, most of the oil was lost, and the mechanics had to make a miraculously rapid main bearing change at a service halt. It was only later, near Harford Llanwrda, that Källström had to swerve to avoid an oncoming truck, ditching the car, and wrecking the front suspension. Somehow, he got it going again, and reached his mechanics. The drama was not over, however, for as time ran out, his car had to be dragged up to and through the time control, with the suspension only partly repaired! Hollywood could never have invented anything quite so dramatic!

Nor was it all over, for between the evening halt in Machynlleth, the Severn Bridge, and the finish back at London airport, Larrousse's Porsche set a series of fastest stage times, Jean-Luc Thérier's Alpine-Renault actually took the lead for a time, before Källström edged back into the lead that he had lost during the night. With only two stages still to run, at the Sparkford control Thérier looked as if he might yet win this RAC Rally – it was not only the first time that Alpine-Renault had contested the British event, but the first time that Thérier had driven on the stages. But it was not quite to be. On the very last stage, close to Camberley (MoD territory), his Alpine-Renault got bogged down in the muddiest of all points in this appalling stage, became stuck, boiled his engine, and soon blew a cylinder head gasket.

And so it was. In spite of everything possible which might have been enough to make him retire, Källström somehow brought the rebuilt, rebuilt *and* rebuilt Lancia to victory, by more than two minutes from Ove Eriksson's 1.9-litre Opel Kadett. Not only that, but the team Opels finished 2-3-4, and thoroughly deserved to win the prestigious Team Prize.

There were several morals to be learned from this event – one being that although starting and finishing in the outskirts of London was good for publicity and media reasons, it meant that much dreary route mileage was involved – either early on, or late, in the itinerary. For the teams, too, this epidemic of transmission failures proved that they still had much work to do to make their cars more reliable for the future, when speeds would inevitably keep on rising.

And so it was, for in 1971 "From Harrogate it started …"

RESULTS

Event held: 14-18 November 1970. One starting point, from London. Finish in London. One overnight rest halt, in Blackpool.

196 starters, 67 finishers.
79 special stages.

General classification		Penalties (min:sec)
1 Källström/Häggbom	Lancia Fulvia HF	541:50
2 Eriksson/Johansson	Opel Kadett Rallye 1.9	544:18
3 Nasenius/Cederberg	Opel Kadett Rallye 1.9	553:18
4 Henriksson/Carlström	Opel Kadett Rallye 1.9	556:08
5 Cowan/Cardno	Alpine-Renault A110	560:20
6 Larrousse/Wood	Porsche 911S	561:04
7 Aaltonen/Easter	Datsun 240Z	567:19
8 Culcheth/Syer	Escort Twin-Cam	580:53
9 Jönsson/Quist	Saab V4	583:41
10 Kleint/Röehr	Ford Capri 2.3	590:33

Team Prize: Opel (O Eriksson, L Nasenius, J Henriksson).
Ladies Prize: BMC Mini-Cooper S (Mrs R Crellin – Mrs P Wright).

1971: "From Harrogate it started"

How many of us – competitors, team bosses, reporters, followers, or mere enthusiasts – will recall the drama surrounding the RAC Rally of 1971, where severe snowfall in the north of the country almost brought the event to a total halt? How many, too, will recall that it was the Scandinavian aplomb, and the experience of all that white stuff, that saw Stig Blomqvist produce a magnificent Saab V4 performance? This all explains the wry remarks made by top co-driver Henry Liddon when questioned in a film interview: "Well, from Harrogate it started …!"

Although the event was still reaching for the peak of its postwar popularity (there were no fewer than 231 starters, which was a postwar record …), Jack Kemsley's organisers had decided to celebrate the 20th 'International' running of the event by thoroughly rearranging the entire layout, for the start and finish had been relocated to Harrogate, and the closest the route got to London was in a time control at Scratchwood Services on the M1 on the final morning.

This allowed a complete change in the sequence of the (mainly familiar) stages to be tackled; the event led almost immediately to the massive Yorkshire forests, and on to Keilder, before striking strongly to

Hannu Mikkola coped remarkably well with his Escort RS1600, in awful weather, in 1971 – finishing fourth overall.

the north, in Scotland, and getting as far as Grantown-on-Spey before turning south again, visiting yet more stages in south Scotland and the Lake District, then returning to Harrogate for a night's rest. 14 hours later, the survivors (and this word meant more in 1971 than in several recent years …) were sent off to Wales, to tackle the giant stages which were now such an important part of this event, before trekking all the way across to Scratchwood, and up via a final handful of 'Mickey Mouse' spectator stages in the Midlands, before they finally returned to Harrogate after 2500 miles and 77 special stages. One highlight (depending on one's attitude to the possibilities of going off the slippery road) was a stage which threaded is way through the Bradford City sewage works!

The entry list was full of the 'great and the good' of European rallying, including four Escort RS1600s from Ford, teams of Lancia Fulvia 1.6HFs (they had won the event in each of the previous two years), Alpine-Renaults, Datsun 240Zs, Saab V4s, and Fiat 124 Sport Spiders, along with Wartburgs, Škodas, and of course the formidably talented Porsche 911S of Björn Waldegård.

As it happened, the sudden onset of truly wintry weather almost submerged the entire event, and in less commercial times (if major sponsors like the *Daily Mirror* and TV schedules had not been involved) it might have been worth cancelling it altogether. As team boss/turned journalist Peter Browning later wrote:

"Nobody took the flurry of snow that fell on the eve of the event very seriously, but when the crews set forth into the Yorkshire moors the following morning they were soon forcing their way through a real blizzard. Thirteen stages had to be cancelled when

Stig Blomqvist and his Saab V4 conquered appalling weather in 1971 to win his first-ever RAC Rally.

Harry Källström tried to make it three Lancia wins in a row in 1971, but the wintry weather defeated him.

they proved impassable, and the rally very nearly ground to a halt despite the extension of lateness allowances ...

"The first leg was a battle for survival against the elements, but the second half, through Wales, across the southern counties, and back up to Harrogate through the Midlands was run in fine, sunny, weather ..."

As it transpired, the first half of the event set the tone for the rest of the five-day event, the result being that 121 crews retired in a matter of hours (40 of them in the Keilder Forest complex alone), and at the event Scandinavian drivers occupied nine out of the top ten finishing positions – for it was only the brave Italian, Sandro Munari, who finally inserted his Fulvia HF into ninth place, no less than 23 minutes adrift of the winning Saab.

This was the sort of event where it was the cars, rather than the drivers, that battled the most against each other. Right from the start, it was the very stable (and nowadays) reliable front-wheel-drive Saab V4s that seemed to relish the conditions, with one of their drivers – either Stig Blomqvist, Calle Orrenius or Per Eklund – looking likely to win at one time, though Per eventually blotted his copybook by rolling his V4 on a Welsh stage, and ending up with a badly crumpled car. Even so, in the end, they took first, third and seventh places, which made the point that where conditions were Scandinavian, then it would probably be a Scandinavian crew that took all the top awards.

Amazingly, the Lancias which had won the previous two RAC Rallies so convincingly, did not really figure so strongly in 1971, for although all three of them made it to the finish – in sixth place (Lampinen), eighth (Källström) and ninth (Munari), they were never able to keep abreast of the Saabs.

And what of the works Wills Embassy-sponsored Ford Escort RS1600s, which boasted 205bhp/1.8-litre engines, and much stronger rear axles than before? Although

The Daily Express sponsored Andrew Cowan in the 1971 RAC Rally, when his Ford RS1600 finished 13th overall.

the previously fancied team cars figured at all strongly in the results. The Alpine-Renaults let themselves down, one of them suffering from a cooling radiator clogged with a combination of mud and snow (which soon encouraged the engine to boil itself into destruction), the other suffering transmission damage on a rock-strewn Welsh stage. The rorty Datsun 240Zs (the spiritual successor to the works Healeys of the 1960s, one felt) could not match the Porsche in its class, nor its traction on the stages, and finished well down. The star of that three-car team was Tony Fall – or he would have been until he went off the track in Penmachno.

On an event like this, there were many tall stories that did the rounds, but one which has stood the test of time was that, as captured in the film made of the event, Peter Clark's Escort plunged into a pond in Woburn Park, and could not be retrieved. His co-driver Tony Mason (who later become more famous for his RAC Rally and TV appearances), ended up on the roof of the partly-submerged car, pleading for help …

RESULTS

Event held: 20-24 November 1971. One starting point, from Harrogate. Finish in Harrogate. One overnight rest halt in Harrogate.

231 starters, 104 finishers.
77 special stages.

General classification		Penalties (min:sec)
1 Blomqvist/Hertz	Saab V4	450:47
2 Waldegård/Nyström	Porsche 911	454:00
3 Orrenius/Persson	Saab V4	460:01
4 Mikkola/Palm	Ford Escort RS1600	460:05
5 Mäkinen/Liddon	Ford Escort RS1600	461:00
6 Lampinen/Davenport	Lancia Fulvia HF	465:16
7 Eklund/Andreasson	Saab V4	469:12
8 Källström/Häggbom	Lancia Fulvia HF	472:47
9 Munari/Manucci	Lancia Fulvia HF	473:49
10 Utriainen/Lehto	Saab V4	474:07

Team Prize: Saab (S Blomqvist, C Orrenius, P Eklund).
Ladies Prize: Opel Ascona 1.9 (Mlle M-C Beaumont/Mlle M de la Grandive).

they finished in fourth, fifth and 11th places, (Hannu Mikkola, Timo Mäkinen, and Roger Clark, in that order), they always seemed to struggle for traction in the wintry conditions, though in the first 24 hours (when conditions were awful) Timo Mäkinen put in one of the astounding performances for which he was famed, and pulled out an astonishing lead that held until the second half of the event began.

In Wales, in more 'typical' forestry stage conditions, Mäkinen was ahead, with the other two cars clawing their way back up the field, when all struck a series of ZF transmission problems. These could only be solved by making total gearbox changes, which was done, but at the cost of considerable time delays. After a delay in the Clocaenog stage in North Wales, which cost Mäkinen more than ten minutes, he slipped back to fifth place, and at the end of the event he still trailed Blomqvist's Saab by about the same margin. These delays not only affected their individual performances, but allowed Saab to move ahead of them to take the Manufacturers' Team Prize too.

Except that Björn Waldegård put up an amazingly consistent show, to place his 240bhp works Porsche 911S in second place (he eventually finished more than three minutes behind the winning Saab), none of

www.veloce.co.uk / www.velocebooks.com
All current books • New book news • Special offers • Gift vouchers

Chapter 4

1972-1980

THE ESCORT ERA

... and the first of the 'World Championship' RACs

In 1973 the RAC Rally most deservedly became one of the founding events of the official World Rally Championship, and from then until the end of the decade the results lists were always dominated by a series of works Escorts. Their shape changed once, and their mechanical specification progressed slowly, but in most other respects the Escorts set a standard which the world of motorsport struggled to match. In most other respects, however, the face and format of the rally seemed to change very little, except that there was a change of sponsors, and the HQ of this event moved around from city to city.

Pentti Airikkala, well sideways, in his DTV Vauxhall Chevette HS in the 1977 event.

The pundits (or so they often claimed) had seen it coming, for a single quasi-factory Escort (driven by Timo Mäkinen) had led its maiden outing for more than half of the 1968 RAC Rally, while from 1969 to 1971 a series of full Ford team efforts had been thwarted, often by weather but mostly by mechanical frailties. It was only a matter of time, it seemed, before the Escort would start to win – and keep on winning.

And so it was. From 1972, when Roger Clark's RS1600 won outright, to 1979, when Hannu Mikkola's much-developed RS chalked up the brand's eighth consecutive victory, there was really little that the world's opposition could do about this. Not even the mighty mid-engined Lancia Stratos, nor the expensively supported Fiat team, could take over. Neither could Nissan-Datsun, nor Alpine-Renault, nor Saab.

To beat the Escorts – at least in an event where gravel stages, a total ban of reconnaissance, and the likelihood of relatively mild weather – it became clear that a 'better Escort' would be needed – and in the end this proved to be possible. Even so, Fiat failed with the 131 Abarth, as did Opel with its nimble Kadett GTEs, and although Vauxhall came close with its 16-valve Chevette HS and HSR types, it was not until 1980 that a rather humbly-developed machine – the Talbot Sunbeam-Lotus – finally proved the point. Even then, it was only the brilliance of the Talbot's young Scandinavian driver, Henri Toivonen, allied to the fact that Ford had finally withdrawn its 'official' team of Escorts, which made it all possible.

The other major change was that after a praiseworthy reign of 12 years as 'Mr RAC Rally', in 1972 Jack Kemsley finally persuaded the RAC to find, and hire, a bunch of new and more enthusiastic organisers to help him. The single most important recruit was the experienced co-driver, Jim Porter (he was, of course, well known as Roger Clark's popular and successful co-driver), who became Clark of the Course. In later years, cynics (quite emphatically wrong, of course) suggested lightly that the reason Roger Clark won two RACs in that period – 1972 and 1976 – was because Jim had been able to provide

Jim Porter, who had already been Roger Clark's co-driver for a successful decade, took over as the RAC Rally's principal organiser in 1972.

him with ideal stages in ideal conditions, but this belittled a period when Roger set all the standards, along with a host of Scandinavians, to the scores of British hopefuls who wanted to begin beating him soon. It would not happen, of course, for Roger retired at the same time as the Escort retired, and a new generation then followed on.

The other major change was that the *Daily Mirror* finally withdrew gracefully from its sponsorship deal after 1973, when the 'Energy Crisis' had upset every type of motorsport – but they were immediately replaced by Lombard North Central, the finance house which had already been supporting the rally for a number of years and thus Britain's biggest rally became the 'Lombard-RAC' – a title which it would enjoy well into the 1980s.

As for the cars themselves, apart from the sensational Lancia Stratos (will we ever forget that engine note, or that styling?) their technical progress, and change, was slower and almost entirely predictable, for the sport's governing body (the FIA, based in Paris) stuck rigidly to its Appendix J Groups 1/2/3/4 (and occasionally Prototype Group 6), and continued to ban the use of four-wheel-drive machines. The RAC organisers, for their part, were utterly against the idea of allowing any reconnaissance of the special stages, or of the use of studded tyres on Forestry Commission stages.

It was during the 1970s (and then only until the end of 1977) that it was possible for determined manufacturers to homologate alternative 16-valve cylinder heads for their less sophisticated engines, and the application of the rules of homologation were as lax as ever. How many Vauxhall Chevette HSs had been built when the car was homologated? Just two, they say. And how many V8-engined TR7 V8s in 1978? None had been delivered, for sure.

The slow pace at which rallying developed during the 1970s can be summed up perfectly by considering how the works Escort stayed

ahead of all its rivals. In 1971 the RS1600 already had the rugged five-speed ZF transmission that all its successors would use, but still only had a 1.8-litre iron-blocked BDA engine which produced 205bhp. From 1972 the alloy-blocked 2-litre engine took over, producing about 230bhp at first, though it was only the (oft-troublesome) development of fuel-injection that allowed it to rise to perhaps 260bhp by 1980. Along the way, in 1975 the newly-styled RS1800 took over from the RS1600 (though the existing platform and all the running gear remained), the package was re-homologated as 'Escort RS' in 1977, after which the ever-familiar two-door saloons continued all the way to 1979 (as works cars), and to 1981 when independently-built cars were financially backed by Rothmans.

So, if the rallies themselves did not change dramatically during the decade, the major opposition to the Escorts most certainly did. Until the mid-1970s, it was the valiant, but under-powered, front-wheel-drive Saab V4s which so nearly matched the pace of the Escorts, while Alpine-Renault and Lancia's Stratos both threatened to overcome both of them. To follow this, Toyota produced its first Celicas, Vauxhall the Chevette HSs, and Nissan-Datsun the 160Js, but surprisingly, the well-financed Fiat 131 Abarth saloons never really figured.

The car that looked likely to match the Escorts, until the brave drivers discovered that there were major snags to be mastered, was the 300bhp Triumph TR7 V8, but it never handled as well as the makers hoped, and eventually fell back. It would not be until 1980 that Talbot (for which, read 'Chrysler' or 'Peugeot' under other names) finally produced the 'better Escorts' that the sport had needed for so long.

In the end it was Henri Toivonen and the Talbot Sunbeam-Lotus that finally took over from the amazingly long-lived Ford Escort. But only for a single year, for it was also in 1980 that the world's rallying authorities were astonished to see the arrival of the fantastic four-wheel-drive Audi Quattro. With turbocharging and more than 300bhp on tap from this car, and the promise of more to come in the 1980s, world-class rallying would never be the same again.

1972: Roger Clark's first victory

Just a year after the hub of the RAC Rally moved out of London, to Harrogate, it shifted, yet again, to York. This was the second of a whole series of relocations of Rally HQ which would follow in the 1970s, all of which helped to make the event a little more compact, yet still able to reach all the classic special stages of Great Britain. Clearly the world of rallying approved of this, for in 1972 there were more than 150 starters, with drivers coming from no less than 15 countries.

By any standards, this looked like a no-nonsense event, with 69 special stages totalling 350 miles in an 1800-mile overall route, there were only to be a handful of 'Mickey Mouse' or 'show business' stages to set the scene on the first day, with the real rallying set to start in North Wales on the first evening. 'Mickey Mouse' this year included a run up and down the tiny Harewood stage, near Leeds, a circuit of the sewage farm 'estate' near Bradford, and a welcome visit to the serpentine Great Orme tarmac loop, immediately to the west of

Timo Mäkinen's challenge in 1972 ended on the first day, when his new alloy 2-litre BDG went out due to wheel stud failure.

Roger Clark won the 1972 event in this Escort – the first of eight Escort wins on the rally.

Llandudno. As so often, the *Daily Mirror* newspaper provided generous sponsorship.

Although Lancia had just completed a victorious attack on the Constructors' World Championship (the FIA World series did not begin until 1973), and in spite of the shambles that the snow-struck 1971 event had been, the RAC Rally was now so popular that a full invasion of works teams turned up. Two of the four Escort RS1600s featured the new alloy-blocked 2-litre engine, and fuel-injection, and were faced with three Saab V4s (including 1971 winner Stig Blomqvist), two 1.6-litre Lancia Fulvia HFs, three Fiat 124 Spiders, three Datsun 240Zs, five Opel Asconas, three Vauxhall Firenzas, and other important entries from Chrysler UK, Toyota, Citroën, Wartburg, Škoda and British Leyland. Unhappily, the works Alpine-Renaults which had been promised did not turn up, and there was no sign of Björn Waldegård, who might have been formidably fast in the latest Porsche 911. Even so, this was probably the most star-studded entry seen so far on this increasingly-prestigious event.

Even though the event had been moved back a couple of weeks – it was the first time the RAC had ever been run off in December, the weather was much less wintry than it had been in 1971. Even so, and to quote one of the specialist magazines: "… almost continuous rain, turning to sleet, and wind sometimes at gale force made driving unpleasant, but did not put the premium on engine-over-the-driving-wheels traction that ice and snow demand."

Right from the start, Roger Clark, in his 230bhp Esso-sponsored RS1600, set about building a lead – not only because the stages, and the conditions, suited him and his Escort, but because he was out to confound his earlier team boss Stuart Turner, who had once said that he might be Britain's best rally driver, but he was not yet in the same class as the top Scandinavians.

Although there was a handful of 'spectator stages' laid out on the first (Saturday) morning – Bramham Park, Harewood and the Esholt sewage works – the event then made tracks for made for Wales, and it was here that the first major (and, for the spectators) disappointing retirements took place: by the time the event emerged from the Welsh forests, and crossed the M4 Severn Bridge, three of the works Escorts – those driven by Hannu Mikkola, Timo Mäkinen, and Andrew Cowan – had all disappeared, leaving Clark all alone to face an onslaught from Stig Blomqvist's Saab V4 and Anders Kulläng's 1.9-litre Opel Ascona, along with the Lancias and Datsun 240Zs. Even so, Roger moved into the lead during that first afternoon, and never lost it thereafter.

Roger Clark and Tony Mason starting the 1972 event in LVX 942J from York.

Roger Clark was Britain's rallying hero in the 1970s, winning the RAC twice in Escorts – in 1972 and 1976.

Amazingly, another threat to Clark's lead came originally from Håkan Lindberg's Fiat 124 Sport Spider, a works car hitherto known to be fast but (by RAC Rally standards) fragile, but after one off-the-road incident, followed by the need to change the rear differential, he was forced out. His colleagues, Rafaele Pinto and Alcide Paganelli, were also eliminated on that first day.

Clark's lead, from that point, was always under attack from Stig Blomqvist's Saab V4 – and those who discount the chances of the Swedish car should know that by this time the Saab's Ford V4 engines had been stretched to 1.8-litres, where they produced about 150bhp. Even if this does not sound competitive with the Fords, one should then add in the advantages of front-wheel-drive, the rugged strength of the Saab's hull, and the utterly astonishing driving talents of Stig Blomqvist. The fact that his car hit a sheep on the Eppynt stage, and a park bench in Sutton Park did not help his cause, but the Saab mechanics, who seemed to be able to repair anything, anywhere, in no time at all, shrugged all this off.

The Sunday run back to the overnight rest halt in York saw the cavalcade visit several more 'Mickey Mouse' (or 'spectator') stages – and a measure of their popularity was that the police counted at least 30,000 people flocking in to the Sutton Park stage in Birmingham: the 'gate' at Silverstone was just as crowded.

By the time the rally reached York, Clark's Escort had stretched its lead over Blomqvist to 1min 33sec, but behind Stig came Per Eklund's sister Saab, Harry Källström's Lancia Fulvia, Tony Fall's Datsun 240Z

and Kulläng's Opel Ascona. Apart from Clark's leading car, the highest-placed British car was currently Will Sparrow's Vauxhall Firenza.

No fewer than 136 cars restarted from York, and were immediately faced with long stages in North Yorkshire, followed by no fewer than nine in the massive Keilder complex (not for nothing did the rallying fraternity call this 'Killer Keilder') – and almost all of them were ideal for the 230bhp Esso-sponsored Escort to flex its five-speed transmission and high top speed. Not only that, but Tony Fall's charismatic Datsun 240Z seemed to be in its element, sweeping past Källström's Lancia and Eklund's Saab to take third place, but was not likely to challenge the leading cars from there. Eklund tried hard to fight back, but during the night in south Scotland he rolled his Saab and was forced out, while Fall's Datsun soon suffered a fuel blockage and lost a massive 11 minutes.

Was it all over? By no means, for after the rally crews stopped for their brief refreshment halt at Turnberry Hotel, there were more stages to tackle before the event crossed the border again into England, and no fewer than five Lake District stages were then scheduled before the pressure was off, and all that then remained was a cross-country cruise through Skipton, to reach York once again.

Roger Clark's lead over Blomqvist – of more than three minutes – looked secure, while behind them Anders Kulläng's Opel Ascona was now in third place, more than six minutes behind Blomqvist. The two works Lancias – driven by Harry Källström and Simo Lampinen – were no doubt mechanically tired, but still going, for at long last those pretty little coupés were being outclassed, way down on the performance of their more modern rivals.

So it was all over. Or was it …? Part way to York from the Newby Bridge control, Clark's Escort suddenly lurched, the front suspension issued a grinding noise, and a wheel bearing totally seized. Fortunately, Ford had arranged for Andrew Cowan's already-retired works car to follow Clark home, and a service car soon arrived, complete with Boreham mechanics – thus allowing a speedy repair to be made at the side of the road. So all was well in the end – though there was great tension on the finishing ramp at York Racecourse when the winning Escort did not arrive at the front of the field!

Every Ford follower likes to remember this day and date – Tuesday, 5 December 1972 – as the occasion on which Ford domination of the RAC Rally began. At the time, they can have had no idea of the period that would follow.

RESULTS
Event held: 2-5 December 1972. One starting point, from York. Finish in York. Overnight rest halt in York.

157 starters, 102 finishers.
69 special stages.

General classification		Penalties (min:sec)
1 Clark/Mason	Ford Escort RS1600	410:07
2 Blomqvist/Hertz	Saab V4	413:32
3 Kulläng/Carlsson	Opel Ascona Rallye 1.9	419:57
4 Källström/Häggbom	Lancia Fulvia HF	421:38
5 Lampinen/Andreasson	Lancia Fulvia HF	422:30
6 Eriksson/Carlström	Opel Ascona Rally 1.9	424:53
7 Nasenius/Cederberg	Opel Ascona Rally 1.9	426:18
8 Blomqvist/Mrs Blomqvist	Opel Ascona Rally 1.9	430:34
9 Andersson/Phillips	Toyota Celica GTV	431:08
10 Walfridsson/Nilsson	Volvo 142S	431:35

Team Prize: Opel (A Kulläng, O Andersson and L-B Nasenius).
Ladies Prize: Opel Ascona Rallye 1 9 (Mlle M-C Beaumont/Mlle C Giganot).

1973: Mäkinen wins, at last
Although it had taken him more than ten years (his first run in the RAC Rally had been in 1962), Timo Mäkinen finally got to win the event in 1973 – and would then go on to emphasise his talents by winning again 1974 and 1975. Timo, need it be said, was driving a newly-built works Ford Escort RS1600 – and made it all look like a routine outing.

During the season, leading up to the RAC, this was a year in which a second Ford Escort success – to follow up Roger Clark's victory of 1972 – had come to look inevitable. In the UK, not only had the entry in British events become dominated by fleets of privately-prepared RS1600s, but their 2-litre 16-valve BDA engines were demonstrably the most powerful in the sport. One car in particular – LVX 942J, Boreham's Esso-sponsored car, which seemed to be the personal property of Roger Clark – was so successful that it seemed to win every rally it started during the season.

Fate, however, had other plans for the sport, and the RAC Rally in particular, as in the weeks leading up to the 1973 event, world power politics suffered an upheaval, yet another Middle East war broke out, and, by November, what became the 'Energy Crisis' (please note the very apt capital letters of this cataclysmic event) was already in full swing. Petrol prices were on the rise, shortages were forecast, and even the black cloud of petrol rationing was also being mentioned.

In summary, therefore, the event for which the world's most prominent rally teams had entered cars in the early autumn would turn out to be rather different from what they had expected, the national media (the BBC in particular) turned against the sport by querying the morality of running an event which would 'waste' precious petrol. The carefully crafted route, therefore, had to be trimmed back, the completely justifiable claim that one transatlantic flight in a Boeing 747 used up a vastly more serious amount was made, and the event finally ran off without much of an organisational hitch.

Before world politics, and (often misguided) public opinion got

The Escort's second win (of eight) came in 1973, when Timo Mäkinen used this Milk Marketing Board liveried car.

Harry Källström wrestling with the heavy, brutish Datsun 240Z in the 1973 event.

Björn Waldegård abandoned Porsche in favour of a BMW for the 1973 event.

in the way, in fact, the 1973 RAC Rally promised to be an even more popular event than that of 1972 had been. No fewer than 198 cars would take the start, and before last-minute changes were made to the route, 80 special stages were listed. In 1972 the choice of York as Rally HQ had been such as success that it was adopted once again for 1973, this time with two overnight rest halts scheduled. On this occasion, however, few 'Mickey Mouse' stages were listed – the first two being Bramham and Sutton Park on the first day - for the vast majority of the flat-out motoring would be in central Wales, the Lake District, South Scotland, the Keilder complex and – only on the final day, in full daylight – the ultra-fast stages of the Yorkshire moors. 20 of those stages were concentrated in Wales on the first night, and no fewer than seven stages (all of them in daylight) later on, in Keilder.

The entry from factory teams all around Europe was enormous, as expected. Ford, having won in 1972, prepared no fewer than six Escort RS1600s, all with alloy 2-litre engines and three of them brand-new, so when the opposition saw the driver line-up (Clark, Mäkinen, Mikkola, Markku Alén, Vic 'Junior' Preston and Russell Brookes) they might have wondered whether it was worth turning up to confront them! Two of those Escorts, incidentally, were sponsored by the Milk Marketing Board, which did not sit very well with the well-known socialising habits of any of Boreham's leading drivers!

Nevertheless, there were three Saab V4s (Blomqvist, Eklund, Lampinen), two Alpine-Renault A110s ('Thérier and Nicolas), BMW 2002s (Björn Waldegård and Achim Warmbold), three Datsun 240Zs (Källström, Tony Fall and Shekhar Mehta), two sturdy Chrysler Avenger GTs (Colin Malkin and Andy Dawson), two Toyota Celica 1600s, three Opel Ascona 1900s for Aaltonen, Eriksson and Kulläng, two Fiat 124 Rally Abarths for Sergio Barbasio and Maurizio Verini), a single Lancia Fulvia HF for Amilcare Ballestrieri – not forgetting a host of experienced British and Scandinavians, all determined that Ford could be beaten, just as it had been beaten several times before 1972.

In a climate which was cold, damp, but virtually devoid of snow (one somehow expected snow to appear in 'RAC weather' at this time …), the event began to unfold in an entirely predictable way, with Ford's works cars leading, squabbling among themselves (there were no team orders – then, or in later years), and with all their rivals except Björn

On a rare visit to contest the RAC Rally, J-P Nicolas took fifth place in his Alpine-Renault A110 in 1973.

1972 winner Roger Clark came so close to repeating the trick in 1973, finishing second behind team-mate Timo Mäkinen.

Waldegård's 16-valve BMW 2002 struggling to stay on terms. As ever, it was Timo Mäkinen who led the charge from Waldegård, and although Roger Clark would lie third at the half-way halt, he was struggling to fight off a flu bug that he had picked up on a recent East African holiday.

Early in the event, however, Clark sparkled in front of big crowds (10,000 at Bramham Park, for instance) to lead from Stig Blomqvist's surprisingly fleet Saab V4, though both the tiny Alpine-Renaults and

the boldly characterful 240Zs were disappointing at this point. It was at Sutton Park that Mikkola (unlucky as he always seemed to be at this period in his RAC Rally career) crashed his Escort, and broke a bone in his right hand, Russell Brookes rolled his works-loaned Escort RS1600, while Adrian Boyd (who had recently bought the famous LVX 942J from Ford) also crashed and ruined his chances. Markku Alén, in his first Escort works drive, also crashed and spent six minutes off the road, which dropped him to 177th place at a stroke, and saw him spending the next four days fighting hard to get back on the leaderboard.

It was only after the 'real' rallying got under way during the Welsh night that Clark eased his way back into the lead, with Mäkinen very close behind him; these two, harassed by Waldegård's BMW for the next three days, would provide all the headlines. On the other hand, the three leading Opels all retired, as did two of the Datsun 240Zs, while Blomqvist's Saab also dropped out after a shunt in Coed-y-Brenin. However, back at York, for the first overnight rest halt, many other leading drivers survived punctures and similar mishaps, so that after 37 stages had been completed Timo Mäkinen was back in the lead, about three minutes ahead of Waldegård's BMW, and Roger Clark's Escort, with a relatively unknown young German driver called Walter Röhrl (Opel Ascona 1900) in fourth place. Markku Alén had already clawed his way back to 13th overall – and there was more to come.

The next phase of the event – the northern loop taking in all the toughest stages which Keilder could offer – was all about Mäkinen's battle with Clark, Waldegård's unhappy demise when he rolled his BMW, and Markku Alén's dramatic fight, all the way up to third place. And how to sum it up? Let's just say that Alén had lost six minutes off the track in Sutton Park on the first day, but ended up only eight minutes from outright victory.

In the early hours of this loop, the biggest drama (or perhaps one should say 'rumour') was that the government might suddenly cause the event to be stopped, there and then, or to ban the sale of petrol to anyone connected with the rally itself, but, in spite of some typically misinformed politically-slanted comments made by the BBC, this never happened. Although Mäkinen's lead in the event never seemed to be in doubt, it was fascinating to see the way that Alén set fastest time after fastest time on so many stages at this point, how Clark's flu seemed to have retreated, and how so many rally cars somehow kept on going, in spite of the battering which was being doled out by this extremely tough event. Technically, one of the features of this event was that the 'engine-over-driving-wheels' brigade (mainly the Saabs and Alpine-Renaults) were not faring at all well, but on the other hand, the good news was that Keilder in daylight (in previous years it had been tackled in the darkness of night) seemed to be more benevolent that usual, and most crews survived.

Back at York, with the luxury of a second night in bed beckoning, there was still time for extensive repairs and service – and with Ford still in first, third and fifth places, they made haste to change dampers, struts and anything else which might just wear out.

General classification		Group	Penalties (h:m:s)
1 Mäkinen/Liddon	Ford Escort RS1600	G2	6:47:08
2 Clark/Mason	Ford Escort RS1600	G2	6:52:23
3 Alén/Kivimaki	Ford Escort RS1600	G2	6:55:26
4 Walfridsson/Jensen	Volvo 142	G2	7:01:13
5 Nicolas/Roure	Renault Alpine A110	G4	7:03:08
6 G Blomqvist/ I Blomqvist	Opel Ascona	G2	7:05:44
7 Waldegård/Thorzelius	BMW 2002	G2	7:06:14
8 Carlsson/Peterson	Opel Ascona	G2	7:09:19
9 Fowkes/Harris	Ford Escort RS1600	G2	7:09:46
10 Barbasio/Macaluso	Fiat Abarth 124	G2	7:10:14
16 Danielsson/Sundberg	BMW 2002	G1	7:19:30

In his first-ever Escort drive, Markku crashed early on, dropping to 177th place, but fought back to take third place overall.

Team Prize: No teams finished.
Ladies Prize: Volvo 142 (Ms E Heinonen/Ms S Saaristo).

The final day's run – York to York by way of just eight special stages to be tackled in six hours in full daylight – produced the final dramas, with Markku Alén setting fastest time on five of them, and Clark beating Timo Mäkinen five times too (Timo, to be fair, seemed to be cruising …). The biggest upset of all was that in the Pickering stage, just two speed tests from the end, Waldegård had left the track (so badly that a tree had to be cut down to allow his car to be retrieved …), picked up a maximum penalty for that excursion, and fell back to seventh overall, 19 minutes in arrears.

In the end, however, not even the challenge of two of the longest stages in the event – Dalby South, which took Alén no less than 18min 21sec, and Cropton, where he took 12min 3sec – could inflict further changes. Not only did Timo Mäkinen therefore win his first RAC Rally (there would be two more victories to come), but works Escorts finished first, second, and third overall.

Would the balance change in 1974? If only we had known …

RESULTS
Event held: 17-21 November 1973. One starting point, from York. Finish in York. Two overnight rest halts, both in York.

198 starters, 91 finishers.
80 special stages.

1974: The Escort's hat-trick victory
After all the traumas, the altercations, and the sheer bad feeling which had been generated between the world of rallying, and the economy-obsessed media in general, the RAC Rally deserved to run in a more tranquil manner in 1974. Fortunately for all concerned, they got their wishes.

The most significant change was already well-publicised, for after some years of rather lack-lustre sponsorship, the *Daily Mirror* newspaper had withdrawn its support (the many controversies surrounding the 1973 rally cannot have helped), and had immediately been replaced by the finance house of Lombard North Central. Theirs would be both popular, and rather more obvious, for some years to come, and everyone seemed happy with the deal.

In almost every other way, however, this was the 'mixture as before,' for once again the event was to be centred on York, where the local populace seemed to enjoy hosting such a colourful event, there were two overnight rest halts, and with the exception of Alpine-Renault, BMW and Datsun, the same phalanx of works teams turned up. Ford, as expected, entered four Escort RS1600s (three of which were brand-new), on what was thought to be their swansong outing, as a new-generation/new-style Escort would shortly be launched.

There was, in addition, a very colourful and publicity-worthy attack from Italy, for not only did Fiat enter a trio of its latest 200bhp/16-valve engined Abarth 124 Rally two-seaters, but Lancia had just got the fabulous mid-engined Stratos homologated, and brought one along for Sandro Munari to drive, where it carried colourful Marlboro sponsorship. Although Munari had little previous form in the UK as a blind-stage/loose-surface exponent, the very special Stratos had already made such an explosive start in its career (it

The first appearance on the event by a Lancia Stratos came in 1974, when Sandro Munari took a very courageous third place.

Simo Lampinen in his front-wheel-drive Lancia Beta Coupé in 1974, on his way to tenth place.

won two World Championship rounds immediately after achieving homologation) that many of the sport's pundits suggested it might be capable of winning in Britain, first time out.

The Stratos, in fact, had everything a modern rally car needed, and

was not merely a special tuned-up version of a more ordinary family car. On the other hand, Lancia, and its influential rally team boss Cesare Fiorio, had worked things out in the opposite direction, had schemed up the rally car they really wanted, then persuaded Lancia to set about building the 500 cars needed to ensure its homologation in Appendix J Group 4. The fact that homologation was granted well ahead of the requisite number of cars being manufactured, was well-known at the time, but no one (not even Lancia's big rivals) seemed to object, for they were all up to the same sort of tricks themselves!

The Stratos was everything that every rally driver wished he could afford, with a stubby and sturdy monocoque platform, a mid-mounted 2.4-litre 240bhp Ferrari 308-type vee-6 engine, rear-wheel-drive, ideal weight distribution, and superb traction.

As ever, this rally was set to be gruelling in so many ways, for the official mileage of the event was 2215 miles, and no fewer than 84 special stages, totalling at least 400 miles, were scheduled. Most were on loose-surfaced Forestry Commission tracks (many of which were now well-known to British competitors), but those that were collectively known as 'spectator stages' were as diverse as the passage of the roads in stately homes such as Bramham Park and Dodington House, a blast through the infamous sewage works near Bradford, and the high-speed circuit of Sutton Park, close to the heart of Birmingham.

Once again Jim Porter was in charge of the general organisation, and made sure that the event would begin gently, with a 9.00am start from York Racecourse, a visit to the Bramham Park stately home, a rush through the Harewood hillclimb, and passage of the Esholt stage, before making for North Wales, and the start of the first forestry stages. Straight away, the sight, the exhilarating sound, and the exuberant spectacle of the Stratos made many instant converts, though as the first forest stages loomed, Ford's Hannu Mikkola held a 12-second lead in the event, while Stig Blomqvist was already prominent in the 160bhp 1.8-litre Saab V4.

That was the good news, but the bad news for Opel was that two of its ever-improving Asconas dropped out at an early stage – Tony Fall in Esholt (which was, quite coincidentally, very close to his home …) and Tony Pond – while the German driver, Walter Röhrl, had to seek assistance to repair the fuel-injection system.

At this point it all began to go wrong for Ford: Mikkola's car suffered a broken rear wheel, which departed from the Escort together with wheel studs, in a Dovey stage, Markku Alén's car suffered a failed BDA engine, and even the maestro, Roger Clark, went off the road for 12 minutes in Dovey 2, which dropped him to 32nd place, and invited a great fightback (which he duly delivered). Clark blamed the 15in wheels which Mäkinen and Mikkola had persuaded Ford to use, but which seemed to cause trouble (see the panel on page 89), and were speedily dropped in favour of the usual 13in wheels instead.

Other high-profile retirements on that eventful first night included Ballestrieri's Fiat (engine), Culcheth's Triumph Dolomite Sprint (accident, the tree won …), Cowan's Vauxhall Magnum (engine), and

There was an epidemic of rolling Saabs in 1974 – this being Per Eklund's battered 1.8-litre V4.

Björn Waldegård put up an amazing performance in 1974, finishing fourth overall in his TTE-built Toyota Corolla.

Timo Mäkinen's second Escort victory in the rally came in 1974.

a youthful Pentti Airikkala's Escort (accident), so as the cars streamed out of Wales across the Severn Bridge, the battle for the lead was between Mäkinen's Colibri Lighters-sponsored Escort, the amazing Stratos, and the equally-amazing Per Walfridsson in his weighty but agile Volvo 142. In the meantime, Saab's team leader, Stig Blomqvist, had blotted his copybook by rolling his V4, but carried on, several minutes off the pace.

After a night's rest back in York, Ford's Timo Mäkinen found himself just 85 seconds ahead of the Stratos, but with the unseen

delights of the high-speed stages in Keilder, south Scotland, and the Lake District still to come on the second loop, he looked quietly confident. With eight different stages packed into the Keilder complex, this was clearly an area where the real heroes would triumph over the poseurs, and it was here that 1972-winner Roger Clark carried on his charge back up the lists after his off-the-stage rest in Wales. 20th at the York restart, he had moved up to 14th by the time the cavalcade reached a control in Carlisle – and Scotland was still to come.

Others were not so lucky, for Ove Andersson's TTE-prepared Toyota Levin broke its suspension after jumping too high and too often, Per Eklund became the second of the works Saab drivers to roll his car, while Colin Malkin struggled to make any sense of the much-vaunted 16-valve Chrysler Avenger BRM, which was way underpowered compared with Ford's ubiquitous BDA.

During an icy but otherwise clear Scottish night, Stig Blomqvist fought his way up from fifth at the York restart, to second overall at the Edinburgh breakfast halt, this relegating the Stratos (which still looked magnificent, and sounded wonderful, though its driver was not familiar with British forests) to third. However, at daybreak, the balance of fortune changed yet again, as it began to snow.

Mäkinen, Blomqvist and Walfridsson loved all this, and even Clark (complete with a car which had needed – and got – a complete rear axle change) made good progress, but Munari's progress in the Stratos became rather miserably precarious, for he lost yet another place to Björn Waldegård's Toyota. Later, as the morning progressed in the Lake District, Tapio Rainio rolled his Saab, Eklund's Saab V4 was immobilised with a broken driveshaft (and could not limp out of the rest of that stage), but the order now seemed to have settled down.

After a second night's rest back in York, the much-depleted field had to face up to a 14-hour dash around the forests in North Yorkshire, some of which were not only long, but whose nine stages included some legendarily-long straight stretches. Munari was still hoping to get the Stratos back into third place, Roger Clark was aiming for a top six finish, while Mäkinen, for once, was driving in a serene fashion, so unlike his usual character.

Following the restart, the drama began almost at once, when both of the works Fords reported that their new-type clutches were wearing out, both descended at high-speed on their service areas, and both were equipped with new components in double quick time – Mäkinen's in 50 minutes, and Clark's in just 34 minutes. Clark would finally move up to seventh place.

Although Stig Blomqvist astonished many observers by being fastest on five of the stages (and Munari twice) nothing could disturb Mäkinen's calm, especially as his ultra-experienced co-driver, Henry Liddon, kept a close check on his rivals' progress. Not even a rather unnecessary (show-bizzy) visit to a control at the Flamingo Park Zoo could spoil the anticipated result, except that a sparkling morning's drive by Munari finally put the Stratos into third place.

For Ford it was a great relief to get just two of their fleet of works Escorts back to the finish, especially as one of them was in first place. Their joy in making this a hat-trick of victories was unlimited – but surely they could not have known that another five outright victories were yet to come?

RESULTS

Event held: 16-20 November 1974. One starting point, from York. Finish in York. Two overnight rest halts in York.

190 starters, 83 finishers.
84 special stages.

General classification		Group	Penalties (h:m:s)
1 Mäkinen/Liddon	Ford Escort RS1600	G2	8:02:39
2 Blomqvist/Sylvan	Saab 96 V4	G2	8:04:19
3 Munari/Sodano	Lancia Stratos	G4	8:11:55
4 Waldegård/Thorszelius	Toyota Corolla	G2	8:13:54
5 Röhrl/Berger	Opel Ascona	G2	8:15:32
6 Walfridsson/Jensen	Volvo 142	G2	8:16:09
7 Clark/Mason	Ford Escort RS1600	G2	8:19:06
8 Coleman/O'Sullivan	Ford Escort RS1600	G2	8:20:29
9 Sclater/Holmes	Datsun Violet TC	G2	8:21:56
10 Lampinen/Andreasson	Lancia Beta Coupé	G2	8:21:57
16 Sparrow/Crellin	Vauxhall Magnum Coupé	G1	8:33:14

Team Prize: Datsun (C Sclater, H Källström and P Faulkner).
Ladies Prize: Toyota Celica GT (Ms P Moss-Carlsson/Ms L Crellin).

13in OR 15in WHEELS

From time to time, even in world-class rallying, there was a bright idea which turned into a trend, a trend into normal acceptance, and then a gradual disappearance of the feature. In 1973 and 1974 the fortunes of the formidable works Escorts were tinged with one of these.

It all started in 1972/1973 when two of the team leaders, Timo Mäkinen and Hannu Mikkola, started to nag Boreham to try something different from the 13in diameter Minilite wheels which were normal wear on their cars. Mäkinen, in particular, lobbied hard, pointing out just how effective was the roadholding and the traction of two Scandinavian brands – Saab and Volvo – with the 15in wheels which they habitually used.

Test sessions with Dunlop on the Bagshot rough-surface proving track in 1973 were inconclusive, but Mäkinen was insistent, demanded (and got) 15in wheels and tyres for the Finnish 1000 Lakes rally of 1974, and finished second overall (behind Mikkola who, incidentally, also used 15in wheels!).

For the RAC Rally of that year, therefore, Ford prepared four cars, all of them fitted with 15in wheels. The team's three Finns (Mäkinen, Mikkola and Markku Alén) were sure that this strategy was correct, but Britain's Roger Clark was not. He, of all people, was grateful for the team's service planners to take on supplies of 13in wheels and tyres too.

As one of the authors later wrote:

"Before long, Roger Clark made one of his rare mistakes, found himself out of control at a point where he knew he would have been in charge on 13in wheels, and went off the road. He then spent the next three days trying to get back on terms, and finally fought his way back to seventh place ...

"Clark, however, only made his dash by switching back to 13in wheels, and once Timo saw that he was being beaten on individual stages he made the swap himself! The supply situation was a bit complicated, and there is at least one authenticated case of Mäkinen's car completing several stages with 13in wheels on one side of the car and 15in wheels on the other ..."

After this, it was not long before Ford took the sensible decision to revert to 13in wheels on all events. In modern times, however, it seems that 'modern-built' 'classic' Escort rally cars regularly use 15in wheels. Make of that what you will.

1975: Timo's third win

One can almost visualise what went through rally enthusiasts' minds in that decade. November in York? Ah yes, that must mean that the RAC

Rally will be in town, and that a works Ford Escort will win again. In 1975, for sure, they would not be disappointed, for in an immaculate performance in the new shape Escort RS1800, Timo Mäkinen won for the third consecutive year.

If the truth be told, Ford's rivals were beginning to get frustrated by this sort of consistent performance, for although the cars were certainly no faster than those of their opponents (the Stratos, in particular), and did not often win in 'special stage' events elsewhere in Europe, in the forests of Great Britain they had begun to seem untouchable. This year, though, was it likely that the status quo could be upset?

Except that Ford had launched a new-shape Escort at the beginning of the year, and was (as usual) running with new individual sponsors on its cars, the scenario of the 1975 event was very similar to that of 1974 … or 1973 … or 1972 … A quick trawl through the list of special stages – 72 of them were scheduled in a total route of 1800 miles – revealed many familiar names, and many familiar sequences, though for 1975 the action would begin in the ultra-fast Yorkshire stages, and would end after a final gruelling passage of the Keilder group in the England/Scotland border area. Groups of 'show business' or 'Mickey Mouse' stages would feature not once, but twice – on the first day near York, and on the second day on the trek down to the West Country, and back into Wales.

Before the start, much of the rumour-mongering centred on Lancia's formidable mid-engined Stratos, which had already won a number of World Championship events in 1975, had almost beaten the odds by taking second and third in the Safari, and was clearly capable

of winning the RAC – if, however, one of its 'superstar' drivers could master the mysteries of unpractised special stages. Ford, for sure, had no illusions about the Stratos' promise, but could only hope for wet (or preferably, icy and even snowy) weather to equal the struggle. Lancia, for its part, sent two Alitalia-sponsored cars for Sandro Munari (he had been third in 1974) and Björn Waldegård to drive, backing them up with two Lancia Beta Coupés. Ford, running new-shape 240bhp Escort RS1800s, had Roger Clark, Timo Mäkinen, and a still-little-known Finn called Ari Vatanen in 'Boreham' cars, with a phalanx of supported, or purely private types to back them up.

With a battle royal like this already looking certain, the teams from Saab (fuel-injected V4s led by Stig Blomqvist), Toyota (with Hannu Mikkola now on its driving strength), Fiat (124 Spiders), Opel (Kadetts), Vauxhall (Magnum Coupés), Triumph (Dolomites, built at Abingdon) and Chrysler (a BRM-engined Avenger for Colin Malkin) could only hope that Lady Luck was on their side.

All this promise, however, was soon overshadowed by two inter-related events – one being the existence of a double 110mph hump in the Clipstone stage, the other being the fact that Waldegård's Stratos spent at least 24 hours running without its rear bodywork (and, therefore, without showing a rear number plate or any rear lights!)

Even so, the first day's rallying had begun with remarkably little unexpected drama. Although the 1.8-litre Saab V4s had begun well, once the Escorts and Stratoses reached the high-speed sections in the Yorkshire moors, they rapidly filled all the leading positions, and it was Waldegård's Stratos, as expected, which led the event back to York after the first 14 stages. Toyota and Opel, on the other hand, had already

Sometimes winning is difficult – Timo Mäkinen's Escort on its way to winning the 1975 event.

Maurizio Verini took this works Fiat Abarth 124 Spider to eighth place in 1975.

seen their teams (driven by Ove Andersson, Hannu Mikkola and Rauno Aaltonen) decimated.

Then came Clipstone forest, on the second morning, where Ari Vatanen (who had already set two fastest stage times) crashed his Escort while flat out in fifth gear, Roger Clark's Cossack-sponsored

Escort almost joined him, Stig Blomqvist rolled his Saab V4 (but Saabs were used to that sort of thing, and the Swede was soon under way once again …), while Waldegård also suffered a broken driveshaft on the same stretch of track.

For Ford, and Timo Mäkinen, that was the good news, as he took the lead, and never again relinquished it (his team-mate, Clark, had a brand-new car which suffered multiple minor problems during the event, including glitches in a new braking system, and broken strut and rear dampers …), but for Waldegård it was a disaster. Not only did he need a change to a transmission driveshaft (this was a lengthy process on the Stratos), but this seemed to take ages, so finally he was obliged to rush back into the fray, more than an hour late, and without the complete rear section of the bodyshell. Disqualification, on both counts, should have followed at once, but the wily Lancia team management somehow kept him going for many hours before officialdom finally took away his road book, and the precious time cards which accompanied it.

For the next several hours, and into the Welsh night, the drama continued to unfold, with the

So near, yet so far – Roger Clark brought a new 'Cossack' car to the 1975 event, fought a stage-by-stage battle with team-mate Timo Mäkinen, and finished a close second place, overall.

Björn Waldegård set the majority of fastest times in the 1975 rally in this Lancia Stratos, but was eliminated for running out of road schedule time during the event.

After Björn Waldegård's Stratos broke a driveshaft on the 1975 rally, it took so long to be repaired that he ran out of time, and had to be eliminated.

In 1975, Brian Culcheth not only won his class in this Triumph Dolomite Sprint, but won the entire Group 1 category outright.

ungainly stripped-for-the-part Stratos setting fastest time after fastest time (the crowds of spectators loved this, though any of them must have known that disqualification would eventually follow …), with Mäkinen driving smoothly and serenely into a secure lead, and with Roger Clark battling hard to overcome a positive flood of new-car problems.

Behind them, Stig Blomqvist was driving his under-powered Saab in a way that no-one else could possibly match, Walter Röhrl proving that he was a better driver than his still under-developed Opel Kadett could match, while two Escort privateers, Russell Brookes and Tony Fowkes, were showing that they were all on the brink of greatness. The biggest shock, however, followed in the wintry daylight surrounding Dovey forest, where Sandro Munari crashed the second of the flamboyant Stratoses, thus ruining the Italian concern's week.

By the time the much-depleted field returned to York for the second overnight rest halt, the leaderboard had virtually settled down, and because there seemed to be such a generous amount of time available for service and repairs before the cars were locked away for the night, the third, demanding, leg began to look like a new rally. Mäkinen's APG-liveried Escort was just 81 seconds ahead of Blomqvist's Saab, Clark's Cossack-liveried Escort was third, closely followed by Tony Fowkes, Russell Brookes, and Billy Coleman (in yet another of the Boreham-provided RS1800s. Waldegård, in the Stratos (for which he had somehow 'found' another rear bodywork section), was up to a theoretical seventh place, but was finally disqualified for being out of time so many controls ago.

Even so, the drama was not yet over. After the restart, Mäkinen needed a new front suspension strut (the work of just a few minutes

to the works mechanics …), Blomqvist's gallant Saab broke its engine crankshaft, while Brookes' car suffered a seized rear differential, broken rear wheel studs, and eventually ran out of time.

The Keilder complex, tackled in the dark as usual, then hosted the final unexpected problems, for in true Hollywood style it began to look as if Mäkinen's drive might be in danger. First of all, his aluminium-blocked 240bhp BDA engine began to lose oil pressure, then the oil gradually began to be lost (up to a gallon would be needed every hour or so!), and with no question of team orders being applied, Roger Clark was then allowed to start making up the gap.

Somehow or other, the loss of oil (it was not burning away, but leaking away …) in Mäkinen's engine was contained, Clark ended up a mere 73 seconds behind him (that was the equivalent of one second per special stage), while the amazingly resourceful, and under-financed, Fowkes in his old-shape privately-prepared Escort RS1600 took third place, four minutes further back. With Tony Pond taking fourth overall in his 1.9-litre Opel Kadett a further six minutes adrift, it was nevertheless a really triumphant show by British crews.

The European works teams, and their drivers, must surely have left York wondering if, and how, they could break what was beginning to look like a Ford Escort monopoly. Little did they know that they would have five more years to wait.

RESULTS

Event held: 22-26 November 1975. One starting point, from York. Finish in York. Two overnight rest halts in York.

250 starters, 104 finishers.
72 special stages.

General classification		Group	Penalties (h:m:s)
1 Mäkinen/Liddon	Ford Escort RS1800	G2	6:00:44
2 Clark/Mason	Ford Escort RS1800	G2	6:01:57
3 Fowkes/Harris	Ford Escort RS1600	G2	6:06:11
4 Pond/Richards	Opel Kadett GT/E	G2	6:12:26
5 Aaby/Nyborg	Ford Escort RS1600	G2	6:14:14
6 Coleman/O'Sullivan	Ford Escort RS1800	G2	6:16:38
7 Nilsson/Carlrstrom	Opel Ascona 1900	G2	6:17:53
8 Verini/Rossetti	Fiat 124 Abarth	G4	6:17:59
9 Sparrow/Crellin	Vauxhall Magnum	G2	6:18:04
10 Lampinen/Maiga	Lancia Beta Coupé	G4	6:18:59
16 Culcheth/Syer	Triumph Dolomite Sprint	G1	6:30:41

Team Prize: Vauxhall (W Sparrow, P Airikkala, P Faulkner).
Ladies Prize: Ford Escort 1600 Sport (Ms T Jensen/Ms M Brathen).

Can there ever have been a more popular victory than this? Roger Clark in POO 505R on the 1976 event.

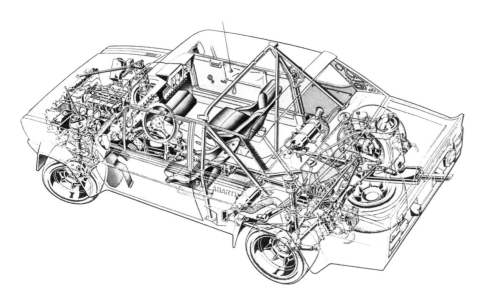

By the mid-1970s, Group 4 rally cars had become very sophisticated – this being the anatomy of the new Fiat 131 Abarth of that period.

1976: Roger Clark, the people's champion

When Roger Clark eased his flamboyantly liveried Escort RS1800 across the finishing line of the 1976 event in Bath, to win a hard-fought event, he finally delivered on all the promises which had been obvious for more than ten years. A Ford works driver for more than decade, a winner of countless other International rallies in all that time, his second RAC victory still felt long overdue. The spectators, and even the oft-cynical media, were all delighted to see this. The Leicestershire-lad had proved what many of us had known for years – that he was Britain's best rally driver – ever. Although he had a rather unsuccessful season, his outstanding performance in the UK in December proved that for all time.

In many ways, this event was one which delivered more glamour, more incident, and more controversy than ever before, and it was evident that the RAC was finally bringing its prestige event into the absolute limelight. By this stage, not only were the cars the stars – for sponsorship was producing all manner of different hues for the photographers and enthusiasts to enjoy – but the drivers had become superstars in the sport, the works teams flocked to take part in the event, and the venue was tailored to suit them.

This year, for the first of what would eventually be four visits in a decade, the Lombard-RAC event was based on Bath (Lombard had had much to do with recommending this change, from York …), a move which was popular with many – although the route was also changed significantly, so that there was to be virtually no time for a visit to Scotland, and there was also what looked like a rather pointless circuit of the West Country.

Although Ford was looking forward avidly to notching up its fifth consecutive victory, a whole host of factory teams seemed determined to stop them, for there were serious and formidable entries from Triumph/British Leyland, Chrysler-UK, Datsun, Fiat, Lancia, Opel, Saab, Škoda, Toyota and Vauxhall, along with several serious privately-

Things could only get better. For 1976, DTV's Vauxhall Chevette RS was brand-new, and lasted only one special stage – but many rally successes would follow in the future.

prepared Escorts from Russell Brookes, David Sutton, and Billy Coleman.

Fiat, however, though well-financed and already bent on winning the World Championship in future years, had a new car (the 131 Abarth saloon) which was not yet suited to forestry stage rallying. Lancia for some reason only sent one Stratos (for Sandro Munari to drive), Triumph was still trying to shake the bugs out of its new TR7 sports cars, while Vauxhall had entered a new model called the Chevette HS, which was still a totally unproven machine. Toyota, on the other hand, not only had Hannu Mikkola on its driving team, but was using fuel-injected 235bhp Celicas, while Saab arrived with new-type, larger and heavy front-wheel-drive 99 EMS types, complete with 225bhp 2-litre engines that looked, and were, extremely competitive.

All of which ensured that this was probably going to be the most exciting, closely-fought, high-profile RC rally which had so far been seen, and when the cars departed in a flourish from Bath's beautiful Great Pulteney Street, the crowds were already out in force, simply buzzing with anticipation. It would prove to be an enthralling event, which might at one time have gone to Pentti Airikkala's privately-built Escort RS1800 if the clutch had not let him down, and would almost certainly have been won by a Lancia Stratos if Björn Waldegård had not recently been sacked from the works team for proving that he was faster than the charismatic Sandro Munari in the same type of car (and had immediately been signed to drive a very hastily-prepared works Escort …).

Whoever might have written the script for this event had to tear it up and start again after only two special stages, for on the Speech House section (in the Forest of Dean), three-times winner Timo Mäkinen got it all wrong, rolled his brand-new Escort RS1800, damaged the rear axle badly, and was forced to retire shortly afterwards. Not only that, but team-mate Ari Vatanen was fastest on two early stages, then over-revved his engine, and struggled into the evening halt in York with a misfiring engine. Not even engine development guru Brian Hart, on the spot to offer assistance, could solve the problem of a broken valve spring, and the car was forced to retire. Two Fords down in the first day … was something unimaginable happening?

Although there were several other Escorts all near the top, it was Pentti Airikkala (already leading as the cars left York) who began to shine, Blomqvist astonishing everyone with the pace of his new Saab, and Hannu Mikkola already getting the very best out of his Toyota who made all the headlines as the field disappeared into the Yorkshire forests.

By this time no fewer than three of the works Opels had retired with mechanical dramas, Eklund's Saab was out after duelling with a tree stump, Russell Brookes' Escort was about to blow its engine in a big way, and Bacchelli's Fiat 131 Abarth was suffering from damaged suspension, while Mikkola's Toyota had problems with its fuel-injection system – so with Airikkala fastest on five of the Yorkshire stages, and fastest on no fewer than five of the six stages all labelled as 'Keilder,' and Tony Pond setting some very fast times in his 2-litre-engined Triumph TR7, it looked as if an upset might be on the cards.

Chrysler's Avenger GT became a competitive Group 1 car in the 1970s; this is Robin Eyre-Mounsell.

By the time the rapidly-dwindling field struggled out of the Keilder/Kershope stage complex, and with 33 of 76 stages already behind them, Airikkala was more than two minutes ahead of Clark, who might have looked serene, but was clearly not able to do anything about that gap. Six stages later, when the cars finally arrived at the overnight rest halt in Bath, and with 39 stages completed, Pentti had stretched that gap to 2min 41 seconds, while Blomqvist's Saab was almost panting over Clark's shoulder, Billy Coleman (Escort RS1800) was fourth, Sandro Munari's Stratos fifth, and Waldegård, in his first drive in a works Escort, sixth and about to move up the field.

Before the cars could get into Wales for the final gruelling night of forestry stage rallying, they had to tackle a number of 'Mickey Mouse' stages, including visits to Cricket St Thomas (stately home), Wiscombe Park (hillclimb), and Porlock (the toll road), but by this time Airikkala's lead was under pressure as the highly-tuned BDA engine began to misfire at high revs, and came in for a lot of attention from David Sutton's mechanics at the control in Weston-Super-Mare.

Here, then, was where Airikkala's luck ran out, for so much time was spent in fettling the engine (to little avail, as it transpired), that the car ran out of time at this location, and was later disqualified, for being more than an hour later than their scheduled booking time at the next time control. Although Sutton kept the car running, even in Wales where its clutch was eventually so far gone that a concerted push was needed to get it off the starting line (and no fewer than four further unofficial fastest stages times were recorded), it finally lay down and died near Machynlleth.

So now the headline-writers had a different story to tell, for Roger Clark was now definitely, and irrevocably, back in the lead, but only about one minute ahead of Stig Blomqvist in the Saab 99, though Stig was then comfortably ahead of his close rivals: Billy Coleman was one of them, but he slipped back after suffering an accident on the open road with a non-competing car. It was from Machynlleth that Clark settled down to make one of his long-famed charges (it was almost as if someone had rewound his main-spring and urged him on), for he then set fastest stage times on six of the final seven stages, all of which were in classic, well-known, Welsh forests.

There was nothing, it seems, that the ever-optimistic Blomqvist could do about this, for the gap soon exceeded two minutes again, and ended up at no less than 4min 37 seconds. And, for Ford, there was more to celebrate, for throughout the event Waldegård had demonstrably seemed to learn more and more about the Escort, and finally muscled his way up to third place overall, just 52 seconds behind the Saab. Sandro Munari finished a rather dispirited fourth in the Stratos (Björn Waldegård admitted that he could 'probably' have won if he had been entrusted with his old mount!), while Ove Andersson/Martin Holmes took an excellent fifth in their 1.6-litre Toyota Corolla.

And so it was that Ford had won its fifth successive RAC Rally – a sequence in which only two drivers (Clark twice and Mäkinen three times) had made a contribution. Surely the Escort 'tradition' could not be continued further? Björn Waldegård, still overjoyed with his first-ever performance in a works Escort, thought otherwise …

RESULTS
Event held: 27–30 November 1976. One starting point, from Bath. Finish in Bath. One overnight rest halt in Bath.

200 starters, 71 finishers.
76 special stages.

General classification		Group	Penalties (h:m:s)
1 Clark/Pegg	Ford Escort RS1800	G4	6:02:26
2 S Blomqvist/Sylvan	Saab 99EMS	G4	6:07:03
3 Waldegård/Thorszelius	Ford Escort RS1800	G4	6:07:55
4 Munari/Maiga	Lancia Stratos	G4	6:08:49
5 Andersson/Holmes	Toyota Corolla	G4	6:11:43
6 Coleman/O'Sullivan	Ford Escort RS1800	G4	6:11:48
7 Kulläng/Andersson	Opel Kadett GT/E	G4	6:15:13
8 Dawson/Marriott	Datsun Violet	G4	6:22:07
9 Culcheth/Syer	Triumph TR7	G4	6:22:54
10 Danielsson/Sundberg	Opel Kadett GT/E	G1	6h24:28
16 Haugland/Gallagher	Škoda 130S	G2	6:44:01

Team Prize: Saab (S Blomqvist, H Gustavsson, J-P Perusse).
Ladies Prize: Jill Robinson/Pauline Gullick (Ford Escort RS1800).

1977: Same car, new winner
Björn Waldegård wins for Ford

In 1977, it seemed, the world of rallying had almost assumed that a Ford Escort would once again win the RAC Rally – even though the Lancia Stratos had already beaten it in other events across Europe. But if an Escort could win, who would be driving it? Roger Clark, the 'Old Master,' Ari Vatanen, the 'New Kid On The Block,' or Björn Waldegård, who had surprised so many observers with his debut drive for Ford in 1976?

As to the opposition, the only new face which appeared to dispute this likelihood was the team of 16-valve Vauxhall Chevette HSs, which had somehow been homologated into FIA Group 4 on the flimsiest of evidence (and would eventually be cast out of the sport, for a time, in 1978). Even so, the balance of the entry list looked as formidable as ever, because Lancia once again entered two of the charismatic Stratos (although that car's works career was soon to be terminated …), there were promised to be two works Saab 99s, no fewer than seven Fiat 131 Abarth Rallye saloons, three rugged Toyota Celicas, two works Triumph TR7s, along with a host of well-financed private entrants in competitive cars to add to the uncertainties.

As to the event itself, in 1977 the organising team played safe, not only by retaining almost all of the familiar special stages, but moving the centre of the rally back to York, where it was intended to have two overnight rest halts. Even so, for obvious publicity reasons, the start was laid out at the dear old Wembley Stadium in London on the first morning, though the cars would not even approach the Metropolis after that! The fact, too, that this was the final qualifier for the World Rally Championship meant that there was a great deal of interest from the 'circus,' and the international media. For the organisers, too, it was heartening to see that no fewer than 120 of the 180 entries came from overseas, and that the lists included 22 FIA seeded drivers.

At first glance, this looked like a rally which was going to be interminable, for after the Sunday morning start from London, there would be special stages for the next five days, 69 of them, totalling more than 400 miles. Nor were many of these all small and fiddly, for (as one of the authors wrote in his pre-rally survey in *Autocar* magazine: "This year's event is transformed. After several years of decline, the stage mileage has been sharply increased … The length of many individual stages has been increased, some stages now being more than 20 miles long …"

Amazingly, it all managed to look quite compact too, for most of Monday and Tuesday was spent in Wales, most of Wednesday was spent in the Lake District and south Scotland, while that night and Thursday took in the gruelling expanses of Keilder and the North Yorkshire group of forests. The last stage of all – it was to be at Wykeham, near Scarborough - was only scheduled for 90 minutes before the first car was to reach the finish at York Racecourse.

The weather, thank goodness, showed no sign of spoiling what promised to be a superb event, though it was seasonably cold and windy – all of which may explain the huge crowds who turned out to watch the early' spectator stages' at venues such as Blenheim Palace, Sutton Park and the Donington race circuit. Although they clearly expected the Lancia Stratos to set the early pace, and the works Escorts to squabble immediately behind that, it was originally Hannu Mikkola in the 240bhp Toyota Celica (the last appearance of this car, as its homologation was about to expire), and the flamboyantly liveried Fiat 131 Abarths (which had just lifted the World Rally Championship) that caused the most interest.

All that, however, was just for starters, as the first of two overnight rest halts in York soon followed. Ford, almost as expected, seemed to be placidly ready for the forestry stages which were to follow in Wales,

Björn Waldegård's Escort success in the 'British Airways' liveried Escort in 1977 was the sixth consecutive victory for that model, achieved without problems.

Stig Blomqvist had taken second place in the 1976 rally in the Saab 99 EMS, and looked like repeating that performance in 1977 until the car let him down.

and if its three 'First Team' drivers were not quite yet on top form, there seemed to be a phalanx of supported private owners (Andy Dawson, Russell Brookes and Kyosti Hamalainen among them). And so it proved as soon as the cavalcade reached the Machynlleth control on the Monday evening, for Björn Waldegård (his brand-new car carrying British Airways sponsorship) had moved smoothly and serenely into the lead, with Airikkala's Chevette HS and Munari's Alitalia-sponsored Stratos close behind. Not that this order persisted for long, as the Chevette went off and lost many places, the Stratos needed to have a broken fan belt replaced, and the Fiat Abarth team began to fall into a variety of mechanical problems. Fiat, it seemed, was never likely to win such a rough-and-ready event (the team's speciality was in 'tarmac' rallies where pre-event reconnaissance was allowed) – though they kept on trying.

Within hours, Fiat's fortunes nose-dived further, as Alén's car, once in second place, lost all its engine oil and a blow-up was inevitable, while Timo Mäkinen (ex-three-time victor in Escorts) rolled his and lost much time. He was in good company, for Ari Vatanen (who had already experienced a crash-prone season) took to a firebreak at high speed and crippled his Escort, while Chris Sclater went ditch-hunting in his Vauxhall Chevette, and Per Eklund rolled his bulky Saab 99. Ice on some stages had much to answer for.

By the time the cars got back to York, Waldegård had consolidated his lead over Hannu Mikkola's Toyota, Andy Dawson (running a works Escort, but one which his team had prepared for themselves) was in an astonishing third place, Russell Brookes' Escort and Roger Clark's works car were close behind, and it was beginning to look like

another Escort benefit was on the cards. Away from the limelight, the Fiats always seemed to be in some sort of trouble, Opel's Group 2 Kadett GTEs were simply too slow, and the works TR7s were, frankly, disappointingly right off the pace. So what did the second half of this five-day marathon, which would include the very worst that the 'Killer Keilder' complex had to offer, be likely to do to the Escort's dominance?

Not much, it seemed, for although Roger Clark could do no more than to consolidate a sturdy fourth place (he would end up 15 minutes behind the winning car, due to needing clutch and other remedial changes along the way) and Dawson lost time when he flew off a track, losing ground from what looked like a remarkable third position, there seemed to be little that the opposition could do to make up the deficits.

The weather turned spiteful for the third long leg of the event, for which no team managers had seemed able to plan. Not only was there torrential rain in the Lake District, and a short-lived and localised blizzard of snow in Scotland and Keilder, but – amazingly – a complete change in the last few hours would then see the 'Yorkshire giants' (Ingleby, Cropton, Dalby and Wykeham) bathed in wintry sunshine, and perfect visibility.

Not even a determined assault on Waldegård's lead by Hannu Mikkola in the Toyota Celica (he set several fastest stage times in the final hours …) could provide any major upsets to the leaderboard, although Timo Salonen brought further misery to the massive Fiat team when he crashed his 131 Abarth in the Whinlatter forest. It was only two stages later, though, that Andy Dawson went off the road again, fortunately inflicting only suspension damage to his Escort (which his mechanics could repair), and he dropped to fifth place, more than three minutes behind Roger Clark's *Daily Express*-sponsored Escort. But there was more, for Chris Sclater rolled his Vauxhall Chevette HS, Brookes' Escort suffered a loose front strut which threatened to punch its way out through the bonnet – and even Waldegård needed a Ford doctor's treatment for a strained wrist.

As ever, it was the Keilder complex (which included three 20-mile stages, all taken in darkness) which spoiled the chances of even more determined crews – including Tony Pond's Triumph TR7, which (according to Tony) was: "… finished. Engine and gearbox have been gone all day …" John Taylor's Haynes of Maidstone Escort suffered a failed electrical system, and both the works Renault 5 Alpines broke their transmissions. In the end, though, Björn Waldegård, most ably backed by Ford's large and well-spread servicing operation, came home the winner, beating Mikkola by just 2min 23 seconds, making this the Escort's sixth successive victory in Britain's premier rally.

At the finish, though, there was less discussion of what had just happened, than to what would look like happening in 1978. Major changes to homologation rules meant that Lancia's Stratos would lose its 24-valve engine option, neither Saab's 99 EMS or Toyota's Celica would be eligible to compete, Hannu Mikkola was moving to Ford, and Markku Alén looked set for a full UK season in a works Fiat 131 Abarth. We could hardly wait for the winter to end, and for the new battles to begin …

RESULTS
Event held: 20-24 November 1977. One starting point, from Wembley Stadium in London. Finish in York. Two overnight rest halts in York.

180 starters, 67 finishers.
69 special stages.

General classification		Group	Penalties (h:m:s)
1 Waldegård/Thorszelius	Ford Escort RS	G4	8:21:26
2 Mikkola/Hertz	Toyota Celica	G4	8:23:49
3 Brookes/Brown	Ford Escort RS	G4	8:31:55
4 Clark/Pegg	Ford Escort RS	G4	8:36:21
5 Dawson/Marriott	Ford Escort RS	G4	8:39:46
6 Hamalainen/Scott	Ford Escort RS	G4	8:42:17
7 Lampinen/Andreasson	Fiat Abarth 131	G4	8:44:24
8 Pond/Gallagher	Triumph TR7	G4	8:45:04
9 Eklund/Cederberg	Saab 99EMS	G4	8:46:02
10 Danielsson/Broad	Opel Kadett GT/E	G4	8:46:22
12 Wilson/Palmer	Ford Escort RS2000	G1	8:58:06
15 Kulläng/Berglund	Opel Kadett GT/E	G2	9:02:50

Team Prize: Ford (B Waldegård, R Brookes and R Clark).
Ladies Prize: Ford Escort RS2000 (Ms J Robinson/Ms D Selby-Boothroyd).

1978: Ford again – with no help from a works team
Although this particular Lombard-RAC Rally will not go down in history as an enthralling contest – Ford Escorts, after all, finished first, second, third, and seventh, and no other type of rally car looked like beating them – it was one that included much drama, intrigue and sheer 'show-business' elements. Not only did all of Ford's works drivers have to turn up and grapple with unfamiliar 'privately-prepared' machines, but British Leyland was still smarting from the damage caused by saboteurs on the recent Tour de Corse. Once again, Lancia produced a pair of Stratoses, and Fiat's 131 Abarth innovations included the use of a 'back-seat passenger' at one time!

Look left, look right, and look back with interest – and one found innovations that promised to make this particular event rather historic. For the first time ever (the event and its ancestors had now been running for more than 40 years) the rally was to be based on Birmingham, there were new cars from British Leyland (the 300bhp TR7 V8s), Saab (99 Turbos), and Datsun (the 160J).

This, and the promise of tackling no fewer than 450 miles of special stages – 76 of them – attracted up to 200 entries, with a 1900 mile route, two overnight halts in Birmingham in a five day event. With a route that opened up with eight 'stately-home' stages on the first day, it was the sort of challenge which seemed to appeal to everybody. The general layout, however, was really rather different from the traditional one, for although familiar stages in North Yorkshire, Keilder, and the Lake District all figured, as usual, the final Welsh loop was truncated near Llandrindod Wells, before the survivors then made a bee-line for the finish in Birmingham.

Before the start, the major talking points revolved around two competing brands – Ford and Fiat. Weeks earlier, Ford had found its pre-rally preparations thwarted by the company-wide pay strike, and in the end a series of extreme emergency deals were struck to allow the star drivers to turn up with any hope of winning. The details of this are covered in the panel 'Dealer Team Ford' on page 101 and, as will become obvious, it worked remarkably well. Fiat, on the other hand, having already won the World Rally Championship that year, sent Walter Röhrl to compete in a newly-prepared 131 Abarth, where his co-driver Christian Geistdorfer was located in a seat behind him, on the centre line of the car: this was done, Fiat insisted, to maximise the traction of the driven rear wheels.

Not that a casual observer could have concluded that Ford's 'superstars' were driving unfamiliar cars, for they were competitive from the very beginning, were almost all very reliable, and were helped by a superb service umbrella from companies like Dunlop, who seemed to have the right tread and the right carcass for all conditions. It also helped that both the Lancia Stratos cars retired with mechanical derangements, as did the two Saab 99 Turbos, the three works Vauxhall

Chevette HSs, and one of the Triumph TR7 V8s, while Röhrl spent much time off the road in a Welsh stage, losing what looked like a definite third place.

Russell Brookes' 'Andrews Heat for Hire' sponsorship appeared on many Escorts in the1970s, this car being on its way to third in 1978.

Amazingly, too, this was the first year for some time that the weather – ice and snow in particular – did not get in the way of the event, so on the first day's rallying, from Birmingham's City Centre, a loop involving nine mainly 'spectator' stages before the event returned to Birmingham for the first of two rest halts was held in streaming wet and slippery, but not wintry, conditions.

On that first day, all the stages featured all-tarmac or part-tarmac surfaces, so the pure performance cars were expected to dominate – yet, amazingly, this was a day when DTF (Dealer Team Ford) lost Vatanen, whose co-driver failed to visit one particular passage control, and suffered badly when John Taylor's fuel-injected Escort suffered not one, but two fuel-injection pump failures. Markku Alén's Lancia Stratos, however, led the way from Röhrl's Fiat 131 Abarth, with Pentti Airikkala showing well in a Vauxhall Chevette HS, the other Stratos seventh, and with Blomqvist's Saab 99 Turbo in tenth place, two-and-a-half minutes off the pace. As for Tony Pond and the formidable TR7 V8, his car suffered a smashed rear braking system, which cost him dear. The Taylor/Escort disaster, which saw them having to be pushed out of the Trentham Park stage, left Taylor in 122nd place – and he would spend the next four days clawing his way back up the field.

And that was only the beginning, for once the second day's stages began – the cars first of all making their way up to Yorkshire, then taking a deep breath and making for a night-time assault on the Keilder complex – the troubles really set in. Both the Saab 99 Turbos retired with broken driveshafts, which stranded them in mid-stage, and Munari's Stratos was hit by insoluble engine problems, also in mid-stage, while Röhrl's Fiat still seemed unable to beat the Escorts in what,

Roger Clark drove one of John Taylor's Escorts for 'Dealer Team Ford' in 1978.

to them, was very familiar going. Alén's Stratos was finally overtaken by Hannu Mikkola's Escort in the darkness of the Scottish stages, but then ground to a halt. When a Lancia mechanic was asked what the problem had been, he gave a typically eloquent Latin shrug, stirred his hand around in a typical gear-changing manner and uttered just one word: "Mayonnaise!"

Everyone – Ford, Vauxhall, and their rivals – seemed to have big troubles before they could get back to Birmingham for the second rest halt. Mikkola's Escort suffered a failed water pump (replaced), Brookes' car lost its brakes (which was very exciting on the fast stages!), while both Roger Clark and Björn Waldegård needed clutch changes on their DTF machines. As to the once-fancied Vauxhalls, they all retired, afflicted by electrical problems, an engine oil pump failure, and a high-speed dash down a forestry firebreak, respectively.

At that second rest halt, in Birmingham, the die had almost been cast, for Hannu Mikkola's Eaton Yale-sponsored Escort led his team-mate Björn Waldegård by more than eight minutes, Walter Röhrl was still driving immaculately, but was unable to beat Waldegård. And in spite of worries about an engine with what felt like a failing head gasket, Roger Clark was still in fourth place, while John Taylor

was already looking to break back into the top ten. The two other outstanding performances, though, were surely by Tony Pond (sixth

By 1978 the rally organisers celebrated a finish in spectacular fashion – this being Mikkola with an Eatons-sponsored Escort in Birmingham in 1978.

Tony Pond put up a brave show in 1978 against a mass of Escorts, driving this Triumph TR7 V8, and was rewarded with fourth place.

in the unwieldy TR7 8), and Brian Culcheth in the amazing little Opel Kadett GTE, which was well on the way to winning the entire Group 1 category.

Which left the Welsh loop, which encompassed 30 rallying hours, and about four hours of flat-out special stage motoring to get rid of the halt, the lame, and the wounded. Yet in all that frantic time, only two cars which had featured in the top ten at the rest halt – Roger Clark's Escort and Leif Asterhag's Toyota Celica – disappeared. As far as the throng of British-car supporters was concerned, it was Clark's retirement which was such a disappointment. Even though he had started the final leg with his ailing engine patched up, and an urge to pass Röhrl's Fiat, by the time he started the Burwarton stage in Shropshire, his car's clutch had failed, and when he arrived at an angular approach to a rather narrow gateway with what he later described as 'a box-full of neutrals,' the Li-Lo-sponsored Escort crashed, rolled, and would move no further.

Tony Pond, on the other hand, urged his TR7 V8 up from sixth to fourth overall by setting several fastest stage times, while John Taylor finally broke through into the top ten at the evening control at Bala. Even so, it was in this part of the rally that Röhrl and his Fiat 131 Abarth slipped back from a fighting third to a dispirited sixth, not because he went off the track, but because he had to halt in mid-stage to deal with a fuel blockage, only to find that his car then took 15 minutes to be extracted from the muddy edge on to which he had parked it. Lief Asterhag, however, crashed his Group 2 Toyota Celica even more emphatically in the Dovey stage, and could go no further.

For much of this, the third and final leg of what had been a memorable rally, the DTF Escorts were almost totally in control, and although there were no team orders to be obeyed, it never looked as if the finishing order would change. Mikkola, driving immaculately in a Sutton-built car which never seemed to need more than routine attention, let his lead degrade by three minutes, while Clark's and Röhrl's misfortunes allowed Russell Brookes to move up to third place. The grittily determined John Taylor (few saw him smile for five days, so determined was he to get back on terms …), eventually reached seventh (from 122nd on the first morning).

Amid all this excitement, a little-known young man from Finland, called Henri Toivonen, achieved a remarkable ninth overall in a Group 2 Chrysler Sunbeam (this car still used the 'Brazilian' version of the conventional Chrysler Avenger model). We would be hearing much more of him in the future.

RESULTS

Event held: 19-23 November 1978. One starting point, from Birmingham. Finish in Birmingham. Two overnight rest halts in Birmingham.

168 starters, 61 finishers.
76 special stages.

General classification		Group	Penalties (h:m:s)
1 Mikkola/Hertz	Ford Escort RS	G4	8:47:23
2 Waldegård/Thorszelius	Ford Escort RS	G4	8:52:41
3 Brookes/Tucker	Ford Escort RS	G4	8:58:55
4 Pond/Gallagher	Triumph TR7 V8	G4	9:03:09
5 Kulläng/Berglund	Opel Kadett GT/E	G2	9:13:48
6 Röhrl/Geistdorfer	Fiat Abarth 131	G4	9:17:47
7 Taylor/Short	Ford Escort RS	G4	9:19:20
8 Dawson/Harryman	Datsun 160J PA10	G2	9:20:51
9 Toivonen/Korhonen	Chrysler Sunbeam	G2	9:27:23
10 Daniellson/de Jong	Opel Kadett GT/E	G2	9:31:52
14 Culcheth/Syer	Opel Kadett GT/E	G1	9:41:57

Team Prize: No finishers.
Ladies Prize: Ford Escort RS (Ms J Simpson/Ms D Selby-Boothroyd).

DEALER TEAM FORD – A 'PRIVATE' ESCORT VICTORY IN 1978

Graham Robson's memory of a unique occasion

I will never forget the build-up to the 1978 RAC Rally, for I had been drafted in to 'run' a two-car team, at arm's length from Ford. This was because Ford's plans had been thrown into confusion by a company-wide strike, called by the unions to back their rapacious pay demands. Because every works Ford mechanic was obliged to back his union, pickets were mounted outside the department, so that there could be no movement of people, cars or parts in and out of the famous workshops.

That, at least, was the theory, but things did not quite work out like that. Ford's Peter Ashcroft was determined that 'his' team – somehow - would take the start in November, to defend the Escort's excellent record in the event. The drivers were all available, the expertise and experience were certainly available - but the problem was to get six cars built, and to train a non-factory back-up team to keep them going - all in just six weeks …

None of Boreham's workforce, especially the pickets, could see much point in paralysing the rallying effort, so many of them proved to be surprisingly 'blind,' or sometimes seemed to abandon their posts: there was much movement - of cars and components - before the strike officially began, and during the evenings and weekends during the strike itself!

Workshop foreman Mick Jones (who was not a union member) once told me what actually happened:

"Before the strike we shipped the cars out to people like David Sutton and Haynes of Maidstone, to prepare them. I came close to building one car in my own garage at home. Peter Ashcroft, Charles Reynolds, and I used to raid the stores at night when the pickets weren't looking ..."

But it was all very much of a 'patch and mend' operation. I will never forget the evening meeting before the start, when Peter Ashcroft's coordinator, Charles Reynolds, looked up wearily from his brief and said, rather sadly: "Welcome to Dealer Team Ford." He looked, and no doubt was, utterly exhausted.

Ashcroft, Reynolds, Jones and engineer Allan Wilkinson could only watch as the 'private' effort unfolded, but four of the cars finished first, second, third and seventh – and incidentally the strike finished during the same week. All in all, the service 'train' included eight privately-owned Transit vans, two Boreham Granada estates, two caravans and a Dunlop tyre truck.

Three pairs of cars were run by three team managers. David Sutton, Hannu, and Ari, therefore, had to stay away from Haynes of Maidstone, Roger Clark and John Taylor, while Andrews Heat for Hire, Russell Brookes and Björn Waldegård made up the other team. Even so, at some service points everyone dived in to help everyone else.

But would it work? The cars were good enough, the drivers were the best in the world – but would this be a 'lucky' team? Peter Ashcroft could only hope so. Every single one of the drivers thought so (and I talked to all of them), and felt that another victory was likely.

In the end everything worked out well. In five days of rallying, from Birmingham to Birmingham, by way of all the forests of the Lake District, Keilder, Yorkshire and Wales, these so-called 'private' Escorts proved that no-one had forgotten the experience gained by six previous RAC Rally wins.

It was Markku Alén's Lancia Stratos that worried the Fords – and though Hannu Mikkola faced up to the Lancia, neither Waldegård, nor even Walter Röhrl's Fiat 131 Abarth, could match their pace. But it was the five stages in Keilder which made the difference, where Alén progressively lost nearly three minutes to Mikkola's Eaton Yale Escort. As *Autosport*'s Rupert Saunders later wrote: "The damage was done, and Alén was a shattered man. From that moment he was struggling to stay in touch ..." Then the Stratos suddenly broke its transmission, and after that the battle was between the Escorts themselves.

Two of the six 'private' Escorts dropped out. Ari Vatanen's car was disqualified after his co-driver missed a passage control on the first day, and Roger Clark's car rolled while the driver was grappling with a car whose clutch had seized – but the other machines kept rolling along. Of the 76 special stages, Hannu Mikkola was fastest no fewer than 30 times, second on 18 stages, and third fastest on ten more. Waldegård

notched up 21 fastest times, Russell Brookes 12 times, John Taylor five times and Roger Clark three times.

The lesson behind this story was that after a decade of Escort development, both at Boreham and out in the wide world, so much was known about the way to make a Mikkola-standard car ready for an RAC Rally that Boreham only had to whistle up a plentiful supply of components, a fleet of part-completed rally cars, and a great 'will to win,' for a private team to spring out of the ground, ready to do the job.

Which, indeed, they did – and in that fraught week there never seemed to be an occasion when the lack of a Boreham 'umbrella' was crucial. Tyres, mechanics and sheer out-there experience seemed to be everywhere, the team's once-troubled two-way radios all worked well, and all the drivers seemed to get on well with each other. During that week, there were times when the rest of the rallying 'circus' stopped expecting mass problems to afflict this operation, but just stood back to admire what had been achieved. They were hoping – and their hopes were actually delivered – that such an operation would not need to be demonstrated again ...

The six cars
SJN 830R (Hannu Mikkola/Arne Hertz)
This mysterious car was seen only once. According to the registration, SJN 830R was a 1977 car, but this plate came off a previously-written-off Escort road car. David Sutton had just run a Boreham car, STW 200R in Cyprus, and for the RAC Rally that car got a new bodyshell – and a new identity.

Hannu Mikkola's success in the 1978 event was a victory for 'Dealer Team Ford' – this car was never to be used again.

MLD 999P (Ari Vatanen/Peter Bryant)
This Sutton-owned car's original identity was old (it dated from 1975/1976), but for this event it was effectively a brand-new car, with a fresh bodyshell, sponsored by Marlboro.

UNY 956S (Russell Brookes/Derek Tucker)
Originally this was new, being built up in the Russell Brookes/Peter Harrison workshops for re-sale. The UNY 956S identity came from a written-off Escort Popular from Jeff Churchill's hire fleet.

WTW 568S (Björn Waldegård/Hans Thorzselius)
This was a genuine works car, spirited out of the workshops before the pickets arrived, and hidden away in Mick Jones' home garage for weeks. Mick then spent much time part-completing the build, before delivering it to Thomas Motors of Blackpool for completion.

Whoops. Björn Waldegård had shunted his Escort in 1978 (but he still finished second). Author Graham Robson sympathises.

OKK 380P (Roger Clark/Neil Wilson)
This was John Taylor's original RS1800, dating from July 1975, and ready to be retired in 1978. For this RAC the gallant old car was wheeled out again, thoroughly refreshed at Maidstone, and entrusted to Roger Clark.

SKK 625R (John Taylor/Phil Short)
This car was brand new in mid-1978 (built up at Haynes of Maidstone for John Taylor to drive). Taylor chose to run it with Lucas fuel-injection on the RAC Rally (all the other cars ran with dual-choke Weber carburettors), which gave trouble throughout.

1979: Escort swansong, and victory

Even before the 1979 rally began from Chester, Ford had announced that it was to withdraw from World Championship rallying at the end of the season. For Ford, therefore, the Lombard-RAC Rally was to be its last works appearance for several years. To the team's joy, of course, splendid performances at other events during the 1979 season had already meant it was certain to win the 1979 Makes Championship, and that either of its leading drivers – Hannu Mikkola or Björn Waldegård – would win the Drivers' Championship too.

As a celebration, therefore (some cynics described it as 'getting rid of the empties' …), Boreham entered or supported no fewer than seven cars, one of which was a brand-new machine, and several others (with new bodyshells) virtually so. In an effort to upset this formidable attack, it was faced by rival works team entries from Audi, Datsun, Fiat, Lancia, Opel, Saab, Talbot, Toyota, Triumph and Vauxhall, all of whom were convinced that, given the breaks, they could match Ford's 'steamroller' record on this event.

The only real surprise in that line-up was that Fiat-Lancia's Markku Alén was so determined to win the event that he had persuaded Lancia to liberate a Stratos from its museum collection, have it refurbished, and sent to help him in his ambition: to everyone's amazement, although works Stratoses had competed in every one of these events since 1974, they had never yet come close to victory.

Although it looked no more likely than ever that the well-developed Group 4 Escorts could be beaten, the competition appeared fiercer than usual: apart from the Stratos, the Saab 99 Turbos were claimed to be more reliable than before, the Talbot Sunbeam-Lotus *and* Vauxhall Chevette HS types were now claimed to be 'better Escorts,' while the TR7 V8s were so now so powerful (300bhp was claimed from their torquey vee-8 engines) that if only they could be persuaded to transmit all that torque to the ground they must surely be competitive.

For the very first time, the event was based in Chester, with a single overnight rest halt (also in Chester) to split the event into two long and arduous loops. After tackling the original handful of 'show-business,' or 'Mickey Mouse' stages on the first Sunday, the cars then made for the familiar loop through the Yorkshire, Keilder, southern Scotland, and Lake District stages, while after the overnight halt there would then be a concentrated loop taking in what seemed like every one of the famous Welsh stages. For the first time in years, it seemed, Jim Porter's organisers had decided to ignore the West Country completely, and the event never got closer to London than Birmingham (and Sutton Park) on the first day. Because this event was by now world-famous, it attracted an enormous entry, with the organising team forced to nominate no fewer than 48 reserves, only a handful would be allowed to take the slots vacated by non-starters. In the end, a total of 175 hopefuls took the start.

Because there was tarmac surfacing on the 'show business' stages that occupied much of the first day, the Stratos and the TR7 V8s barked and grappled their way into the lead at first, but no sooner had the competitors disappeared into the forests of North Yorkshire

than the 'usual' order re-asserted itself, with Hannu Mikkola's Escort setting fastest on 11 of the next 15 stages. Waldegård and Airikkala both crashed their cars, but kept going, while Tony Pond (Talbot Sunbeam-Lotus), Stig Blomqvist (Saab, accident) and Markku Alén (Stratos, accident) all fell away. Only Timo Salonen (driving a 180bhp Group 2 Datsun 160J) seemed to keep in touch, and before long there were seven Escort RS1800s (six of them works machines) in the Top Ten.

As far as the enormous crowds were concerned, it was the five TR7 V8s which were the most disappointing of all, for they rarely seemed to be competitive, even on tarmac: they suffered badly from punctures, and mechanical niggles, and were often heckled by some of the spectators who had seen this team's traumas all before. Their description as the 'BRMs of rallying' in *Autocar*'s rally report said no more, and no less than they deserved.

Even after a mere 20 stages or so, it no longer looked as if any works Escort could be matched by any of its serious rivals, and for the media, and for the most knowledgeable spectators the challenge was to pick which of the multi-liveried Escorts was going to get closer to Hannu Mikkola, let alone overtake him. Conditions, in any case, were rugged enough, and fewer than one hundred runners would return to Chester for the overnight halt.

Back there, the Leaderboard reinforced the impression which

had been demonstrated out in the forests, in the mud, on the ice, and very occasionally in some snow, of the northern section of this event. Hannu Mikkola, for sure, looked to be unstoppable (the fact that his car had not suffered a single puncture must have been a factor), for he already led team-mate Ari Vatanen by more than five minutes, and Russell Brookes by nine minutes. There was no question, nor any need, for Ford to consider applying any team orders, for Mikkola's nearest non-Escort rival, Tony Pond in his last drive in a Talbot Sunbeam-Lotus, might have been fourth, but was ten minutes adrift. Roger Clark, although knowing that he would soon bid his beloved Escorts goodbye, was motoring happily along in a car which carried the same registration number as that which he took to win in 1976, was in eighth place, seemingly happy that he was no longer in the publicity spotlight. John Taylor, as grimly determined as ever, was struggling to carry on despite a painful back injury (a re-occurrence of the injuries sustained in his earlier steeplechasing career days), while Malcolm Wilson was up in fifth place, in a privately-prepared Escort RS.

Unhappily, most of Ford's hard-luck stories seemed to be inflicted on Björn Waldegård's brand-new car, for the Swede had spun on the first special stage of all (Knowsley Safari Park, near Liverpool), damaging the bodywork, and deranging his back axle, after which he seemed to pick up a series of time-absorbing punctures – ten in all during the event, five of which necessitated wheel changes in mid-

Björn Waldegård was well on his way to becoming World Rally Champion when he started the RAC Rally of 1979. Here he was in a brand-new Escort RS, which nevertheless suffered from many punctures. He could only finish ninth, while colleague and rival Hannu Mikkola won.

stage. Ninth at Chester, 16 minutes off the pace, he never looked like being able to reduce that gap.

Malcolm Wilson (who had recently won the Castrol-*Autosport* Championship in an ex-works Escort RS) ran out of luck in Pantperthog, when he slid off the road for 17 minutes, dropping to 20th place, while Ari Vatanen lost his second place when his co-driver made an administrative mistake at a Time Control which cost over ten minutes.

And what about Markku Alén and the Lancia Stratos? Having plunged off the track in the Dalby stage of Yorkshire, which cost him 14 minutes' delay, he eventually got going again, but was down in tenth, now 17 minutes off the pace.

Mikkola and the Ford team – all still hale and hearty at this juncture – then started out again to tackle the Welsh stages, which would be compressed into 30 hours. Mikkola, need it be stressed, carried on just as rapidly, and as smoothly, as he had started, so most of the headlines were then created by other people's misfortunes. Tony Pond crashed his Talbot, and was forced to retire while Roger Clark's Esso-sponsored car suffered a catastrophic engine failure (Roger then becoming the only works Ford driver to have to retire).

On the other hand, both Timo Salonen (in the under-powered Datsun 160J), and Alén's Stratos began a spirited fight back, which saw them both drag their way upwards towards the otherwise invincible Escorts, while Pentti Airikkala's Vauxhall Chevette HS appeared, for the first time, among the leaders. Walter Röhrl's Fiat 131 Abarth, too,

seemed to shrug off a lack-lustre beginning, by suddenly appearing among the front runners, muscling its way into the top ten before the Machynlleth halt, then clawing its way further up, to finish eighth at the close.

Even so, as far as the works Ford team was concerned, this event seemed to be 'business as usual,' especially as it had brought along more than a dozen service and support vehicles, and stood ready to tend to its cars at more than 70 points. By the end of the event, the opposition might have been full of reluctant admiration for the Escort's performance, but most were now looking forward to rallying between themselves, rather than facing up once again to a drubbing. One telling point, however, made in the various post-events summarised that if there had been no Escorts in the lists, the top ten would have been populated by Datsuns, Lancias, Vauxhalls, Fiats, Toyotas and even Triumphs.

Which was scant consolation, for in 1980 four-wheel-drive would be allowed, and who knew what might happen after that…?

RESULTS
Event held: 18-21 November 1979. One starting point, from Chester. Finish in Chester. One overnight rest halt, in Chester.

175 starters, 74 finishers.
59 special stages.

General classification		Group	Penalties (h:m:s)
1 Mikkola/Hertz	Ford Escort RS	G4	8:03:38
2 Brookes/White	Ford Escort RS	G4	8:14:07
3 Salonen/Pegg	Datsun 160J	G2	8:16:22
4 Vatanen/Richards	Ford Escort RS	G4	8:19:53
5 Alén/Kivimaki	Lancia Stratos	G4	8:20:23
6 Taylor/Short	Ford Escort RS	G4	8:24:01
7 Airikkala/Virtanen	Vauxhall Chevette HS	G4	8:25:57
8 Röhrl/Geistdorfer	Fiat Abarth 131	G4	8:26:37
9 Waldegård/Thorszelius	Ford Escort RS	G4	8:29:12
10 Carr/Gocentas	Ford Escort RS	G4	8:30:31
19 Carter/West	Ford Escort RS2000	G1	9:04:01

Team Prize: Ford (H Mikkola, R Brookes and A Vatanen).
Ladies' Prize: Ford Escort RS2000 (Ms M-L Kerpi and Ms E Heinio).

1980: Toivonen's Talbot triumph

When it was all over, with the champagne already sprayed, and the rallying 'circus' ready to leave Bath, many rallying enthusiasts looked at each other in amazement, and spluttered: "Well, we weren't expecting that!" For the first time in a generation, it seemed, an Escort had not won the RAC Rally.

Even so, what the spectators had just seen was not a rallying revolution, but merely a restatement of a familiar scenario. The truth was that the Talbot which *had* won was really no more than 'a better Escort,' and was already at the peak of its potential – and everyone, somehow, realised that in 1981, the arrival of a four-wheel-drive turbocharged Audi Quattro would make all the difference.

Even so, in Bath, there was certainly no shortage of Escorts – competitive Escorts at that – to try to notch up a ninth successive victory. The principal reason for this was that at the beginning of the year, the rich and ambitious cigarette company, Rothmans, had set out to win rallying's World Championships – Drivers' *and* Constructors', if possible – and with money reputably no problem it had gathered up much of Ford's works expertise, some of its cars, and some of its superstar drivers, to do that job. David Sutton was its chosen instrument, and along with another sponsor – Eaton Yale – was all ready to win the RAC Rally if he could.

The opposition, however, was not about to be frightened by this ambitious, but somehow cold-blooded approach, and turned up in big numbers. Facing Rothmans/Sutton/Ford, therefore, there were competitive entries from Datsun, Opel, Saab, Talbot (was Chrysler-UK), Toyota, Triumph and Vauxhall, so the competition was bound to be fierce, and well-matched. Looked at coldly, in statistical terms, one could see that Saab and Triumph had more powerful cars, that Opel, Talbot, Toyota and Vauxhall all had machines with similar

In 1980, Hannu Mikkola's Escort was prepared by David Sutton, and took second place behind the winning Talbot Sunbeam-Lotus.

Dealer Team Vauxhall developed the Chevette HSR to match the Escort, which ultimately it did, on performance but not reliability.

power outputs – but none of them had that important factor which was going to make such a difference in the next five days – experience. This year, for the first time in ages, it seemed, there was no team entry from Fiat (whose 131 Abarths had just won the World Constructors' Championship), or from the charismatic Lancia Stratos.

Compared with previous years, the Escort suddenly found itself faced with several 'clones' which might just be able to match it – and so it proved during the event. Not only had Talbot and Vauxhall finally

Talbot team boss, Des O'Dell (right) with his protégé Henri Toivonen, who was on his way to winning the RAC Rally in 1980 – the first time an Escort had been beaten for nine years. He would stay on at Talbot for 1981 ...

... using sister cars to the Sunbeam-Lotus which he had used to win in the previous year.

got on terms, with cars having as much power, and in small-enough packages, but Toyota was back with the very latest 16-valve Celica GT, ex-Boreham engineer Allan Wilkinson leading its technical development, and 1979 World Champion Björn Waldegård leading the charge. Opel, too, (under Tony Fall's guidance) had seen the Ascona 400 (complete with 250bhp Cosworth-developed 2.4-litre engine) finally achieve homologation.

If the mixture of entrants and superstar drivers was much as before – what other rally in the world would start with Messrs Mikkola, Waldegård, Salonen, Vatanen, Kulläng, Blomqvist and Airikkala at the head of the field – how were Tony Pond, Russell Brookes, or a young man called Henri Toivonen likely to cope with those individuals just ahead of them? It was only Fiat's two most illustrious drivers – Walter Röhrl and Markku Alén – who were missing.

Although the route itself measured 1810 miles, and included 70 stages totalling 467 miles, the fact that it was based in Bath meant that its 'shape' was rather different from usual. For sure, the first day encompassed several 'show-business' special stages (including such popular venues as Longleat Safari Park, where the lions would be locked away for the day, Blenheim Palace, Silverstone and Donington Park), the meat of the first half of the event would take in the usual colossal challenge of the North Yorkshire, Keilder and Lake District special stages – but the overnight rest halt was then located, for the first time in the event's history, in Windermere. The final outcome, if it was to be close, would be settled in the classic stages of central and south Wales, before the depleted cavalcade returned to Bath, four days after they had originally left it.

When the event started, from the glorious Regency splendour of Bath's Great Pulteney Street, we could not have known that for the first time in years there would not only be a battle between drivers, and cars, but between two major tyre manufacturers – Dunlop and Michelin. Dunlop and Ford had enjoyed something of an unbreakable partnership throughout the 1970s, but in 1980 Michelin came to the RAC Rally with Talbot and Opel to see what could be done about it.

Almost immediately, this factor became obvious, and although Mikkola, driving a Sutton-built Escort which had already completed three British International rallies during the year, was as fast as ever, he personally admitted that as he had done a lot of testing (in private) of the still-new Audi Quattro during the year, he had to come to terms with the Escort all over again. And, as he admitted in mid-event: "No excuses, but the tyres have a lot to do with it – those Michelins have a lot to do with it ..."

Rothmans-sponsored Escorts with this livery featured in the 1980 and 1981 rallies. This was Ari Vatanen fighting for the lead in 1980 – shortly before he rolled the car out of contention.

By the time the field entered the Yorkshire forests, the first retirements, and major problems, had been reported. Tony Pond's thundering Triumph TR7 V8 had virtually scalped itself in Longleat, where the car skidded off the tarmac, and dived under a lion's feeding table, Malcolm Wilson's engine had blown its engine spectacularly at Silverstone, Ari Vatanen had rolled his Escort (and promptly retired), while Pentti Airikkala's Vauxhall Chevette HSR had broken its transmission.

By the time the much-depleted field arrived at Windermere for its rest halt, it was Anders Kulläng (whose contract with Opel was not to be renewed …) who led the event in his Opel Ascona 400, with Björn Waldegård's Toyota Celica only 13 seconds behind him. The dashing young Finn, Henri Toivonen (whose famous ex-works driver Pauli was among the spectators looking on …) was third, just 80 seconds off the pace, and Hannu Mikkola was already no less than four minutes behind the leaders. The car-breaking passages of Yorkshire, the Lake District and Keilder stages (six of them, totalling 70 miles) had caused their usual upsets, so only 75 cars (of the 142 starters) were still running.

It was in the Grizedale stage, just across the water from Windermere itself, that the order was up-ended – terminally, as it transpired. On that stage, Kulläng's Opel suffered not one, but two punctures, losing 17 minutes due to enforced work by the drivers in the middle of the impenetrable forest, while Waldegård's Toyota deposited an oil filter bowl on the track, which instantly allowed the engine to destroy itself. This instant upheaval gifted the lead to Henri Toivonen,

but Mikkola, only 2min 40 seconds adrift, seemed determined to close that gap in the Welsh stages that followed. Talbot, for its part, was grimly determined to make this chase unsuccessful, with Guy Fréquelin (works car) and Russell Brookes ('Andrews Heat for Hire' car) providing close-up support.

And there the matter rested for the final 24 hours, for every time Mikkola set a fastest stage time in his Escort, Toivonen would grin cheerfully, and go out to set an even faster time on the next stage. Kulläng, to his credit, was still plugging away, but was at least 15 minutes off the lead, and would finally grapple his way back up to fifth place, while Tony Pond, still with rippled-roof of his TR7 V8 in evidence, just failed to break into the top ten. Timo Mäkinen, of all people, enjoyed his solo 'guest' drive in a Rothmans Escort, by taking sixth place, with few of the dramas connected with his team-mates.

Talbot could not have been more delighted, for when the 47 finishers crossed the line in Bath, its team had taken first, third and fourth places, this achievement being so well received by Peugeot (the parent company), who approved a compact, but none-the-less effective, World Rally Championship programme for 1981.

And so a decade of Escort supremacy in the RAC Rally came to an end, though the cars which had finally matched it would have only a short time to enjoy their success. In 1981 the Quattro was coming …

RESULTS

Event held: 16-19 November 1980. One starting point, from Bath. Finish in Bath. One overnight rest halt, in Windermere.

142 starters, 47 finishers.

General classification		Group	Penalties (h:m:s)
1 Toivonen/White	Talbot Sunbeam-Lotus	G2	8:17:33
2 Mikkola/Hertz	Ford Escort RS	G4	8:22:09
3 Fréquelin/Todt	Talbot Sunbeam-Lotus	G2	8:31:24
4 Brookes/Bryant	Talbot Sunbeam-Lotus	G2	8:32:16
5 Kulläng/Berglund	Opel Ascona 400	G4	8:33:47
6 Mäkinen/Holmes	Ford Escort RS	G4	8:43:41
7 Pond/Gallagher	Triumph TR7 V8	G4	8:46:43
8 Dawson/Gormley	Datsun 160J	G2	8:48:08
9 Danielsson/Booth	Ford Escort RS	G4	8:55:58
10 Hill/Varley	Vauxhall Chevette HS	G4	8:58:40
11 Raymond/Daniels	Ford Escort RS2000	G1	9:14:54

70 special stages.
Team Prize: No finishers.
Ladies Prize: No finishers.

TURBOCHARGING, FOUR-WHEEL DRIVE, AND GROUP B

The whole face of World Championship rallying completely changed in the period of 1981 to 1986. 1981 saw the last time a small factory (Talbot, based in Britain) won the World Championship for Manufacturers, a victory which was never commercially valued by the company. Ari Vatanen's title in the World Championship for Drivers was the first and only time the title had gone to a driver funded by a private sponsor as opposed to a manufacturer and also the first time a car driven by the champion was a model long before rendered obsolete by the team which had developed it.

The impending changes went far deeper. 1982 was the year when technical advances took over the sport. The first turbocharged cars had first made a cautious mark in the sport when Stig Blomqvist won the 1979 Swedish Rally, and right from the start of the WRC in 1973 eligible cars had been limited to two-wheel drive models. Then pressure from the German federation persuaded the international authorities to admit four-wheel drive cars for WRC use in 1979. At that time there was no four-wheel drive production car which would be competitive in WRC rallying, until the Audi Quattro came along. The Quattro featured turbocharging and total traction. The traditional design of top level rally cars was changed forever.

At the time when rally car technology ventured into new territory, the international authorities set about completely reshaping the class structure of the sport. About to disappear were the old Groups 1, 2, 3 and 4 which categorised the cars eligible for international rallies, to be replaced by a new concept of Groups B, A and N. General principles were completely different: instead of permitting any modifications unless they were forbidden, now no modifications were permitted on cars unless they were specifically authorised, or came within identified freedoms. These changes became necessary not only for greater clarity,

Although Henri Toivonen only won three WRC events he dramatically captured the spirit of the early '80s and the Group B era before he died in 1986.

Scrutineering became a don't-miss occasion for rally spectators. This was the scene in Nottingham in 1985.

Rothmans vigorously promoted rally sport, including a campaign of roadside posters in 1981.

but were brought about due to the increased degree of legislation affecting cars on roads, and because of the increasing responsibility of manufacturers in the event of accidents for cars carrying the name of their company. There was a two-year period when the top rally cars could run under either grouping, but the new rules were here to stay in 1984.

The technical future looked settled until the wording of the new rules was closely examined, and a massive loophole became evident. This was the 'Evolution' clause – a facility aimed innocuously at allowing modification of the basic homologated designs of the cars to cater for facelift changes introduced to the basic design of the mass production cars. The items that could be changed were listed, in the hope the list covered any change the manufacturer might wish. Instead of the 200 examples which the basic Group B rules required, an allowance was given for 10% of that number (20 cars) to use the Evolution option. This was heaven for the newly expanding breed of rally team engineers, who sought to take full advantage of every permitted Evolution item – for competition purposes, not for the intended production car market purposes. It was a dramatic moment when the FIA President, Jean-Marie Balestre, was asked in a Press Conference in Sweden in 1981 how come such a U-turn was permitted. The FIA President angrily replied that the enquiring journalist was wrong, and should read the rules properly. The early 1980s saw a never-predicted Group B boom time, which only eventually wound down at the end of 1986.

Through all this, one of the stable factors of the sport was the continued popularity in Britain of the RAC Rally. There were various pressures, most particularly from international teams, to abandon the event's cherished secret route format, and allow pre-event route inspection. Until now the use of pacenotes was not allowed. The opportunity to compete on a low-cost World Championship rally, however, was much enjoyed by private competitors. Meanwhile the chance of watching the rally at venues across much of Britain encouraged a new passion among spectators. Increasing spectator traffic became a major element in planning the RAC Rally in the '80s. A concept of specially-controlled stages was instigated to run selected special stages at stately homes or theme parks, which were better able to

Long before the days of central servicing, teams set up service points anywhere that was convenient. This is in the Scottish village of Newcastleton in 1986.

manage masses of spectators. In other respects the style of the event was much the same as before. The town locations of race headquarters continued to be rotated year by year. Almost every year different teams were in the sporting spotlight, and interest in the constant changes in the sport helped strengthen the spectator culture.

1981: First 4WD turbo RAC win

The end of the 1981 season finally saw Audi winning in the style they had promised all year: running away without any challenge. From the second stage to the finish, only an indiscretion by Hannu Mikkola gave the opposition any chance of leading during the final round in the World Championship. It was a remarkable finale to an equally remarkable year; a year which swept away forever the traditions of the sport and opened the door to a most exciting future. The only car able to challenge Mikkola and the Quattro was the Vauxhall Chevette 2300HSR of Tony Pond, which retired with transmission failure. An unusually subdued Ari Vatanen cruised to second place gaining the title in the World Championship for Drivers, after the Talbot driver Guy Fréquelin had been delayed by a puncture and then crashed. Talbot won the Manufacturers' series by finishing third, the only one of its four team Sunbeam Lotuses to reach the end, clinching the series when the Datsun Violet GT of Timo Salonen had engine trouble and ran out of fuel during a stage.

For the Audi Quattro team this was a new challenge (though Mikkola had frequently driven over the stages on other British rallies). The Lombard RAC was the first time these four-wheel drive cars would face secret routes that required enhanced manoeuvrability to handle

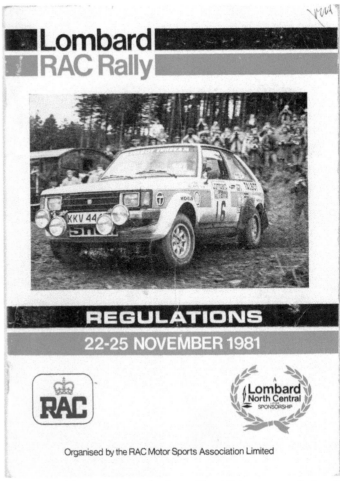

A picture of the previous year's winner, Henri Toivonen, was featured on the regulations for the rally.

the frequently unexpected hazards. For the foreign drivers lack of experience in British forests increasingly seemed to count for less. The organizers took great care to warn of unexpected hazards. For them it was often more important to have the right tyres rather than prior knowledge of the stages. The previous year the Michelin users had the best equipment but this year Audi used Kleber – having previously found that its superior traction made tyre choice less critical. Pirelli brought a special type of tyre which helped Vatanen keep his high position without taking risks. Indeed when the Rothmans Escort team driver Pentti Airikkala changed to Pirelli in mid-event he immediately went faster.

The rally base at Chester facilitated a figure of eight route configuration around the country, the northern loop preceding the loop around Wales. As usual there were various publicity stages held on private land aimed at containing the amazing crowds who

Ari Vatanen's Escort took second overall in the 1981 event, but he secured the World Drivers' Championship.

The Vauxhall Chevette had been the only challenger for the Ford Escort cars. This is Tony Pond braving the British weather.

attended the event. The theory was that spectators going to these stages would reduce the traffic pressure around the forests, which were often accessed by narrow lanes. British national rallymen always made a good showing on these sections: this year Jimmy McRae (Opel Ascona 400) and Tony Pond (Vauxhall Chevette 2300HSR) led after the first stage, whilst close behind was Malcolm Patrick in his dealer team Ascona 400. On the second stage Mikkola put his Quattro ahead, and steadily increased his advantage until Grizedale Forest, when he put his car on its roof. Spectators pushed it back upright, the four-wheel drive enabled it to climb back on to the road and he set about making up for the mistake, but Pond took over the lead. Henri Toivonen, last year's winner, also overturned (distracted when he noticed his oil pressure was failing), and Russell Brookes also went off the road: both retired. As soon as the rally reached the Kielder complex of stages on the Scottish borders, Mikkola had made good his delay and was leading again: by stage 16 he was over three minutes in the lead.

The stormy weather on the first night was as incredible as the determination of the spectators to brave it. Wind lashed the falling rain so it fell down almost horizontally, and it was a relief when morning began to break on Monday. Mechanics had an hour to work on the cars in the desolate car park near the Washington control, and already several more drivers were missing. Björn Waldegård broke two radius arms on his Toyota Celica and could not continue, both Malcolm Wilson (Ford Escort RS) and Patrick went helplessly off the road and one stage before Washington, Markku Alén went off the road when driving his Chardonnet team Stratos with a puncture. Soon after the cars restarted Andy Dawson had to abandon the rally with the Bluebird Turbo when the engine suffered after ingesting water in the ford at Hamsterley – whilst Salonen also retired shortly afterwards. But saddest for British hopes was when Pond lost second place in the 30-mile stage in Dalby with transmission trouble, and had to give up.

At the midway point Mikkola led Vatanen by over nine minutes. Michèle Mouton, on her first visit to a British rally was third, over one minute ahead of Stig Blomqvist. Fréquelin was in tenth place, ready to attack. The weather, finally, was now dry, but it was getting colder by the hour. It looked as if there could be snow to come. On the way out of Chester, Per Eklund stopped to change his oil pump, curing the cause of the clouds of smoke which followed behind his Celica. His anxiety to regain the lost time – and the consequent drop down the running order – led to trouble when he clocked into

Hannu Mikkola won the RAC Rally the first year the Audi Quattro competed on the event.

a control three minutes too early, leading to a penalty of one and a half minutes. The weather, meanwhile, promised the most horrible night to come as the cars reached the evening halt at Brecon, snow was already lying on the ground. Leading British driver McRae was soon to retire from an excellent fourth place with a broken halfshaft. Mouton was in serious transmission trouble, having to tackle some stages in rear-wheel drive only before the gearbox could be changed. Eventually this was done, but in the snowy Beddgelert stage in North Wales at dawn on the final morning she slid down the bank and could not regain the road. Fréquelin's challenge began well, but then he went off the road at Dovey. Airikkala was now fourth, ahead of Jean Ragnotti's Renault, which was delayed earlier through shock absorber problems, and Eklund's Toyota was sixth. After a final burst of speed from Roger Clark, on this event in a private team's Escort, on the closing stages. Mikkola cruised to an 11 minute victory. It was the end of the season. It was the 99th World Championship Rally and the final World Rally run fully under the old Appendix J car rules. This was the final WRC event for David Richards and Jean Todt (co-driver for Guy Fréquelin) – and for Martin Holmes … !

THE NEW TURBO CARS

Only Saab had come to the RAC Rally with a turbo car before and they had not been successful. This year suddenly there were six makes of turbo car: Audi, Mitsubishi, Renault, Datsun, Peugeot and Volvo. The Audi had systematically been developed to make the car more agile, whilst Mitsubishi entered Lancer Turbos in the hope that it could improve on the already promising recent result on the 1000 Lakes.

Renault's intention was to develop its already successful 5 Turbo cars for customers, and provide a back-to-back test between the two alternative models of 5 Turbo, the outright Group 4 car, and the less powerful customer specification model. Datsun used the rally to try out the Bluebird Turbo model, in the hope that the Group 2 car would block the Talbot championship title challenge, whilst the Peugeot dealers in France supported the 505 Diesel Turbo of Laurent. Finally from Sweden came the Volvo engineer Bengt-Inge Steffansson with a Group 1 Volvo 240 Turbo.

RESULTS

Event held: 22-25 November 1981. 10th and final round in Manufacturers' and 12th and final round in Drivers' championships. Start/Finish: Chester. Overnight halt: Chester.

151 starters, 54 finishers.
65 special stages – 450 miles (total 1791 miles).

General classification		Group	Penalties (h:m:s)
1 Mikkola/Hertz	Audi Quattro	G4	8:30:00
2 Vatanen/Richards	Ford Escort RS	G4	8:41:05
3 Blomqvist/Cederberg	Talbot Sunbeam Lotus	G2	8:43:36
4 Airikkala/Short	Ford Escort RS	G4	8:43:43
5 Ragnotti/Holmes	Renault 5 Turbo	G4	8:53:55
6 Eklund/Spjuth	Toyota Celica	G4	8:54:54
7 Nilsson/Olsson	Nissan Violet GT	G4	8:57:20
8 Kaby/Arthur	Toyota Celica	G4	9:01:18
9 Kulläng/Berglund	Mitsubishi Lancer Turbo	G4	9:05:22
10 Clark/Serle	Ford Escort RS	G4	9:08:24
15 Pankhurst/Freeman	Ford Escort RS	G1	9:37:58

Leaders: Pond and McRae stage 1, Mikkola 2-6, Pond 7-10, Mikkola 11-65.

Riding with Ragnotti

Quite unexpectedly I received a call from Renault's rally manager Patrick Landon in Paris. Landon briefly said that the Renault Sport Elf team wanted to come to the RAC Rally again (its first time in four years), and asked if I could help. I thought I had abandoned the world of high-speed competition after my previous year's ride on the RAC with Timo Mäkinen, but the idea of riding with Jean Ragnotti, that year's Monte Carlo Rally winner, in one of rallying's next generation rally cars, was very tempting. Okay, I said, maybe I would be interested, but only if Ragnotti would agree to speak English. Landon said we had better speak further when I had time to be more rational!

Renault's greatest worry had been its lack of knowledge about the actual stages themselves, but in that respect the current style of route instructions was so good on the secret roads that virtually all the nasty corners were advised. In reality, the special help that the foreigners

needed more was in the advanced preparation for the event. Certainly the Renault rally service manager Marcel Callewaert, for many years one of France's most successful co-drivers, had anticipated some of the problems, but never realised what pre-event late night miseries would soon await him in England before the rally.

The liaison sections route for the rally was announced some ten days in advance. For 1981 the service restrictions were tightened. The official service areas were seldom ideally located, and the types of vehicle allowed to go to each was carefully limited. Servicing however was also allowed in garages along or near the route, if personal permission was given in advance. At the moment the road books were issued, therefore, crews representing each of the teams set off looking for strategically placed garages to seek permission for their vans to stop on their forecourts. Experienced British co-drivers knew where to start looking for garages, and for this event Renault joined forces with Team Datsun Europe. Every few hours people on the road would telephone to a central base we had set up in the Northfleet Hotel in Woking, so we could then collate the arriving information, and send confirming letters to the garages involved.

From Thursday through to Monday, Marcel, the late Jean-Marc Andrié, and myself were ensconced in the hotel, waiting for these calls. Andrié was Ragnotti's usual co-driver, with whom he had won Monte Carlo, but this time he was riding with Bruno Saby. As the complication of the work became apparent, the strain mounted. In moments of despair Marcel would thrust his hands in the air, uttering words which condemned the concept of British style rallying. The manager of the hotel (who had no reason to know what we were doing: we could have been planning a mercenary invasion of an African republic) would nervously

SKC036
RENAULT 5 TURBO
J. RAGNOTTI / M. HOLMES
LOMBARD RAC RALLY 1981

enquire if all was well, and would go away pretty sure it wasn't. But gradually things settled down, patterns of vehicle movements became plain, and by the following Tuesday the work of preparing the service road book was finished.

Meanwhile I had already been to the Renault rally headquarters at Antony, near Paris, to sit in its cars. Our car was one of the original 'Tour de Corse' version Renault 5 Turbos, fully modified to the Group 4 rules, which had won the Monte Carlo Rally, while Saby had one of the many clubmen 'Cevennes' version cars. It was the first WRC event on gravel with the car. It was obvious that because of my height I could not compete in the car unless the seat was lowered and placed further back. This was done, and extra room was found by removing the padding – and getting me to sit on bare glass fibre. Actually this proved bearable. Left-handed co-drivers had the advantage in Renault cars. The position of the side of the seat prevented a normal right-handed person from writing on his road book during the rally. There were unusual sensations like when the night-time countryside suddenly lit up, when flames came out of the exhaust, or the arrival of wonderful warmth in the cockpit when the team removed the lid over the engine in the service park.

Being a co-driver in the new generation of turbocharged technology, I was not allowed near the steering wheel of the rally car, but during the rally Ragnotti explained the quirks of the car. The most noticeable was the uncertainty of the response of the turbocharger as he entered a corner. Jean explained that this gave a lot of trouble. On secret routes the driver traditionally likes to hedge his bets on the accelerator, just in case the corner is more severe or there is an obstacle he did not expect. This takes the form of feathering the throttle just before he would normally wish to accelerate. This was a terrible problem for the original turbo cars, because you could not exactly judge when the power would arrive again.

The uncertainty of the secret route corners forced 'Jeannot' into many moments of emergency, which were safely handled with the help of the hydraulic handbrake. In terms of tackling unexpected corners, I could not remember any recent rally car in which I felt so safe. Normally co-drivers follow the rally routes on their maps in case the instructions on the official timecards fail to warn about a bad bend to come, but as the rally progressed I gained a curious impression that there was no normal unexpected hazard which the Renault, in Ragnotti's hands, could not overcome. Many of the sideways liberties could only be taken because of the tyres – the Michelin TRX tyres had amazingly strong sidewalls. True, we suffered two punctures during the event – one of which threw us off the road into a ditch at high speed at Esgair Dafydd – but this style of driving on other tyres would have led to a puncture every stage. At the Kilburn stage we spun off the road within 100 metres of the start line, whilst in the wilds of Dovey forest we nearly had an awful accident. The organisers had placed huge signs at the roadside saying 'Doctor' (where medical aid was available), and the Renault spun helplessly towards the group of officials standing at this point. Ragnotti's black humour rose to the occasion. He asked me to see if there was a special penalty for running over a doctor.

The traction with the mid engine layout (for a two-wheel drive car) was impressive. Drivers waiting on the start lines of stages stated that only the Quattros could take off with anything like as little fuss as the 5 Turbo, and, of course, wherever there was a muddy exit from a corner, the Renault would shoot away. In the 5 Turbo you really knew you were leaving the corners quicker than the others. The remarkable available traction must have been one reason for choosing such wide section rear tyres, but when a limited number of narrower-section rear tyres were tried later in the event, they gave a nicer feel for the driver.

The greatest fun was not the forest rallying – or even the enjoyment of working with the team. It was the sheer magic of the car. That little Renault on the tarmac stages was sheer delight. Ragnotti was second quickest on the spectator stages at Sutton Park and Knowsley, each time behind Hannu Mikkola's Audi Quattro, and quickest at Lambton Park, Oulton Park, and Great Orme at Llandudno. Of these, Great Orme was the best. The motion of a beautiful machine, driven precisely and in perfect accord with the twists and turns of the cliffside road, was full justification for leaving my typewriter for one final attempt at rallying.

1982: Lancia challenges the Audi Quattros

Hannu Mikkola's second successive win on the Lombard RAC Rally eventually proved effortless, but came only after Markku Alén's new Group B rear-drive Lancia 037 had led on the first day, before suffering troubles with his car's supercharged engine. Mikkola's Audi Quattro team-mate, Michèle Mouton, took second place after many delays earlier in the event with turbocharger trouble, although she finally beat Henri Toivonen's 2.4-litre Opel Ascona 400 by nine seconds. Every Audi driver, except Mikkola, had problems. John Buffum, Harald Demuth and Mouton all damaged cars going off the road. Malcolm Wilson also lost considerable time while Opel lost three of its four works cars as well. After a pre-rally disagreement with its new world champion, Opel told Walter Röhrl his services would not be required – so his fellow German Jochi Kleint was invited to compete in his place. Kleint and the newly-signed Rothmans Opel driver Ari Vatanen both went off the road, while British champion Jimmy McRae stopped with transmission failure.

This year the rally was based in York and concentrated the route in the north of the country, with stages in Wales, and a quick visit to Scotland. Foreigners again dominated this secret route rally. The only British driver to challenge for the lead was Terry Kaby (2.3-litre Vauxhall) who held second place on the first day, and, at the end, fellow Vauxhall driver Russell Brookes was the highest-placed at sixth. The Opel Rothmans team had become the first team to contest all the WCR events in a season, but used a selection of different drivers. Having already gained the Drivers' title for Röhrl, its hopes of also becoming Manufacturers' champion required a catastrophe on the part of Audi.

Despite the foregone conclusion that Audi, or maybe Opel, would win the Manufacturers' championship, there was a remarkably strong manufacturer entry from elsewhere. From Japan came Nissan, Toyota,

The rear-wheel drive Mitsubishi Lancer Turbo was powerful, but poor handling and traction doomed its chances of success.

The Yorkshire Dales provided a splendid backdrop for Markku Alén's compressor Lancia 037.

Mitsubishi and a Mazda, from Britain came the Group 2 Talbots and the Group 4 Vauxhalls, while from Eastern Europe came Škoda and Lada. There was also an interesting selection of privateers battling for the Group A class.

Pentti Airikkala took his Mitsubishi to an equal fastest time on the first stage, but it did not last; by that evening he had retired with a wheel torn out of the car in an accident. His team-mate Anders Kulläng later abandoned with clutch failure, and for the Japanese team stage 1 was its only happy memory. Their fellow Japanese teams had varying experiences. Nissan entered a 2-litre Violet GT and a Silvia Turbo: Timo Salonen in the former, but he never got going properly and Andy Dawson in the latter car had many troubles: both retired. The Toyotas had no troubles, but they lacked the power to be competitive whilst Rod Millen's powerful rotary engined Group 2 Mazda never went well in conditions which demanded torque rather than power.

Mikkola thought he had taken control of the rally on the second stage, one of the traditional publicity stages, but Alén's speed later that evening when he took the lead in the first batch of forest stages (in the Forest of Dean) was a rude awakening. Alén was thrilled. The idea of his rear-drive Lancia beating a four-wheel drive Quattro, particularly one driven by a fellow Finn, was quite unexpected. On the second day however Alén's challenge started to fade. The distributor timing loosened whenever the engine got too hot, the driver having sometimes to slow up even more – because of flames in the engine compartment just behind his head. On stage 9 another Quattro had made a quickest time – Buffum's car, fitted with American BF Goodrich tyres. Mikkola soon got himself into form, and retrieved the lead when Alén had troubles.

On the third day Alén lost more time with distributor problems, letting Demuth and then Toivonen pass him. Mouton, meanwhile, had begun to go well. Through the first half of the rally her car never ran well (a turbo change put that right), and following the Kielder stages she had taken third place behind Mikkola and Toivonen, ahead of Demuth who lost two more places after going off the road in the Lake

Hannu Mikkola seen on his fourth and final victory on the RAC Rally.

District. On the final stages in Yorkshire, Mouton gradually overhauled Toivonen, but both of them (and several others) had nasty moments when they momentarily went off the road at the end of the Langdale stage. Plenty of body repairs were called for! Russell Brookes gradually pulled up to fifth place before being retaken by Demuth, and after various problems the Talbots came through in ninth and 11th place. Alén held the Group B lead throughout.

Mikkola had a delay on one stage where he punctured a tyre, but from that moment on he was in complete control, winning by nearly five minutes. Vatanen had now climbed to second place and Toivonen was third – surprisingly good Opel performances, but in North Wales Vatanen went off the road. Alén, therefore, held third place as the cars returned to York at the end of the first leg, while the best non-Finn was the German Demuth. The lead in the new Group A was held alternatively by the Manta GT/E of 23-year-old Juha Kankkunen (a protégé of Timo Mäkinen) and the Swede Bror Danielsson in a Mazda RX7, but finally the group was won by the 22-year-old Swede Mikael Ericsson with an Audi Coupé.

Audi became the 1982 Manufacturers' champion even though they had decided to miss the Safari Rally and had scored less points than Opel because of the 'best-seven scores' rule. The Drivers' championship had already been won by Walter Röhrl in Ivory Coast after a season-long rivalry with Michèle Mouton.

WHERE WAS RÖHRL?

An embarrassing confusion over attendance at a pre-rally forum arranged by GM Dealer Sport two days before the start, led to the premature end of the Röhrl-Opel association. Vauxhall-Opel had arranged a major public forum on the Friday evening at which the three new Opel rally champions (Walter Röhrl, the new world champion, 'Tony' Fassina, the European champion, and Jimmy McRae, the double British Open champion) would appear. Röhrl did not attend. He expressed his confusion, stating that if he only had been asked by the Opel Sports Relations manager Tony Fall to go, he would have been happy to oblige, but he was not asked! On Saturday morning the decision was taken to replace Röhrl and his co-driver Christian Geistdorfer with Opel's German crew and occasional WRC competitors Jochi Kleint/Gunter Wagner. Fall said: "Röhrl's heart is not totally in this event." Kleint was happy to substitute for Röhrl, but early in the rally he went off the road, and Audi took the Manufacturers' title.

Drivers came to the RAC Rally from all over the world. This is New Zealander Rod Millen in a Mazda RX7.

RESULTS

Event held: 21-25 November 1982. 11th and final round of Manufacturers' and 13th and final round in Drivers' championships. Start/Finish: York. Overnight halts: York.

149 starters, 63 finishers.
69 special stages, but one cancelled – 436 miles (total 1853 miles).

General classification		Group	Penalties (h:m:s)
1 Mikkola/Hertz	Audi Quattro	G4	8:01:46
2 Mouton/Pons	Audi Quattro	G4	8:06:03
3 Toivonen/Gallagher	Opel Ascona 400	G4	8:06:12
4 Alén/Kivimaki	Lancia Rally	GB	8:11:43
5 Demuth/Daniels	Audi Quattro	G4	8:14:10
6 Brookes/Broad	Vauxhall Chevette 2300HSR	G4	8:14:50
7 Waldegård/Spjuth	Toyota Celica	G4	8:16:29
8 Blomqvist/Cederberg	Talbot Sunbeam Lotus	G2	8:17:12
9 Eklund/Whittock	Toyota Celica	G4	8:21:42
10 Wilson/Greasley	Audi Quattro	G4	8:22:32
21 Ericsson/Sandström	Audi Coupé	GA	9:18:27

Leaders: Mikkola & Airikkala stage 1, Mikkola 2-6, Alén 3-11, Mikkola 12, Alén 13-16, Mikkola 17-69.

1983: Audis lead all the way. Success for Swedes

The 1983 Manufacturers' championship had already finished in Lancia's favour, and the Drivers' series was decided, so the RAC held little of its usual magic. The weather itself was unusual. This time there was no fog, wind, snow or rain to greet the competitors as they normally expect. It was hardly like an RAC Rally at all!

Like Lancia, Audi also had no reason to come to the final round of the season as its second place behind Lancia was assured, and everyone

There was no chance for a hat trick win for Hannu Mikkola after suspension failure on the tarmac stage at Liverpool's Knowsley Safari Park stage.

Gradually, spectator friendly stages were developed as delightful family occasions. This is Per Eklund's rear-drive Toyota Celica twin-cam Turbo.

A rare smile from Stig Blomqvist on his second and final RAC Rally win – 12 years after his first win.

Forests came in many guises. This is Blomqvist driving through a private forest estate on the rally.

knew that Mikkola could not be overtaken for the Drivers' title. Happily Audi did turn up, dividing its attack between its official Ingolstadt team with Mikkola and Mouton and Blomqvist, and the British David Sutton run team. It soon turned out to be not so much a battle between drivers, or even the teams that ran them, but between tyres. The Ingolstadt team ran Michelins, David Sutton and the privateers used Pirellis.

Against the Audi teams were the Rothmans Opel team on the last outing for the official international appearance, and the Toyota on its first major test with the new turbo car. Toyota knew that its car's poor traction and the consequent short tyre life would make work difficult, especially as the event this time had stages of up to 40 miles in length. Apart from these teams the entry this year was full of also-rans. This was the final official Vauxhall entry with a Chevette for Brookes and Kaby, the 2300HSR now in Group B form while Nissan had a 240RS for Salonen.

At the end of the first day Blomqvist took advantage of a steering problem of Mikkola to take the lead, and he held this through to the end of the rally. Mikkola made things worse for himself by wrecking a tyre on the second day, on a tree stump, which forced him to stop and remove the remains of the wheel. He fell to 26th place but was soon up to second, although well out of touch. Blomqvist had built up an enormous buffer as rivals fell out. In the dry conditions, retirements were mostly a matter of accidents or engine failures. 40-year-old Jimmy McRae proved that age was no barrier to fast, safe driving, but Vatanen and Toivonen went off the road; they both restarted only to go out later with engine trouble. Waldegård retired when he left the road in the Lake District's Grisedale stage, and Eklund mercifully stopped with engine trouble after struggling with a wrenched hand, and his co-driver David Whittock's back suffered in various untoward incidents.

No rally in those days seemed to pass by without at least one Audi fire. Antero Laine's fire caused such a problem that the stage had to be cancelled, whereas Weidner's problems were caused by turbo failure. Hopes for a glorious finale for the Chevettes were dented when both Brookes and Kaby went off on the same stage; the former losing third place as a result, though Russell Gooding won the Group 4 category in his Vauxhall.

In Group A there was a remarkable battle between Kalle Grundel with a works Golf, and Mikael Sundström in a private Ascona, which used Firestone tyres of an obsolete design! The latter was a young Finn whose Ascona progressively became more ragged – his biggest damage coming on a stage that was later cancelled! His luck and determination brought memories of another Finn, Ari Vatanen, who nine years previously had used a similarly ragged Opel, and who later became World Champion in 1981 … The three works Ford Escort 1600i cars (Wilson, Aitken and Mark Lovell, who won himself the ride after victory in the single make Escort Turbo championship) could not keep pace. Grundel suffered various punctures and excursions but finally won the group by four minutes.

Success for the Swedes continued when Susanne Kottulinsky inherited her ladies' win, firstly after Michèle Mouton left the road twice in quick succession, and then Louise Aitken stopped with distributor trouble. Mats Jonsson went into the Group 2 lead as soon as the rally reached the forests – he and Susanne were members of the Junior team and yes!, the Swedes won that competition as well.

What do we make of Mikkola? Undisputably the greatest driver of his days, in 1983 he won his world title after years of endeavour, but try as he might he never got everything his own way. This time he had hoped for a hat-trick of RAC Rally wins, but it was not to be. The quiet Swede, Blomqvist, was on the warpath like never before; 1984 was going to be his year. His 1983 Lombard RAC win was just a taste of what was to come!

RESULTS
Event held: 19-23 November 1983. 10th and final round of Manufacturers' and 12th and final round in Drivers' championships. Start/Finish: Bath. Overnight halts: Bath and Windermere.

129 starters, 61 finishers.
59 special stages but two cancelled – 491 miles (total 1386 miles).

General classification		Group	Penalties (h:m:s)
1 Blomqvist/Cederberg	Audi Quattro	GB	8:50:28
2 Mikkola/Hertz	Audi Quattro	GB	9:00:21
3 McRae/Grindrod	Opel Manta 400	GB	9:12:19
4 Lampi/Kuukkala	Audi Quattro	GB	9:16:57
5 Brookes/Broad	Vauxhall Chevette 2300HSR	GB	9:19:01
6 Buffum/Wilson	Audi Quattro	GB	9:21:16
7 Kankkunen/Piironen	Toyota Celica Twin-cam Turbo	GB	9:31:49
8 Grundel/Michel	VW Golf GTi	GA	9:38:20
9 Sundström/Orrick	Opel Ascona	GA	9:42:18
10 Jonsson/Johansson	Opel Ascona	G2	9:45:07
52 Cooper/Taylor	Fiat Ritmo 105	GN	11:44:08

Leaders: Mikkola stages 1-4, Blomqvist 5-59.

1984: Peugeot win on first attempt
With both world titles already decided it was a delight how many teams came to the RAC Rally. The only major teams absent were Lancia and Renault, while Audi left David Sutton to maintain its interests, running Hannu Mikkola in an old long chassis Quattro and Michèle Mouton in a Sport Quattro. Last year's winner Stig Blomqvist did not take part so competition number one was left vacant. Toyota sent three cars for Björn Waldegård, Juha Kankkunen and Per Eklund, on his final event for Toyota Team Europe. Nissan sent Timo Salonen and Shekhar Mehta, Opel relied on British crews.

Novelties for 1984 were few but important. This was the first time the RAC had doubled-up on the use of special stages, encouraging spectators to stay and watch cars through twice rather than congest the surrounding roads going from one stage to another. The stages themselves had seldom been so long, the average length of each high-speed section being a little under ten miles and the longest, in north Yorkshire, was 28.

Based once more at Chester, the RAC was again a five-day event, the first being run on stages local to the start, with a heavy emphasis on spectator facilities. Much of the short first leg was run on asphalt roads. Ari Vatanen's car even retained its normal gravel road setup, but was

Eight years after he won his second and last RAC Rally, Roger Clark was invited to drive this Porsche and finished 11th.

still nearly two seconds a mile quicker than the opposition. The first stage held at Knowsley Safari Park, which last year saw Mikkola go off the road, this time not seriously, but the drama came for Tony Pond's works Group A Rover whose suspension was irreparably damaged; the accident caused disappointment, as this was Rover's first works entry on a World Championship rally.

Early on Monday morning the 'real' RAC Rally started, when the cars were sent first to make a two-day loop of the Lake District, the border country and then North Yorkshire. Starting with Grizedale at dawn, Kankkunen (then lying fourth), among others, had punctures, and Mouton broke a front differential. Waldegård then made another fastest time at the Lowther Park stage, but on the next stage his Toyota's engine broke. Four-wheel drive cars held the top five placings until Malcolm Wilson's Quattro had gearbox troubles and fell back. Vatanen was cruising ahead of the Quattros of Mikkola, Mouton and John Buffum, while fifth now was Eklund – the top Toyota.

The Kielder stages were long, lonely, and as unyielding as ever, though among the top runners there were few incidents. Jimmy McRae momentarily fell behind Russell Brookes after a puncture, but then Brookes fell back to tenth after going off the road and rolling. Both Mazda RX7 team cars retired: Phillipe Wambergue, when losing a wheel, and Ingvar Carlsson with axle failure. Coming into the top ten was a great battle, between Nissan's team leader Salonen, and the semi-works driver Terry Kaby, which was to continue into the final night

Despite the huge publicity for outright winners, the RAC Rally was seriously tackled by teams anxious for class wins. This is class winner Mark Lovell in a four-wheel drive Citroën Visa Mille Pistes, seen in the Sutton Park special stage.

It would be six years before Toyotas would become consistently competitive in European rallying, although these cars had already started winning in Africa.

On his tenth attempt, victory on the RAC Rally finally came to Ari Vatanen, seen here with co-driver Terry Harryman.

The Welsh loop started on the Wednesday morning with Vatanen over four minutes in the lead, and Mikkola exactly eight in front of Mouton. Even before the first forest stage of the loop was tackled, Strömberg was out, his Saab broke the clutch input shaft and the crowds were unable to push the car to the finish. But Grundel could not enjoy this change of circumstance, because almost immediately his steering broke and he crashed. After the Forest of Dean the rally headed for the South Wales stages, which was where the excitement built up. Treacherous for drivers with their deceptive corners, these new-found stages have become some of the RAC Rally's most demanding. Kaby was going slowly, struggling with a jammed gearbox, and both he and Mouton had to stop and change a puncture in mid-stage. Buffum was up to third place at the Aberafan rest halt, while Kankkunen crashed heavily and was out.

After Aberafan the excitement mounted considerably into the night as news came through that Vatanen had rolled, and thrown away his lead to Mikkola, but then Buffum went off the road. Suddenly the face of the event had changed. Vatanen had a challenge for the first time, though he regained his lead after only three more stages. Mouton was now lying behind Eklund, and started a long process of trying to regain third place. The central Welsh stages had no more effect on the order, and when cars arrived at Dolgellau in the final morning the order seemed stabilised. But life with Vatanen is always full of surprises. This time he had a broken driveshaft at the start of the two long Dovey stages, and once again lost his lead to Mikkola! This time he took it back again after only one more stage and kept it until the finish. It had been an enjoyable RAC, something interesting everywhere. Roger Clark came out of three year's retirement to drive a Porsche for Rothmans and came 11th, while 12th, after many problems with the British Citroën Team's Visa 1000 Pistes, was Mark Lovell.

1984: A YEAR OF CHANGE

One could dismiss 1984 as the 'Year of Peugeot,' but Peugeot simply identified what we had been looking forward to for a long time – the chance to develop a rally car as an instrument for sport, rather than an adaptation of a road car. As Ford and Lancia started to show later in the year Peugeot represented a beginning rather than an end. Audi became the first team to win both world titles for four years, but they did this literally weeks before the Peugeot era started.

when the British driver had gearbox problems. In the Yorkshire stages Buffum had to slow with gear problems. Four-wheel drive cars held the top four places, Eklund led McRae and Salonen, and after Kaby spun, the Finn was now 61 seconds ahead of the British Nissan driver. In the surprisingly dry conditions, still the only top driver to have retired was Waldegård. In Group A the FISA champion Ola Strömberg (Saab 99) pulled ahead of Kalle Grundel, who was being pressed by Mikael Ericsson (Audi 80 Quattro).

RESULTS

Event held: 25-29 November 1984. 10th and final round of Manufacturers' and 12th and final round of Drivers' championships. Start/Finish: Chester. Overnight halts: Chester.

120 starters, 52 finishers.
56 stages – 536 miles (total 2008 miles).

General classification		Group	Penalties (h:m:s)
1 Vatanen/Harryman	Peugeot 205 Turbo 16	GB	9:19:48
2 Mikkola/Hertz	Audi Quattro	GB	9:20:29
3 Eklund/Whittock	Toyota Celica Twin-cam Turbo	GB	9:37:07
4 Mouton/Pons	Audi Sport Quattro	GB	9:37:28
5 Brookes/Broad	Opel Manta 400	GB	9:48:06
6 Salonen/Harjanne	Nissan 240RS	GB	9:49:37
7 McRae/Nicholson	Opel Manta 400	GB	10:04:20
8 S Mehta/Y Mehta	Nissan 240RS	GB	10:07:01
9 Fisher/Frazer	Opel Manta 400	GB	10:14:19
10 Ericsson/Billstam	Audi 80 Quattro	GA	10:15:03
28 Wiggins/Shepherd	Vauxhall Astra	GN	11:35:23

Leaders: Vatanen stages 1-39, Mikkola 40-42, Vatanen 43-49, Mikkola 50, Vatanen 51-56.

Three years after his dramatic walkout from the RAC Rally, Walter Röhrl was back again for one last time, but crashed. He never returned. On the left is Audi team chief Roland Gumpert.

1985: Victory for the Lancia Delta S4

This had been the longest-ever stage-format RAC Rally with nearly every stage run only once. It was difficult to know which team created the greatest interest. Lancia with its turbo-compressor Delta S4, or the debut of the big-engined, normally-aspirated MG Metro 6R4, where British interest was whipped up by the Austin Rover press agency. "I have never seen spectators clapping at service points before," said Austin Rover's team manager John Davenport. The Metro 6R4 cars held second place in the hands of both Malcolm Wilson, and later Tony Pond, whose eventual third place was the best non-Lancia result. Henri Toivonen's team-mate Markku Alén led much of the way, but lost time off the road on the final night. He finished a fortuitous second.

By now, opportunities afforded by the Group B rules had arrived in the WRC in full force. New generation Group B cars were entered by Lancia, MG, Audi and Peugeot, while Ford demonstrated its new Group B car before the event, and Mitsubishi entered its prototype (but eventually stillborn) Starion car in the auxiliary rally. By now Audi was very well advanced in transmission development. It was difficult to predict who would win the event, but Audi driver Hannu Mikkola was easily the most experienced RAC Rally driver. Every year since 1979 he had finished the event in

Final time on the RAC for Henri Toivonen brought his second WRC victory. Here he is on a cold, icy morning on Scotland's Cardrona Forest.

either first or second position, and on the second day he started pulling ahead, but then electronic problems stopped the car and he was out. Walter Röhrl was less at ease, not having entered this specialist event

The proud British MG Metro 6R4 team had tremendous British media and fan support, but Tony Pond's third place was the team's best result on the RAC.

Škoda was a fervent supporter of the RAC Rally, winning its class on average every year it entered, often in more than one class. This is Norwegian driver John Haugland's 130 LR, which this time ran under Group B rules.

for six years, but he immediately found that the new gearbox made the Audi easier to control on secret route rallies – until, that was, he went off the road on the first night.

The pressure was off Peugeot for this event. It came with two second-evolution cars for Timo Salonen and Kalle Grundel. When Grundel and the British dealer team Peugeot of Mikael Sundström went off the route, team manager Jean Todt pointed an accusing finger at the British organisers, saying the event had no place in the world series, emphasizing that many leading drivers were complaining about inconsistent arrowing, thus increasing political uncertainty about the event's unique format. In the end neither of the works Audis nor Peugeots reached the finish.

Two-wheel drive cars were completely uncompetitive. No two-wheel drive cars scored any fastest times, but comfortably the quickest of them was Juha Kankkunen's Toyota. The British-run Opel Manta 400s of Jimmy McRae and Russell Brookes were challenged by Terry Kaby's Nissan, who got ahead of Brookes when the latter went off the road on the first night, and all of these were quicker than the Mazda RX7s. Group A, however, had normally been two-wheel drive territory. Leading for a long while was Mats Jonsson's rear-drive Opel Ascona, but following him were several front-wheel drive Vauxhall Astra GT/Es. The only important 4 x 4 Group A car was Mikael Ericsson's Audi 90 Quattro on its World Rally debut, but this suffered chronic overheating and soon retired.

By midday on the second day, Lancias were unchallenged in first and second places, Pond was ahead of Sundström, Eklund's private Quattro and Kankkunen headed the rear-drive cars. Things were going wrong for the Lancias, however: for several stages Toivonen only had two-wheel drive, and had already changed a gearbox. As conditions got colder the surviving crews were subdued by the challenge of the conditions. "It was quite a night to drive on ice with 400bhp," said Alén. Another cold night was to come.

With two journeys into Kielder Forest in the second half of the rally, there was every expectation that the carnage had not stopped yet, but despite Kielder's awesome reputation little happened the first time through that region. The rally made a loop into Scotland and this was where Peugeot lost its last Group B car (Sundström's) and then on the second loop the fun really started. The leader, Alén, slid off the road and was helpless until fellow Finn Kankkunen arrived to rescue him, and this let Toivonen into the lead. Alén dropped to third, so Pond was again up to second, but the Lancia was able to pull back time and recover that place. Then, two stages after Alén's error, Mats Jonsson went off, losing enough time to let the young British driver Andrew Wood into the lead of Group A. In the small classes, rear-engined Škodas scored class wins in both Groups A and B. The latter was predictable but the former, against more powerful front-drive fuel-injected Opel Corsa Sprints was a big surprise.

The format of the event itself remained close to its traditions, being even longer than previous years, with stages averaging ten miles. The question now was whether the RAC organisers should continue with their old individualistic secret route policies direction, or adjust to the pressure from the sport. Many errors were made which put the organisers at a distance from regular competitors, and journalists were angry at indifference to their grievances. However, FISA had already pledged its consent to continue secret routes for the 1986 RAC.

THE PERILS OF SECRET ROUTES BY WALTER RÖHRL

Audi asked if we would go to the RAC Rally, as it was a good chance to get more experience of its new transmission development. My regular co-driver Christian Geistdorfer was not at all happy about going, so I went with the British co-driver Phil Short. Just to have someone with you who knew each stage was a great help; it was something to make my life safer. I had not been to England to compete on the RAC since 1979, and in recent years had tried to avoid going to the event. The first time I came to the RAC (in 1973) secret route rallying seemed the only right system of rallying, but I lost my opinion when other people knew the stages from national championship events. I had been lucky that championships in other years had been decided before I had to go to the RAC Rally!

Once we started the rally I chose a reliable speed, rather than take risks, but we had various troubles in the opening stages when a front strut broke, a turbo pipe came off, and then with the gearbox itself. On one longer stage we were about 5km into the stage when the gearlever came off in my hand, and the car was stuck in first gear. Phil sorted through his carry-on bag and eventually produced a screwdriver. We inserted this in the gearlever hole and operated the gearbox with this to the end of the stage!

We did not find too many problems with the secret stages, but the corner where I eventually went off was very tricky. It didn't look very difficult when we approached it. About 50 metres into the corner I realised it was a sharp tightening bend; I thought I could still make it safely, but the left rear wheel had already slid into the ditch. When I pressed the pedal to get the power on, the car was already going sideways, then it hit a tree stump. It began to roll over and over down the hillside at about 80km/h. I thought we would never stop. When the car came to rest Phil and I got out, and I considered we were fortunate not to have been hurt seriously, though my neck was aching from a previous injury sustained during my accident at Sanremo in 1984. Despite rolling over some eight or ten times, the car's antenna was still working and I radioed for help. Hannu was first to answer. He asked me if it was the corner a mile and half before the finish. I said yes, and he said he knew the corner, because he had been off there some years before ...

RESULTS

Event held: 24-28 November 1985. 11th and final round of Manufacturers' and 12th and final round of Drivers' championships. Start/Finish: Nottingham. Overnight halts: Nottingham and Carlisle.

155 starters, 62 finishers.
65 stages but two cancelled – 547 miles (total 2179 miles).

General classification		Group	Penalties (h:m:s)
1 Toivonen/Wilson	Lancia Delta S4	GB	9:32:05
2 Alén/Kivimaki	Lancia Delta S4	GB	9:33:01
3 Pond/Arthur	MG Metro 6R4	GB	9:34:32
4 Eklund/Cederberg	Audi Quattro	GB	9:58:35
5 Kankkunen/Gallagher	Toyota Celica Twin-cam Turbo	GB	10:10:53
6 McRae/Grindrod	Opel Manta 400	GB	10:16:01
7 Kaby/Gormley	Nissan 240RS	GB	10:24:08
8 Brookes/Broad	Opel Manta 400	GB	10:25:50
9 Millen/Rainbow	Mazda RX7	GB	10:29:39
10 Carlsson/Melander	Mazda RX7	GB	10:29:57
12 Wood/Nicholson	Vauxhall Astra GT/E	GA	10:43:18
21 Wiggins/Shepherd	Vauxhall Astra GT/E	GN	11:42:07

Leaders: Alén stages 1-12, Mikkola 13-20, Alén 21-53, Toivonen 54-65.

1986: Group B cars – last event in Europe

It wouldn't be like this for a long while. The super-strong Group B Supercars provided an amazingly close event in which seconds separated the leading positions right to the end. The lead changed no fewer than seven times involving five different drivers at the wheel of three different makes of car. "I can't remember having had to drive flat-out from start to finish before," said the usually slow-starting Timo Salonen, while his future boss, Achim Warmbold of Mazda, said "I don't think cars in future will ever stand being driven flat-out like these Supercars". As testimony to the special challenge of driving these cars, this was the first time drivers did not have to drive all through the night. Only a third of the stages were held in darkness. Mazda cars won the Group A and Group N categories. Entries included two works Lancia Delta S4s, three works Peugeot 205 Turbo 16s, four works Ford RS200, and five MG Metro 6R4s. It was a splendid farewell to these remarkable cars in Europe.

The night before the start Lancia threatened its second driver Mikael Ericsson, Alén's team-mate, that he would be out of a job next year. It certainly stirred the young Swede into action and he was in the lead by half way. Rally leader after stage 1 was Stig Blomqvist in a Ford RS200 before Kankkunen's Peugeot went ahead. A second-day

Only once did Ford have the chance to enter its ground-breaking RS200 car on the RAC Rally, but good results escaped them. This is Stig Blomqvist who retired with engine trouble.

Cold early mornings did not deter spectators watching Ingvar Carlsson's Mazda 323 4WD.

puncture dropped Blomqvist well down the field, and, although he pulled back to fifth, an overheating engine caused retirement on the third day. From the second stage nobody could overtake the Peugeots through Sunday's 'Mickey Mouse' spectator stages. There was a quick change of fortunes in the Kielder stages on the Monday, which saw first Alén, then Salonen, and finally Ericsson in the lead before the overnight halt at Ingliston was reached. At half distance, the only top retirements had been Marc Duez's works-supported Metro 6R4 and the works-supported RS200s of Mark Lovell and Stig Andervang. On the way south, however, fortunes were due to alter more frequently.

Immediately the event restarted, Kankkunen was back in front again, but he felt off form, and two slips cost him respectively the lead and then put him on his roof. He continued, encouraged that many previous RAC winners had been upside down en route. Ericsson led as the rally made its way south back to England, but he made two errors on successive stages, letting the consistent driving of Salonen take the lead – which he was to hold all through the Welsh stages back to the finish. On the final day Salonen kept in front, but the slightest slip would have seen Alén through, although he was under increased pressure by the retirement of Ericsson two stages from the end.

The final stage was the most testing of all. Salonen slowed down as much as he dared, almost past caring about his rivals, and brought the car safely through to the Bridgend rest halt, before the return to Bath. He held his breath for seemingly ages until Alén arrived, and found the Lancia driver had been even more cautious. Markku said that his motive was simply to stay two places in front of Kankkunen. Unknown to the Lancias,

Splendid line up of rally cars at the start in Bath's historic Great Pulteney Street.

Early evening shot of winner Timo Salonen in the heart of the daunting Kielder Forest, driving a Peugeot 205T16 Group B car.

the Peugeots were manipulating their drivers' championship prospects. Kankkunen was moved up from fourth to third, behind fellow Peugeot driver Sundström; the points gap between the Championship contenders was not five but three; however, Alén's caution still put him ahead in the series for the moment.

Russell Brookes' Opel Manta 400 was the top placed rear-drive car for more than two days, but his stage times were seven seconds a mile slower than the leaders. The semi-official and private Metro 6R4s disappeared for various reasons, while a lone Harald Demuth's Group B Audi Sport Quattro, entered at the last moment by David Sutton, retired two stages from the end with engine failure. David

Llewellin had to run far down the field, after police delayed him on the second day, while Malcolm Wilson ran even further back having slid off the road suffering transmission trouble. Punctures and transmission troubles also slowed Tony Pond, and finally the honour of the best of British-built Supercars went to the fifth placed Ford of Kalle Grundel.

Group A saw three main contenders, Ingvar Carlsson's Mazda which toured round with insolent ease, Lasse Lampi's Coupé Quattro which suffered transmission problems and Kenneth Eriksson's 16-valve VW. Eriksson's remaining rival for the special one-off Group A World Championship, Rudolf Stohl, never entered, and the moment he failed to start Eriksson secured this title. Ford's three Sierra Cosworths, entered in Group B, were prepared in the same specification as the works cars expect to be in Group A next year; these were converted one-make Championship cars which had gained useful pre-homologation stage experience, but transmission and suspension trouble sidelined them.

After the end of the rally the press communiques started to appear. Honouring rallying's tradition of not announcing next year's plans until the previous programme had ended, and notwithstanding the American Olympus WRC Rally was still to come, Warmbold announced that Salonen would be his number one driver next year. Lancia jumped the gun by boasting they had captured Kankkunen. As to who would win the World Championship for Drivers, the rally world would have to wait another month. This year saw the last fully secret route Rally GB.

SUPERCAR ERA

The Supercar era will be remembered as a Golden Age in rally sport, but the Group B challenge took its toll. Peugeot progressed from success to success, while its associated company Citroën soon realised it had underestimated the technical level required, and soon cancelled its WRC programme. Early in the season Austin Rover's normally-aspirated Metro 6R4 was plagued by problems with the engines, which should have been the most straightforward part of the design, but Ford's RS200 faced problems even more serious. Despite the company's prior public misgivings about Group B safety, a Ford featured in the Portugal tragedy. Then its cars suffered a series of fires, but the cars gained many successes in national level events. Alarmed at the events in Portugal, coupled with a nagging worry about its competitiveness with its front-engined car, Audi withdrew in mid-season.

Performance of the Group B cars was an amazing 0-100km/h in around 2.5 seconds, power outputs of over 500bhp, and, perhaps the most incredible of all, was the reliability of the cars, especially of the Lancias and Peugeots. Particularly when the WRC rally routes were shortened in mid-season, we saw quite the closest rallying ever. Traditional elements of rallying endurance were discarded, and every stage fought to the second. It was a fantastic time.

RESULTS

Event held: 16-19 November 1986. 11th and final round of Manufacturers' and 12th and penultimate round in Drivers' championships.
Start/Finish: Bath. Overnight halts: Harrogate, Ingliston and Liverpool.

150 starters, 83 finishers.
45 special stages but 1 stopped – 321 miles (total 1577 miles).

General classification		Group	Penalties (h:m:s)
1 Salonen/Harjanne	Peugeot 205 Turbo 16 E2	GB	5:21:11
2 Alén/Kivimaki	Lancia Delta S4	GB	5:22:33
3 Kankkunen/Piironen	Peugeot 205 Turbo 16 E2	GB	5:27:16
4 Sundström/Silander	Peugeot 205 Turbo 16 E2	GB	5:27:42
5 Grundel/Melander	Ford RS200	GB	5:29:32
6 Pond/Arthur	MG Metro 6R4	GB	5:30:14
7 Eklund/Whittock	MG Metro 6R4	GB	5:33:12
8 J McRae/Grindrod	MG Metro 6R4	GB	5:35:08
9 Llewellin/Short	MG Metro 6R4	GB	5:40:38
10 Carlsson/Bohlin	Mazda 323 4WD	GA	6:00:33
39 Maslen/Balfour	Mazda 323 4WD	GN	6:56:57

Leaders: Blomqvist stage 1, Kankkunen 2-15, Alén 16+17, Salonen 18-21, Ericsson 22, Kankkunen 23-25, Ericsson 26-30, Salonen 31-45.

Chapter 6
1987-1996

THE GROUP A ERA

The speed with which the Group B formula was abandoned was brutal, but, in retrospect, for the most part understandable. The reigning manufacturer champion Peugeot, who had no competitive Group A cars and expressed fierce disapproval at the FIA's method of altering the rules, had taken the change personally. It sued the FIA, lost, and immediately diverted its accumulated high-performance rally car experience into the burgeoning alternative of cross country rallying. This problem was widespread. No other team had satisfactory suitable Group A cars available for the 1987 season. There was an urgent rush to develop and then homologate cars that would be competitive. With Peugeot gone, Lancia had the best suited machinery, namely the Delta HF 4WD. Designed as a niche product for marque enthusiasts, it had the two essential ingredients for success: a turbocharger, and four-wheel drive. However, it fell well short of the performance levels that success in WRC was predicted to demand, but it provided a basis on which to proceed. Immediately it was the best car on the WRC market, winning nine of the 13 WRC events in 1987. Rival cars were the Mazda 323 4WD model, which had a smaller engine, while Audi had its equally underpowered 200 Quattro. Ford had a choice, an equally underpowered, normally-aspirated Sierra XR4x4 or its two-wheel drive, turbocharged Sierra RS Cosworth. Cars that featured both normally-aspirated engines and two-wheel drive were headed by the BMW M3 and Volkswagen's Golf GTi 16v. Gradually Lancia pulled ahead in the 1987 championship, and in 1988 its cars won ten WRC events. Meanwhile other teams started to catch up.

At the start of the Group A formula, the most active Japanese manufacturer in the WRC was Mazda, but its colleagues soon started to take an interest. It was attracted by the relative ease of manufacturing suitable turbocharged, four-wheel drive models in numbers required for homologation, while European manufacturers found it hard to achieve the minimum production requirements for homologation. Toyota was initially the most prominent. In 1988, it launched its Group A turbocharged, four-wheel drive Celica range, but

its engineers found the technical demands of WRC competition were very challenging. Quickly following was Mitsubishi with its Galant VR-4, followed later by its incredibly successful Lancer Evolution series, and then came Subaru in early 1990. By 1990 Japanese cars started winning WRC rallies, and by the mid-'90s, they were winning titles.

Spectacular 1988 Finish ceremony for Markku Alén in Harrogate.

The Group A era saw the sport surging forward in popularity. The RAC Rally routes remained largely familiar each year, with spectator-friendly stages preceding visits to the best available forest regions in Wales, Yorkshire, the Scottish border counties, tackled in a suitable order according to which town was chosen to host the event. The event had an advantage compared with other events in the championship. Because of the secret stages, the overall timeframe at the event for the professional teams was very short. This prevented crews embarking on time costly pre-event reconnaissance. This format came under pressure, being at variance with other events included in the WRC calendar. Gradually the organisers' resistance to change eroded, and the rally changed irrevocably to become an orthodox format event where stages could be pacenoted.

Elaborate format change was still far off, though various organisational changes were made to ensure that the event smartened up, fit for its position in a major international sport. Over this period the age range of winning drivers widened. Henri Toivonen had won the 1980 RAC Rally at the age of 24 years, but nine years later Pentti Airikkala won the event when he was 20 years older, the oldest driver to win a WRC rally in Europe for nearly 30 years. Internationally there was also shift of winning drivers from Scandinavia to elsewhere in Europe. In the period of this chapter, the sport hailed World Champions from other countries, such as Italy, Spain, and France – many finally clinching titles in Britain – so during this time the winners of the RAC Rally came from Finland, Spain, Britain and Germany!

For the writers of his book, perhaps the most exciting development was the success of young Colin McRae who took on the mantle of the legend created by Roger Clark. The successes of McRae, and later Richard Burns, re-ignited the enthusiasm of the popular national media around the world, which had faded away at the end of the Group B era. And as we will see in this chapter, it was all about to get more exciting than ever.

1987: Juha Kankkunen wins rally and title
The new Group A rally formula found Lancia the most well-prepared team with its Delta HF 4WD, and an impressive drive lineup. Under Lancia's 'equal opportunities' scheme, its three official regular drivers (Markku Alén, Juha Kankkunen and Miki Biasion) would have the same chance of becoming World Champion, though for the RAC Rally Mikael Ericsson replaced Biasion. For the Italians, however, the most important target (the World Manufacturers' title) had long ago already been achieved, after Argentina. Under Group A rules turbochargers were immediately found to be essential, as was four-wheel drive traction, though the only 4WD team to enter the 1987 RAC Rally was Lancia.

There was no serious opposition to the Lancias. Mazda had originally hoped to challenge Lancia, but suffered transmission

Rallying for all! Victory for veteran Pentti Airikkala (right) and businessman co-driver Ronan McNamee.

Draughty ride after his roll in the windscreen-less Lancia of Markku Alén.

Floral celebration for Juha Kankkunen.

Open stretches between the forests for Carlos Sainz in his rear-wheel drive Sierra RS Cosworth.

homologation trouble during the year and did not enter. Lancia's only competition came from less competitive sources – the powerful rear-drive Ford Sierra RS Cosworth (which was also available in Group N), the less powerful private four-wheel drive Audi Coupé Quattro, and a collection of 2-litre front-drive cars from Opel, Peugeot and VW. The other main novelty of the event was that they allowed reconnaissance of the 'stately home' stages held on the Sunday (but not the forests). After Stig Blomqvist had made fastest time on the opening stage in his Ford at Oulton Park, Lancias led all the way, hounded by the Fords. Kankkunen finished the first day with an impressive 40-second lead. Alén had his first accident of the event, very slowly sliding onto his roof in front of the national network television cameras, but the short day was noted more for poor weather than hot competition. The British GM team suffered badly, and after problems in a water splash, the Opel Kadetts of Derek Bell, Malcolm Wilson, Pentti Airikkala and Dave Metcalfe all retired. The GM Euro Sport Opels of Sepp Haider and Mats Jonsson, however, had no trouble as their air intakes were located differently to the British-prepared cars.

On the Monday the rally headed for the forests. Once again the rally abstained from driving all through the nights, but each night halt was brief, with cars restarting extremely early each morning. The crews restarted for Monday's route at 4:15am! Alén was the first car on the road, and he had to drive, and to open the road over the snowy stages at Clocaenog before dawn. This cost him more time and let team-mate Mikael Ericsson into second place behind Kankkunen. Blomqvist, running second on the road, also suffered badly, dropping to ninth. Behind the leading Lancias now was Eklund's private Audi Coupé Quattro with Blomqvist catching up fast. On the third day the rally headed (at 3:15am!) into the Yorkshire forests. Alén overturned again, and Ericsson also went off the road for some while. After Yorkshire came the daunting stages in Kielder, where conditions in the early evening were very unpleasant, with rain in the lower regions, and snow higher up. Eklund had brake trouble, which let Blomqvist rise to second. One corner deceived both Kankkunen and Alén; the former went off the road and was lucky to do no damage when the car crashed over rocks. Alén was stuck for some minutes, throwing away all chances of the title for him. Wednesday, the final leg (with an easier 6:45am start), took cars from Carlisle down to the Lake District. Only Eklund

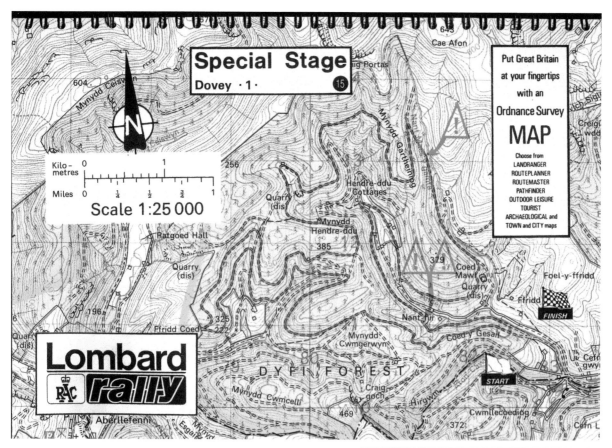

Special Stage

Dovey · 1 · ⑮

Kilo- 0   1
metres

Miles 0   ¼   ½   ¾   1

Scale 1:25 000

Put Great Britain
at your fingertips
with an

Ordnance Survey

MAP

Choose from
LANDRANGER
ROUTEPLANNER
ROUTEMASTER
PATHFINDER
OUTDOOR LEISURE
TOURIST
ARCHAEOLOGICAL and
TOWN and CITY maps

Lombard rally

Major innovation was the supply of official maps of the once-secret forest stages. This shows a part of Dyfi (originally called Dovey) Forest in Central Wales.

and Blomqvist were putting up a show. With Kankkunen now three minutes in the lead. As the rally headed back to Chester with Eklund in second place, there was one final drama to play. After the rally, the scrutineers discovered the inlet manifold on Eklund's privately prepared Audi was oversized, and he was excluded, so Blomqvist ultimately finished second.

For a sportsman like Blomqvist, gaining second place at the expense of his friend, and in circumstances such as these, was upsetting. There were many happier sides to the rally, however. Carlos Sainz drove his Cosworth to an impressive eighth place, the first Spaniard to get a top placing on this event in memory – and on his first attempt. But perhaps the nicest tale was that of Scotsman George Donaldson who won Group N in a works-loaned Cosworth. 15,000 enthusiasts had entered Ford's Sierra Rally Search in the hope of winning this drive, and it was Donaldson who succeeded. He won the group by no less than seven minutes from his nearest rival. The ban on Group B cars only applied to bigger-engined cars, and small engine Group B cars were still admitted in WRC events. This provided Pavel Sibera with another decisive category win on the event for Škoda.

DONALDSON'S GROUP N DREAM

29-year-old rally mechanic George Donaldson, from Edinburgh, thought his dreams had come true when he was selected as the Ford Sierra Rally Search '87 champion. His prize of an expenses-paid drive on this event seemed almost incidental. When he finished 15th – and won the rally's second most important prize (the best Group N car) he achieved successes far greater than he expected.

For the Lombard RAC Rally, Donaldson was privileged to have an old friend with him. This was professional co-driver Fred Gallagher, with whom Donaldson had often worked when he was rally mechanic at Toyota Team Europe, and was a fellow Edinburgh resident. George had first entered an international rally on the Scottish in 1981 when he won the newcomers' award. In 1983 he took his Mini to the Swedish, and his work as a mechanic with TTE took him all over the world. He never became a professional rally driver but went on to become one of the most experienced team managers in rallying.

RESULTS

Event held: 22-25 November 1987. 11th and final round of Manufacturers' and 13th and final round of Drivers' championships. Start/Finish: Chester. Overnight halts: Chester and Carlisle.

165 starters, 83 finishers.
48 special stages but one cancelled – 307 miles (total 1630 miles).

General classification		Group	Penalties (h:m:s)
1 Kankkunen/Piironen	Lancia Delta HF 4WD	GA	5:26:36
2 Blomqvist/Berglund	Ford Sierra RS Cosworth	GA	5:30:16
3 J McRae/Grindrod	Ford Sierra RS Cosworth	GA	5:33:15
4 M Ericsson/Billstam	Lancia Delta HF 4WD	GA	5:35:11
5 Alén/Kivimaki	Lancia Delta HF 4WD	GA	5:35:26
6 Llewellin/Short	Audi Coupé Quattro	GA	5:45:41
7 Jonsson/Johanson	Opel Kadett GSi 2.0	GA	5:48:36
8 Sainz/Boto	Ford Sierra RS Cosworth	GA	5:49:16
9 Eriksson/Diekmann	VW Golf GTI 16v	GA	5:51:20
10 R Ericsson/Rosendahl	Subaru RX Turbo	GA	5:58:36
15 Donaldson/Gallagher	Ford Sierra RS Cosworth	GN	6:05:22
27 Sibera/Gross	Škoda 130LR	GB	6:24:30

Leaders: Blomqvist stage 1, Alén 2+3, Kankkunen 4+5, Alén 6, Kankkunen 7-48.

1988: Four different leaders, three on final day

"Everyone goes off the road on the RAC Rally sooner or later. You are not going fast enough if you don't!" explained outgoing World Champion and former winner Juha Kankkunen. The 1988 event lived up to its reputation with a vengeance. All the top drivers went off the road at one time or another, and two of them, Hannu Mikkola and Kankkunen himself, retired on the final morning for just this reason when in the lead. It was a most extraordinary rally, a fitting climax to a season which had started quietly, and gradually accelerated in interest.

Although Lancia and Miki Biasion had clinched their respective World Championship titles a month before at Sanremo, there had been a much stronger entry in Britain than the year before. There were four-wheel drive turbocharged teams – Lancia (now running Delta Integrales), Mazda (323 4WD), Toyota (Celica ST165) and Mitsubishi (Galant VR-4). There were three different cars in the podium places.

A frosty morning road section in Northern England for Markku Alén.

Ford, however, once again persevered with its turbocharged rear-drive Sierra RS Cosworth cars.

This was Toyota's fifth World Championship Rally entry with its new-generation car and the fourth consecutive event on which Kankkunen had led only to retire. "This time we were even in the lead on the final leg," the Finn joked. In this instance retirement was not mechanical but self-inflicted; with only eight stages to go he went off the road, and a tree broke the oil cooler. Markku Alén's Lancia eventually won the event (the tenth victory for the official Italian team out of 11 starts in 1988, his first win on this event in 15 attempts) even though he had himself spent five minutes off the road, during the event. It was an important success for him.

Unpredictably icy conditions reduced the emphasis on the performance and reliability of the cars. Both works Mazda 323 4WDs were still going strong on the morning of the final day, it looked like Mikkola was going to win, but he then put his car off the road when suddenly blinded by sunlight, and broke the transmission getting back on again. Correct tyres were more important than the power under the bonnet. Lancia and Mazda (headed by second placed Timo Salonen) had a significant edge with Michelin tyres, which were more effective on the hard ice of the second day and the soft slush of the third and fourth days, over the Pirellis of Toyota; they were also more puncture resistant. On his way to eventual third place, but towards five minutes behind the winner, was Björn Waldegård who twice had to stop on stages to change a flat tyre.

This was the first WRC event for the British-based Mitsubishi Ralliart Europe team, with a single entry for Ari Vatanen, quite a

Sunset backdrop for Mark Lovell's Ford Sierra Cosworth.

Timo Salonen's Mazda high up in the Lake District.

landmark occasion in which eight of the top 12 seeded entries were for Japanese cars. Vatanen was to be plagued with problems – the steering, clutch and finally (due to an electronic fault) the engine, but before his fourth-day retirement he had set two fastest stage times with his Michelin tyres.

There were many surprises further down the field. Pentti Airikkala drove a privately-run ex-works Delta Integrale which achieved fourth place, but only after going off the road. He arranged for the car to be rolled over three times to a place from where it could be driven back to the road. On his first-ever WRC event, future works driver Armin Schwarz was fifth in a privately run Audi 200 Quattro. The icy conditions gave a new lease of life for the old Škoda cars: John Haugland's car won the A5 class for Škoda, the company's 16th class win on the event in 16 years. After being headed earlier by Malcolm Wilson's 16-valve Astra, Stig Blomqvist (Ford Sierra RS Cosworth) was the top two-wheel drive finisher, his Pirelli shod car beating Carlos Sainz's similar car on Michelins.

This was the second year there was an official FIA Cup for Group N, and this year it was the only title to be decided at the RAC Rally. The Argentinian Jorge Recalde came to the event in his Top Run Lancia Delta Integrale with a seven-point deficit against the Belgian importers' Mazda 323 4WD of 23-year-old Pascal Gaban. As the rally progressed Recalde kept going, overcoming a gearbox problem which cost him road penalties, but still staying just ahead of the Belgian. Then Gaban had troubles, firstly two punctures, and on the fourth day he also went off the road for 20 minutes. These delays put him down to ninth best Group N car while Recalde remained a steady

Worrying moment as Björn Waldegård changes a flat tyre as a Mazda slithers downhill towards his Celica on studless tyres.

General classification		Group	Penalties (h:m:s)
1 Alén/Kivimaki	Lancia Delta Integrale	GA	7:15:37
2 Salonen/Silander	Mazda 323 4WD	GA	7:19:43
3 Waldegård/Gallagher	Toyota Celica ST165	GA	7:22:16
4 Airikkala/Murphy	Lancia Delta Integrale	GA	7:25:06
5 Schwarz/Hertz	Audi 200 Quattro	GA	7:26:43
6 Blomqvist/Melander	Ford Sierra RS Cosworth	GA	7:34:22
7 Sainz/Rodriguez	Ford Sierra RS Cosworth	GA	7:36:53
8 Walfridsson/Barth	Audi Coupé Quattro	GA	7:41:06
9 Jonsson/Backman	Opel Kadett GSi	GA	7:44:56
10 Grundel/Johansson	Peugeot 309GTI	GA	7:49:38
11 de Mevius/Manset	Mazda 323 4WD	GN	7:51:40

Leaders: Kankkunen & Salonen stage 1, Kankkunen 2-9, Alén 10-30, Kankkunen & Mikkola 31, Mikkola 32+33, Alén 34+35, Mikkola 36-38, Kankkunen 39-43, Mikkola 44-46, Alén 47-52.

1989: First win for Japanese manufacturer

There was disarray when entries for the 1989 event were about to close, as Mitsubishi discovered its intended team-mate for Ari Vatanen, Mikael Ericsson, who had recently won the 1000 Lakes Rally for them, had already been entered to drive for Lancia. Hastily it recruited Pentti Airikkala, the British national Group N champion, and a non-priority driver. Days later, Lancia cancelled its entries for the event which left Ericsson and his team-mate Markku Alén without drives. Without Lancia, the entry of top line works cars was restricted to Toyota in full force with three Celica ST165s, three now outclassed Mazda 323 4WDs, two Mitsubishi Galant VR-4s, and one uncompetitive rear-drive Ford Sierra RS Cosworth. At Mitsubishi, Airikkala was full of energy on his first competitive professional WRC drive for six years, making up for Vatanen who was off-form. Vatanen finished the rally, but only after he put his car on its roof en route, and he could seldom match the times of the team's newcomer. Airikkala said his Group A car was completely different to the Group N version which he had been driving in the British national championship, and much easier to drive.

Once again all the WRC titles, even the Group N Cup, had already been earmarked, and this event was set to provide a lot of interest. Lancia's absence meant that there was no hope of European teams preventing a Japanese victory, which had never been gained on this event before.

It was Toyota, not Mitsubishi, which made the running, leading for 51 of the rally's 55 stages, except, that is, for the three final stages. Celicas held the top four placings at the end of the first day. British Open Champion David Llewellin led initially, but was then delayed

third. If they finished like this the Championship would end up equal, but then Gaban pulled back one place to be eighth – and shortly before the finish rose by the retirement of another driver to be seventh. By just two points was a year-long struggle resolved!

It had been an event in a lifetime for racing driver and former World Endurance Champion Derek Bell, who reached the finish in an 8-valve Astra, which as a promotion was using lead-free fuels. "I have been out of control in this car for hours on end. I'm never going to do this sort of thing again." More top drivers entered this event than any World Rally for the past six years. With excitement such as this maybe 1989 was set to see a challenge for the world titles on a level not seen for quite a few years.

RESULTS
Event held: 20-24 November 1988. 11th and final round of Manufacturers' title and 13th and final round of Drivers' championships.
Start/Finish: Harrogate. Overnight halts: Telford, Harrogate and Carlisle.

178 starters, 87 finishers.
52 special stages – 374 miles (total 1743 miles).

by turbocharger problems, later crashing, but, after two days, Toyotas still held 1-2-3. Airikkala was fourth, 94 seconds behind the leader. At this point the drivers were reclassified, Airikkala would restart the first non-Toyota, ahead of Vatanen and all the Mazdas. It was in the Scottish border Kielder forest complex where Toyota's troubles started to become more serious. Rally leader Juha Kankkunen had alternator trouble on the first night stage and then lost the brakes as well. Carlos Sainz inherited his lead. Toyota's number three driver Kenneth Eriksson also had brake troubles, and these delays meant that Airikkala edged up to second place, 96 seconds behind Sainz, with Kankkunen third.

On the Scottish stages, on the fourth day, battle was joint between Sainz and Airikkala. The Mitsubishi had its rear suspension lowered and the veteran Finn started going really fast without taking risks. He nibbled away at Sainz's lead, so by the time the rally reached the final night halt at Newcastle, he was only 31 seconds behind the Spaniard. After winning the Cartel Rally held in the Yorkshire Forests, which the rally tackled on the final day, Airikkala felt confident about taking that remaining half-minute – but it didn't happen like that. Sainz started holding off the Finn, then, three stages before the end, things went wrong for the Spaniard, this time a broken propshaft. Mechanical woes had now afflicted each of the once dominant Toyotas. Just as Airikkala had mentally adjusted to finishing second, he found himself in the lead. Toyotas finished 2-3-4, each of them having held the lead at one time or another, but been denied the chance of victory by mechanical problems. Vatanen was a distant fifth while Mazdas took the next four places, reliable but well off the pace.

Toyota had also been heartened in the early stages when its British driver Graham Middleton was leading Group N, but, like Llewellin, his hopes were dashed in Wales. Englishman Simon Stubbings took over with his Mazda, though the similar car of Grégoire de Mevius was in front by the end of the second day. The Belgian took second place in

Daihatsu achieved impressive results in rallying with their three-cylinder turbocharged Charade GTti. This is the car of Terry Kaby, this time delayed by a turbo failure.

Pentti Airikkala's victorious Mitsubishi Galant VR-4 seen in Scotland.

Hannu Mikkola (left) enjoyed a happy 15-year partnership with Swedish co-driver Arne Hertz, finally with Mazda. This year, four Mazdas finished in the top ten, though Mikkola was delayed by gearbox trouble on this event.

Final day disappointment for Carlos Sainz and his Toyota team. Hopes were dashed after leading for a total of 26 stages.

the FIA Group N Cup, behind Alain Oreille who had taken the title on the Ivory Coast Rally, when Gustavo Trelles was slowed and then had to retire because of engine trouble.

Malcolm Wilson strived hard in his front-drive Vauxhall Astra GTE, finally finishing the best European car and the best two-wheel drive or normally-aspirated car, reaching tenth place when Per Eklund's Lancia was excluded for running too late on the final day. Russell Brookes had also been tenth on the second day before his rear-drive Cosworth retired with engine trouble.

Rallying in the 1980s had now come to an end. Despite Llewellin's two fastest stage times (the first by a British driver on this event for three years) British drivers were no nearer repeating the win achieved by Roger Clark on this event in 1976, and now the once all-conquering British cars were absent at the top level as well. The four-wheel drive Cosworth was eagerly awaited, but what hope would this offer against the reliable technology and universal commitment to motorsport from Japanese teams, while the European two-wheel drive cars were still suffering engine failures? Through it all a 44-year-old Finn won the rally. The cars and the people change, but the magic of the Lombard RAC Rally and the sport remained.

ONE MAN AND HIS CO-DRIVER
Victory on the RAC Rally 1989 was the climax of the maverick rally career of Pentti Airikkala. At the time he was the second oldest driver to win a WRC event. Beyond his British championship drives for Vauxhall, which extended off and on for six years and led to podium results on one-off WRC events in Sweden and Finland, he had no long-time relationships with WRC teams. He lost some opportunities when he was injured in a crash in New Zealand in 1980, and his professional career ended when he was injured again in a crash on the 1990 Lombard RAC Rally. Sadly his health started to fail, and after a long illness he died in 2009. He

had many different co-drivers, but through the '80s he regularly rallied with an Irish businessman, Ronan McNamee. McNamee was well established through the Cuisine de France company, for which he was a joint main shareholder. This company pioneered the par-baked concept of freezing pre-baked bread loaves and cakes, distributed and then re-heated in shops. At the end of the '90s the business was sold for around £40m, which McNamee and his partner shared.

RESULTS
Event held: 19-23 November 1989. 10th and final round of Manufacturers' and 13th and final round of Drivers' championships. Start/Finish: Nottingham. Overnight halts: Telford, Nottingham, Carlisle and Newcastle upon Tyne.

187 starters, 84 finishers.
55 special stages – 375 miles (total 1925 miles).

General classification		Group	Penalties (h:m:s)
1 Airikkala/McNamee	Mitsubishi Galant VR-4	GA	6:19:22
2 Sainz/Moya	Toyota Celica ST165	GA	6:20:50
3 Kankkunen/Piironen	Toyota Celica ST165	GA	6:23:11
4 Eriksson/Parmander	Toyota Celica ST165	GA	6:25:30
5 Vatanen/Berglund	Mitsubishi Galant VR-4	GA	6:27:44
6 Salonen/Silander	Mazda 323 4WD	GA	6:28:19
7 Sundström/Repo	Mazda 323 4WD	GA	6:30:56
8 I Carlsson/P Carlsson	Mazda 323 4WD	GA	6:32:54
9 Mikkola/Hertz	Mazda 323 4WD	GA	6:35:52
10 Wilson/Grindrod	Vauxhall Astra GTE	GA	6:40:11
20 de Mevius/Lux	Mazda 323 4WD	GN	7:05:52

Leaders: Sainz stage 1, Llewellin 2, Kankkunen 3-8, Kankkunen & Eriksson 9, Eriksson 10, Kankkunen 11-15, Sainz 16-19, Kankkunen 20-31, Sainz 32-52, Airikkala 53-55.

1990: Pacenotes in the forests at last
Given permission to stay at home after already gaining the 1990 Drivers' title, World Champion Carlos Sainz still came to Britain, and avenged his last day defeat the year before. The final hours were just as eventful, Sainz only confirming his command of the rally seven stages from the end, when Juha Kankkunen's Lancia crashed due to unexpected sheet ice. It was the moment when the last remaining Finn in the event, despite being in the lead, was forced to retire, allowing a non-Scandinavian to win the event for the first time in 14 years.

The big news was that pacenotes were admitted on the RAC Rally for the first time for the whole of the route, not just for the publicity stages. It had been a brave step forward for the British organisers, who were aware that their stubborn resistance to constant demands from the international authorities may have been misjudged. Not everyone welcomed the change, however, but many others did, several finding the whole concept of a non-secret event in these remote forests unexpectedly enjoyable. The overall winning speed was only fractionally faster than before, despite the impression of drivers that they were going much faster. One factor which gradually emerged – was that the rally was not necessarily safer, judging by how many drivers left the road.

Although Lancia and Sainz had become respective champions six weeks earlier, top entries came from Toyota, Mitsubishi, Lancia, Ford (now finally with four-wheel drive), Mazda and Subaru teams, and the battle between drivers was intense. No fewer than 11 made best times, while five drivers (in four different types of car) held the lead at one time or another. And the British event was wide open in another sense, the top seven starters came from six different countries. Markku Alén's early lead was a major encouragement for Subaru. Sainz led at halfway, before he lost the lead with a puncture, Kenneth Eriksson had fallen back for a wrong tyre choice, while Ari Vatanen pulled to the side of the road to allow another driver to pass – and broke the steering, and so on.

Not until Kankkunen's accident did a driver hold a lead of greater than 22 seconds, and usually it was less than ten. The wide range of drivers and manufacturers entering the event with such equal chances of success was a major feature. "I could only keep up by driving flat-out" said Timo Salonen, who later went off the road in the underpowered Mazda. Ford was again making some best times, including semi-official driver Colin McRae, who made three fastest times as soon as the leaders' pace slackened near the end. Both of Mitsubishi's drivers held the lead, while all three top European drivers making their British debut (Miki Biasion, Didier Auriol and Alex Fiorio) made at least one best time. After two of Ford's drivers crashed, and with Fiorio still learning his way round the forests, sixth place McRae was best Ford finisher and gained Manufacturers' championship points for Ford.

If the overall lead saw a remarkable battle, Group N turned out to be a disaster. The reigning Group N champion Alain Oreille did not take part, the muddy forests of Britain were not a

First of two wins on Rally GB for Carlos Sainz.

Fifth place finish for Didier Auriol in his Jolly Club team Lancia.

The Lombard RAC Rally made many new friends this year; the pacenote system forced the organisers to make the route more compact, but focussed on the speeds now involved. One stage was effectively annulled when many top drivers averaged over 70 miles an hour; despite the ice (and no-studs rule), and the slow publicity stages, the total event was run for the first time at just over 60mph (almost 100km/h). But the mould had been broken, the resolute RAC Rally organisers had in one stroke shown itself willing to adjust and meet the international criteria with a smile.

Soon to become a familiar sight – Colin McRae with a crumpled rally car! He finished sixth, best Ford.

8 o'clock on a Sunday morning but the fans still turned out in Harrogate in numbers.

suitable place for his front-drive Renault. He waited for news about his championship rivals. While the Ford works driver Gwyndaf Evans was untouchable, Tommi Mäkinen's Mitsubishi was struck down with gearbox failure and the third championship rival Gustavo Trelles (Lancia) crashed. Evans apart, all the top Group N drivers retired, and for a long time a remarkable second place was held by Robbie Head in a Honda Civic, until he hit a bridge on the final morning and the Daihatsu Charade of Terry Kaby took his second place. So, as Oreille stood and watched his rivals self-destruct, the title came to him for a second time.

SAFER AS A SECRET?

The high number of accidents to competitors during the 1990 Lombard RAC Rally, in particular to the top drivers, has raised queries whether the decision to abandon the long-cherished secrecy of the routes through the forests was right. Of the 14 full professional entries received from the six top teams, eight of them were forced to retire, six either directly or indirectly as a result of going off the road. What did the drivers think?

Ari Vatanen (1981 World Champion and 1984 RAC Rally winner): "The system of checking the roads beforehand worked better than expected. Actually I thought there would be more accidents than there were." European competitors had always eyed the British round of the series with suspicion. Pacenotes significantly improves driver psychology, showing whether forests are 'failsafe.' And in fog the advantage is vast.

Drivers said they enjoyed the chance to see the places during recce, which they would normally only dash past at top speed. The organisers found, to their surprise, the rally was over-subscribed. 81 competitors inspected the whole route, another 40 inspected some of the route – and those who could not spare the time accepted the offer of pacenotes supplied by the organisers, made specially by former World Champion Björn Waldegård. Clerk of the Course Malcolm Neill said, "We did it to give equal opportunities to competitors, we just took a long time getting around to doing it."

Double World Champion Miki Biasion said "It was a very fast rally, but I must say I really enjoyed my first visit to Britain." But too fast? FISA Rallies Commission President Guy Goutard said "Where the rally went past areas with many spectators it was too fast. They could easily make changes, they are not short of available roads." One traditional feature remained. If a driver averaged over 110km/h (68mph) on a stage, they were given a standard minimum time and gained no advantage for being quicker. The rules stated competitors could only make two reconnaissance passes through each stage at specified times for each stage over a nine day period, and there was a maximum speed limit of 25km/h on all stages in reconnaissance, increased in later years.

RESULTS

Event held: 25-28 November 1990. 10th and final round of the Manufacturers' and 12th and final round of Drivers' championships. Start/Finish: Harrogate. Overnight halts: Harrogate and Newcastle upon Tyne.

176 starters, 94 finishers.
41 special stages – 352 miles (total 1466 miles).

General classification		Group	Penalties (h:m:s)
1 Sainz/Moya	Toyota Celica ST165	GA	5:43:16
2 Eriksson/Parmander	Mitsubishi Galant VR-4	GA	5:44:58
3 Biasion/Siviero	Lancia Delta Integrale	GA	5:47:22
4 Jonsson/Olsson	Toyota Celica ST165	GA	5:49:40
5 Auriol/Occelli	Lancia Delta Integrale	GA	5:51:02
6 McRae/Ringer	Ford Sierra Cosworth 4x4	GA	5:53:17
7 Schwarz/Wicha	Toyota Celica ST165	GA	5:54:56
8 Llewellin/Short	Toyota Celica ST165	GA	5:56:43
9 Fiorio/Pirollo	Ford Sierra Cosworth 4x4	GA	5:59:22
10 Droogmans/Joosten	Lancia Delta Integrale	GA	6:05:31
11 Evans/Davies	Ford Sierra Cosworth 4x4	GN	6:11:40

Leaders: Vatanen stage 1, Kankkunen 2, Alén 3, Kankkunen 4, Alén 5-8, Kankkunen 9-12, Eriksson 13-17, Sainz 18-29, Kankkunen 30-33, Sainz 34-41.

1991: Kankkunen wins, Sainz's disappointment

It was like a Hollywood epic: country boy against society sportsman, Finn against Spaniard. Whoever beat the other was going to be the 1991 World Drivers' Champion. No fewer than seven top teams took part, but nobody had expected anyone to match the pace of Toyota or of Lancia (who had won the Manufacturers' title at Sanremo Rally). And there was a lot of technical developments in the sport. This was the last event in which 40mm turbocharger restrictors were allowed, before 38mm ones became mandatory. Subaru had British developed engines for the first time, prepared in just six weeks, for which an extra 40bhp were claimed. Nissan had specially blended fuels to replace pump fuels previously used, and immediately claimed a 'minimum' increase of 30bhp. The evolution Mitsubishi, which had been the powerhouse at the mid-season Acropolis, was no longer the fastest car any more.

In 1990, the accidents of top drivers were the talking point of the Lombard RAC, and it was the same again this year. Drivers who

Didier Auriol led the rally before he lost time off the road.

One more chapter in Colin McRae's rally adventures, as Stig Blomqvist passes by in his Nissan Pulsar GTI-R.

are normally quite safe on their wheels went upside down during the course of this event. One driver who had spent his season on a strict leash, and was given the go-ahead to do his best, was Colin McRae. He repaid Subaru's support by proudly leading the event for a couple of stages. The first British driver to lead the event in the forests since Roger Clark 15 years before. Eventually he crashed twice, and had to

Toyota had a close working relationship with tyre supplier Pirelli. Here Carlos Sainz (left) takes advice from Pirelli's technician Fiorenzo Brivio.

Another upside-down moment for Markku Alén, this time in the Lake District.

retire, but his and his car's potential had been clearly noted. Alén shot into an early lead, but a puncture at stage 4 set him back. By then Juha Kankkunen was warming up and took the lead, only to fall behind on the second day when his steering worked itself loose. In Wales, McRae, despite running a long way down the field, was slowed down during an especially muddy stage. Another victim of a puncture had been Lancia driver Didier Auriol, but he was catching up fast, taking 24 seconds off everyone else at Hafren, the longest Welsh stage.

Auriol took the lead in Dovey Forest, but suffered another puncture in North Wales. Carlos Sainz was safely through Wales but as the rally moved northwards to the Lake District, he was uneasy. The water temperature on his Toyota was soaring to 130 degrees for no apparent reason, even though his stage times were not yet affected. His team eventually had to change the head gasket, and Sainz safely brought his car back to Harrogate that night, but the engine problem would be his downfall. He went off the road momentarily when he glanced at the water temperature gauge, enough for Kankkunen to overtake him. Sainz then allowed mechanics to take their time to get the car as reliable as they could in the hope that Kankkunen would in turn strike trouble.

Kankkunen entered the Kielder complex of special stages in third place and came out as the leader. The Kielder stages were to influence not only the course of the rally, but also the outcome of the '91 Title season. Rally leader Auriol was stuck off the road for a half-hour, and fell out of the top ten. Others who fell foul of Kielder included Markku Alén, Tommi Mäkinen (Mazda), Colin McRae and Stig Blomqvist. Blomqvist, whose Nissan team-mate David Llewellin had shown new pace, each gaining one fastest time, although their cars were not yet reliable. Mitsubishis finished strongly in second and fourth places, though Salonen was still ill at ease with the Galant, even after a season. In the end only one Subaru finished. Ari Vatanen, now back again with a different Japanese company, returned to Harrogate with a car that was unusually unmarked. Ford, however, was as unhappy as ever. Gwyndaf Evans crashed, unfortunately just one stage short of passing through his home town village in mid Wales, Malcolm Wilson retired after an unpleasant moment when the front transmission seized, and team-mate François Delecour struggled against almost overwhelming odds, including electrical discharge, fire extinguisher trouble, complete brake failure on his Ford, and a moment of indiscretion with the police to finish sixth. After countless gearbox changes Robbie Head was able to win Group N in his Ford Sierra Cosworth 4x4, and two similar cars took the next two places. Stig-Olov Walfridsson went off the road and damaged his Mitsubishi's engine. Group N Championship Ford driving contenders Fernando Capdevila and Carlos Menem Jr were out early on, while Grégoire de Mevius (Mazda) dropped from second to fourth on the last morning with turbocharger trouble.

CHANGE AT THE TOP

1991 was the year when 51-year-old Englishman Max Mosley became President of the Fédération Internationale du Sport Automobile (FISA), an autonomous committee delegated by the FIA for the organisation of motorsport. This was to be a stepping stone towards progressing to become President of the FIA in 1993. His background was in circuit racing and team management, leading on to playing a major role in the restructuring of Formula 1, but Mosley brought into the FIA a considerable amount of original thinking about rally sport. A large amount of this filtered through to change the format of rally sport, especially the WRC. Among Mosley's initial opinions about rallying was regret that there were not enough available places in teams for drivers competent to fill them. He also had an abhorrence of the visible financial wastage in the sport, and an urgent need to make the sport safer for spectators.

RESULTS

1991 Lombard RAC Rally
Event held: 24-27 November 1991. 10th and final round of Manufacturers' and 14th and final round in Drivers' championships. Start/Finish: Harrogate. Overnight halts: Chester and Harrogate.

151 starters, 82 finishers.
37 special stages – 349 miles (total 1464 miles).

General classification		Group	Penalties (h:m:s)
1 Kankkunen/Piironen	Lancia Delta Integrale 16v	GA	5:46:43
2 Eriksson/Parmander	Mitsubishi Galant VR-4	GA	5:49:35
3 Sainz/Moya	Toyota Celica ST165	GA	5:52:43
4 Salonen/Silander	Mitsubishi Galant VR-4	GA	5:55:34
5 Vatanen/Berglund	Subaru Legacy 4WD Turbo	GA	5:56:50
6 Delecour/Grataloup	Ford Sierra Cosworth 4x4	GA	6:02:04
7 Mikkola/Johansson	Mazda 323 GTX	GA	6:02:41
8 Duez/Wicha	Toyota Celica ST165	GA	6:08:44
9 Saby/Fauchille	Lancia Delta Integrale 16v	GA	6:10:42
10 Aitken-Walker/Thorner	Ford Sierra Cosworth 4x4	GA	6:23:29
11 Head/Roy	Ford Sierra Cosworth 4x4	GN	6:27:00

Leaders: Alén stages 1-3, Kankkunen 4, Alén 5, Alén & Kankkunen 6, Kankkunen 7-11, C McRae 12+13, Sainz 14+15, Auriol 16-19, Sainz 20-22, Auriol 23-31, Kankkunen 32-37.

1992: Lombard's 19th and final year

Didier Auriol's title challenge came to an end with burned out plug leads on his Lancia on the last evening in Kielder. After earlier delays he had been hauling in the leading Carlos Sainz at such a rate that ultimate victory looked assured. With his other challenger Juha Kankkunen falling behind, Sainz then had the championship within his grasp, and he finally clinched this at the finish of the four-day event. Toyota's rival team Martini Racing had already gained the Manufacturers' title for Lancia, but bad tactical errors in the Drivers' battle at Lancia had begun six weeks previously. They had taken their eye off the tactics of their driver line-up. The chances of the Auriol team losing the championship title (which would happen only if he scored virtually no points in either Spain or Britain) seemed too remote to consider seriously. Sainz, however, proved unbeatable in the forests of Britain and gained his second title – this time for Toyota.

The 1992 Lombard RAC Rally seemed to have everything: more entries than last year, a record pace of the winner, and two world titles which would only be resolved in the closing hours of the event. There was also the inspired idea of a contingency prize of £100,000, should a British driver win the event outright. Three drivers began the event

Success for Alister McRae, winning Group N in his Ford Sierra Cosworth 4x4.

with expectations of gaining the World Drivers' title. Sainz however had been surprised at the pace of Colin McRae's Subaru, particularly on the second day in Wales when McRae took the lead, which was magic stuff for the British spectators who turned out in huge numbers in the border country regions on the third day. The spectators were to cause trouble later on.

The Lancia Martini cars were off the boil on this occasion. The cars had given the impression all year of near-invincibility, but here they were unable to handle the wet greasy surfaces of the British forests in November. Michelin's men took drastic steps in darkest Wales as they carved full tread blocks from their tyres when the Pirelli shod Toyota and Subaru pulled away from them. It was only when conditions started to dry out on the third day that things began to go the way they liked. But just as it looked like Sainz would be overtaken by Auriol, the Frenchman's car failed and he abandoned his car in the stage.

Second place for Subaru was compensation, after McRae had been leading for five stages but had a puncture on the first stage of the third day, losing the lead to Sainz. Rally rules prevented a thorough check of the car at this point, and on the next stage he lost the front brakes. Colin reset the transmission to compensate, but this overloaded the system and lost the drive to the rear wheels. Four minutes cost him any chance of victory and claiming Lombard's financial bounty. McRae's misfortunes helped to dismay the spectators who had thronged the Kielder stages the next evening. Things took a sombre turn through unexpected problems faced by the organisers. Twice within three stages there were delays because spectators were ill, and then when crews were told to drive through the cancelled stage 24 at non-competitive speeds, spectators gave vent to the competitors. Later they caused stage 28 to be stopped as well.

There was a poor showing by the Nissan Group A team which led to the team being wound up for good. Any sparks of performance from its drivers were smothered by tyre troubles, coupled with demoralising realisation that its privately run Group N cars were more successful. The Ford team suffered strange suspension troubles (although Malcolm Wilson showed surprising flair between misfortunes: between him and Colin they collectively scored more best times than drivers from any

The beauty of a British forest in autumn.

This was the final appearance for the troubled Nissan Motorsports Europe rally team which was disbanded after this event. Stig Blomqvist retired off the road and Tommi Mäkinen (pictured) finished a disappointing eighth.

Final RAC Rally victory for Carlos Sainz, who led most of the way.

other nation), but the legendary consistency of Miki Biasion brought Ford fifth place. The Mitsubishi of Kenneth Eriksson never looked good or fast. So ended the strange season-long enigma of Auriol. The man whose career was going perfectly until he announced his wish to change camps next year, after which he had serious problems every rally, and was seemingly unconcerned. He simply put it down to bad luck.

In Group N three championship contenders started the event while another stayed at home. Alister McRae's Ford won the category on the event, and Grégoire de Mevius won the Group N Cup (the only WRC title to be won by Nissan). Tuesday evening ended in organisational confusion when Dave Metcalfe jammed a stage causing a build up of blocked cars behind. Metcalfe, who had been leading the unofficial 'formula 2' category in the new Astra GSi 16 valve, had lost a wheel; strangely this was also the fate of the Peugeot 309GT1 of his nearest two-wheel drive rival, Richard Burns. The 2-litre category was then dominated by the 1.3-litre Škoda Favorits.

1992 marked the end of the Group A programme for the Nissan Pulsar GTI-R team after two disappointing years in the WRC. The team's only podium result had been third place on the 1992 Swedish Rally.

Other factors, however, were not equal. The quality of fuel took on a new significance; the use of special fuels was estimated to give an increase of 60/70bhp over pump fuel, meaning that the advisory 300bhp limit was still easily exceeded by all the top teams. In 1995 the restrictor size was reduced to 34mm, in 2011 to 33mm.

RESULTS

Event held: 22-25 November 1992. 10th and final round of Manufacturers' and 14th and final round in Drivers' championships. Start/Finish: Chester. Overnight halts: Chester and Carlisle.

157 starters, 101 finishers.
34 special stages but one cancelled – 331 miles (total 1551 miles).

General classification		Group	Penalties (h:m:s)
1 Sainz/Moya	Toyota Celica ST185	GA	5:23:06
2 Vatanen/Berglund	Subaru Legacy 4WD	GA	5:25:22
3 Kankkunen/Piironen	Lancia HF Integrale	GA	5:25:51
4 Alén/Kivimaki	Toyota Celica ST185	GA	5:26:35
5 Biasion/Siviero	Ford Sierra Cosworth 4x4	GA	5:26:47
6 C McRae/Ringer	Subaru Legacy 4WD	GA	5:31:14
7 Eriksson/Parmander	Mitsubishi Galant VR-4	GA	5:33:26
8 Mäkinen/Harjanne	Nissan Pulsar GTI-R	GA	5:35:07
9 Wilson/Thomas	Ford Sierra Cosworth 4x4	GA	5:35:26
10 Aghini/Farnocchia	Lancia HF Integrale	GA	5:37:58
14 A McRae/Senior	Ford Sierra Cosworth 4x4	GN	5:57:37

Leaders: Sainz stages 1-14, C McRae 15-19, Sainz 20-34.

1993: Juha Kankkunen wins on the ice

Juha Kankkunen won his 20th World Championship Rally, making him the most successful WRC driver. Three of the four top teams that entered, Toyota, Mitsubishi and Subaru, all led, but Ford was off the pace, though it dominated Group N. The use of studless tyres on sheet ice made this quite the most treacherous rally this season, but without suffering the usual mechanical stress, all the top cars except for Colin McRae's Subaru finished. "Almost every corner could have been our last!" was all that four times World Champion Juha Kankkunen could say to convey the drama of driving on sheet ice and snow in his Toyota Celica Turbo 4WD without studs. His third RAC Rally win was

François Delecour in the snow with his officially entered Escort RS Cosworth. This new model was introduced earlier in the year.

Splendid second place for Kenneth Eriksson's Mitsubishi Lancer Evo. This was the first year of competition for the remarkable series of Lancer Evo cars, and the model's best result in the WRC to date.

quite the hardest. "We had a bad moment on every stage," Kankkunen said. He had battled for the lead with Armin Schwarz, and finally stayed ahead when McRae broke his radiator, damaged by a foreign object, and the engine suffered terminal overheating. Graciously the Finn told the Scotsman not to be too disappointed. "It had taken me 11 years before I eventually won my own home event." It would take Colin seven attempts.

After poor results earlier in the season the Mitsubishi Lancer Evolutions went well; Armin Schwarz led on the opening day before going off the road on Day 2. Always close behind the leaders, and after revelling in the icy conditions team-mate Kenneth Eriksson eventually scored his third second place on the event in four years. Ford, however, despite successes in the championship earlier this year with its new Escort RS Cosworth, had an unhappy time. The team had the embarrassment of the semi-official car of third placed British driver Malcolm Wilson, admittedly on his 18th attempt on this event, finishing ahead. Of Lancia there was no sign, the championship challenge of its privately run team in tatters after its entry for Carlos Sainz was excluded on the Sanremo Rally for fuel offences.

Some of the most surprising people had disappointments. Frenchman Didier Auriol was completely off form in his Toyota, although he finished third in the World series for the third year in succession. Swede Mats Jonsson in the works-run Toyota could not re-adjust himself to driving without studs, while, also under stress, Ari Vatanen hoped for a good result to prove his continued value to Subaru. In fact, Sainz announced he was moving to Subaru, notwithstanding the announcement of his contract with the company for 1994. Vatanen went off the road and could only come fifth, he moved over to Ford the next year. Ford's saving grace was in Group N where it finished 1-2-4 and that Gwyndaf Evans' winning Group N car made the first fastest time on a WRC rally for six years.

The effect of the weather was endless. The studless tyres of the passing rally cars polished the icy surfaces. At the furthest north stage of the rally there was a complete blockage of cars and stranded crews were given permission to restart the rally after the next overnight halt in Gateshead. The road sections were just as dangerous as the stages. Vatanen said he went off the road avoiding a road accident collision – with his own service vehicle!

In the two-wheel drive 'Formula 2' the Vauxhall Astra of David Llewellin finished five minutes ahead of the Škoda Favorits of Emil Triner and Pavel Sibera. Grégoire de Mevius had engine trouble after a fanbelt pulley failure with the new Group A Nissan Sunny GTI when leading, and

Toyota's winning team relied on extensive servicing arrangements, with service points sometimes in quite remote locations.

Third place Malcolm Wilson finished the best Escort RS Cosworth entered by Michelin Pilot Team Ford. Here he tackles the very slippery Myherin stage.

Jimmy McRae's VW went off the road after suffering tyre problems and retired. Llewellin's Astra team-mate Mark Higgins fell back after going off the road.

NEW RULES FOR 1993

Many new rules were introduced for the 1993 season, divided into sporting and technical rules, many instigated by the new Sporting President Max Mosley, with cost saving in mind. In the sporting realm there were only 13 rallies in the World Championship with the restriction, allowing points scoring participation in only ten events for both Drivers' (as in 1992) and Manufacturers.' This new limit for teams in turn demanded a system of prior registration. Manufacturers gave FISA (now disbanded and incorporated within the FIA itself) the names of the drivers who would represent them.

The season also saw the start of restrictions on servicing, with a limit allowing only one turbocharger change per day, plus only having one spare transmission per rally: the latter could only be changed at the end of a day. These rules heavily increased the burden on scrutineers. Midway through the season the FISA had introduced a 'Flying Squad' of technical inspectors, able to carry out spot checks wherever they pleased. Performance reducing measures came into force. The most significant was the use of lead-free control fuel, produced by a single supplier (Carless in Britain), and mandatory for events in Europe for top teams.

The next measure was to increase minimum weights: for the class in which the top teams were running (3.5-litre Group A) the minimum rose to 1200 from 1100kg. At first it was assumed that rally cars would be running ballast all the time, but in reality the cars were running in heavier specification because of other factors. The new rules required a replacement turbocharger to be carried on board all the time. No-servicing rules meant crews had already started carrying some spare parts. Because crews often changed tyres in no-service areas, stronger jacks were fitted. The decision among Michelin users to run with ATS inserts all the time also increased the total weight.

Wheel widths were also reduced, usually by one inch, and overall diameter of the tyre could not exceed 650mm. These changes caused the tyre manufacturers to concentrate on 15 inch tyres for gravel use and 17 for asphalt. There was an early difficulty for Michelin having to produce new size anti-deflation ATS inserts for the first two rounds of the championship. Heavier weight and narrower tyres were a double problem! By the 1000 Lakes, there was such confidence in the anti-deflation ATS inserts they were used even on the fastest stages.

RESULTS

Event held: 21-24 November 1993. 13th and final round of Manufacturers' and Drivers' championships. Start/Finish: Birmingham. Overnight halts: Birmingham, Lancaster and Gateshead.

165 starters, 94 finishers.
35 special stages – 338 miles (total 1633 miles).

General classification		Group	Penalties (h:m:s)
1 Kankkunen/Grist	Toyota Celica Turbo ST185	GA	6:25:48
2 Eriksson/Parmander	Mitsubishi Lancer Evolution	GA	6:27:32
3 Wilson/Thomas	Ford Escort RS Cosworth	GA	6:31:26
4 Delecour/Grataloup	Ford Escort RS Cosworth	GA	6:32:57
5 Vatanen/Berglund	Subaru Impreza 555	GA	6:33:59
6 Auriol/Ocelli	Toyota Celica Turbo ST185	GA	6:39:39
7 Burns/Reid	Subaru Legacy 4WD Turbo	GA	6:47:25
8 Schwarz/Thul	Mitsubishi Lancer Evolution	GA	6:51:02
9 Jonsson/Backman	Toyota Celica Turbo 4WD	GA	7:00:48
10 A McRae/Senior	Subaru Legacy 4WD Turbo	GA	7:02:12
11 Evans/Davies	Ford Escort RS Cosworth	GN	7:10:44

Leaders: Kankkunen stage 1, Schwarz 2-4, Schwarz & Kankkunen 5, Kankkunen 6-18, C McRae 19-21, Kankkunen 22-35.

1994: 50th RAC Rally, Auriol a surprised Champion

This was a rally of two dimensions: firstly, the WRC Drivers' title battle in which Didier Auriol, avenging his bitter disappointment of two years earlier, became the first French World Rally champion, and secondly, the first RAC Rally win for Colin McRae at his eighth attempt – the first home victory for 18 years. This was an event which McRae's Subaru team-mate Carlos Sainz should have won. Auriol had started the rally 11 points ahead of Sainz, but he had a very troubled event and the title was only clinched by Auriol when the Spaniard went off the road on the last morning. The Frenchman was then able to cruise to the end. He finished sixth after losing four minutes on the first day after hitting a rock, and ten minutes when he rolled off the road later on, and on Day 2 lost another four minutes when the turbo failed. "For me a perfect event is when I have driven perfectly to win. To become Champion in these circumstances is amazing, but I'm not complaining!" After all this had happened McRae was in the lead, having gone well on slippery stages where his Subaru's Pirelli tyres worked well while the Michelins of rival teams lost their consistency in mid stages.

There had been tension throughout the four-day event. On the first day, Sainz escaped a penalty despite reports he had been pushed by other competitors after losing water from his engine when the radiator broke. As Auriol encountered one problem after another, few

Juha Kankkunen shows the sleek (if dirty) lines of the Celica ST205 on the way to second place.

Nissan was now represented on events by two-litre, two-wheel-drive 'Formula 2' Sunny GTI cars. Here is Tommi Mäkinen on his way to winning his class, ninth overall.

predicted he could retain his Championship lead. At one point he was 94th overall but the Frenchman was not fazed. He continued at a pace he felt safe to pursue. At the end of the event Auriol was half an hour behind the leaders, but still won the title. Elsewhere at Subaru, Day

Everything was finally coming together for Colin McRae. Here he is gaining the first of his three Rally GB victories.

2 saw an early exit for Subaru's third driver Richard Burns when he went off the road on stage 9, after he hit a rock and broke the suspension. This, the final event for the Ford Boreham team, was a disaster. Its best result was only third place for Bruno Thiry, on his first ever RAC Rally. François Delecour went home in disgrace. He went off the road during a stage, became disorientated, mistakenly cut out a large portion of the stage route, and was excluded. Miki Biasion had engine failure, Malcolm Wilson crashed, and on the final day the team's radio relay plane was forced to land with engine failure.

The RAC Rally brought other championship categories to a climax. Jesus Puras cruised to third place in Group N and won the Production Car title in front of Isolde Holderied, who had already secured the Ladies' title, but confusion still continued in the 2-litre Cup. Protracted delays in deciding what to do about the wrong fuel used by the GME team in Australia meant the teams left Chester with the 2-litre title still unresolved.

In the contemporary debate about the future formulae for rallying, 'Formula 2' (2-litre front-wheel drive) cars performed better than ever expected. The major battle between the Nissan Sunny GTI of fastest driver Tommi Mäkinen, the unproven Ford for Gwyndaf Evans, and the championship contending Opel Astra of Grégoire de Mevius, brought all three of them into top ten overall positions. Evans drove the Gordon Spooner team's development RS2000, a car which had never shone in earlier, smaller events, and so his 'F2' win provided a clear hope for future success. Leader in this category on stages 1 and 2 was Alister McRae, but his Nissan stopped with electrical trouble on Day 2. Mäkinen inherited the lead then lost it to Evans when he suffered a puncture. Evans lost the lead after stage 17 when the gearbox failed, but regained it on stage 24 from Mäkinen when the Finn overturned. Nevertheless, Mäkinen fought back after his excursion and climbed up to finish second. Škoda cars finished sixth and seventh in the category (taking 1-2-3 in their class) and claimed their 22nd class win on the event in as many years. There was a lucky finish for Martin Rowe in the British Peugeot 306S16 whose car was fitted with sequential gear

Unlucky event for Miki Biasion, his Ford retiring on the second evening.

change that was virtually untested before the start. In the last two stages a wheel fell off and a suspension strut broke, but still he maintained his fifth place. There was disappointment for David Llewellin in a new model Astra which could not match the speed of de Mevius' old style version. Not until after this event did the Stewards of the preceding Rally Australia meet to debate the Opel's fuel offence on their event. Before then the championship ended with three manufacturers separated by two points, but Opel eventually lost its points from Australia, leaving Škoda to win the 2-litre title.

After scoring his first two WRC victories both far away in New Zealand, Colin McRae scored his first WRC win in Europe. "My lasting memory of this year's RAC Rally was the final day, after my team-mate Carlos Sainz retired. It became clear that I had a real chance of being allowed to win the event! On every stage it seemed more and more people were on the sides of the road. Towards the end people were standing all the way down the stages, cheering, waving flags. My co-driver Derek Ringer and I had the feeling that if the car had suddenly stopped, it would have been physically carried to the end of the stage! The car was fitted with a hydraulically-controlled front differential system. This new system, which Prodrive only developed during the year, meant you can tuck the front of the car inside the corners without fear that the rear will spin you round. It worked well especially on highly cambered roads in the forests!"

This was the final event for Ford's competition activities at Boreham in Essex which ceased after the end of 1994. Ford entered no fewer than six Escort RS Cosworths.

ROTATION

This was the first of three years in which a WRC event rotation system applied. The FIA had become overwhelmed by increasing pressure from new rallies for inclusion in the WRC calendar each year. The plan was to rotate eligibility for the full WRC series with the FIA's 2-litre series. When it was the turn of a WRC event to be rested from the series, that event would qualify for the 2-litre series. Events would count for both series or one or the other, events counting only for the 2-litre events were called "W2L." The RAC Rally's turn to be rested would come in 1996, after which the whole system was dismantled.

RESULTS

1994 Network Q RAC Rally
Event held: 20-23 November 1994. 10th and final round of Manufacturers' and Drivers' championships and 8th round of World 2-Litre Championship for Manufacturers.' Start/Finish: Chester. Overnight halts: Harrogate and Chester.

178 starters, 97 finishers.
29 special stages – 323 miles (total 1469 miles).

General classification		Group	Penalties (h:m:s)
1 C McRae/Ringer	Subaru Impreza 555	GA	5:17:25
2 Kankkunen/Grist	Toyota Celica ST185	GA	5:20:58
3 Thiry/Prevot	Ford Escort RS Cosworth	GA	5:27:37
4 Blomqvist/Melander	Ford Escort RS Cosworth	GA	5:30:13
5 Vatanen/Pons	Ford Escort RS Cosworth	GA	5:34:25
6 Auriol/Occelli	Toyota Celica ST185	GA	5:47:57
7 Evans/Davies	Ford Escort RS2000	GA	5:52:24
8 Habig/Judd	Ford Escort RS Cosworth	GA	5:53:16
9 Mäkinen/Harjanne	Nissan Sunny GTI	GA	5:53:25
10 de Mevius/Lux	Opel Astra GSi	GA	5:53:54
12 Milner/Turvey	Ford Escort RS Cosworth	GN	5:57:37

Leaders: Sainz stages 1+2, C McRae 3-29.

1995: Colin McRae – Britain's first Champion

What a difference a year made! Only 12 months ago Subaru had its first RAC Rally win, and was wondering if and when it would eventually win one of the sport's supreme titles. This year Subaru cars finished 1-2-3, driver Colin McRae was World Champion driver, and its team was World Champion Manufacturer! Colin was 27 years and 109 days old when he won the title, a record as the youngest ever winner of the title (still valid as this book was written nearly a quarter century later), beating the record by four months set by Juha Kankkunen nine years earlier, and over two years younger than Ari Vatanen when he won in 1981. The exploding career of Colin McRae attracted considerable fan interest in the rally. There were large crowds lining the streets around Chester race course even before the 8 o'clock start, cheering when Colin drove past, and politely clapping for Carlos!

With teams now entering every event and expecting their drivers to compete for them regularly through the season, the FIA launched a system of season-long dedicated competition numbers. A neat idea, with an unfortunate consequence at the end of 1995! It was always a lottery being the final rally in the championship. In previous years either every team rushed to the RAC Rally, or teams who had already achieved their championship objectives did not enter, or worse still cancelled their entries. In 1995, Toyota cars (as reigning champion Manufacturer) carried numbers 1, 2 and 3. The RAC Rally traditionally reserved its prestigious number 1 start, often for last year's winning driver. It was therefore a nightmare when Toyota was banned from competing in the WRC after Catalunya Rally because of its celebrated turbocharger indiscretions. Missing from this rally, therefore, were numbers 1 Auriol, 2 Kankkunen and 3 Schwarz. The hastily revised entry list now started at number 4!

Catalunya Rally three weeks earlier witnessed team orders that had

This picture could have been staged – but it wasn't! Colin McRae storms through Kielder forest on his way to the World title, encouraged by fellow Scots fans.

created inevitable tension, leaving McRae and Sainz equal on points going in to the RAC. This time there were no reasons for the Prodrive team to issue team orders, no ulterior objectives remaining to achieve. Subaru knew one of its drivers would be champion before the event started, and that it could beat Mitsubishi to the Manufacturers' series as well. This was to be a classic shoot-out. Whichever driver beat the other would be Champion! Once the rally reached the forests Subaru's team-mates Sainz and McRae led all the way. After Sainz had damaged his car at a water crossing, the first day spectator stages saw a battle between the Mitsubishis of Mäkinen and Eriksson. From then on it was Subaru all the way. McRae fought hard after a second-day puncture let Sainz lead, before he finally overtook Sainz two days later, when McRae became uncatchable in the wet and foggy conditions.

Mitsubishi's title hopes ended when Tommi Mäkinen crashed on the second day, and Kenneth Eriksson then crashed into a river on day three. Although its third entry of Rui Madeira in a Group N car finished a remarkable sixth overall, its total points were too small to threaten Subaru. Best non Subaru was the Ford of Alister McRae which was run privately by Malcolm Wilson's company, despite a roll on day two. The Sole surviving semi-official RAS team Ford of Bruno Thiry finished fifth after Malcolm Wilson crashed and François Delecour had transmission trouble while sixth overall, the top 'Formula 2' car for the second year running, was Gwyndaf Evans' Ford Escort RS2000. Renault entered kit car versions of the Clio Maxi for its first major event on gravel surfaces, and finished third in the category with Alain Oreille behind Evans and the Nissan of Jarmo Kytölehto. The Škoda

French driver Alain Oreille finished tenth overall, second best 'Formula 2' competitor in this Renault Clio Maxi. It was his first time on this event and his last WRC appearance.

Bruno Thiry's works-supported Ford Escort RS Cosworth was entered and run by the RAS Ford team in Belgium.

team scored a class win in the 1600cc division of 'F2' in the hands of guest driver Stig Blomqvist. Stig finished sixth in 'F2.' The wet and slippery conditions were again ideal for Pirelli-shod cars, with the first four overall finishers and the Group N winner all using its tyres. Both Michelin and Pirelli users fitted the anti-deflation mousse inserts throughout, but both had significant failures on the very fast stages in northern England on the second leg.

The Network Q RAC Rally ended the season on a wistful note. The recent exclusion of Toyota from the World Championship left former World Champions (Didier Auriol and Juha Kankkunen) without drives for 1996. Mitsubishi had already only confirmed one regular WCR driver for 1996 (Tommi Mäkinen), and Ford none at all. At the end of the RAC Rally, the only team with a fully defined future programme and line-up was Subaru, which had Colin McRae, Kenneth Eriksson and Piero Liatti already signed up. Toyota meanwhile stayed at home examining the possibilities of a return to WRC competition under the World Rally Car regulations in 1997.

GM announced that Britain's Vauxhall Sport Rally Team was to be disbanded at the end of the 1995 season. Vauxhall would, however, continue to support the Rally of Wales, which was the first round of the British championship, and, through its associated company Network Q, the RAC Rally.

THE MOSLEY EFFECT

By now the electoral promises for WRC reform made by FIA President Max Mosley were beginning to be seen everywhere. Engine power outputs were now further controlled with both Group A and Group N cars having the diameter of their turbo restrictor sizes reduced by 4mm, to 34 and 32mm respectively. Pre-rally recce times were substantially shortened from an 11 day period to a seven day period, with each stage limited to three passes per crew. Ways of limiting servicing were being trialled. Now servicing was to be permitted in: (a) official service parks, normally after every 50/60km of special stages, where any authorised work could be carried out; (b) auxiliary service areas where only refuelling and tyre changing, using only spare wheels carried onboard the car, could take place, or (c) other places where any work done had to be carried out only by the crew using spare parts and tools carried in their rally car. New rules limiting the number of tyres each competitor could use during an event were controlled by teams bar-coding their tyres. The sport was gradually being brought under control.

RESULTS

1995 Network Q RAC Rally
Event held: 19-22 November 1995. 8th and final round of Manufacturers' and Drivers' championships.
Start/Finish: Chester. Overnight halts: Leeds and Chester.

176 starters, 95 finishers.
28 special stages – 317 miles (total 1446 miles).

General classification		Group	Penalties (h:m:s)
1 C McRae/Ringer	Subaru Impreza 555	GA	5:09:19
2 Sainz/Moya	Subaru Impreza 555	GA	5:09:55
3 Burns/Reid	Subaru Impreza 555	GA	5:15:58
4 A McRae/Wood	Ford Escort RS Cosworth	GA	5:20:34
5 Thiry/Prevot	Ford Escort RS Cosworth	GA	5:21:11
6 Evans/Davies	Ford Escort RS2000	GA	5:42:07
7 Madeira/Silva	Mitsubishi Lancer Evolution III	GN	5:44:04
8 Kytölehto/Kapanen	Nissan Sunny GTI	GA	5:45:19
9 Kamioka/Gormley	Subaru Impreza WRX-RA	GN	5:50:21
10 Oreille/Boyere	Renault Clio Maxi	GA	5:50:40

Leaders: Sainz & Mäkinen stage 1, C McRae 2, Eriksson 3, Mäkinen 4-7, C McRae 8, Sainz 9-20, C McRae 21-28.

The Icon of the Age – Colin McRae

No one person can be said to epitomise the spirit of the Group A rally age more than the British driver Colin McRae, who in 1995 became his nation's first FIA World Rally Driver's Champion, but, sadly, died in a helicopter accident in 2005, aged 39. This appreciation was published by *The Independent* newspaper:

There was always something very special about Colin Steele McRae. He was the first British driver not only to popularise rally sport in Britain and then elsewhere, but at the same time to succeed at it as well. His win or bust approach to the sport, coming in the days of a developing television platform, captured the imagination of the public. The stories of his many crashes, usually free of personal injury, were vividly portrayed for all to see. It was therefore ironic that he died in a flying accident, a discipline in which he always claimed he never took risks.

Colin was brought up in a motorsport family. Father Jimmy had a plumbing business and enjoyed motorsport for a hobby, before developing it into a professional activity in which he became British rally champion five times. But even as his father was discovering his own prowess in the sport, the next generation was coming along fast. Colin was born with speed in his blood and his successes on wheels started at age 13 when he was Scottish schoolboy motocross champion. At 16 he won

West Scotland autotest championship. As soon as he reached the age of 17, he borrowed an Avenger from a friend in his local Coltness Car Club before the inevitable happened. They went off the road and were stuck in a peat bog. At that time Colin's only competition car was one he used for autotest (high speed driving test manoeuvres) competition, and to go one step further he decided to buy a Talbot Sunbeam. His first rally in his own car was in 1985, a traditional end of season social event called the Galloway Hills Rally, and once again he went off the road, but this time with greater severity than before. The 1986 Scottish championship beckoned. His father saw Colin's latent potential and lent him his own co-driver Ian Grindrod. Colin started to finish rallies! Part way through the season he was joined by Derek Ringer who went on to work with Colin off and on throughout his career.

There were so many enthusiasts in the Scottish world of rallying, and many of them played a part in the Colin McRae story. Colin was still only 19 when he took a lady co-driver with him on a local event. It was the start of many chapters. It was his first ever overall victory, and the lady who brought him success was Alison Hamilton, who later went on to become Mrs Colin McRae. Colin went on to win the 1988 Scottish championship, an achievement his father never managed, in the same year when his father won the British championship for the fifth and final time. It was time to move onwards and upwards. Through the help of the British Junior Rally Team Colin already had the chance to take his Nova to the Swedish Rally, which he finished and came third in his class, his first World Championship event. In 1988 he had the chance to find his feet in British championship rallies as well. At this time the national Peugeot rally team were anxious to help develop young British rally driver talent. The prize for winning his class on the national championship was the use of a 205 GTI on the 1988 Lombard RAC Rally, the engine however failed. This was the end of his days in small two-wheel drive rally cars. From 1989, he turned to bigger cars.

The moment Colin McRae began to progress through 1989 and 1990 with Ford Sierra rally cars was fundamental to his career and led to the invitation to drive for the official Subaru team in the 1991 British championship. He then became integrated into the Subaru World Championship team, an association which took him and Derek Ringer through to the end of the 1998 season. The Colin McRae legend had already begun. The alternation between success and badly damaged cars was developing, and much of this was inspired by Colin's fascination with the career of Ari Vatanen, who had a similar approach to the sport. It was a moment of great satisfaction when Colin became Ari's junior team-mate at Subaru. They worked well together and results came. In 1993 Colin scored Subaru's first World Championship victory, in New Zealand, the year before the company embarked on its Impreza competition programme. It was widely stated at the time that the Impreza rally programme would never have started unless Subaru scored at least one victory with the older Legacy model …

These were formative days in the sport when the World Championship adopted very specific concepts. The championship rules now required full driver commitments, regulations were being modelled after Formula 1, technical regulations led to the World Rally Cars which continue to this day and the manufacturer interest in the sport was booming. Colin played a major role in these days. His New Zealand victory in 1993 was a British driver's first World Rally victory for 17 years, Colin went on to become the first British World Rally champion in 1995, a feat followed six years later by his friend and rival, the late Richard Burns.

Colin's move to Ford in 1999 was the start of another major step forward. It was never officially confirmed but it is clear that Colin became easily the world's highest paid rally driver to date with an annual fee stated to be over £3M. Over the years Colin developed a team-mate rivalry and an immense mutual respect with Carlos Sainz during their times at Subaru, Ford and later at Citroën. Ironically it was a cost cutting contraction of the sport, instigated by the international sporting authorities, which spelled the end of Colin's full-time career in World Championship rallying. Citroën had to choose between Colin and Carlos for its number two seat for the 2004 season, and Sainz's stronger commercial connections left McRae out in the cold.

He never lost his flair, as demonstrated on his occasional drives with Škoda, especially when he looked like taking a Fabia onto the podium in Australia in 2005 before mechanical troubles intervened. His final World Championship rally was in Turkey in 2006 when he substituted for Sébastien Loeb, and again he was forced to retire.

Colin created considerable worldwide acclaim through the computer game to which he gave his name. There was a sector of enthusiasts who knew the McRae name through the game and assumed that Colin was a male version of the fictional Lara Croft! After his World Championship career ended, Colin took part on various cross country rally events. He was awarded the MBE by the Queen in 1996. His father continues to compete on rallies, usually with historic cars, his younger brother Alister was himself British champion in 1995 and still competes. Colin had a second brother, Stuart, who never followed Colin and Alister into the sport. For a long time the family lived together at Lanark, before Colin moved for financial reasons for a while to Monte Carlo before moving back to Lanark, while Alister married and settled in Perth, Western Australia.

1996: RAC Rally's championship "rest year"

Making up for its absence the year before, Toyota entered cars for Juha Kankkunen and Armin Schwarz although the "2-litre-only" event status meant no full WRC points could be won on this event. It was the only top level WRC team present. While Kankkunen slid off the road on the first day and retired, Schwarz cruised effortlessly in treacherous conditions to victory. He became the first driver recorded as leading the RAC Rally from start to finish, as did Škoda's 50-year-old veteran driver Stig Blomqvist in the 'Formula 2' (W2L) category, which he also led all the way. He came third overall, 25 years after he first won the event outright. The strength of entry this year lay not only with the 'F2' cars, with official or dealer entries from Škoda, Ford, Volkswagen, SEAT, Renault, Honda and Nissan, but with the private drivers. The 182 cars that started were far in excess of any WRC event for almost two years. It was also the chance for private teams to run full Group A specification cars without being swamped by the big teams headed by Japanese Subaru driver Masao Kamioka. The event was boosted in the public image by the entry of the Formula 1 driver Martin Brundle with a Ford Escort RS Cosworth. No current Grand Prix driver had ever finished the RAC, though future F1 driver Vic Elford had finished third in 1964.

Snow and ice made this an amazing event. After a series of misfortunes on the opening stages, the top Finnish drivers Kankkunen, Ari Vatanen and Jarmo Kytölehto all retired as a result of going off the road. Many of the top team drivers were forced to retire after going off the road – apart from two works Škodas which suffered engine failure, and the Polish champion Krzysztof Holowczyc, who retired out of time after taking a wrong turning. On no previous occasion could the conditions at the beginning of the event have been more daunting for a newcomer. Brundle twice went off the road before he retired, though on one rare occasion in clear conditions he had scored a second best stage time. "I have driven competition cars at night at Le Mans, Sebring and Daytona, but I have never driven a competition car out of a hotel on sheet ice before!" One stage was abandoned altogether, and many competitors on another had to be diverted.

The rule forbidding studs on British forest events caused considerable difficulties

Even his magical Formula 1 driving skills and the experience of co-driver Roger Freeman did not keep Martin Brundle on the wintry roads. They retired off the road.

Gearbox trouble thwarted Jörgen Jonasson's event in this Volkswagen Golf GTi 16v.

Wintry conditions plus the '2-litre only' status of the 1996 event gave Škoda a heaven-sent chance of a podium result with this Felicia Kit Car 1600.

Armin Schwarz's ST205 (pictured) walked away with a victory of almost eight minutes ahead of the Subaru of Masao Kamioka, the highest result on the RAC Rally for a Japanese driver.

for organisers and drivers alike. Impending difficulties became obvious when crews reported before the start that they could not cover every special stage in their recce in the time allowed because of snow. The problem was that when temperatures fell in late afternoon the stage surfaces became glazed. Three years earlier, similar problems had struck the event in the Kielder forest stages. This time the problems struck the rally further south in Hamsterley forest. Overall time allowances had to be retrospectively adjusted, and some drivers completed a whole day before knowing if they should have been excluded earlier in the event. These problems had a serious effect. Drivers such as Vatanen and Alister McRae retired from the event, out of time, later claiming they had given up for no good reason.

Until seven stages before the finish Škoda was confidently expecting to take the W2L title. Its only misfortune until then had been an engine failure for the Czech driver Emil Triner. But when Triner's team-mate Pavel Sibera also had engine failure, the race for the title opened up for Renault and SEAT. Renault had entered a four-car team, but only one driver (Grégoire de Mevius) finished, so it was the superior consistency of SEAT through the season, despite losing its star driver Jesus Puras on the first stage on this event, that won Renault the title. Seven of the top ten W2L cars at the finish were from different manufacturers. All in all, it was a most extraordinary event, the end of the Rotation era and in many ways the right moment to welcome in a brave new future next year!

This was the end of the Group A era as we knew it! World Rally Cars were coming …

A WINTER NIGHTMARE
The organisers explained their insuperable problems in a statement. "42 crews went beyond their maximum permitted lateness on Saturday (the opening day when the route went to the Scottish Borders, then down to the overnight halt in Leeds) due to the extreme and worsening weather conditions. As a result of which the rally convoy was extended from the normal three and a half hours (cars running at one-minute intervals) to over six hours. Wishing to protect the interests of as many competitors as possible, the organisers proposed an extension of maximum lateness to the FIA Stewards before the end of Leg 1. As a direct consequence of the extended convoy length, it was impossible for the Stewards to consider the matter before the

start of Leg 2 (Sunday) without prejudice to the affected crews. All 42 crews were therefore permitted to take part in Leg 2 under notice of possible exclusion. The FIA Stewards met on Sunday night and decided to take the exceptional step of extending the maximum permitted lateness between controls on Leg 1 from 15 minutes to 45 minutes. Some crews were able to continue in the rally without threat of exclusion. Unfortunately this left another 19 crews having exceeded their maximum lateness on Leg 1. They were therefore not permitted to continue on the rally."

RESULTS

Event held: 23-25 November 1996. 8th and final round of World 2-Litre Manufacturers' championship.
Start/Finish: Chester. Overnight halts: Leeds and Chester.

182 starters, 82 finishers.
27 special stages but 1 cancelled – 243 miles (total 1113 miles).

General classification		Group	Penalties (h:m:s)
1 Schwarz/Giraudet	Toyota Celica GT-Four ST205	GA	4:46:50
2 Kamioka/Gormley	Subaru Impreza 555	GA	4:54:42
3 Blomqvist/Melander	Škoda Felicia Kit Car 1600	GA	5:02:02
4 Higgins/Mills	Nissan Sunny GTI	GA	5:09:11
5 de Mevius/Fortin	Renault Maxi Megane	GA	5:11:20
6 Easson/Cook	Ford Escort RS Cosworth	GN	5:13:59
7 Buckley/Ewing	Subaru Impreza WRX-RA	GN	5:16:54
8 Rovanperä/Repo	Seat Ibiza Kit Car	GA	5:20:40
9 Weber/Hiemer	Seat Ibiza Kit Car	GA	5:22:24
10 Baumschlager/Wicha	VW Golf Kit Car	GA	5:23:25

Leader: Schwarz stages 1-27.

WORLD RALLY CARS

The period of 1997 till 2002 was a very special time for Rally GB, the period which ran across the new millennium. These were the last years when entry levels were guaranteed to run well into three figures. Till the time of writing, except momentarily for two years (2006 and 2007), the event has never since fielded anything like so many competitors. It was a period in which the layout of the routes substantially changed. 1999 was the last time for nearly twenty years that the rally had any stages outside Wales. It saw the arrival of commercialism in the sport with spectators having to pay to watch the rally in the forests. This

chapter covers the last years of the ten year event partnership with Network Q.

There were constant important changes in the sport which impinged on Rally GB, not least the progressive requirement to limit the opportunities for servicing rally cars. This together with limiting the time spent in the recently introduced pre-rally reconnaissance period led to the emergence of a whole scale duplication of special stages. The event became a Friday till Sunday activity to accord with standardisation in the sport, which effectively spelt the end

Richard Burns FIA World Rally Champion 2001.

Marcus Grönholm (right) FIA World Rally Champion 2000 and 2002 with co-driver Timo Rautiainen.

of the popular spectator friendly Superspecial Sunday tradition. There was also the arrival of the new generation World Rally Cars, a project which was conceived in order to make top level rallying more accessible for manufacturers. This successful move provided an increasing variety of shapes and colours of cars running at the head of the rally and increased attention in the World Championship cars in the rally.

This six year span saw four different drivers win Rally GB, including a hattrick of victories for Richard Burns and three different makes of car won the event. Each year the event was again the final round of the series and four times the Drivers' title was only decided in Britain. For home fans there was the excitement of greeting a second British World Champion. Six years after the Scottish driver Colin McRae became world champion, Englishman Burns followed on. On both occasions they gained their titles on home soil on Rally GB. Burns provided a never ending variety of intriguing situations. In the short period of this chapter he drove for three different manufacturers, but tragically the 2002 event was the last time he competed on Rally GB. Shortly before he was due to compete in the 2003 event he suffered an illness which took his life away.

It may have only been six years but a lot was going on! World Rally Car regulations were a new concept of vehicle homologation, an alternative option for the prevailing Group A rules which were too strict when designing competitive cars, deterring all but the biggest car producers from entering the sport. It was a huge success, the WRC expanding from three manufacturers in 1996 to seven in 1999. The trick was allowing basic mass production cars to be fitted with turbochargers and four-wheel drive kits. Subaru was first out with World Rally Cars in time for the start of the 1997 season. World Rally Car was not the only new formula of the times. This was the era when various new formulae were being considered. The 2-litre two-wheel drive, normally-aspirated, Kit Car formula was being encouraged as the FIA sought, rather optimistically, to develop a set of rules which might balance rally winning capability for two-wheel drive cars with the total traction cars. However, with the exception of two WRC wins, on asphalt rallies in 1999, the endeavour failed. The last victory for two-wheel drive on Rally GB was Henri Toivonen's win with a Talbot Sunbeam Lotus in 1980. In the period of this chapter we saw the emergence of Super 1600, which provided the foundation for the whole FIA Junior driver initiative. Super 1600 and then Kit Cars brought a plethora of manufacturers into the framework of the WRC at a time when the Group N formula brought no different manufacturers into top level sport. Group N began to fade from the limelight though it did not disappear completely for another 15 years.

1997: Colin McRae wins, title for Mäkinen

The first quarter century of World Rally Championship competition came to an end on a far higher level of awareness than could ever have been imagined in 1973. The 1997 RAC Rally, despite its ever-reducing overall length, and despite the Manufacturers' title having already been won by Subaru, maintained its popularity among manufacturers. Encouraged by the new official 2-litre championship 11 teams made official entries. Centre stage on this event was taken by Mitsubishi's Drivers' championship leader, Tommi Mäkinen, and Subaru's hopeful Colin McRae. Mäkinen's eventual one-point title victory was the end of the closest battle for the Drivers' title since 1979. For British fans, however, the prominent interest was that a new home star was emerging, another British superstar driver was on the scene. This was the first time that Richard Burns had led the RAC Rally. His bid for victory was wrecked by a puncture and McRae's title challenge by the relentless presence of Mäkinen. Despite McRae's heartiest efforts, Mäkinen won the championship for the second consecutive year.

McRae and Juha Kankkunen (Ford) fought for the lead on Sunday's opening 'Mickey Mouse' sections. On these Kankkunen had held the lead for four stages when McRae slipped behind, having eased his pace because of a loose wheel. In the forests on the Monday, McRae, running first car on the road, was one of a few who tackled the opening stage while it was still dark; daylight soon arrived, but the fog in the hills lingered. Fourth running Burns (Mitsubishi) now led while McRae dropped to eighth, 79 seconds further back. McRae was then

Italian driver Piero Liatti's Subaru displays its wounds. Liatti won the Monte Carlo Rally earlier in the year, the first rally to be won by a new generation World Rally Car.

*Superspecials were held in good weather and bad, and still the spectators came along.
This is a shot of a very murky stage at Silverstone race course.*

More Subaru damage! This time Colin McRae is missing a rear window.

consistently the faster driver on the rally. By the end
of leg 2 he had caught Burns, and at the night halt was
exactly equal (to the second), ahead of Kankkunen.
The final day was spent in forests in the south of Wales
on stages none of the top drivers had rallied before.
Burns finished fourth behind Carlos Sainz's Ford
which had had transmission problems for much of the
way.

Having led three rallies already during the season,
the new Toyota Corollas continued to show promise
but the team failed to deliver the result it wanted. Its
drivers, Didier Auriol and Marcus Grönholm, made
competitive times on stages even though Grönholm
had never competed on the RAC before. Auriol was
unhappy with the gearshift, wanted to withdraw, and
finally crashed.

It was a curious end to the season. Reflecting on
the effect of the new World Rally Cars on the sport,
it was noticeable that the World Champion's car was
prepared to the old Group A rules. It was an event
where the World Champion scored no fastest times
and where there were no team orders! When McRae
went well, he was unbelievable. Even from far away,
spectators could see his Subaru dancing from ditch to
ditch, never in a straight line, jumping off the ground
where no other car was jumping, and never staying in
the middle of the road. While Burns was driving neatly
and consistently in a classical style, McRae looked
the hero. After losing time early Monday morning
in the fog, he jumped from eighth to third place in
one stage. Two stages later he was second, and when
Burns incurred a time control penalty (caused by a
delay at service after a bolt was cross-threaded) he
was equal in the lead. And the champion Mäkinen? "I
cannot remember ever driving as slowly as I did here.
There were three moments I was worried. We missed
our braking point in the fog at Silverstone and went
straight into a chicane. In Hafren forest, on the second
morning, I had a top gear spin and then that evening
the clutch started slipping so badly I thought we could
not finish the Sweet Lamb stage. Otherwise all went
according to plan."

In World 2-Litre, it looked as if VW would finally
end SEAT's recent run of successes: Harri Rovanperä's
SEAT finished second behind Alister McRae's VW,
which had led almost from the start, but McRae was
later excluded for illegal front suspension pieces. In
the early stages Mark Higgins challenged in the new
Nissan Almera on its very first event, but retired on the
final day after an accident while lying third. In SEAT

Polish driver Krzysztof Hołowczyc in a water crossing.

General classification		Group	Penalties (h:m:s)
1 C McRae/Grist	Subaru Impreza	WRC	3:54:31
2 Kankkunen/Repo	Ford Escort	WRC	3:57:18
3 Sainz/Moya	Ford Escort	WRC	3:58:24
4 Burns/Reid	Mitsubishi Carisma GT	WRC	3:59:30
5 Grönholm/ Rautiainen	Toyota Corolla	WRC	4:00:43
6 Mäkinen/Harjanne	Mitsubishi Lancer Evolution	WRC	4:01:31
7 Liatti/Pons	Subaru Impreza	WRC	4:03:11
8 Vatanen/Freeman	Ford Escort	WRC	4:11:59
9 Rovanperä/Silander	SEAT Ibiza KC	GA	4:17:34
10 A.Medeghini/B. Medeghini	Ford Escort	WRC	4:18:06
12 Climent/Romani	Mitsubishi Lancer Evolution	GN	4:22:12

Leaders: C McRae stages 1+2, Kankkunen 3-6, C McRae 7-11, Burns 12-17, Burns & C McRae 18, Burns 19+20, C McRae 21-26.

Gwyndaf Evans went well, but retired, as did Oriol Gomez, while David Higgins had many problems and was sixth in the category. Renault had a lucky second place as both cars had driveshaft trouble with Martin Rowe eventually crashing. Neil Wearden scored W2L points for the second World Rally in succession when he took third place with his Honda; Per Svan's five-year-old Astra GSI had many problems, but finished fourth ahead of Jimmy McRae who was fifth with the little Hyundai Accent which had not been rallied for over a year.

ONLY WELSH FORESTS

The decision to use forests only in Wales was a bold step in the format for the rally. The move threatened to reduce substantially the event's much-vaunted spectator levels, but the increase in promotion of the Sunday stages did something to balance this. The concentration on Welsh stages provided the opportunity to use forests in south Wales. The second major change was the choice of Cheltenham, not only as the headquarters for the event, but as a place to which the event would return every night. The event headquarters were at the world renowned racecourse, where there was a well attended rally show before the event, and the opportunity to run a special stage in and around the horse race course.

RESULTS
1997 Network Q RAC Rally
Event held: 23-25 November 1997. 14th and final round of Manufacturers' and Drivers' championships.
Start/Finish: Cheltenham. Overnight halts: Cheltenham.

162 starters, 92 finishers.
26 special stages – 239 miles (total 1146 miles).

1998: Richard Burns wins first Rally GB

Both major rally world titles were decided in Britain. Richard Burns (Mitsubishi) inherited the lead of the rally when Colin McRae's Subaru engine failed, gradually pulling ahead as his rivals fell by the wayside. McRae came to the rally already out of the race for the Drivers' title but with a strong chance of dictating the outcome of the series. To beat Tommi Mäkinen to the title, his rival Sainz had only to reach the finish in fourth place, but then Mäkinen retired when he damaged his car. The rally came to a sensational conclusion when Sainz, who appeared to be cruising to the Drivers' title in third place, retired 500 metres before the end of the last stage, gifting the title to Mäkinen. The Mitsubishi team was only cautiously hopeful of winning the rally, though more confident at winning the Manufacturers' series. When Toyota lost Didier Auriol and then Sainz, the Drivers' and the Manufacturers' titles both went to Mitsubishi.

After the two McRae brothers tied on the opening stage, Superspecial Sunday saw a close fight between Subarus and Toyotas. By the end of the day Mäkinen was out, when he crashed on a patch of oil on a tarmac stage, and a forlorn attempt to continue to the next stage on three wheels was mercifully stopped by the police. Burns was slowed by differential trouble down in sixth. Colin McRae was easily fastest but then broke a wheel. Day two stages in central Wales saw Burns shoot up to second on the first stage, Colin had engine failure while leading, and Burns took over. Auriol was uncharacteristically quicker than Sainz, but then his engine stopped at the water crossing in Sweet Lamb stage. When McRae spun twice, two stages later, Burns momentarily took the lead. McRae took back the lead again, but could not pull far away from Burns. Later that afternoon McRae felt a misfire in his engine, and suddenly noticed smoke pouring from the exhaust. Burns strengthened his lead in foggy conditions on the final day as Alister McRae crashed, Sainz was cruising in third place when his engine failed within sight of the end of the last stage. When Alister stopped, Sainz settled for third, enough for the title, but never at a speed which threatened the leader Burns. Burns' differential trouble returned on the final day, but by then he had a buffer in front of the pursuing Fords, and despite foggy conditions held the lead to the end. For the SEAT WRC team, the retirements of the other crews gave the company the chance of sixth place in the hands of Harri Rovanperä, but it lost guest driver Gwyndaf Evans with gearbox trouble on the second day.

The excitement for the Drivers' championship meanwhile overshadowed the fine drive by Burns, who had fought back after his troubles. The attrition rate was incredible. The three works Subarus and the three works Toyotas all retired, allowing Ford to gain second and third places, as it had done in 1997, but, like the Toyotas, the Fords were off the pace. Sainz had been driving with model consistency, for a long time lying second, close behind Colin McRae, but slipped back at the end of the second day when he slid off the road.

Group N was won by Manfred Stohl, but close behind was the Subaru of David Higgins. In the new Teams' Cup the Toyota Saudi Arabia driver Abdullah Bakhashab won the event, though the absent HF Grifone won the title. The Spanish company SEAT World 2-Litre

Cup team needed only to finish in the points to take the title from Peugeot. For a long time the Vauxhall of Jarmo Kytölehto led the field, but all the time the Renault of Tapio Laukkanen was pressing hard, and halfway through the event took the lead and went on to win. So

Joint rally leaders after the first stage! Colin McRae (left) and younger brother and team-mate Alister.

Dramatic moment on Millbrook stage when Tommi Mäkinen wrecked his Mitsubishi's suspension, threatening to jeopardise his chances of retaining his World Title.

Harri Rovanperä drove the only SEAT WRC to reach the finish.

many 'F2' teams were entered. Hyundai had its usual two car team, but both retired with the differential problem that had been anticipated before the event. Nissan had one team car for Mark Higgins, but the engine consumed foreign material and failed. Pavel Sibera had a Škoda Octavia Kit Car, but crashed on the same oil slick that had destroyed the hopes of Mäkinen. SEAT had two entries which finished third and fourth and won the W2L title. A private Ford came fifth, and after a long season of troubles in the British championship, the 1600cc Proton Satria of Mats Andersson finished sixth.

There was some sense of justice at the misfortune of Sainz, because of the nature of the first day crash that eliminated Mäkinen. The Finn slid on a patch of oil into concrete blocks, which the stage marshals knew of but never warned the drivers about. It seemed very unfair, even though Sainz lost no time adjusting to his windfall opportunity. For Mäkinen the final day was one he never expected to enjoy. After the shock of his retirement two days before and the apparent hopelessness of his title aspirations, he was packed and ready to go home from Cheltenham. As he was making one final television interview, his brother telephoned with the news of his title. "I told him this was a far too serious matter to joke about, but it was true!" It was his third successive World title, a triumph for Finland which that year had already welcomed the Formula 1 Drivers' title for Mika Häkkinen. 1998 was the final event for Ford's original World Rally Car, which had been converted from the old Group A car.

The final time Richard Burns rallied a Mitsubishi. After winning this event he promptly moved to Subaru for the next season.

NEW TITLE NAME AND TIMING TO TENTHS
The Network Q RAC Rally had now become the Network Q Rally of Great Britain, launching the habit of calling the event "Rally GB." And as from the start of the 1998 WRC season, timing on every special stage, except the Safari Rally, was to the tenth of a second. This produced a remarkable situation when the first Rally GB special stage saw a tie between drivers – the two Subaru team-mates Colin and Alister McRae, the first time two brothers had led the same World Rally.

RESULTS
Event held: 22-24 November 1998. 13th and final round of Manufacturers' and Drivers' Championships.
Start/Finish: Cheltenham. Overnight halts: Cheltenham.

168 starters, 81 finishers.
28 special stages – 236 miles (total 1176 miles).

General classification		Group	Penalties (h:m:s)
1 Burns/Reid	Mitsubishi Lancer Evolution	WRC	3:50:30.6
2 Kankkunen/Repo	Ford Escort	WRC	3:54:17.1
3 Thiry/Prevot	Ford Escort	WRC	3:55:58.1
4 de Mevius/Fortin	Subaru Impreza 555	WRC	3:58:25.4
5 Lindholm/Aho	Ford Escort	WRC	3:58:46.2
6 Rovanperä/Pietilainen	SEAT	WRC	4:01:03.9
7 Schwarz/Hiemer	Ford Escort	WRC	4:02:47.3
8 Holowczyc/Wislawski	Subaru Impreza 555	WRC	4:03:37.3
9 Martin/Kitsing	Toyota Celica GT-Four	GA	4:07:41.6
10 Stohl/Muller	Mitsubishi Lancer Evolution	GN	4:09:37.8
12 Laukkanen/ Lindström	Renault Maxi Megane	GA	4:11:36.1

Leaders: C McRae & A McRae stage 1, C McRae 2-15, Burns 16, C McRae 17-19, Burns 20-28.

1999: 18-hour second day

This was a rally for fun! With the top two championships settled in Australia this was billed as the showdown of them all. When Richard Burns and Colin McRae, between them Britain's two best drivers, would publicly decide who was the best. The British media enjoyed the expectation, and because of the promised absence of any team orders, it was a promotional dream rally. The excitement was there right to the end. McRae had many problems, and finally crashed off the road into

Much better visibility this year in Silverstone for Bertie Fisher who finished 21st overall, the highest placed pre-World Rally Car Subaru to finish.

Guest driver for the Germany-based Toyota Castrol team was Martin Brundle, but he was off the road again. Seen here on the Blenheim Palace special stage. Martin never returned to the World Rally Championship …

a rally car abandoned from a previous stage, while Burns won the rally as he pleased. Burns had a dramatic incident on the second day when a fire started in the engine compartment of his Subaru, 12 months to the day and in the same place that McRae's Subaru had disappeared in clouds of smoke and then retired in 1998. Burns was lucky, however, and lost no time while a broken oil filter bowl was repaired.

It was the shortest rally in the 1999 World Championship in terms of time from start of reconnaissance until prize-giving, with the second day almost 18 hours long. There were different service parks for works teams and for privateer drivers, to ease pressure on available space. Each stage of Leg 1 was held on mixed surfaces, but with only one midday Service Park visit during the day.

Apart from the short stage at the Cheltenham racecourse right at the start, Subaru drivers led the whole rally, Juha Kankkunen taking the lead on stage 2 on the day of the publicity stages, Burns taking over when the rally reached the forests. Peugeot did well with its ultra short wheelbase 206 WRCars on the publicity stages, but gradually fell back in the forests, though Marcus Grönholm led the rest of the field until he crashed on the final day. François Delecour fell back with transmission troubles. Ford had high hopes, but could sense things were going badly when McRae smashed the side of his car on the first stage and Thomas Rådström did the same the other side on the second. Rådström then incurred a one minute penalty for a time control mistake. McRae was holding fourth place at the end of the second day but then crashed, while Rådström drove carefully to finish. Mitsubishi allowed Tommi Mäkinen the chance of tackling the rally at his own preferred pace. Although forced to fit catalytic converters for the first time, Mitsubishi watched Mäkinen gain two best times on the Cheltenham racecourse tests, but then smashed his suspension and had engine electrical troubles. He had climbed up to fifth before the engine failed. Freddy Loix was struggling on his first British rally, bemused at the way his rival drivers cut corners with abandon.

The two World Championship teams from VAG were promising. Harri Rovanperä, who had already been told that he no longer had a drive with SEAT in the following year, finished a remarkable third overall, while Toni Gardemeister, who was to be Didier Auriol's regular team-mate in 2000, retired with clutch failure. Škoda had no sooner seen both its Octavia World Rally Cars in the top ten places when Armin Schwarz had a crash and retired, leaving guest driver Bruno Thiry just outside the points. This was a rally with few novelties. Škoda had a development differential on Schwarz's car, while the only two new team cars on the event (McRae's Ford and Grönholm's Peugeot) both ended up badly crashed!

As in the previous year there was an amazing climax to the rally. Three of the top ten drivers did not complete the final stage. Delecour ground to a halt with another gearbox failure. Auriol, having apparently hit the same rock as team-mate Carlos Sainz, tried hard to repair the damage but ran out of time, and Gwyndaf Evans' engine failed on the final stage, so he freewheeled to the end of the stage. Then Markko Martin's car burst into flames at the end of the stage from an oil leak, but he was able to reach the end.

The Network Q lived up to its notorious reputation for spectator attendance, leading to huge jams on the roads outside the stages, and to delays while safely issues were solved! Ultimately the last two stages on the second day were stopped and interruption times created. Burns won in full glory and confidence. "Even when the car was on fire I knew the mechanics at the service park would sort it all out!" Wow, beat that for the quote of the millennium.

Renault clinched the World 2-Litre Cup when Alister McRae went off the road on the second day. Tapio Laukkanen led for half the rally before running out of fuel on a road section. Three cars registered in the Teams' Cup were at the start line, Luis Climent's Valencia team car, Abdullah Bakhashab's Saudi car, and Krzysztof Hołowczyc's from Poland. Although unsure exactly of his necessary objective, Climent led the category from the first day and reached the finish to win the Cup. If there was any disappointment it came from the confusion surrounding both the 2-Litre and the Teams' Cup contestants. Many

contradictory official guidelines on how points were to be awarded led to greater, not less confusion. Contestants in both series started the event not knowing what to do to succeed, but in the end events resolved themselves. Renault was the W2L title holder, Valencia Terra y Mar the best Team.

End of an era

It would never be quite the same again … As from 2000, this event was expected, for the foreseeable future, to be held only within the boundaries of the Welsh Principality. This was the final time the rally would use stately home or promotional stages. Various new directives by the FIA meant this was the final World Rally due to finish in mid week. It was to be the end of the competition career for the Toyota rally team for 18 years, and the end of the career for the British Renault team. So far as the championship platform was concerned, this was also the final rally for the World 2-Litre series, as this was being abandoned for 2000.

Spectating had gradually become a highly sophisticated and all-embracing activity!

RESULTS

Event held: 21-23 November 1999. 14th and final round of Manufacturers' and Drivers' championships.
Start/Finish: Cheltenham. Overnight halts: Cheltenham.

160 starters, 89 finishers.
22 special stages – 389 kilometres (total 1815 kilometres).

General classification		Group	Penalties (h:m:s)
1 Burns/Reid	Subaru Impreza	WRC	3:53:44.2
2 Kankkunen/Repo	Subaru Impreza	WRC	3:55:31.5
3 Rovanperä/ Pietilainen	SEAT Cordoba	WRC	3:58:39.5
4 Thiry/Prevot	Škoda Octavia	WRC	4:02:11.7
5 Loix/Smeets	Mitsubishi Carisma GT	WRC	4:03:19.5
6 Rådström/Barth	Ford Focus	WRC	4:03:47.5
7 G Panizzi/H Panizzi	Peugeot 206	WRC	4:04:17.8
8 Martin/Kitsing	Toyota Corolla	WRC	4:05:21.5
9 P Solberg/Mills	Ford Focus	WRC	4:06:54.0
10 Kahle/ Schneppenheim	Toyota Corolla	WRC	4:08:48.2
15 M Higgins/ Thomas	VW Golf Kit Car	GA	4:15:37.0
18 Rowe/Ringer	Renault Maxi Megane	GA	4:16:47.3
22 Ferreyros/Saenz	Mitsubishi Lancer Evolution	GN	4:22:27.5

Even after three wins (this was one) and three second places, Burns was still unable to beat Tommi Mäkinen to the Drivers' title.

Leaders: Mäkinen & Grönholm stage 1, Kankkunen 2-7, Burns 8-22.

2000: Hat-trick win for Burns, Grönholm wins title

One year ahead of the time schedule Peugeot had set itself for winning the title, it swept the board in the 2000 World Rally Championship! Having already clinched the Manufacturers' title, now it also gained the Drivers' title. Amid the crescendo of curiosity about the race to the title, Richard Burns' Subaru almost incidentally won the rally for a third time running. Victory had seemed far away on the first forest stage of the event, when Burns hit a rock as he cut a corner, and damaged his rear suspension. By the second afternoon, however, the leader Colin McRae had crashed off the road in his Ford, and Burns gained a lead he held to the end of the event. Virtually every top driver had spent time off the road, often costing little more than damaged cars or lost time.

Apart from two runs round a purpose-built superspecial course in Cardiff, it was forest racing all the way. This year the rally was limited only to the forests of Wales: gone were the superspecials that were previously held on the opening day. Weather conditions seemed to change every moment of the event. From heavy rain through fog to low autumn sunshine, drivers faced everything except ice – but the stage surfaces were treacherous in their inconsistency! It was the first RAC or Network Q Rally to be won at over 100km/h average – despite the slippery conditions, and the first to end rather than start on a Sunday.

For the second year running, all seven WRC registered teams entered the event, SEAT on its last appearance in the series, brought no fewer than four entries. Three Cordobas finished, but all were out of the points, as were both Škoda Octavias, and the one remaining Hyundai Accent in the event. Ford lost two of its three drivers (McRae

and Tapio Laukkanen) and Mitsubishi lost Freddy Loix through crashes. Outgoing champion Tommi Mäkinen drove a very confused event, several times going off the road, but made a storming finish at the end to beat Carlos Sainz into third place. Sainz chased his teammate McRae through much of the event, despite two dramatic crashes, but the team finally finished second place in the Manufacturers' championship, just ahead of Subaru.

Subaru's drivers all went off the road on the first morning of the rally, except for Petter Solberg, who crashed on the last day, gaining championship points. New to the WRC this year had been the Hyundai Accent WRC. Toyota Corolla WRCs were used by the two best privately run entries of Markko Martin and Henning Solberg. Martin finished an amazing seventh overall, after finishing ninth and then eighth in previous years. Another private Toyota was driven by Janne Tuohino, who jointly led the event overall at the end of the first stage.

The event started dramatically. By the end of the third stage no fewer than four drivers had been leading the event! Many cars went off the road in the slippery conditions: Loix crashed on the first forest stage, Burns had dropped down to 27th, Didier Auriol's third place SEAT then suffered a loose turbo pipe, McRae was the fastest driver on the event in the early stages, but Marcus Grönholm took over the lead when McRae twice spun and stalled his engine. Grönholm had a near-miss on stage 5, after which he decided to go more easily – and then hit a sheep on stage 6!

On the second day McRae took the lead back and started to pull ahead with confidence. He spoke about going steadily and not taking unnecessary risks – before the car found itself upside down with a

Top non-works driver to finish was seventh-placed Markko Martin, in an ex-Sainz Toyota Corolla WRC.

VIP visitor to the rally was FIA President Max Mosley, here talking with Richard Burns.

Quickly identified by the red flashes on their helmets are winners Richard Burns and co-driver Robert Reid.

burst radiator on stage 12. Grönholm momentarily held the lead, but all the time Burns was recovering lost ground, and on stage 13 Burns took the lead which he held to the finish. Alister McRae holed his Hyundai's sump. On the final day, Grönholm cruised to second place behind Burns, and gained his title. Both Petter Solberg and Tapio Laukkanen crashed out of the event.

Three of the four titles in the World Championship remained unresolved until the final round. The Group N title went to the 28-year-old Austrian Manfred Stohl who led from start to finish. When four times champion Gustavo Trelles stopped with a double puncture, Toshihiro Arai (Spike Subaru) only had to qualify by starting the event to become Teams' Cup champion, although he later retired while Hamed Al Wahaibi (Arab World team) won the category. Vauxhall was the only strong contender in the Formula 2 division, but things went badly wrong when both Mark Higgins and Neil Wearden crashed close to each other on the second day. Higgins then crashed again on the final day and had a fraught journey back to the finish with an overheating engine while Wearden had total engine failure on the very last stage. The 1600cc class was won by Sébastien Loeb on his first RGB appearance.

2000 saw Vauxhall's last planned official entry in rallying, and Markko Martin's last non-professional drive as a privateer. Also in 2000, the SEAT company planned to 'reshuffle' its motorsport activity away from the WRC.

The most frequent WRC driver from the Sultanate of Oman was Hamed Al-Wahaibi, seen here at the Margam stage.

CHANGES TO THE RALLY OF DREAMS

Far more competitors entered the Network Q Rally of Great Britain than any other World Rally in 2000 – a trend threatened by the planned changes to the format of the sport in future years, which were expected to take away much of the amateur adventurous spirit in competitors. For years, the spirit of the event had been epitomised by the thousands of amateur enthusiasts involved in all aspects of the rally. The young Finnish driver Janne Tuohino entered his private Toyota Corolla WRC – and led the rally after the first stage, equal with his hero Juha Kankkunen. He retired early on the second stage but already his dream had come true. The new millennium would bring changes to the event, but it was unclear whether it was proof of national commercialisation of the event or as a result of the spectator traffic jams 12 months earlier. The 2000 Rally of GB was an all-ticket affair for spectators, ending four decades of free spectating entertainment. There was to be no more freedom to roam in the forests.

RESULTS

Event held: 23-26 November 2000. 14th and final round of Manufacturers' and Drivers' championships.
Start/Finish: Cardiff. Overnight halts: Cardiff.

150 starters, 79 finishers.
17 special stages – 381 kilometres (total 1509 kilometres).

General classification		Group	Penalties (h:m:s)
1 Burns/Reid	Subaru Impreza	WRC	3:43:01.9
2 Grönholm/Rautiainen	Peugeot 206	WRC	3:44:07.5
3 Mäkinen/ Mannisenmaki	Mitsubishi Lancer Evolution	WRC	3:44:16.9
4 Sainz/Moya	Ford Racing Focus	WRC	3:44:35.4
5 Kankkunen/Repo	Subaru Impreza	WRC	3:44:48.8
6 Delecour/Grataloup	Peugeot 206	WRC	3:44:50.4
7 Martin/Park	Toyota Corolla	WRC	3:46:26.3
8 G Panizzi/H Panizzi	Peugeot 206	WRC	3:46:37.5
9 Auriol/Giraudet	SEAT Cordoba	WRC	3:47:29.4
10 Rovanperä/ Pietilainen	SEAT Cordoba	WRC	3:48:12.0
17 Stohl/Muller	Mitsubishi Lancer Evolution	GN	4:07:45.3
32 Higgins/Thomas	Vauxhall Astra Kit Car	GA	4:27:48.0

Leaders: Kankkunen & Tuohino stage 1, P.Solberg 2, C McRae 3+4, Grönholm 5+6, C McRae 7-11, Grönholm 12, Burns 13-17.

2001: Englishman Burns takes the 2001 title

Colin McRae, Tommi Mäkinen, Richard Burns and Carlos Sainz all started the rally with a chance of going home champion. In all the celebrations of the new British champion being crowned, Marcus Grönholm's rally victory passed without much attention as did the announcement that his Peugeot team had won the Manufacturers' title for the second time. Of the four title contenders Mäkinen was the first to go. A bolt in the suspension snapped as the car bottomed in a dip in the road, and he struggled out of the first forest stage. McRae led the rally for three stages before he crashed heavily on the fourth stage. Two of the four had retired on the first morning. Sainz's chances were, admittedly, remote, compounded by having brake troubles, and on the second day his entry was withdrawn leaving Burns needing only to finish in the top four places to take the title. It is difficult to know how Richard Burns will be remembered in history. Will it be for being the first English World Rally champion – or the first champion in the 29-year history of the series to gain the title having won only one of the 14 qualifying rounds?

A more compact route than ever, demanded more double-usage of stages. In wet, foggy and slippery conditions the event favoured drivers who knew the stages, had cars that handled well, and drivers who made no mistakes. Burns made none, though he had two bad

The McRaes had a very privileged fan, who was always welcome when he brought his bagpipes. Here he is serenading Alister.

The Welsh spirit of the event was prevalent. Ford Focus RS WRC driver Mark Higgins' Welsh co-driver Bryan Thomas meets a fan clad in local attire.

moments, firstly when the car was difficult to restart leaving parc ferme on Saturday morning, and again when the starter motor failed on Saturday evening. Grönholm was already over a half minute ahead of Burns on the first day. The top end of the field was already becoming thin. The works cars of Petter Solberg (Subaru, no fuel), Piero Liatti (Hyundai, clutch), Markko Martin (Subaru, engine), Roman Kresta (Škoda) and Gwyndaf Evans (SEAT) were all missing. The second day saw fourth-placed Didier Auriol delayed off the road, then Freddy Loix (a gradual fall of turbo boost pressure, then lost gears) retired after his Mitsubishi team tried to cannibalise his gearboxes to no avail. After the withdrawal of the Ford team, Grönholm was over a minute and a half in front of Burns, while on the final day Harri Rovanperä passed Burns to create a Peugeot one-two result.

There was a thrilling finish in Group N when David Higgins scored a landmark victory for Subaru over a horde of Mitsubishis, finishing 2.8 seconds in front of the Peruvian driver Ramon Ferreyros, who was driving the car rallied earlier this year by former four times champion Gustavo Trelles. Swedish driver Kenneth Backlund was lying third until the final stage when the transmission failed. For the second year running, the 1600cc class was won by Sébastien Loeb in a Citroën Saxo, this time counting for the new Super 1600 series which he had already clinched earlier in the year, but which proved another disaster for Ford. Only one of its five S1600 starters reached the end of the event. Its only consolation was that François Duval led the category for

Easily the fastest Peugeot on the event was winning Marcus Grönholm who easily outpaced his teammates.

Plenty of prizes for Ulster driver Niall McShea, who finished second in the class for the new Super 1600 cars behind another Citroën Saxo driver, Sébastien Loeb.

two stages before crashing. This was a completely new championship, the first time the FIA had introduced money as one of the factors in the specification of a competition car, a concept which was to continue in many future rally car formulae.

No sooner had the rally finished than a major change in the long established driver line-ups began involving Mäkinen (Mitsubishi), Kenneth Eriksson and Alister McRae (Hyundai), and Armin Schwarz (Škoda). Only Ford hoped to retain its line-up for the forthcoming year, for a third consecutive season. Some drivers, like Didier Auriol and Bruno Thiry, went home not knowing where or when they would drive rally cars again. The press became curious about Burns' future plans, on account of Subaru refusing to acknowledge his contractual freedom to leave the Banbury team in order to go to Peugeot. The WRC drivers' contracts recognition committee received notifications from Subaru and Peugeot that they had nominated Burns for their teams. All the teams were eager to find out the identity of the team whose car would carry competition number one next season.

MISUNDERSTANDINGS GALORE!
In the stormy conditions of the Saturday afternoon came reports that Carlos Sainz had slid off the road and impacted spectators, who were standing in an unauthorised place. With spectators now paying to watch the event, this was especially worrying for the organisers who were aware that any stage cancellations would have financial complications. The Ford team was also alarmed for image reasons, and ordered that its team of cars should be withdrawn forthwith. The Ford team withdrew both him and Mark Higgins, the third factory Ford, out of sympathy with those who were reported to have been injured in the accident. Sainz, who was visibly shaken, saw his championship aspirations ended. It was some time before an FIA official disclosed that, contrary to earlier reports, no spectators were injured in the Sainz incident. All those involved were non-paying voluntary marshals, who were not obliged to stand in the places reserved for spectators. Earlier there had been another very worrying incident. An official FIA fuel rig had given a false reading, causing Petter Solberg to run out of fuel on the second stage, leading to retirement. Eventual winner Marcus Grönholm then also arrived at service with an absolutely empty tank because of this problem.

RESULTS
Event held: 22-25 November 2001. 14th and final round of the Manufacturers' and the Drivers' championships.
Start/Finish: Cardiff. Overnight halt: Cardiff.

117 starters, 50 finishers.
16 special stages – 355 kilometres (total 1715 kilometres).

General classification		Group	Penalties (h:m:s)
1 Grönholm/Rautiainen	Peugeot 206	WRC	3:23:44.8
2 Rovanperä/Pietilainen	Peugeot 206	WRC	3:26:11.9
3 Burns/Reid	Subaru Impreza	WRC	3:27:00.2
4 A McRae/Senior	Hyundai Accent	WRC	3:30:33.6
5 Schwarz/Hiemer	Škoda Octavia	WRC	3:31:16.1
6 Eriksson/Parmander	Hyundai Accent	WRC	3:31:55.8
7 Auriol/Giraudet	Peugeot 206	WRC	3:32:05.9
8 Thiry/Prevot	Škoda Octavia	WRC	3:34:40.4
9 de Mevius/Boyere	Peugeot 206	WRC	3:38:02.5
10 Arai/Sircombe	Subaru Impreza	WRC	3:38:51.2
11 D Higgins/Thorley	Subaru Impreza WRX	GN	3:44:56.7
15 Loeb/Elena	Citroën Saxo	S1600	3:50:37.3

Leaders: C McRae stages 1-3, Grönholm 4-17.

2002: First win for Petter Solberg and Norway
With both major titles already settled, this was once again promoted as the ultimate head-to-head battle between British champions Richard Burns and Colin McRae, but both were delayed off the road on early stages, then Burns went off permanently. McRae ended his career with Ford with an unconvincing fifth place, and it was the reigning champion Marcus Grönholm who started the rally with determination to show who really deserved the World Champion status. He won stage after stage for the first half of the event, until the Eppynt (Epynt) army ranges where he found a jump with his name written on it … Then it was the still little-known Estonian Ford team driver Markko Martin who took the lead before Petter Solberg caught up with him.

For the top drivers, every forest stage this year was held in daylight. Every special stage was run at least twice for the first time. After weeks of rain, the most surprising thing about the event was that it never rained once. It was amazing that drivers now complained about the sunlight in the early morning and then late in the afternoons! On the very first forest special stage the guest driver Valentino Rossi was blinded by sunlight, and his Peugeot slid off the road. On the next stage the reigning British Super 1600 champion Justin Dale in his works Mitsubishi World Rally Car did the same, this time overturning.

Martin took an initial lead, but then Grönholm pulled ahead impressively while both Burns and McRae left the road. Stage 4 was cancelled through spectator problems. Hyundai lost Armin Schwarz when his car caught fire, and team-mate Juha Kankkunen, following next, stopped and helped extinguish the fire. The organisers even gave the Finn a time allowance for his trouble! Schwarz continued, but then retired unwell from smoke inhalation. The asphalt roads on the second day at the army ranges at Eppynt attracted countless spectators. They got good value. Grönholm, Jani Paasonen (Mitsubishi), David Higgins

The end of the first Mitsubishi works drive for Justin Dale, when scrutineers forbade him from continuing because of roll cage damage.

The first of many WRC wins for the future champion Norwegian Petter Solberg.

(Subaru) and Tomasz Kuchar (Toyota) all destroyed their World Rally Cars at this place, and only two kilometres further on, Delecour had a pacenote misunderstanding, and the remaining two works Mitsubishis were wrecked as well. Martin retook the lead, battling with Solberg. Harri Rovanperä was delayed by wheel bearing and brake trouble.

For more than a day there was excitement in the knowledge that either Solberg or Martin were expected to score a maiden World Rally. Sébastien Loeb, now a factory World Rally Car driver for Citroën, had a broke wishbone, and team-mate Thomas Rådström retired with a hole in the side of the engine. Solberg beat Martin by 24 seconds. Peugeot arrived in Britain confidently having already won the title, but Harri Rovanperä finished seventh, the only works Peugeot driver to finish, after long delays with a broken wheel bearing which wrecked the handling as well as the braking. At Ford, the sensation of the rally was that Martin, in the standard blue colour scheme car, was leading the two Martini cars all the time. A half year later, he won his first WRC event! The quiet man from Estonia fulfilled all the expectations of him. In the end Ford finished with four cars in the top six. Looking back on the 2002 event, it is sad to realise this would be Richard Burns' final British WRC event. Before the 2003 event he was struck down with the aneurysm which led to him passing away three years later, exactly five years after he had scored his final win on this event.

Interest in Group N activities had been sidelined by the new official Junior World Rally Championship for Super 1600 cars, the Junior series being the one remaining title of the 2002 season to be won. The Citroën drivers Andrea Dallavilla and Daniel Sola started the event one point apart, but Dallavilla had a double puncture on stage 8, and that sealed his championship fate. For much of the early stages Janne Tuohino was in the lead, but then a puncture put him back, so Daniel Sola went ahead to win. It was a bad event for many teams. All three Suzukis went off the road in the first two forest stages (after Kangas had finished second on the opening stage), none of the four Fords reached the finish and of the 19 Junior drivers to take the start only six reached the finish, four of them with Citroën cars. Gwyndaf Evans' MG led impressively on the short superspecial which opened the event, but gradually fell back, and finally retired with a broken rear suspension hub. In the end Niall McShea's Opel benefited from electrical troubles for Mirco Baldacci and a puncture for Giandomenico Basso, to finish second in the category, the best finish for Opel. Tuohino finally finished fourth,

Mayhem in the Eppynt Ranges. Photographer Mark Griffin captured the moment when the Corolla WRC of Polish driver Tomasz Kuchar joined the carnage.

enough to gain him third place in the championship and give Citroën an impressive 1-2-3 placing in the series. Dallavilla, who had started with such hopes, finally came sixth and last. The non-championship driver Simon Jean-Joseph was again the fastest Super 1600 driver in his Renault Clio.

More Welsh delight for winning co-driver Philip Mills and young daughter Sioned.

TROUBLE BREWING

Drivers found to have committed speeding offences in Shakedown on this event had their cases heard by Neath Magistrates Court on 10th November 2003, one day after the end of Wales Rally GB 2003. The Court agreed to hold the proceedings on this day in order to minimise the effect on the drivers' professional careers, considering that six-month driving bans were likely to be imposed. Three drivers were banned from driving in Britain for the six month period, on account of being caught for speeding more than three times. The financial penalties also imposed were for Loix (seven offences) £1725, Schwarz (five) £1000 and Carlsson (four) £800. Other drivers caught in this multiple speed trap were both Hirvonen and Paasonen (three, £600 each), both Mäkinen and Sainz (two, £400 each), and for the Spanish driver Txus Jaio, Martin, Colin McRae, Rowe, Stohl, Burns and Delecour (one time and £150 each). For other offences; Meeke was banned from driving for one year and fined £300. This caused the FIA to investigate why the police considered the event should use public roads that were evidently so dangerous that speed cameras were required in the first place. One of rallying's strongest supporters was the Government Minister Peter Hain, leader of the House of Commons. A compromise was agreed. Following assurances from the police that the location of speed traps on road sections would be disclosed in advance, as a more genuine way to cut speeding and increase safety, a comprehensive list of every possible location was to be published in future, and in March 2004 the event was confirmed as a round of the 2004 WRC.

RESULTS

Event held: 14-17 November 2002. 14th and final round of Manufacturers' and Drivers' championship.
Start/Finish: Cardiff. Overnight halts: Cardiff.

85 starters, 38 finishers.
16 special stages but one cancelled – 367 kilometres (total 1636 kilometres).

General classification		Group	Penalties (h:m:s)
1 Solberg/Mills	Subaru Impreza	WRC	3:30:36.4
2 Martin/Park	Ford Focus RS	WRC	3:31:00.8
3 Sainz/Moya	Ford Focus RS	WRC	3:32:12.1
4 Mäkinen/Lindström	Subaru Impreza	WRC	3:33:13.9
5 McRae/Ringer	Ford Focus RS	WRC	3:33:37.9
6 M Higgins/Thomas	Ford Focus RS	WRC	3:35:38.3
7 Rovanperä/Pietilainen	Peugeot 206	WRC	3:35:52.2
8 Loix/Smeets	Hyundai Accent	WRC	3:35:52.3
9 Kankkunen/Repo	Hyundai Accent	WRC	3:36:05.5
10 Gardemeister/Lukander	Škoda Octavia	WRC	3:36:39.3
18 Svedlund/Nilsson	Mitsubishi Lancer Evolution	GN	4:01:57.4
19 Jean-Joseph/Boyere	Renault Clio	S1600	4:02:08.8
21 Sola/Romani	Citroën Saxo	JWRC	4:03:06.6

Leaders: Martin stage 1, Grönholm 2-9, Martin 10-13, Solberg 14-17.

Chapter 8
2003-2012

HOME, IS WALES

This chapter covers the period when Rally GB was entrenched in Cardiff, where it had already been based from 2000 to 2002, and the event proudly started to insert the name Wales into its title. In the sport this was a period of established superstars, and, in this ten year period, two drivers – Petter Solberg and Sébastien Loeb – each won the event three times, Jari-Matti Latvala won it twice, and Marcus Grönholm and Mikko Hirvonen once each. Ford cars won Rally GB four times, Subaru and Citroën three times, while the national anthems of Norway, Finland and France were regularly played at the finish ceremonies.

Cardiff is the capital of Wales, located in the far south of the country, and is its largest city, chief commercial centre, and the seat of the National Assembly. As the biggest city in the country, it fulfilled the wish of the FIA for WRC events to have strong connections with major cities. There was a lot of logic in concentrating the rally in Wales, where there was an abundance of available forest for special stages, but the only difficulty is that the forests were not close to Cardiff. Fitting Cardiff into the current requirements of central service parks, double usage of stages, and requiring rallies to have at least 25% of the total

Cardiff City Hall, a majestic location for rally headquarters.

route on special stages was awkward. With Cardiff being the cultural epicentre of the country, conflicting demands meant it was not always possible to take advantage of the many features of the City. There were no available large areas near Cardiff to locate the service park, and the limit of the length of road sections restricted the areas where the rally could go. Stages in North Wales could not be used, and it was very difficult to travel even to central Wales. The days of a round-Britain rally when huge numbers of spectators saw the cars passing by were long gone. The event had to be held not just in Wales, but was also limited to certain parts.

2003: Fastest ever Rally GB. Solberg Champion

After 17 years of Lombard support, then ten years of Network Q Rally GB, there was a new sponsor, the Welsh Development Agency. Support also came from the Welsh Assembly Government. The official headquarters in the Cardiff City Hall was the site for parc ferme, the trade and display areas, and the official start and ceremonial finish. The stages were, essentially, all to the north and west of Swansea, and the service area was at Felindre, with the Shakedown stage nearby. Everything was located in the south of the Principality. Generally dry conditions made for a fast event.

The British round of the series was non-stop drama for a week. First headline was the withdrawal of Richard Burns, the man Peugeot had entrusted to help them leapfrog Citroën to the Manufacturers' title. Burns had been one of four drivers able to win the World Drivers' title,

though this depended on misfortunes for rivals Carlos Sainz, Petter Solberg and Sébastien Loeb. On the first morning there was a series of shocks. Firstly Sainz retired in bizarre circumstances. Wiring to the official in-car camera was faulty, and led to an internal fire. This in turn led to a continuing smell of burning which distracted the twice former World Champion to such an extent that he lost concentration and crashed, his first and only retirement of the year. The outgoing World Champion Marcus Grönholm clipped a pile of logs which damaged the steering, and the police ordered that he retire from the rally and not drive to the Service Park. Markko Martin's engine overheated due to a water leak and failed, and his Ford team-mate Mikko Hirvonen slid off the road. The race for the world title settled down into a head-to-head battle between Solberg and Loeb, then Citroën confirmed rumours that the company had ordered Loeb not to take risks. It was better that he take second place, because fighting for the lead could damage its prospects of beating Peugeot to the Manufacturers' title. Solberg enjoyed the scene. He had already learned, 12 months ago, the technique of winning this event, now he was engaged in learning how to become a world champion. By the final day it was clear he was going to be a popular hero for the sport; winning at an average speed of 108.19km/h, the fastest to date.

Solberg's title came as an unexpected turnaround in the fortunes of Subaru this year. It had taken so long to make the 2003 model reliable. It was only in the second half of the season the car had become a winner at all. From there on things went Solberg's way, this was his

Luca Cecchettini entertains the spectators at the Walters Arena in his Fiat Punto Super 1600.

Finally the time had come when the popular British Mini homologation ran out. Neil Burgess finished 39th and won his class! Minis had competed on Rally GB for well over 40 years.

The gloomy side of Wales! This was the temporary service area for competitors driving on the pre-event Shakedown.

Three-way title fight between Carlos Sainz, Petter Solberg and Sébastien Loeb. Solberg was to become the last non-French World Champion for 15 years.

fourth win in the final seven events of the series. Citroën gradually improved the performance of the car to become one of the best all-rounders in the sport. Peugeot was the last remaining team able to beat Citroën to the Manufacturers' title, but when Burns withdrew and Grönholm retired, they had only Harri Rovanperä for any points. Coming up fast as the rally progressed, however, was Freddy Loix, who on his debut for the Peugeot team finished a superb sixth when Rovanperä retired. Overall this had to be a disappointing end to the career of the remarkable 206WRC.

Ford and Škoda came to Wales with no chance of winning a title this year. Ford had won only two events so far, and Škoda was still learning about the Fabia WRC preparing for a full WRC attack in 2005. While Didier Auriol reached the finish and scored championship points, his Škoda team-mate Toni Gardemeister went off the road on the final day and retired. Meanwhile, as Subaru's Solberg battled away, a lot of attention was focussed on his team-mate Tommi Mäkinen on his final rally before retirement. It was to be one of his best results all year. For a long time he was locked in battle with Colin McRae, who also announced his planned withdrawal from championship rallying. It was

wonderful to see these two old-timers fighting each other all through the rally, ahead of everybody except the championship contenders! Another special memory of the event was the final chance to compete with a 'classic' Mini on a World Championship rally before FIA homologation consigned these cars to history. Neil Burgess and Jim Holder won their class in a private car first time out. Back in the late '50s and early '60s it took the official BMC team five attempts before it won its class on this event in a Mini!

Renault driver Brice Tirabassi started the final event as odds on favourite for the Junior title. Both he and his non-championship team-mate Simon Jean-Joseph suffered a lot of shock absorber troubles, and it took all of Brice's efforts to hold on to fourth place in the category before he retired. Racing for the lead were Daniel Carlsson (Suzuki), Kris Meeke (Opel) and Mirco Baldacci (Fiat), but things did not go well for the Suzuki cars. All four of its cars suffered gearbox troubles for no evident reason, it was a struggle to keep the cars going. At one point Salvador Canellas Junior had no gears left, and needed to be pushed into the Service Park, eventually settling for seventh place. Then came Tirabassi's retirement, and suddenly the championship fight livened up. If Suzuki driver Canellas finished second, he would be champion. It seemed an impossible task, but gradually things seemed clear. With three Suzuki drivers ahead, team orders could elevate Canellas into third place and maybe take the title for Suzuki. The pressure became acute when Meeke swerved to avoid some rocks, and went off the road on the final morning. Suzuki could not avoid the facts. The company was consulted, and did not allow the team to issue team orders in Canellas' favour, and gambled on Baldacci, the San Marion driver, striking trouble. In the end Baldacci survived the event, Carlsson won the category, and Tirabassi took the title.

2003 was the last rally for Tommi Mäkinen. It was goodbye to gravel crews and goodbye to registered three-car points-scoring teams.

TRAGIC ILLNESS FOR BURNS

World Champion Richard Burns suffered a blackout when driving from London to Wales Rally GB. Markko Martin was a passenger and steered their car to safety on to the hard shoulder of the motorway. Richard was hospitalised and immediately given tests to discover the trouble, and withdrew from the rally. When medical explanations did not materialise, there were increasing worries about his career as a competitor in his sport, which sadly had come to an end. Freddy Loix was nominated as the replacement driver for Peugeot. Loix had never expected to compete in Britain this year, and the first time he drove a 206WRC on gravel was the day before the start.

RESULTS

Event held: 6-9 November 2003. 14th and final round of Manufacturers' and Drivers' championships.
Start/Finish: Cardiff. Overnight halts: Cardiff.

75 starters, 40 finishers.
18 special stages – 377 kilometres (total 1575 kilometres).

General classification		Group	Penalties (h:m:s)
1 Solberg/Mills	Subaru Impreza	WRC	3:28:58.1
2 Loeb/Elena	Citroën Xsara	WRC	3:29:41.7
3 Mäkinen/Lindström	Subaru Impreza	WRC	3:31:56.9
4 C McRae/Ringer	Citroën Xsara	WRC	3:34:26.2
5 Duval/Prevot	Ford Focus RS	WRC	3:36:14.2
6 Loix/Smeets	Peugeot 206	WRC	3:37:04.6
7 Stohl/Minor	Peugeot 206	WRC	3:37:46.5
8 Kresta/Tomanek	Peugeot 206	WRC	3:38:00.7
9 Pykalisto/Mannisenmaki	Peugeot 206	WRC	3:38:51.7
10 Latvala/Anttila	Ford Focus RS	WRC	3:41:23.4
14 Carlsson/Andersson	Suzuki Ignis S1600	JWRC	3:57:29.8
18 Jones/Lewis	Subaru Impreza	GN	4:02:15.1

Leaders: Solberg stage 1, Loeb 2+3, Solberg 4-18.

2004: Solberg's penultimate stage victory

Petter Solberg kept alive his chances of retaining the Drivers' title when he won the Wales Rally GB for the third successive time, beating championship leader Sébastien Loeb after a long and very close battle which finally went in the Norwegian's favour on the long penultimate stage. Solberg started the rally as the only driver capable of challenging Loeb, although François Duval snatched an early lead on the opening superspecial. The conditions in Wales meant running first car on the road did no harm for Loeb, who was able to pull well ahead on the first two forest stages, while Solberg made a poor start. After stage 3, Loeb was 19.5 seconds in front of Marcus Grönholm. Petter began the long job of catching back lost time. The differences in times between Loeb (Michelin) and Solberg (Pirelli) were essentially down to tyres.

This was a mid-September event held on a route very similar to the 2003 rally with only one completely new stage. Previously difficult relationships between competitors and the Police were absent in 2004 after the Police agreed to delegate all traffic offence matters to the organisers. The Stewards fined Group N driver Peter Bijvelds £600, and JWRC driver Kris Meeke £500 for speeding. Less satisfactory was the decision to take the rally cars away from Cardiff's splendid City Hall, the building which previously made a superb backdrop to the start and finish. Reclaimed land at the docks, adjacent to the Superspecial course, was chosen to host these occasions instead. The warmer and presumably drier conditions meant that tyres played a remarkable part all through the rally. Nobody really knew whether it would be wet or dry, and teams regularly found themselves running short of the correct tyres when the weather turned out to be very mixed. Loeb played a bold hand when he elected, on the Saturday morning, to run six stages on the same set of very soft tyres, reaching the end with the tyres worn down to zero. First time through Margam stage (the penultimate stage on the Saturday) Loeb had a puncture. Then for the second time at Margam, the penultimate stage of the rally itself, Solberg had expected dry conditions and fitted hard, wide tyres, and this was where he took the lead.

Peugeot had a three car team of 307s, Marcus Grönholm and Harri Rovanperä with five-speed gearboxes, and Daniel Carlsson a four-speeder. Grönholm retired when he cut a corner and hit a gatepost, Carlsson slid off but the clutch failed as he tried to regain the road, and Peugeot's only finisher was Rovanperä who had power steering failure (luckily losing very little time), and then gear selection failure, after a rock impacted the underneath of the car.

In the Ford team, Markko Martin was lying third for most of the rally but fell well back on the second day when a turbocharger failed. Duval had been delayed when a rock damaged the pedal box and caused problems with the clutch and the brakes, but he made some good times after taking a bold gamble with ultra soft tyres. The non-registered Škoda team was present with three cars, but suffered badly from not having tested the Fabia in the British forests. All three of its cars experienced handling problems, the cars of Armin Schwarz and Toni Gardemeister going off the road as a result, although

Wet one moment … Alister McRae won the Group N category in his Subaru …

… and sunny the next! Cars line up in the service park in Felindre, north of Swansea.

Gardemeister eventually finished 19th, while Jani Paasonen retired when the clutch failed.

Even behind the leaders the quality of the entry was high, 26 WRC cars started the rally, and once again Manfred Stohl finished the highest placed non-works entry, again in a very old Peugeot 206WRC. On his first full attempt at a gravel rally, the world downhill mountain bike champion, Nicolas Vouilloz finished just outside the points in his Bozian B-team Peugeot. In an ex-works Ford Focus WRC Matthew Wilson, 17-year-old son of M-Sport chief Malcolm, made his World Championship debut, finishing 13th overall. Mark Higgins, also in a Focus WRC, was heading for a points finish when he hit a tree on the penultimate stage. Ironically it was the famous tree which ended Richard Burns' rally in 2002.

There were two special dramas. The first, the day before the rally started, when the FIA refused to allow various 1600cc cars to start, on account of a Junior WRC regulation, new for 2004. This meant arranging, at 24 hours' notice, a supplementary rally to cater for the two unlucky competitors! Secondly there was a political protest by pro-hunting agitators on the second day, which could have been catastrophic for the rally, until the Police blocked main roads and gave an official escort for the rally cars.

Petter Solberg was once again elated, explaining that he never lost his belief that he could win, "I was very worried, even to know if we could finish the rally, because a wheel bearing was failing, but we did not give up hope. My luck came halfway through the last long stage when suddenly the stage, which until then had been very wet, became drier. This immediately gave us the chance to push our car to the limit, and this was where we passed Sébastien. I don't think our manager David Lapworth thought it was ever going to be possible to win but I knew we could – if only the conditions changed. But, I admit, we did leave it all very late …"

Suzukis led the Junior WRC all the way, and for some time were lying 1-2-3-4, then Mirco Baldacci threw away the lead when he rolled, giving team-mate Guy Wilks the lead, which he held to the finish. Per-Gunnar Andersson crashed when his brakes failed. Meeke (Opel) recovered from early misfiring problems, finishing second, having passed Kosti Katajamaki who finished third. Jari-Matti Latvala was slowed by clutch trouble on the first day, but finished fourth. Best Fiat was Xavier Pons in 5th place, normally an asphalt rally specialist. Renaults were unlucky, only the non-championship car of Gareth Jones finished. Nicolas Bernardi went off the road, Larry Cols lost a lot of time when the sumpguard became detached, and Oliver Marshall broke his engine mountings. Winner Guy Wilks

Colourful cars. Teammates Matthew Wilson (behind) and Mark Higgins in their M-Sport team Ford Focus WRC cars.

General classification		Group	Penalties (h:m:s)
1 Solberg/Mills	Subaru Impreza	WRC	3:42:39.5
2 Loeb/Elena	Citroën Xsara	WRC	3:42:45.8
3 Martin/Park	Ford Focus RS	WRC	3:45:33.2
4 Sainz/Marti	Citroën Xsara	WRC	3:46:21.6
5 Duval/Prevot	Ford Focus RS	WRC	3:47:20.8
6 Rovanperä/Pietilainen	Peugeot 307	WRC	3:49:24.4
7 Hirvonen/Lehtinen	Subaru Impreza	WRC	3:49:47.8
8 Stohl/Minor	Peugeot 206	WRC	3:52:59.6
9 Vouilloz/Giraudet	Peugeot 206	WRC	3:57:51.8
10 Warmbold/Price	Ford Focus RS	WRC	3:58:28.8
14 A McRae/Patterson	Subaru Impreza WRX	GN	4:07:36.1
18 Wilks/Pugh	Suzuki Ignis S1600	JWRC	4:16:25.6

Leaders: Duval stage 1, Loeb 2-17, Solberg 18+19.

2005: Michael Park died. Loeb forfeits win

The tragic accident on the final morning of the rally overshadowed the memory of another fine battle in the forests. At a time when the top drivers had settled into their positions with Sébastien Loeb safely in the lead, Petter Solberg doing better than he expected in second place, and Marcus Grönholm back to third after suffering first morning brake problems, the rally seemed like being played out to an anticlimactic end. Then, early on Sunday, came news of a terrible crash involving Markko Martin, Peugeot's number two driver, in which co-driver Michael Park died. It had been 12 years since there had been such a black day in World Championship rallying, a tragedy that touched everyone. Team-mate Grönholm immediately withdrew from the event, which meanwhile had been shortened so that only the run to the Finish in Cardiff remained. Peugeot's great rival driver at Citroën, Loeb made up his own mind. He had no wish to win a rally and particularly to become Champion on such a day. He accordingly arranged to check in at the next control two minutes early, thus incurring a two minute time control penalty, demoting himself to third place. This allowed Solberg to win the event (for the fourth successive time) and Loeb's team-mate François Duval to come second.

This year the rally headquarters was located at the Millennium Stadium in Cardiff. No special stage was held on the Thursday evening. There was free transit for the cars from the Ceremonial Start in Cardiff to the restart the next morning at Felindre service park near Swansea. A special stage was held in Cardiff of just 1.1km, on a concrete surface, and finished in the Millennium Stadium on the Saturday night. This was a one-at-a-time section, not a Superspecial. The shortest stage in the world?

The 12th round of the 2005 World Rally series had promised much. Rally GB is traditionally one of the smoothest gravel

now led the series with two rounds to go. Biggest drama was when Mathieu Biasion's Renault crashed off the road on the first Rheola stage, then on the second run of this stage, Guerlain Chicherit (Citroën Saxo) went off at the same corner and rolled right over the stricken Clio.

THE EVER CHANGING CHARACTER OF THE WRC

Every WRC rally now had a new shorter timespan (between Wednesday morning through to Sunday afternoon) into which everything, including recce, had to be fitted. This involved a new time-saving recce programme called the '1000 Pistes' system. The number of tyres used by each crew was strictly controlled by barcoding the identities of tyres nominated by the teams. Flexi service where competitors declared at what time after the final stage they would work on their cars eased pressure on mechanics.

RESULTS

Event held: 16-19 September 2004. 12th round of 16 of Manufacturers' and Drivers' championships.
Start/Finish: Cardiff. Overnight halts: Swansea.

83 starters, 42 finishers.
19 special stages – 394 kilometres (total 1298 kilometres).

Little doubt where you are!

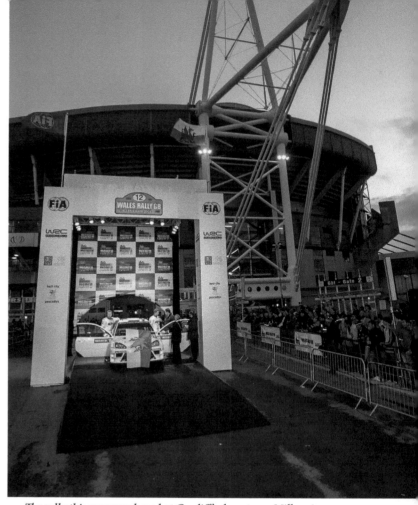

The rally this year was based at Cardiff's downtown Millennium Stadium. Antony Warmbold and Michael Orr (Focus RS WRC) wait their turn to start.

championship events, where sheer car performance and driver skills are paramount. There was a chance Loeb could win the World Drivers' title, and there was a continuing and tense struggle between Citroën and Peugeot for the Manufacturers' title. There was a chance that three times event winner Solberg might pull off a rare fourth successive victory. In fact there was a cautious approach from the potential leaders. Citroën was well aware this was an event it had never won before, and as it had discovered to its cost the year before, unexpected things could always happen. Petter had been testing parts for the '06 Impreza before the rally and this made him aware that the current '05 car was not everything it could be, so he felt it would be impossible to match Loeb's times. By stage 2, Loeb was in front and stayed there until the fateful stage 15.

Solberg was the only driver out of Subaru's three car team to complete the course, as both Stephane Sarrazin and Chris Atkinson went off the road. Once again Mitsubishi finished the 'best of the rest.' Harri Rovanperä was this time the faster driver in the team, holding a splendid third place until he lost third gear at the end of the second day while Gianluigi Galli, on his first Wales Rally GB, had been seventh until he also went off the road on stage 15. Ford had an unhappy event with its WRCs. Toni Gardemeister was excluded from a disappointing ninth place when, at the end of Leg 1, his car was found to be underweight, while Roman Kresta could only manage sixth. One moment of cheer was that its promotional formula Group N Fiesta won its class. Škoda played its cards hard. Conscious that none of its previous six team drivers had finished a World Rally this year in the top eight (drivers' points scoring) positions, they gambled on inviting

a 'big name' driver into the team, to see if the weaknesses had been driver rather than car related. Colin McRae was the chosen 'name,' and by the final control he had risen to seventh overall.

The championship therefore remained open, to be decided another day.

The strength of contenders in the Production Car series had started to thin out. Championship leader Toshi Arai nominated this as one of the two events he would miss. The FIA had unilaterally allowed Xavier Pons to withdraw from the series, having been offered a WRC drive instead, and two further drivers were absent: Brice Tirabassi (illness) and Karamjit Singh (apparently on financial grounds), so consequently only eight contenders took the start. Aki Teiskonen led after all but one stage (when he suffered a differential problem) winning both this and the Group N category. The Argentinean driver Marcos Ligato, made his first appearance in Britain, finished second ahead of the recently crowned Middle East champion Nasser Al-

Just a little reminder of heritage. This same Mini Cooper S in the foreground won the event 40 years earlier.

Media officials and tyre technicians greet the eventual winner Petter Solberg at the end of a stage on the Eppynt ranges. Solberg did not win any stages on this event.

Attiyah. Andrea Medeghini eventually finished sixth having lost a lot of time with a puncture on the first day. Going with a style and consistency seldom seen before was Natalie Barratt, who climbed up to fifth place, but then she damaged her rear suspension and did not finish the second day. She finished seventh, scoring her first points in the 2005 series. The competition was livened up by the appearance of non-championship entries from David Higgins and Niall McShea, both of whom initially led the championship cars. McShea fell back on stage 3 when he had a pacenote problem and spent the rest of the event trying, unsuccessfully, to catch Teiskonen, finishing 19th overall and second in Group N. Higgins had a time-consuming puncture on the second stage, when he had stopped to change the wheel and was hard pressed all event to climb back into the top six, finishing 24th overall and sixth in Group N. Non-championship driver Patrik Flodin made three Group N fastest times.

BEATEN BY MUD!

Toni Gardemeister was excluded because his car was not muddy enough! Engineers explained that this was a bad situation where every possible factor was taken into account, but their tolerance of weight changes did not balance each other, but instead compounded each other. One engineer detailed the problems. The cars were weighed at the end of the first leg of six stages. There were two identical loops of three stages, one in the morning and the other in drier conditions in the afternoon. At the end of the first loop, some 40kg of mud was removed by the team from Gardemeister's car but after the second loop, virtually none. Toni added: "For sure, mud was not the only problem. The tyre wear had been more accentuated on the second lap than we expected, so the tyres were slightly lighter than expected when the car arrived for the final service of the day" (at which point the official weighing took place). But there was another factor. On arriving at service, the organisers sent cars into a wash area, one of the objects being to remove mud clinging to the cars, to make the cars cleaner when they entered service. Who knows how much mud had been unwittingly removed – and thereby created the circumstances in which the car was underweight and therefore out of the rally?

RESULTS

Event held: 16-18 September 2005. 12th round of 16 of Manufacturers' and Drivers' championships.
Start/Finish: Swansea/Cardiff. Overnight halts: Swansea.

80 starters, 56 finishers.
15 special stages but two cancelled and one stopped – 297 kilometres (total 1252 kilometres).

General classification		Group	Penalties (h:m:s)
1 P Solberg/Mills	Subaru Impreza	WRC	2:45:57.8
2 Duval/Smeets	Citroën Xsara	WRC	2:47:15.2
3 Loeb/Elena	Citroën Xsara	WRC	2:47:15.7
4 Rovanperä/Pietilainen	Mitsubishi Lancer	WRC	2:47:27.2
5 Stohl/Minor	Citroën Xsara	WRC	2:48:32.8
6 Kresta/Tomanek	Ford Focus	WRC	2:49:15.1
7 McRae/Grist	Škoda Fabia	WRC	2:49:28.2
8 M Higgins/Thomas	Ford Focus	WRC	2:49:38.7
9 Meeke/Patterson	Subaru Impreza	WRC	2:49:39.9
10 H Solberg/Menkerud	Ford Focus	WRC	2:50:18.3
18 A Teiskonen/ M Teiskonen	Subaru Impreza	PCWRC	3:04:03.5

Leaders: Grönholm stage 1, Loeb 2-15. Solberg at finish.

2006: Rally win and two titles for Ford

Marcus Grönholm's seventh win of 2006 may not have been enough to win him the World Drivers' title, but at least he became the most successful driver in the history of the series from Finland with his 25th WRC career victory (he went on to win a total of 30 in all). Ford in turn ended the season with a record number of points scored by a manufacturer in a year to date, Ford and Citroën with eight wins apiece, BF Goodrich tyres had won every round. In the fast, damp and slippery stages in South Wales, Subaru had a disappointing rally as Petter Solberg struggled to keep up, the Norwegian not repeating the wins he had gained over the past four years. Citroën fared even worse, but the OMV Peugeot Norway team had its best result, with an impressively measured second place for Manfred Stohl, while three reliable Škodas rounded off the top ten. The rally reverted to its more traditional late autumn date, perpetuating the tradition of driving flat out over fast, slippery, mountainous forest tracks, but this year the sponsors explored the promotional opportunities presented by the sport, to a greater degree than many were happy to see.

Reverting to the final round in the championship since 2003 meant Wales Rally GB was again run in shorter daylight hours which demanded various route changes. The first time since 1986 that the FIA World Rally Championship had stretched into December, it also had the greatest number of starters on a World Rally for five years, since Finland 2001. Another novelty was the use of a penalty system for missing a stage on a road section, it was not necessary to complete the route to be classified as a finisher and score points, and the 'Five Minute Rule' was also extended. In theory, a driver could be classified (and indeed score points) without tackling any special stages at all – all they had to do was to cross the start line each morning and present the car at the parc ferme after the finish. This was the SupeRally rule, later to become known as 'Rally2' and in 2019 'Restart.'

Stormy weather with heavy rain on the Saturday night left a legacy of lying water, mud, and conditions as slippery as you could imagine.

More Eppynt madness. This time the victim was Connor McCloskey and his Group N Mitsubishi Lancer Evolution IX.

Curious indoor finish ramp at the Millennium Stadium for Marcus Grönholm and Timo Rautiainen. Weird. Note the empty seats …

Even the winner Grönholm made a spin, as did Solberg, which cost him any chance to challenge Stohl for second. Jari-Matti Latvala finished fourth, giving the Stobart team its best overall result of the season. Three Škodas finished in the top ten places while the fourth car, driven by Andreas Aigner, went off the road and damaged its engine. 17-year-old Andreas Mikkelsen went off the road twice, and was not among the finishers. His fellow Norwegian Mads Østberg crashed early on, but eventually reached the finish through use of SupeRally penalties. All six registered teams came to Britain for the final round, the main anxiety in the air being the indecision about the detailed technical rules for 2007. So much waited to happen in 2007. This expectancy was highlighted by the appearance here of Alister McRae in one of the new Super 2000 cars in the form of a Toyota Corolla. On the car's first event outside South Africa, this was essentially an opportunity to learn more about the development potential of the car and the formula, even if it had to compete within the category. After a cautious start, the team removed power-sapping baffles, and made three best stage times on the final day. In the end a ball joint bolt failed, and the car went off the road on the final stage!

The highest placed Super 1600 car on the event was Juho Hänninen's PH Sport Citroën C2. The final battle for the Junior WRC title was incredible. Six drivers were still able to win the title. Leaders on the event were Guy Wilks, until he had four punctures on stage 3, and Kris Meeke, till he went off the road. Wilks again took the lead until he landed heavily and smashed the transmission casing. 19-year-old Estonian Jaan Mölder, was out of the title race, led till he punctured a tyre on the first stage of the final day; Patrik Sandell took over, but

went off the road on the next stage, and Mölder retook the lead to the finish. He was the youngest driver to win a JWRC round. Misfortunes followed the other championship contenders. Jozef Béreš had a broken gearbox while Urmo Aava broke his steering. Finally, both Sandell and Per-Gunnar Andersson were stuck far off the road, and had to wait for rescue. Then SupeRally stepped in. The championship title would not be decided by speed over the stages, but ultimately by rescue vehicles getting broken rally cars back to Cardiff before results were announced. In the end, Sandell's car was transported to Cardiff with an hour to spare. Sandell said "My worry was the breakdown truck bringing our car to the finish was itself going to break down on the way …!"

In 2006, MMSP closed its Mitsubishi World Championship operation based in Rugby, Markko Martin announced, on Estonian national television, his retirement from professional rallying, and it was the end of the line for the Citroën Xsara WRC.

P-G Andersson (Suzuki Swift S1600) threw away his chance of another Junior WRC title with this last morning accident.

François Duval's eighth place Fabia WRC on his final works drive for Škoda Motorsport.

VICTORY FOR A TOW TRUCK

Under prevailing SupeRally rules, rally cars did not have to drive all the stages. They did not even have to be driven to the finish under their power, to be classified as finishers – or win their categories – or the rally – or a championship. It was bad enough that the British championship category winner Ryan Champion used SupeRally rules to qualify as a finisher in a broken down vehicle, he also used the rules so his immobile car could overtake David Higgins and Stuart Jones in the results! Having the eventual Junior WRC champion Patrik Sandell anxiously knowing that his world title depended on the recovery truck safely reaching the finish with his wrecked car on board was absurd. And, because the finish proceedings had long since closed by the time the truck arrived, the champion did not even cross the finish ramp. That was lucky, because it was doubtful if the finish ramp would have been strong enough for the crew to spray their champagne standing on top of a recovery truck.

RESULTS

Event held: 1-3 December 2006. 16th and final round of Manufacturers' and Drivers' championships.
Start/Finish: Swansea/Cardiff. Overnight halts: Swansea.

111 starters, 82 finishers.
17 special stages – 356 kilometres (total 1207 kilometres).

General classification		Group	Penalties (h:m:s)
1 Grönholm/Rautiainen	Ford Focus RS	WRC	3:20:24.8
2 Stohl/Minor	Peugeot 307	WRC	3:22:00.3
3 Solberg/Mills	Subaru Impreza	WRC	3:22:20.0
4 Latvala/Anttila	Ford Focus RS	WRC	3:23:01.9
5 Pons/Del Barrio	Citroën Xsara	WRC	3:23:44.7
6 Atkinson/MacNeall	Subaru Impreza	WRC	3:23:52.3
7 Sordo/Marti	Citroën Xsara	WRC	3:24:33.1
8 Duval/Pivato	Škoda Fabia	WRC	3:24:47.4
9 Rovanperä/Pietilainen	Škoda Fabia	WRC	3:28:25.1
10 Kopecky/Schovanek	Škoda Fabia	WRC	3:29:52.6
13 Alén/Alanne	Subaru Impreza	GN	3:40:49.6
19 Hänninen/Sallinen	Citroën C2	S1600	3:52:51.8
20 Mölder/Becker	Suzuki Swift S1600	JWRC	3:55:04.7

Leader: Grönholm stages 1-17.

2007: Hirvonen winner, Loeb the champion

The Manufacturers' championship had effectively been won on stage 4 in Ireland two weeks earlier when Marcus Grönholm attacked an Irish wall with his Focus, but Sébastien Loeb inherited his ticket to the World Drivers' title on this event, cruising to an easy third place behind the Fords of Mikko Hirvonen and Grönholm. For Grönholm it was the end of a wonderful sporting career, leading the BP-Ford team to its second consecutive Manufacturers' title before handing over the reins of the team to his younger team-mate and compatriot Mikko Hirvonen.

This year the Service Park moved to the Swansea Waterfront development complex while the Start and Finish ceremonies were back at the Cardiff City Hall. The final forest stages on the Friday and Saturday were run in full darkness. There were various new championship rules. On road sections, a competition car had to be driven on four wheels and tyres, no more free-wheeling for rally cars. Each team could only use ten chassis per year for testing and for use on events, fewer if the team had not entered a full WRC season. All registered championship World Rally Cars had to fit two accident data recorders. Remote Service Zones far away from Service Parks could be created, with restricted numbers of crews allowed to work on cars, and using only equipment and parts carried by the competing cars. Testing for manufacturers' teams, was limited to 13 sessions (total of 48 days per year), except at a team's designated permanent testing sites.

Malcolm Wilson presents Marcus Grönholm with a ceremonial gift to celebrate his 150th WRC event. Co-driver Timo Rautiainen (left) looks on.

The cheeky competition creed of future double FIA Group N champion Armindo Araújo.

Right from the start the 2007 event was to be a rally of attrition, where holding station was even more important than taking risks trying to win. It was a splendid chance for Jari-Matti Latvala in his quest to prove once again his credentials for a full works drive in the future. His hopes of a top finishing position were dashed in the heavy storms on the first day, when he lost a lot of time struggling along without windscreen wipers, and like many other drivers, with endless windscreen misting problems as well. When he returned to the competition on the second day, Latvala (driving on his sixth Rally GB) won every forest stage, proving the fastest driver on the event, and did his reputation no harm, at a time when Ford's driver line-up for 2008 was still under discussion.

Despite the challenge of the conditions, this year's British event was where young drivers did better than ever. The non-championship 20-year-old Matthew Wilson finished in a very competent sixth place and best British driver, ahead of five registered team drivers. In the end the top private team driver was the Norwegian Mads Østberg (also 20 years old) in his much-rallied three-year-old Subaru, who was finally overtaken into tenth place by 22-year-old Latvala on the final stage of the rally. Before his retirement 18-year-old Andreas Mikkelsen had been lying tenth overall, 18-year-old Elfyn Evans won his class in his Group N Ford Fiesta ST, finishing the highest placed driver of a two-wheel drive car on the event, while the 19-year-old Darren Gass won his class in his Citroën C2 Super 1600.

There was no technical innovation on the event, but one thing that was as demanding as ever, the inevitable unfriendliness of torrential rain … Also, even though this was not the first time that World Rally Cars had been driven on orthodox stages at night this year, it was the first time there were gravel stages and stages in the rain at night for a long time. There was a lot of dissatisfaction with the performance of cars' headlamps! Subaru was still working hard to improve its '07 cars, and this time all three finished in the top ten – Petter Solberg fourth, Chris Atkinson seventh and Xavier Pons ninth, but still there were problems, especially in the rain. Subaru's co-drivers were forced to make long range mops out of sticks of wood to keep their drivers seeing where they were going. Suzuki brought its SX4 for its competition baptism on gravel. The team gained valuable experience but had its problems, notably loss of hydraulic pressure and brake troubles. It was the first time that Conrad Rautenbach had rallied a World Rally Car, and Mikkelsen had a new ex-works Focus, but both cars ended their events off the road on the army ranges of Eppynt on the Saturday.

Andreas Mikkelsen (Ford Focus RS WRC) learns the art of rally driving the expensive way.

Toshihiro Arai stayed away from the final two rounds in the Production Car series, as his quota of six qualifying events had already been accomplished, waiting back home in Japan for news from Wales as to whether Gabriel Pozzo, his sole remaining challenger, could pull off the category victory that he needed to beat Arai to the title. Pozzo faced an uphill battle. Not only was this, as ever, one of the trickiest rallies in the series, but he was also at a disadvantage. This rally had a side attraction, the final two rounds of the British championship were doubled up with the main event. Because the British championship was run for Group N cars, the organisers, to make things fairer for the BRC competitors, brought two of the three top British competitors into the PCWRC as 'guest' drivers. This meant in order to win the category Pozzo had to beat these additional experienced local drivers as well. Pozzo's hopes came to an end, however, when he went off the road on the first day, and Arai heard the news he had gained the title for a second time. Mark Higgins took an early lead in the Production Car category, but he had a variety of problems. His BRC rival Guy Wilks got ahead to lead all the way to the finish, to win the category on the overall event and take the British title. Challenging hard was Juho Hänninen, top non-British PCWRC driver, who suffered punctures like all the other top drivers, and who eventually finished second.

Wales Rally GB was a turning point in rallying. For example, it was to be the last rally in which tyre insert mousses were allowed, indeed in which freedom of tyre supplier was allowed for four-wheel drive cars, and the last opportunity for cuts to be made in the tread patterns of tyres. Exit Guy Fréquelin, architect of Citroën's remarkable World Championship success story, and goodbye to the OMV team which had brought a new degree of social responsibility to rally sport with its carbon-neutral policy, and finally farewell to 33-year-old Marcus Grönholm, the "father" of the present era World Championship drivers (and whose 20-year career had spanned 150 WCR starts and two World Championships titles) and his brother-in-law co-driver Timo Rautiainen. And, sadly, the sport lost 1995 World Rally Champion Colin McRae, who died earlier in the year.

RESULTS

Event held: 30 November-2 December 2007. 16th and final round of Manufacturers' and Drivers' championships.
Start/Finish: Swansea /Cardiff. Overnight halts: Swansea.

108 starters, 83 finishers.
17 special stages – 360 kilometres (total 1272 kilometres).

General classification		Group	Penalties (h:m:s)
1 Hirvonen/Lehtinen	Ford Focus RS	WRC	3:22:50.9
2 Grönholm/Rautiainen	Ford Focus RS	WRC	3:23:06.1
3 Loeb/Elena	Citroën C4	WRC	3:24:23.9
4 Solberg/Mills	Subaru Impreza	WRC	3:25:48.2
5 Sordo/Marti	Citroën C4	WRC	3:26:05.2
6 Wilson/Orr	Ford Focus RS	WRC	3:30:23.8
7 Atkinson/Prevot	Subaru Impreza	WRC	3:31:20.4
8 Stohl/Minor	Citroën Xsara	WRC	3:31:45.5
9 Pons/Amigo	Subaru Impreza	WRC	3:32:39.7
10 Latvala/Anttila	Ford Focus RS	WRC	3:33:33.3
13 Wilks/Pugh	Mitsubishi Lancer Evolution	PCWRC	3:44:23.7
50 Gass/Shanks	Citroën C2	S1600	4:37:22.2

Leader: Hirvonen stages 1-17.

2008: Citroën wins title on an icy rally

Wintry conditions made the Wales Rally GB, this time run fully within December, a veritable festival of ice, a challenge made more difficult by rules forcing crews to run with wide summer-time gravel tyres, with no studs. On the penultimate stage of the rally Sébastien Loeb snatched the lead to take victory from long time leader Jari-Matti Latvala. When Latvala's team-mate Mikko Hirvonen lost time upside down on Day 1, the FIA Manufacturers' championship was effectively passed to the Citroën Total team. The sensation of the event, however, was Citroën's Junior World Champion Sébastien Ogier, who rallied a World Rally Car for the first time, and led overall after the first four stages. New this year was a complete ban on tyre anti-deflation mousse inserts and Pirelli replaced BF Goodrich as the official control tyre supplier.

There was a bold decision by the organisers to invoke the remote

Spanish Honda Civic Type-R driver Dani Sola, the 2002 Junior WRC champion, demonstrates speedy wheel changing.

M-Sport hierarchy Malcolm Wilson and Belgian chief engineer Christian Loriaux greet guest driver Valentino Rossi.

Second finisher Jari-Matti Latvala who led for much of the rally. It would be another three years before it would all come right for him in Britain.

service park option at Builth Wells, so that the forests in Central Wales could be visited. Going to that region, however, turned out to be a nightmare on account of cancelled stages and disruption for spectators, but, for the now traditional stages further south, the icy conditions provided spectacularly exciting rallying. Running first cars on the road through the event made for many nervous moments for Loeb and Latvala, while later running cars could see in advance where the earlier cars had their worrying antics. For some crews, especially those in two-wheel drive cars, progressively glazing icy surfaces created problems even on road sections.

Severely icy conditions led to huge route cuts on Day 1. On a day when there were supposed to be 123km of stages, all to be tackled without major service, there were finally only 57km, and it was difficult for crews to know what tactics to use. Survival instincts came to the fore, even to reach the starts of stages inside the forests became a challenge too great for some. There were two stars in the opening stages, Ogier and Mads Østberg. The French driver took the lead on the first stage to be run, but dropped back with gearbox problems on Friday. He restarted again on Day 2, only to go off the road. Østberg was lying second overall for a couple of stages before suffering the perennial Subaru problem of misting windscreen! He was lying in fifth place, easily the top privateer, with six stages to go when he met a very icy corner, and that was the end of his event. In trouble all through Day 1 was Hirvonen, delayed after overturning in the publicity stage at Sweet Lamb. By Saturday there was some normal order. While Latvala did his best, Hirvonen only started to make competitive times on Day 2. Latvala led Loeb by 12.9 seconds, while Per-Gunnar Andersson was lying in an impressive third place in his Suzuki ahead of Østberg. Of the Suzukis, Andersson was considerably happier than Toni Gardemeister who was out of the top ten, while Chris Atkinson had a heavy crash on stage 7.

On Day 2 Loeb kept station behind Latvala, ending the day 7.3 seconds adrift, and ensuring once again that Latvala had the misery of running first car on the road on the final day. All the time Dani Sordo supported Loeb, after having made a dream time on the first stage on the Saturday, while Petter Solberg remained in fourth. This was without doubt one of the most exciting contests all year. There was interest everywhere you turned. Loeb scored a record 11th win in a season, Hirvonen became the first driver to score Drivers' championship points on every round of the season. One of the greatest attractions was the return to the 'Rally GB' of MotoGP champion Valentino Rossi, who vowed to make no silly mistakes and give himself the chance to learn more about the sport. What an event to choose! To his

Missed but not forgotten. This plaque was placed on the tree which cost the life of Michael Park three years earlier.

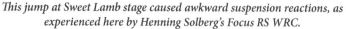

This jump at Sweet Lamb stage caused awkward suspension reactions, as experienced here by Henning Solberg's Focus RS WRC.

credit Rossi finished 12th overall, not far behind Matthew Wilson and Barry Clark who also avoided the pitfalls of the route. At the other end of the celebrity scale came 17-year-old Tom Cave, who only passed his street driving test shortly before the event – and won his class (1600 Group N) by a quarter of an hour!

Juho Hänninen was favourite for the Production Car title, but he had misfortunes on the first day and could not continue. Andreas Aigner then just had to finish in the top three placings in the category to win the title, which he was doing on the final day before Patrik Sandell retired, and he came home second. After Mark Higgins led initially in his Impreza N11, Guy Wilks went ahead with his Evo IX. On the second day Wilks eased his pace, mindful of the British championship which his team were anxious he should win, and this let Patrik Flodin in his Subaru Impreza N14 into the lead. Flodin acquired a handsome lead, as his rivals fell by the wayside, but on the final morning Sandell was catching up fast in his Peugeot S2000, much more suited to the conditions later on in the event. Sandell, however, had engine problems, and retired on the final stage. Of the 25 cars which started in PCWRC, only ten were classified as finishers and of these only six completed the full route. Car after car had trouble in the water crossings, often causing terminal engine failure, but few so spectacular as for Armindo Araújo, who left the road on an icy liaison section and whose car ended up a considerable distance off the road in a river. He was able to carry on, and scored two points! It was a happy day for Aigner, the third Austrian world motorsport champion: "Rindt, Lauda and Aigner. That's got a nice ring to it!"

THE ROSSI FACTOR

No event is without amusing stories when Valentino Rossi is in town, and Wales Rally GB was no exception. "During recce I saw Sébastien Loeb standing beside the track just after the end of a stage" said Rossi, "so I thought I would stop and ask how things were going for him. He seemed normal, was nice, said this and that, nothing special. Then I had a big surprise. Behind where he was standing was a drop down into the trees, and his recce car was well off the road out of sight!" This was Valentino's return to orthodox rallying. He was at the event six years before and it was only his second orthodox rally. "I have always had a great passion for rally. After my father retired from bikes, he took up rallying. He used to take me along and showed me how to go sideways in car!"

Despite some unbelievably tricky conditions, Rossi drew praise from the experts. Loeb, "If I ever tried to race in the MotoGP I would be left far behind. The way he went, considering his lack of experience of pacenotes, and to have only two passes in recce, especially in the prevailing conditions, was remarkable!" Latvala: "The last time he came to WRGB was six years ago. That was also my first World Championship rally. It has taken me all this time to be able to challenge people like Loeb. Valentino's first attempt was all wrong, but this time he did it all correctly. He set out to have fun, to finish, start off slowly – and his 12th place was excellent."

RESULTS

Event held: 5-7 December 2008. 15th and final round of Manufacturers' and Drivers' championships.
Start/Finish: Swansea/Cardiff. Overnight halts: Swansea.

78 starters, 47 finishers.
19 special stages but two cancelled – 275 kilometres (total 1418 kilometres).

General classification		Group	Penalties (h:m:s)
1 Loeb/Elena	Citroën C4	WRC	2:43:09.6
2 Latvala/Anttila	Ford Focus RS	WRC	2:43:22.3
3 Sordo/Marti	Citroën C4	WRC	2:44:30.2
4 Solberg/Mills	Subaru Impreza	WRC	2:45:09.2
5 P G Andersson/J Andersson	Suzuki SX4	WRC	2:47:13.7
6 Duval/Giraudet	Ford Focus RS	WRC	2:48:17.4
7 Gardemeister/Tuominen	Suzuki SX4	WRC	2:48:34.6
8 Hirvonen/Lehtinen	Ford Focus RS	WRC	2:48:48.4
9 Wilson/Martin	Ford Focus RS	WRC	2:51:23.5
10 Clark/Nagle	Ford Focus RS	WRC	2:53:02.7
11 Flodin/Bergsten	Subaru Impreza	PCWRC	2:56:01.3

Leaders: (stage 1 cancelled) Ogier stages 2-5, Latvala 6-17, Loeb 18+19.

2009: Loeb's penultimate stage victory

Sunshine and heavy rain storms swept the southern counties of Wales with reports of broken windscreen wipers and huge puddles forming on the gravel forest tracks. Citroën's Sébastien Loeb and Ford's Mikko Hirvonen won every stage between them. Ford had a testing time with an unprecedented series of broken driveshaft couplings, and on the final day Citroën's protégé driver Sébastien Ogier lost fifth place when he swerved to avoid rocks in the road, which the storms and passing cars had dislodged. A remarkable drive to ninth place overall came from 21-year-old Eyvind Brynildsen. This should have given him victory in both the Group N and PCWRC categories in his Škoda Fabia S2000, but after the event he was excluded for using undersize rear brake caliper pistons. This gave Group N victory to Armindo Araújo, the first such win on a World Rally for an Evo X and victory in the PCWRC category for the Evo IX of Martin Prokop.

The rally was held six weeks earlier than usual, and the FIA's WCR season finished before the end of October for the first time ever. Rally HQ, Ceremonial Start and the Finish formalities were all held at the Wales Millennium Centre in the Cardiff Bay area with the Service Park close by. Changes this year included the size of wheels for use on World Championship events limited to either 15 inch for gravel or 18 inch for

Zimbabwean driver Conrad Rautenbach competed in Rally GB five times, his eighth place was his best result – and the final time he competed in Europe.

2009 was the first year after the end of Subaru's WRC team, leading to Petter Solberg setting up a remarkable private team running works-specification Citroëns. This was only the second time he had a C4 WRC and he finished fourth both times. His motto: "This is my life!"

THE GREAT BRITISH RALLY

The media busily trying to make sense of it all at the post-event press conference.

One of the few stately homes in Wales featured in Rally GB is this house on the Margam Country Park stage. There was a nightmare retirement for Sébastien Ogier, going off the road avoiding dislodged rocks.

asphalt. Only four mechanics could work on cars at the same time, as opposed to six. The title "Wales" had been dropped from the name for Britain's 2009 round of the WRC. Six months before the event the Welsh Assembly Government (WAG) withdrew its sponsorship of Rally GB with immediate effect, and apparently with no prior warning to the organisers IMS who issued a statement saying that this was in breach of the existing contract for the period up to and including the 2011 rally. The event was now funded by the British motorsport federation.

Ford came to Cardiff cautiously confident, the British forests its home ground. The battle between Loeb and Hirvonen was a classic World Championship struggle. At the start there was nothing between the capabilities of either driver and car, the championship would be decided by either errors or unforeseen eventualities. Through Day 1 the two drivers were neck-and-neck, Loeb leading by a 5.3 second margin, but, from the start, strange things were happening for Ford. On the first stage Jari-Matti Latvala had a sudden and dramatic failure of the driveshaft coupling, and lost a lot of time, then later that morning its number three car, driven by Khalid Al Qassimi, had the same problem. On the long road section from stage 6 back to the end-of-day service in Cardiff, Hirvonen suffered the same problem, although he was able to drive the car back to base.

On the opening stage of Day 2 Hirvonen reduced Loeb's lead to 2.9 seconds, then something happened that nobody could understand. Hirvonen found his car just would not perform at its best on stages 8 and 9, it behaved strangely and unpredictably. "Something wasn't right. I just couldn't make good times and I really

do not understand what went wrong," Mikko admitted. On these two stages the official split times told the story, a gradual reduction in Mikko's performance compared with that of Sébastien's. Meanwhile Loeb continued his faultless flat-out progress. Hirvonen regained his competitive speed, albeit some 20-30 seconds behind. Could Hirvonen catch Loeb on the last day? It was doubtful, but he never gave up. The championship was settled on the penultimate stage when the bonnet on Hirvonen's Focus was dislodged after a heavy landing. His vision was completely obscured as they travelled at 170km/h down the stage so he had no option but to stop, and co-driver Jarmo Lehtinen removed the bonnet.

The rest of the field were miles behind the drivers who were racing for the title. There was a fascinating battle between Dani Sordo and Citroën's guest driver, Petter Solberg, who at the end of Day 1 was lying third overall, but was then delayed by windscreen wiper troubles in heavy rain on Day 2. Sébastien Ogier was secure in fifth place, four Citroëns in the top five places, until he crashed on the final stage. Ford's supporting drivers finished fifth and sixth, though Henning Solberg had to drive a whole day with a mysterious misfire, while Matthew Wilson had strange handling only cured at the end of Day 1 by a transmission change. Latvala, who had lost nearly seven minutes with his driveshaft trouble, was eventually unchallenged in eighth place.

Armindo Araújo, already confirmed as Production Car champion, used Rally GB as an opportunity to help his Ralliart Italy team develop its troublesome Lancer Evo X. He went well whenever engine overheating trouble allowed, and made his way to the finish ahead of all the orthodox Group N cars. The sensation of the event was Eyvind Brynildsen at the wheel of a Škoda Fabia S2000 (allowed that year to compete in the PCWRC class), a car the former Mitsubishi driver had only been using for a few weeks. Brynildsen led PCWRC throughout, but after the finish was excluded, wrongly packaged pieces having been supplied by the factory. Apart from an early challenge from Nasser Al-Attiyah, Martin Prokop in an orthodox Group N car was second, in his Lancer Evo IX, while Toshi Arai settled for third. Patrik Flodin lost a wheel on stage 3 and was unable to drive to the midday service, but restarted under SupeRally and was able to finish sixth in the category. Patrik Sandell had no sooner passed Prokop into second than he suffered power steering trouble and slid off the road, he eventually finished seventh.

After the 2009 rally, Suzuki and, days later, Subaru both stopped their WRC activities.

WHY WE LOST – MALCOLM WILSON, M-SPORT, DIRECTOR OF BP FORD ABU DHABI WRT

"I think Mikko lost the championship on stages 8 and 9, not on the final day when the bonnet flew up. It was psychological rather than a mechanical problem. We would have been happy if we could have found some mechanical problem, it would have made things easier for everybody in the team to accept, Mikko and ourselves included, but there was nothing mechanically wrong. Mikko knows it. I believe that after all this Mikko will come back even stronger next year. If you look at how he has progressed over the years it has always been disappointments like this that have made him even stronger. The performances of Sébastien Loeb and Mikko on this rally were in a different class to everybody else. In stage 8 I think Sébastien used all the skills in his book, gained from his five previous championship titles and his 53 rally wins, to best use on those stages. I think it was the Loeb factor that ended up costing us the rally and the title for Mikko."

RESULTS

Event held: 23-25 October 2009. 12th and final round of Manufacturers' and Drivers' championships.
Start/Finish: Cardiff. Overnight halts: Cardiff.

62 starters, 50 finishers.
16 special stages – 348 kilometres (total 1466 kilometres).

General classification		Group	Penalties (h:m:s)
1 Loeb/Elena	Citroën C4	WRC	3:16:25.4
2 Hirvonen/Lehtinen	Ford Focus RS	WRC	3:17:31.5
3 Sordo/Martí	Citroën C4	WRC	3:17:32.5
4 P Solberg/Mills	Citroën C4	WRC	3:17:53.5
5 H Solberg/Menkerud	Ford Focus RS	WRC	3:22:53.4
6 Wilson/Martin	Ford Focus RS	WRC	3:24:11.4
7 Latvala/Anttila	Ford Focus RS	WRC	3:28:37.3
8 Rautenbach/Barritt	Citroën C4	WRC	3:30:53.2
9 Araújo/Ramalho	Mitsubishi Lancer Evolution	N	3:40:44.2
10 Prokop/Tomanek	Mitsubishi Lancer Evolution	PCWRC	3:40:57.0

Leader: Loeb stages 1-16.

2010: Rally-long Loeb-Solberg battle

This was the final event for the 2-litre turbo World Rally Cars before the 1.6-litre formula was introduced. Starting first car on the road served Sébastien Loeb well, enabling him to dictate the road conditions for the cars coming behind him. Jari-Matti Latvala looked like he might win this rally, but was never able to recover time lost from a puncture at the end of the first day. From that moment on Loeb was hard pressed by the private team driver Petter Solberg. Britain's famous autumnal race round the forests once again lived up to expectations of fast-changing weather and unpredictable surfaces.

Due to a local outbreak of tree disease, Shakedown was held on a short asphalt road called 'the Barrage' located within Cardiff Dock, on the Wednesday evening before the rally. This road was then run as the first stage, 24 hours later, again at night. This featured a loop mid stage which meant only one car could be despatched at a time. 'Wales' was back in the event's title name. Location of the service park for the WRC teams was in front of the downtown City Hall in Cardiff. It was the second longest rally in terms of total distance this year, after the Swedish.

The drivers showed a remarkable competence over the hideously slippery forest tracks, with only one top driver (Sébastien Ogier) failing to finish through a driving error, sliding off the road on the very fast Radnor stage. The closeness of the fight for the lead was uncanny, with the lead changing hands four times between Loeb and Latvala on Day 1. On the final stage of the day, however, Latvala had been driving in bad visibility hampered by a misting windscreen when his car touched a rock and punctured. Loeb was back in the lead by 1.8 seconds but it didn't last long with Petter taking the lead on Day 2. Gearshift problems, and the handicap of running position ruled against Solberg.

Both the battling leaders reported misjudgements, one half-spin cancelling out another, only seconds separated them. Loeb was back in the lead during the morning, but after over 153km of stages his lead was only three seconds greater than 24 hours earlier. In the end Petter Solberg came home a quarter minute behind Loeb, Latvala came third.

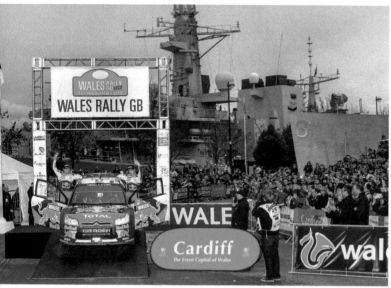

Sébastien Loeb and Daniel Elena show their winning Citroën C4 WRC to the crowds at the finish line in Cardiff Docks area.

The service park was split up across various downtown locations in Cardiff. The WRC crews were located right outside the Wales Millennium Centre in the Cardiff Bay area.

The registered Stobart team drivers Henning Solberg and Matthew Wilson finished behind them in sixth and seventh places. Formula 1 driver Kimi Räikkönen ended the season with a most respectable drive to eighth place. Mads Østberg finally ended up ninth in his old model Subaru, despite a three minute delay with a puncture. Behind the leaders some drivers struggled. American Ken Block dropped back on Day 2, and missed four stages because of a broken driveshaft after lying in tenth place, the Chinese Stobart team driver Chao Dong lost time when his Focus had a fire on Day 1, then on Day 3 his alternator and water pump belt failed.

Once again Citroën privateer Petter was the only driver able to challenge the official Citroën and Ford team monopoly. Solberg's team manager Ken Rees said "Having to drive in dirtier conditions thrown up by Loeb did not itself lose us the rally, our gearbox troubles on the first day already did that, but it was frustrating. At the wheel of his older car, Petter would have been the fastest driver in the event. It would have been lovely if we had the chance to win!" Solberg refused to be too downcast. "Loeb cannot keep this up for ever," he sighed, "His age will eventually catch up with him." Actually, Loeb is less than nine months older than Petter, and Sébastien went on to win one more title!

The domination by Loeb and his Citroëns has been impressive but there was a clear call for a change sooner or later. There were mixed reactions to the passing of the original World Rally Car formula, but certainly there was a large buzz of excitement in the service park about the imminent arrival of the new 1.6-litre turbo direct injection cars.

There were no fewer than 18 entries in the Production Car category, the largest field of the season. Potential champions were the reigning title holder Armindo Araújo (Mitsubishi) and Patrik Flodin (Subaru). Flodin set a cracking pace on Day 1 and in five stages had a lead of more than a minute, but then he touched a rock and damaged a steering arm. He set off on Day 2 in third place, behind the new leader Ott Tänak, the Pirelli Star Driver on his first time on Wales Rally GB, with his rival Araújo contentedly biding his time in fourth place for most of the day. And then just before the end of the day Flodin broke the rear suspension of his car and this effectively handed the title again to Araújo. Tänak's fellow PSD colleague Hayden Paddon brought his car into third place, making this a Mitsubishi 1-2-3. Araújo's only problem was having to run with a turbocharger problem at the end of Day 1.

Three drivers came to Wales able to go home with the Super 2000 award. After some measured results Xavier Pons was favourite, but the fastest driver on paper was fellow Fiesta driver Jari Ketomaa while the outsider was Patrik Sandell. Pons said he wasn't comfortable on this event and Sandell had a bad Day 1 with power steering failure, which set him well back but he fought hard, aware that it was not only the Drivers' title that was at stake, but the Teams Cup as well. While Andreas Mikkelsen (Fabia S2000) was unbeatable in the lead of S2000 Ketomaa settled into second place with Eyvind Brynildsen third in front of Pons. Brynildsen then went off the road on the Eppynt stages and could not get back, thus elevating Pons to third and making his

Eyvind Brynildsen splashes his Škoda Fabia S2000 before retirement off the road. His undamaged car was stuck in mud.

The Citroën of fifth-placed Dani Sordo won only one stage – but it was on the final stage of the rally. This was the last WRC stage to be run under the 2-litre turbocharged rules.

this point Pons eased his speed a lot, and this let Craig Breen pass into second place – which was just what Sandell's Red Bull team needed to secure the Teams Cup. For Mikkelsen, whose season had mostly been at the wheel of a Fiesta S2000 the win was not straightforward. It was the first time he had rallied a Škoda on gravel. At the end of the final stage on Day 2 the engine completely stopped and the crew was only able to restart after changing many parts.

Pirelli's control tyre agreement ended in 2010, and Michelin and DMack became the suppliers the following year.

RESULTS
Event held: 11-14 November 2010. 13th and final round of Manufacturers' and Drivers' championships.
Start/Finish: Cardiff. Overnight halts: Cardiff.

61 starters, 45 finishers.
20 special stages – 345 kilometres (total 1542 kilometres).

General classification		Group	Penalties (h:m:s)
1 Loeb/Elena	Citroën C4	WRC	3:14:54.0
2 P Solberg/Patterson	Citroën C4	WRC	3:15:13.1
3 Latvala/Anttila	Ford Focus RS	WRC	3:16:29.3
4 Hirvonen/Lehtinen	Ford Focus RS	WRC	3:16:47.3
5 Sordo/Vallejo	Citroën C4	WRC	3:17:06.2
6 H Solberg/Prevot	Ford Focus RS	WRC	3:21:20.5
7 Wilson/Martin	Ford Focus RS	WRC	3:23:31.8
8 Räikkönen/Lindström	Citroën C4	WRC	3:25:21.9
9 Østberg/Andersson	Subaru Impreza	WRC	3:27:07.7
10 Mikkelsen/Fløene	Škoda Fabia S2000	SWRC	3:28:55.2
17 Tänak/Sikk	Mitsubishi Lancer Evolution	PCWRC	3:38:31.0

Leaders: Loeb stage 1, Latvala 2, Loeb 3, Latvala 4-6, Loeb 7, P Solberg 8+9, Loeb 10-20.

2011: 26-year-old Latvala wins on tenth attempt
Jari-Matti Latvala's win came after a season of unrelenting and frustrating dedication to the unsuccessful championship challenge of his Ford Abu Dhabi team-mate Mikko Hirvonen. The fight for the Drivers' title was over early, on the second morning when Hirvonen

championship challenge easier. On the first stage of the final day Ketomaa went off the road and rolled, but there was nobody to help his car regain the road. Pons was now second, Sandell now fourth. At

went off the road and damaged his car's radiator, which left Sébastien Loeb with the title for the eighth time. Hirvonen had just taken the lead from Loeb, but when his supporting role was over, Latvala started to attack on his own account, and on Day 2 going into a lead he held until the end. Loeb meanwhile fought hard for the satisfaction of one more victory, but on the final morning retired after an accident on a non-competitive section. Latvala was now far ahead of customer driver Mads Østberg, who finished second and whose only problem was when his car's engine ran on only three cylinders, "I'm so used to driving Subarus, when such a problem proves fatal. I forget that I'm now driving a Ford!" Henning Solberg took third place, his first podium finish for two and a half years. Ford finished 123 and British cars took the top the ten placings.

There had been a mixture of conditions ranging from crisp autumnal mornings with icy roads, and fog at higher altitudes, during recce, but as the rally approached it became warmer and damper. For the first time in five years there was an intruder in the traditional Ford and Citroën battle – the Mini John Cooper Works cars standing by ready to attack them. Dani Sordo went off the road early on Day 2 after lying fifth, but already his team-mate Kris Meeke had been ahead of him. Meeke, however, lost over two minutes on stage 7 when an alternator belt failed, and he spent the rest of the event catching up. At the end of Day 2 Meeke was eighth, at the end of Day 3 he was fifth. When Loeb dropped out, the race was on for Meeke to grab a podium position. It had been ten years since a British driver had gained a top three result on this event. This was not to be, however. Henning held his nerve, even when Meeke had closed to 1.8 seconds behind him prior to the final stage. A spin on the PowerStage for Meeke, however, sorted it out and gave Ford the top three places, keeping Meeke in fourth place. The performances of the Mini were encouraging, given that most of the recent testing had been on asphalt.

The elongated four day format which started at Llandudno, with two night halts in Cardiff, was unpopular because of the extended road section distances, with the final morning restart held at 4:55am, though many popular stages in North Wales that had been missed for many years were included. The central service park was located at the Royal Welsh Agricultural Society Showground in Builth Wells. The Friday and Saturday night halts, and the finish, were in the far south of Wales, at Cardiff. There was no stage in South Wales for the first time since 1996. The short mandatory final PowerStage was held on gravel roads on the Eppynt Ranges. There was a notable lack of British entries being

Top: The winner Jari-Matti Latvala seen on the pre-event Shakedown stage.

Middle: Although ineligible for scoring Manufacturers' World Championship points, the Prodrive-run Mini John Cooper Works car of Kris Meeke finished fourth overall, and won one special stage.

Bottom: Picturesque setting at Cardiff Castle for the finish ceremonies.

The vast Royal Welsh Showground in Builth Wells served as the central service park for the event.

FIFTY YEARS OF FOREST RALLYING

On the 50th anniversary of the first time Britain's premier rally relied on forest roads for its competitive sections, it was fitting that the 2011 event went back to the Dovey forest complex near Dolgellau, which is now known by the Welsh name Dyfi. In the 1960s, long routes laid out in this complex were used, always run in secret format with pre-event recce banned, in the days when fewer tracks were subject to public rights of way or local resident requirements, and therefore unavailable for road closure. Few of the top drivers on this year's event had had any cause to be in that forest before, but two had. One was Matthew Wilson who had a very serious accident in which both legs were broken and put him and his co-driver Scott Martin out of the sport for months on a national British round. The second was Kris Meeke, whose first ever event in his rally career (a prizedrive as the result of a junior driving talent competition) used Dovey as the first stage. What a way to start your career! Meeke: "Different days when I first rallied the little Peugeot. We were not allowed to use pacenotes then. We drove the roads blind!"

only 11 out of the total 78 accepted, which made Meeke's performance all the more important. Matthew Wilson, meanwhile, finished a steady fifth. This was the first year of a new class system on international rallies.

The first season for the 1.6-litre World Rally Car rally formula finished on a high note, with cars showing quite unexpected levels of reliability. Alone among the top running cars the only mechanical failure came to the Citroën DS3 WRC of Petter Solberg, who stopped early on Day 3, when a fuel line fractured and there was an underbonnet fire. Finally there was also a worthy fight in the tyre war, with the alternative official supplier DMack. In the tyre industry, DMack had the chance to provide a special softer 'joker' version tyre for this event, but having already used its 'joker' opportunity Michelin had to continue with proven equipment. DMack tyres were being used for the first time on a World Rally Car with Ott Tänak, who finished sixth.

With Hayden Paddon having already secured the Production Car World title, the battle of this event was for second place in the series. Patrik Flodin led for most of the rally, after Jarkko Nikara went off the road. At some distance behind came Martin Semerád in front of Michał Kościuszko, who had been delayed by electrical trouble. Benito Guerra had been lying third until the final stage, when he rolled and retired. After the end of the event Semerád was excluded for not complying with upper suspension plates. Flodin's victory secured him the runner-up spot for the second year running in the category. The effect of this was that everyone behind Flodin in the event moved up a place, and increased their point scores, which saw Kościuszko now finish third in the championship with Semerád fourth.

RESULTS

2011 Wales Rally GB
Event held: 10-13 November 2011. 13th and final round of Manufacturers' and Drivers' championships.
Start/Finish: Llandudno /Cardiff. Overnight halts: Llandudno and Cardiff.

74 starters, 39 finishers.
23 special stages – 354 kilometres (total 1861 kilometres).

General classification		Group	Penalties (h:m:s)
1 Latvala/Anttila	Ford Fiesta RS	WRC	3:27:03.5
2 Østberg/Andersson	Ford Fiesta RS	WRC	3:30:46.4
3 H Solberg/Minor	Ford Fiesta RS	WRC	3:34:08.6
4 Meeke/Nagle	Mini John Cooper Works	WRC	3:34:15.8
5 Wilson/Martin	Ford Fiesta RS	WRC	3:36:00.8
6 Tänak/Sikk	Ford Fiesta RS	WRC	3:36:30.6
7 Novikov/Giraudet	Ford Fiesta RS	WRC	3:36:51.2
8 Kuipers/Miclotte	Ford Fiesta RS	WRC	3:37:16.2
9 Block/Gelsomino	Ford Fiesta RS	WRC	3:43:04.7
10 Araújo/Ramalho	Mini John Cooper Works	WRC	3:44:05.1
12 Abbring/Vanneste	Škoda Fabia S2000	RC2	3:45:00.8
14 Flodin/Alanne	Subaru Impreza N14	PCWRC	3:49:32.2

Leaders: Latvala stages 1+2, Loeb 3-5, Hirvonen 6, Loeb 7-14, Latvala 15-23.

2012: The smallest ever Rally GB entry

For two long days it really looked as if the mighty Citroën rally empire was going to be comprehensively defeated. 2011 winner Jari-Matti Latvala was leading again, and his Ford team-mate, and initial rally leader, Petter Solberg was in second place. On the final day, however, the Citroëns, which had been woefully slow until then, found their form, and Sébastien Loeb was able to pass Solberg into second place. Nothing could deny Latvala the seventh victory of his WRC career – the 27-year-old sprung into unbeatable form on the first morning, when the Citroëns struggled to find grip in the slippery conditions. Quite the reverse of form.

It was a remarkable event in which every starter (albeit only 31 crews) were still running on the final day, until three stages before the finish. The event, however, was boycotted by British privateer drivers, on whose support the traditional popularity of the event was largely based. The change in date and the insistence on an extended route format forced them away. These problems made the event an unwelcome challenge for championship teams, even if the delight of the popular Welsh forest stages remained. Citroën left Britain defeated, but assured that either Loeb or Mikko Hirvonen would win the Drivers' title, although the Manufacturers' title could not be claimed for the moment.

The date change for the rally, reverting to a September date, caused a lot of knock-on consequences, not only to the entry level but also to climatic factors. Following a similar format to 2011, promotionally styled to suit the interests of the event's sponsor, the Welsh tourism authorities. The epicentre of the event was Cardiff in the south. The only activity in the north of the country was the night time ceremonial start at Llandudno.

It had been seven months since a works Ford, once again Latvala, had stood at the top of the podium of a WRC event. It was a constant matter of 'so near, yet so far.' The shock of the visibly improved traction of the Citroëns in the last gravel event, Finland, had given the M-Sport team an unwanted reality check. So it was all the more surprising that both Loeb and Hirvonen said the stages on the Friday and Saturday were too slippery for them.

The rally soon settled into a pattern with the two works Fords, Loeb's Citroën and Mads Østberg's private Ford pulling away from Hirvonen's Citroën, and a stream of other World Rally Cars. Ott Tänak (Fiesta) held a solid sixth place until three stages before the end when the suspension broke. This elevated Evgeniy Novikov ahead of Thierry Neuville, Matthew Wilson, Martin Prokop, and, eventually, Nasser Al-Attiyah. For more than half the event the rally had been processional, but the final morning saw a fantastic fight for second place, eventually going to Loeb on the penultimate stage.

Østberg yet again finished the top non-works driver, Sébastien Ogier was by far the fastest S2000 driver, and enjoyed battling with various World Rally Cars. Chris Atkinson (Mini) had a series of minor problems, but eventually came home in 11th place after damaging the rear suspension. Team-mate Paulo Nobre stopped on the final day with a broken alternator cable.

The effect of Ford's domination was highlighted by the new enhanced official split timing facility, able to detect the fastest driver on every sector of the rally. On the first two days, Ford drivers were quickest on 53 splits, Citroëns on nine. The real miracle then became clear. Despite the Citroën's amazingly disappointing performance, Loeb contained the situation, and was able to keep in touch with the Fords. So what was the secret behind Latvala's faultless command of the event? Jari-Matti: "Fords have always been quick on this event. When you can get it all together it works. For me,

Petter Solberg emerges from the gloom and finds an unusual surface in front of him.

my feeling I could win came on stage 3, Myherin, my favourite stage, but I wasn't confident of winning however until right before the finish. I was always waiting for Citroën to strike back." Malcolm Wilson said "He was much more relaxed, it was noticeable. There was no pressure on him and it showed!" And as for Loeb, he was contemplative. "You cannot win every time. Winning isn't so easy as some people imagine!"

There were problems for the two Super 2000 championship favourites. Per-Gunnar Andersson in the Proton went off the road on Day 1 and Hayden Paddon had electrical troubles, so both of them drove under SupeRally rules, leaving a great battle at the front between Craig Breen in his old 2-litre Fiesta and Yazeed Al-Rajhi in his 1.6 turbo S2000. Also in trouble on Day 1 was Alastair Fisher, with broken suspension. At the end of Day 2 the Saudi driver was ahead by 0.1

Mads Østberg finished in fourth place in the Adapta team's Fiesta RS WRC, the car in which he had earlier scored an unexpected victory at the Rally of Portugal. The next year he was to become a full time official member of the official M-Sport team.

Popular WRC privateer Martin Prokop from Czech Republic develops his corner-cutting skills.

22-year-old Irish driver Craig Breen poses with his family's Fiesta S2000, the car which set his professional rallying career on a firm footing. On this event he was the top scoring Super 2000 championship driver.

second, but then came the announcement that he had been recorded by the police on two occasions for breaking the road speed limits. This led to a mandatory Five Minute time penalty which left Breen with a lead of over two minutes in front of Andersson's team-mate Tom Cave, with Yazeed in third place. Maciej Oleksowicz had a difficult rally but struggled through to fourth, and the three Day 1 miscreants finished in the three remaining positions. In the SWRC title stakes both the series leader Andersson's and Paddon's problems and their low points scores meant Breen's victory revived his title hopes.

2012 was the last WRGB for Sébastien Loeb to date, and was farewell to Cardiff.

WHERE WERE THE PRIVATEERS?

Whereas the top level entry was as strong as ever, the main news factor was the appallingly small total entry list, with only 31 crews signed up to take part, and with no private British competitors at all. A further 41 club competitors had entered a three day parallel national event which used the same stages once rather than twice, and the total field was bolstered by six entries driving Land Rovers. Traditional support from private entries largely evaporated in 2005, caused by a feeling of being unwelcome. The low number of entries for the WRC event was a tragic situation for this classic fixture, which had been held as a championship qualifying event every year since the World series started in 1973, and this year celebrated 80 years since the event was first run. It attracted less than half the number of WRCar entries to last year.

RESULTS

Event held: 14-16 September 2012. 10th round of 13 of Manufacturers' and Drivers' championships.
Start/Finish: Llandudno /Cardiff. Overnight halts: Cardiff.
31 starters, 29 finishers.
19 special stages – 325 kilometres (total 1604 kilometres).

General classification		Group	Penalties (h:m:s)
1 Latvala/Anttila	Ford Fiesta RS	WRC	3:03:40.3
2 Loeb/Elena	Citroën DS3	WRC	3:04:08.1
3 Solberg/Patterson	Ford Fiesta RS	WRC	3:04:09.0
4 Østberg/Andersson	Ford Fiesta RS	WRC	3:04:50.9
5 Hirvonen/Lehtinen	Citroën DS3	WRC	3:05:09.8
6 Novikov/Minor	Ford Fiesta RS	WRC	3:07:17.3
7 Neuville/Gilsoul	Citroën DS3	WRC	3:07:52.2
8 Wilson/Martin	Ford Fiesta RS	WRC	3:09:40.7
9 Prokop/Hruza	Ford Fiesta RS	WRC	3:10:39.2
10 Al-Attiyah/Bernacchini	Citroën DS3	WRC	3:13:12.4
12 Ogier/Ingrassia	Škoda Fabia S2000	RC2	3:13:24.3
13 Breen/Nagle	Ford Fiesta	SWRC	3:18:22.9

Leaders: Solberg stages 1+2, Latvala 3-19.

THE DAYS IN DEESIDE

2013 was the year that Rally GB moved to North Wales with a service park located on wasteland in Deeside, adjacent to Toyota's British engine manufacturing plant, geographically just inside the Welsh border with England. The move northwards in Wales was an attractive concept because it made the event more accessible to fans in several large conurbations such as Manchester and Liverpool, was not far from special stages in the area, and was not impossibly far from popular central Welsh forests. The closest town to the service park was in Chester where the RAC Rally had been successfully based eight times in the pre-service park RAC Rally days, but which was outside

Author Martin Holmes wrapped up for the bleak anticipated elements, arrives with his special loan car at the Deeside Service Park.

Wales. The nearest Welsh town of significance was the tourist town of Llandudno over 50km away. The event maintained a Wales-only location policy faithfully with few exceptions.

The sport meanwhile had moved on. This was the Sébastien Ogier era, World Champion every year in this chapter and Wales Rally GB winner five of the six times. The sixth time was the delightful occasion when, for the first time, a Welsh driver, Elfyn Evans, won a WRC event. This was the era of the Volkswagen Motorsport team, new in 2013 and Rally GB winners four straight years until 2016. The Hyundai Motorsport team entered the WRC scene in 2014, and Toyota came back in 2017. The World Rally Car category was expanded in 2017 when special performance-enhancing modifications were allowed, which helped make the championship critically expensive for non-

Storms are heading for the Volkswagen service area.

works entries. This trend helped the WRC support championships grow in importance, though growing requirements for competitors to drive fully homologated cars restricted entries by amateur drivers – a

The FIA's regular central service park system gives rise to innovative opportunities. This is Hyundai Motorsport's portable headquarters, a construction which is taken to all the European rounds of the WRC.

Strange trees alongside the rally route in North Wales as Dani Sordo passes by.

requirement which made the concurrently run national category rally popular among clubman drivers. This chapter brings the ever-changing world of Rally GB up to date. From the moment the 2018 event ended the organisers were working on plans for the 75th edition in 2019, while the FIA wasted no time in announcing new car categories, aimed at maintaining the attraction of the sport.

2013: Volkswagen's first WRGB win

The new World Champion Sébastien Ogier headed a second successive Volkswagen one-two result, benefitting from a disastrous event for Citroën, and outpacing the opposition from M-Sport, headed in third place by Thierry Neuville. Much of Wales Rally GB was run this year over fresh territory further north than in recent years, and later in the season than the previous year, but the old familiar fast and slippery conditions prevailed. The northwards relocation of the event was rewarded by hugely increased spectator numbers.

More than twice the number of competitors entered this year than started in 2012, and, most impressively, was again endorsed by British privateers. Last year not a single British privateer driver was on the start list, this year around a dozen were entered. WRGB reverted to its traditional end of season date in the middle of November. This year there were name changes in the sport. The support championship categories S2000 and PCWRC were now called WRC2 and WRC3, but the Junior WRC name remained.

Activities were centred near Chester, just inside Wales, with the service park in newly prepared ground at Deeside. On the Friday a remote service zone was at Newtown, on the Saturday and the Sunday there was no midday service at all. At no time during the daytime did the rally cars return to Deeside. For the first time since the PowerStage became a regular feature of final day activities in the WRC in 2011, it was not held on the final stage of the event, but earlier on the last day (third stage).

VW driver Jari-Matti Latvala started the rally 14 points behind Neuville in the Drivers' series, but he had a difficult rally, finding driving first car on the road challenging on the Friday, and after he made two slow stages Ogier was too far ahead of him for Latvala to hope for a third WRGB victory. Latvala: "Too many small mistakes even if my speed is there. I was hoping for a third WRGB victory but it didn't happen." Once the rally began in earnest on the Friday Latvala passed Neuville, who had a lot of traction trouble, but Latvala's hopes of challenging his team-mate Ogier were out of the window. Neuville's fellow M-Sport colleague Mads Østberg struggled almost to the end of the penultimate day before he found his true speed, to withstand a challenge from the number three VW of Andreas Mikkelsen. Østberg: "In the end I asked my father (Morten) how to overcome my trouble, and he told me to forget about the problems and just go for it! It worked!" Mads' speed suddenly improved, and on the final day he put up better times than the rally leader!

It was a big disaster for Citroën at pre-event scrutineering when an administrative error by Citroën Racing was unearthed. They had

Before moving to Hyundai. Thierry Neuville ended his career at M-Sport with a fine third place behind the dominant Volkswagens.

A novel crowd-funding operation for fifth placed Volkswagen driver Andreas Mikkelsen.

run too many different cars in testing and competition during the season than the regulation allowed. The result was a five minute pre-event penalty arbitrarily levied on Dani Sordo. In the end the penalty only cost Sordo one place, but it set the scene for an event the team would want to forget. Sordo's team-mate Mikko Hirvonen started off well, lying fourth, but on stage 6 his co-driver made an omission in reading his pacenote instructions, and a heavy impact with an earth bank ensued, which put them out of the event. As Sordo steadily climbed back from 54th position to finish seventh, Citroën's number two team driver Robert Kubica had a horrendous time – his first time on the event and his first time with his new driver reading notes in a different language. Kubica finished the opening three night time stages in a promising seventh place, but on the first stage on Friday he went off the road and stopped, and then on the second stage on Saturday he left the road again, this time for good. Happily the crew were fine.

Welsh driver Elfyn Evans was unbeatable in the WRC2 category. The battle for second place was fought between Jari Ketomaa, Mark Higgins and Eyvind Brynildsen, all of whom suffered various misfiring troubles. Yazeed Al-Rajhi challenged until the Saturday afternoon when he had a broken driveshaft, while another DMack user Tom Cave fought hard after delays from gearbox troubles suffered on the opening stages, and incurred a 4m20s penalty for late check-in to parc ferme after the unit was replaced on the Thursday evening, followed by rear differential failure. Eleven of the 12 starters finished, the only retirement was the Ukrainian driver Oleksii Kikireshko, who crashed.

Jari-Matti Latvala churns up the lawns at the Chirk Castle spectator superspecial stage.

Citroën DS3 R3Ts in the Classes were split up into various categories. There were drivers registered for the WRC3, drivers who had entered the Citroën Top Driver series and some British championship drivers who entered under the organisers "Road to Wales" promotional project. Already crowned WRC3 champion,

Sébastien Chardonnet drove in the hope of clinching the Top Driver scheme, as did Quentin Gilbert and Keith Cronin. British Champion Jukka Korhonen qualified as a WRC3 driver, and won the category, the only competitor in the category to complete the route, although at the end of Day 2 he opted to take Rally2 penalty to allow more time for repairs to his car to be made. Of the other three WRC3 competitors Bryan Bouffier stopped in mid rally with a gearbox problem, Jean-Mathieu Leandri after just two stages and fourth was Cronin, who finished but only after crashing. Osian Pryce finished the rally after power steering problems, Hans Weijs and Molly Taylor after overheating problems following a water crossing, but Jonathan Greer crashed.

RESULTS

Event held: 14-17 November 2013. 13th and final round of Manufacturers' and Drivers' championships.
Start/Finish: Llandudno. Overnight halts: Deeside.

56 starters, 44 finishers.
22 special stages – 311 kilometres (total 1501 kilometres).

General classification		Group	Penalties (h:m:s)
1 Ogier/Ingrassia	Volkswagen Polo R	WRC	3:03:36.7
2 Latvala/Anttila	Volkswagen Polo R	WRC	3:03:58.5
3 Neuville/Gilsoul	Ford Fiesta RS	WRC	3:05:01.2
4 Østberg/Andersson	Ford Fiesta RS	WRC	3:05:24.9
5 Mikkelsen/Markkula	Volkswagen Polo R	WRC	3:05:40.1
6 Prokop/Ernst	Ford Fiesta RS	WRC	3:11:14.2
7 Sordo/Del Barrio	Citroën DS3	WRC	3:12:03.6
8 Evans/Barritt	Ford Fiesta R5	WRC2	3:14:49.8
9 Ketomaa/Suominen	Ford Fiesta R5	WRC2	3:15:52.9
10 Higgins/Williamson	Ford Fiesta R5	WRC2	3:16:57.7
16 Gilbert/Jamoul	Citroën DS3 R3T	RC5	3:31:56.7
28 Korhonen/Salminen	Citroën DS3 R3T	WRC3	3:48:32.7

Leader: Ogier stages 1-22.

2014: End to end win for Ogier

Sébastien Ogier led Wales Rally GB end to end, but the fastest driver in the field was his team-mate Jari-Matti Latvala, who dropped from a challenging position for victory when he lost time off the road on Day 2. This allowed Ogier to ease his pace, winning only four of the 23 stages all event. M-Sport driver Mikko Hirvonen finished a popular second on his final WRC event, while Kris Meeke challenged hard but an off road error led to tyre problems, and his potential podium

Alastair Fisher won the single-model Junior WRC category, limited to Citroën DS3 R3T cars on the rally.

position went instead to his team-mate Mads Østberg. Østberg finished the season with the highest number of fastest stage times by a non-VW driver, with Hirvonen the highest placed non-VW driver in the championship. Nasser Al-Attiyah cruised to take the WRC2 Drivers' championship title, leaving Jari Ketomaa powerless to beat him despite leading the category end-to-end.

Special stages were run on three rather than four days. The Ceremonial Start was the Eirias Park stadium at Colwyn Bay. Eight stages (plus the Shakedown) were run in the Clocaenog forest complex. The PowerStage reverted to being the final stage of the event with the venue in the Brenig Forest stage in Clocaenog Forest, where the route passed close by a spectacular reservoir. On Friday there was a midday remote service halt at Newtown in central Wales, and on the Saturday the midday halt was back at Deeside.

The 2014 Rally GB was an event of two parts. The first day witnessed a fascinating battle between the two VW drivers, Ogier and Latvala, in conditions where (unusually for a gravel rally) running first car on the road was an advantage, but hopes of a complete VW domination was denied, firstly when Mikkelsen went off the road on stage 2, then by Latvala's misfortune. After the battle for the lead ended, Days 2 and 3 saw a fascinating fight for second place between Hirvonen, Meeke and Østberg. With only split seconds between them, Meeke was dismayed when given a controversial ten second jumpstart penalty, and later Østberg was given an equally controversial penalty for a late control arrival. In the end it did not matter, Hirvonen was able to cement his position when Østberg had a tyre delaminate unexpectedly late on Day 2, and then Meeke had his own tyre issues on Day 3.

Second place for Mikko Hirvonen, on his final professional rally in the WRC.

Winner Sébastien Ogier led from start to finish.

battle between Hirvonen, Østberg and Meeke for second place during Day 2 changed three times in as many stages, but when the stages became treacherously slippery on the Saturday evening Hirvonen edged ahead. Meeke said the surfaces were like a gravel version of Monte Carlo's black ice. The final day started with Meeke 3.4 seconds behind Hirvonen, but on the first stage of Day 3 he slid into a ditch and damaged his tyres. Meeke's battle was now to ensure his tyres were in good enough condition to complete the remaining stages and the road section back to the finish at Llandudno. Elfyn Evans in the second M-Sport car drove a measured event, and gradually climbed up to finish in fifth place, so M-Sport gained five points more on this event than Citroën, but Citroën took second place in the Manufacturers' title by two points.

Hyundai had its own misfortunes when its second driver, Juho Hänninen, went into a deep ditch on Day 1, and Hayden Paddon had power steering failure, but eventually finished tenth. All three Hyundai drivers said they had traction and handling difficulties, but Thierry Neuville persevered to finish fourth. Of the non-team drivers, top was Ott Tänak in a works loaned Fiesta WRC fitted with DMack tyres (on the company's 50th WRC event appearance), who gave another superb performance on this event after he finished sixth three years ago. It was a big disappointment for fans when WRC driver Henning Solberg, who ran with Pirelli tyres, retired on the final day after lying ninth – and scoring a best stage time – in the regular M-Sport test car renovated for the occasion. Top Pirelli driver was Martin Prokop who inherited ninth position, an impressive result for this private team car.

The one outstanding Drivers' title to be resolved in Wales was for WRC2, where Al-Attiyah only had to finish seventh in the category to be unbeatable, however well Ketomaa did. Ketomaa did his best and won

Both M-Sport and Citroën needed both their drivers to finish the event safely, which in Citroën's case they eventually did. Hirvonen matched high speed with reliability, but early on it was Østberg who gave chase to the Volkswagens. Østberg, however, found his car hard to handle on the Friday afternoon and he slipped back. Positions in the

in his Fiesta R5, after leading from start to finish with Al-Attiyah cautiously tackling the stages when they became exceptionally slippery. For some time Al-Attiyah, in his RRC Fiesta, was lying eighth in WRC2, but finally rose to a safe sixth place when second placed Bernardo Sousa went off the road. Slowly learning the four-wheel

Ukrainian driver Valeriy Gorban on a scenic road section, in his rare RRC specification Mini John Cooper Works.

General classification		Group	Penalties (h:m:s)
1 Ogier/Ingrassia	Volkswagen Polo R	WRC	3:03:08.2
2 Hirvonen/Lehtinen	Ford Fiesta RS	WRC	3:03:45.8
3 Østberg/Andersson	Citroën DS3	WRC	3:04:11.8
4 Neuville/Gilsoul	Hyundai i20	WRC	3:04:23.1
5 Evans/Barritt	Ford Fiesta RS	WRC	3:04:32.5
6 Meeke/Nagle	Citroën DS3	WRC	3:05:11.2
7 Tänak/Mölder	Ford Fiesta RS	WRC	3:05:37.9
8 Latvala/Anttila	Volkswagen Polo R	WRC	3:05:55.7
9 Prokop/Tomanek	Ford Fiesta RS	WRC	3:06:51.5
10 Paddon/Kennard	Hyundai i20	WRC	3:06:56.7
12 Ketomaa/Lindström	Ford Fiesta R5	WRC2	3:14:08.1
26 Fisher/Noble	Citroën DS3 R3T	WRC3/ JWRC	3:31:20.1

Leader: Ogier stages 1-23.

drive techniques in these extremely slippery conditions was Stéphane Lefebvre (in the only Citroën R5 on the event), who went off the road on Day 2, breaking his reverse gear. Lorenzo Bertelli ended his WRC season with a spell of fastest WRC2 times and finished second, ahead of Matthew Wilson on his first rally in over a year. For the tyre companies there were three different makes on the podium: DMack, Pirelli and Michelin.

The eventual category winner in WRC3 led from start to finish. This time it was Alastair Fisher, and he headed Martin Koči, while third place was a surprise – the former Citroën C2 driver Henri Haapamaki, on his first WRC event outside Finland, making some best times in between problems. In the WRC3 Drivers' and the Junior championships the only outstanding question was who would be runner-up in both to Stéphane Lefebvre. Both runner-up places went to Fisher, beating Koči, Quentin Giordano and Christian Riedemann. Mikko Hirvonen's final WRC appearance was in 2014.

RESULTS
Event held: 14-16 November 2014. 13th and final round of Manufacturers' and Drivers' championships.
Start/Finish: Deeside/Llandudno. Overnight halts: Deeside.

63 starters, 53 finishers.
23 special stages – 306 kilometres (total 1364 kilometres).

2015: Rain, wind – a traditional Rally GB!
Wales welcomed the World Rally Championship in the way it knew best, with rain and wind and pitfalls galore in the forests. It was a surprise that Sébastien Ogier led from start to finish, and disappointing that the anticipated battle with his team-mate Jari-Matti Latvala ended on just the second stage of the event. Citroën outdistanced its Hyundai rivals to finish second in the Manufacturers' championship with its driver Mads Østberg the best non VW driver at the end of the season.

This year there were no Thursday evening stages. The Saturday's stages required cars to cover a record distance of 109km on the same set of tyres, including two that were night time forest stages. The Ceremonial Finish for the first time was held in the Service Park at Deeside itself. Missing this year were the traditional stages in the Clocaenog forest complex and it was to be the most recent time the event would be the final round of the WRC.

When Volkswagen chief Jost Capito declared his drivers were free to fight each other for victory. It sounded as if the Wales RallyGB was going to be memorable. It all started out well as Sébastien Ogier and Jari-Matti Latvala battled each other, but it all went wrong on the Friday morning when Latvala went off the road. Andreas Mikkelsen in the third VW found it hard to get into the groove as Ogier drove away. Back at M-Sport, Ott Tänak had trouble finding his rhythm while Elfyn Evans punctured, and also found it difficult to match the speed of the Citroëns, let alone the Volkswagens. So, right from the start there was more focus on the various championship titles. In the Manufacturers' series, the Citroën drivers knew that the future for the team and their own careers probably hinged on this event, and right away Kris Meeke moved into second place, with Mikkelsen third, and team-mate Mads Østberg fourth.

The Hyundai drivers, meanwhile, were already in trouble. Thierry Neuville, demoted for this event to its second team, lost a wheel on Day 1, while Hayden Paddon, promoted this time to a main team drive, had difficulty in the slippery conditions. All this left Dani Sordo, holding fourth place, the top Hyundai driver, with Paddon in fifth. Sordo's main problem was downshifting, which led to him off the road and losing time on Day 2, while Paddon had hydraulic troubles. Østberg meanwhile had his own unpleasant problems, with a hole in the floor of his car which let large quantities of glutinous muddy water into the footwell, and eventually led to him slipping off the road on Day 2 and dropping to eighth place. With Meeke solidly holding on to second place, Citroën's championship chances still looked good, thanks to Hyundai's problems. Meanwhile another curious situation arose, the official race for the 'best-of-the-rest' driver behind the Volkswagen drivers.

At M-Sport, things were not very good. Tänak gradually improved until he held fourth place at the end of Day 2, but then retired off the road. With Evans eventually finishing sixth behind Paddon, the best non-registered driver behind them was Stéphane Lefebvre (Citroën) who had a promising WRC run, finishing ahead of the Fiesta WRC privateers Robert Kubica and Lorenzo Bertelli. Latvala's disappointing rally ended on a happy note, victory on the PowerStage!

Interest in WRC2 was spread in two directions, the race for victory on the event and the battle for the Production Car Cup title. With Nasser Al-Attiyah already WRC2 Drivers' champion, the withdrawal by Škoda Motorsport of its entries for Pontus Tidemand and Jan Kopecky, and a Day 1 puncture for Craig Breen in his family's team Peugeot, attention on the event was focussed on newer names. The two trainee Toyota drivers, Eric Camilli in the Oreca team Fiesta R5 and Teemu Suninen in Toni Gardemeister team's old Škoda Fabia S2000 walked away from the rest of the field. Breen gradually recovered from his setback and finished third. Camilli then had turbocharger problems which allowed Suninen to take victory. Yuriy Protasov was running third in a Fiesta RRC but then went off the road on stage 10. The Production Car Cup battle was fascinating. Max Rendina had entered his quota of points-eligible events but stood to win if neither Gianluca Linari nor Joan Carchat exceeded his total. Linari, however, cruised his way to the finish line and the title on Day 3.

The winning WRC3/Junior championship driver was 19-year-old Norwegian Ole Christian Veiby in a Citroën DS3 R3T.

Stéphane Lefebvre discovers the asphalt delights of the Great Orme stage.

Quentin Gilbert had already secured the Junior WRC title but still the WRC3 title was unsecured, and here in Wales there were three contenders able to score points, two of them (Simone Tempestini and Ole Christian Veiby) who were able to catch him if circumstances allowed. Gilbert led from the start but on the first afternoon he stopped when the water pump belt broke and continued under Rally2 rules. Early on Day 1 Tempestini had brake trouble and had to stop for the day, and he also restarted. Veiby, meanwhile, held a lead of more than two minutes over Chris Ingram and the 21-year-old Peugeot driver Fabio Andolfi. On the road section to the final stage of the event the cars had to pass a swollen river crossing, and Ingram's car retired, as did another WRC3 driver Mohammed Al Mutawaa. Tempestini retired on the final day with engine trouble after surviving clutch trouble, which meant Gilbert won his second FIA title of the year.

2015 marked the end of a championship for the old Group N cars.

The delights of a sunny autumn day in the Welsh forests!

Miserable rally for Thierry Neuville. On the first day he missed stages when he lost a wheel, and then rolled his Hyundai when running first car on the road on the second day.

LINGERING MEMORIES

The winner was a champion who was still shocked by the tragic events in his own capital city back home, following the terrorist attacks on Paris in November 2015, a fact respected by the organisers, who cancelled the champagne ceremony at the end of the event. A sense of achievement by all those hardy souls who had braved and survived the worst weather that Wales could throw at them. Bewilderment in the service park, at best a meeting point for all the winds in the area, as they cleared up after overnight storms. And a fast shift of emphasis. Right up until the second last stage of the rally, this event promised to be a fight to end them all. Latvala versus Ogier versus Mikkelsen, a world title fight to end them all! Malcom Wilson declaring he did not mind if Evans or Tänak crashed, so long as they favourably showed the pace of his cars (Tänak obliged on both counts, he scored a scratch time. Actually there was a title fight that lasted until the finish for the Production Car Cup, a battle that actually went on into the Stewards' room (hastily moved from the storm-wrecked service park to the nearby factory buildings) until quarter to nine on the Sunday evening, finally confirmed one hour afterwards.

RESULTS

Event held: 13-15 November 2015. 13th and final round of Manufacturers' and Drivers' championships.
Start/Finish: Deeside. Overnight halts: Deeside.

70 starters, 57 finishers.
19 special stages – 310 kilometres (total 1469 kilometres).

General classification		Group	Penalties (h:m:s)
1 Ogier/Ingrassia	Volkswagen Polo R	WRC	3:03:02.0
2 Meeke/Nagle	Citroën DS3	WRC	3:03:28.0
3 Mikkelsen/Fløene	Volkswagen Polo R	WRC	3:03:38.2
4 Sordo/Martí	Hyundai i20	WRC	3:05:53.3
5 Paddon/Kennard	Hyundai i20	WRC	3:06:02.5
6 Evans/Barritt	Ford Fiesta RS	WRC	3:06:11.1
7 Østberg/Andersson	Citroën DS3	WRC	3:07:30.4
8 Lefebvre/Prevot	Citroën DS3	WRC	3:08:40.4
9 Kubica/Szczepaniak	Ford Fiesta RS	WRC	3:09:24.7
10 Bertelli/Granai	Ford Fiesta RS	WRC	3:11:07.0
11 Suninen/Markkula	Škoda Fabia S2000	WRC2	3:15:01.4
23 Veiby/Jaeger	Citroën DS3 R3T	WRC3/ JWRC	3:35:38.0

Leader: Ogier stages 1-19.

Eric Camilli only drove Rally GB once in a World Rally Car.

2016: Volkswagen wins fourth world title

Sébastien Ogier's win at Wales RallyGB finally ended the running order nightmare which all season had haunted him, in conditions where tracks which became progressively more slippery actually favoured him. Once again this year, Ott Tänak found the conditions also completely suited his DMack tyres, notwithstanding his later running order, and on this occasion he scored the most number of overall scratch times. Ogier helped Volkswagen forget a nightmare event in which all its cars had driveshaft troubles by leading the team to its fourth successive Manufacturers' title. British drivers fared badly, Citroën driver Kris Meeke had a most unhappy event struggling to finish even fifth, the only British driver to finish in the top 20.

It was the third WRC event to run this year within one month, as the date had been brought forward to October from November. There was one spectator-friendly stage at Cholmondeley Castle, the event sneaking momentarily out of Wales into neighbouring England, for the first time since 1999. After two years, the Ceremonial Start returned to Colwyn Bay, and the Ceremonial Finish returned to Llandudno on the Sunday. There were only four visits to the central service park, on Friday evening, early morning and late afternoon on Saturday and Sunday morning. There was no midday service during the rally, except for a tyre zone on Friday.

For the final 2016 round in Europe, the last time fans saw top drivers in action in the current specification WRC cars, there was a good turnout in the top teams, with the non-registered Citroën team even bringing four examples of its DS3 WRC cars. There were no technical novelties among the cars, and, with continued attention on finalisation of the designs of the 2017 WRC cars, meant very little attention was paid to pre-event testing of the old 2016 cars. Special this

A happier rally for Thierry Neuville when he finished third overall, top Hyundai finisher.

year was a change of date, moving to late October, and competitors were pleased to see clear weather during the recce. There were worries about the longer distance between tyre changing points in potentially warmer weather than the year before, but the weather turned the night before the start – it was now wet and foggy! Someone happy to see the change was the DMack driver Ott Tänak, who knew his tyres would

The nearby English City of Chester was used as a ceremonial passage control location.

Mads Østberg rushing through the North Wales stages. The car's curious cherished immatriculation number was requested by M-Sport, as this car was the 50th Fiesta RS WRC it had assembled.

be splendid on the wet and slippery Welsh roads. Indeed he had already created a shock when he was fastest on the rather softer but dry conditions at Shakedown. There was to be only one rival for Tänak for whom the conditions were also well suited, the recently crowned World Champion Sébastien Ogier. He was happy as it was probably one of the few occasions during the season when running first car on gravel roads was an advantage. As the tracks became damp, the slimy conditions got more and more slippery with each passing car, and Tänak found the conditions gave his DMack tyres an even greater advantage!

So it was that Ogier set off ahead on another rally, this time leading Tänak from start to finish. Tänak lost touch when he dropped about a quarter minute with a puncture late on Friday afternoon, after when Ogier was in full control. Tänak ended up with 12 fastest stage times against seven for Ogier. Volkswagen was in for a rally of stress with driveshaft issues, in the case of the champion a failure came just before the end of the final stage of the day. How about that for luck? This trouble offered a lot more hope for Hyundai, which ended up with three cars in the top six places, while Mads Østberg's Fiesta struggled to keep up with Hyundai's Dani Sordo. While Andreas Mikkelsen suffered bad time loss with his VW transmission trouble, Latvala was still able to join the top ten cars, and eventually overtook Østberg into seventh place by the finish. The top ten ended up with Stéphane Lefebvre ninth on his first event since the Germany crash, and Eric Camilli tenth.

There were 19 competitors in WRC2 but the 2016 British national champion Elfyn Evans was not among them, having been displaced in the M-Sport WRC team by Eric Camilli. Best WRC2 driver at Shakedown was Teemu Suninen but it was Esapekka Lappi who soon passed into the lead, despite damaging the rear of the car and particularly the rear aileron, a major handicap on the fast Welsh stages. Suninen continued in second place until the final stage when he was pipped by Pontus Tidemand. Tidemand was up to third behind Lappi and Suninen midway through Day 1. Although Tidemand had already lost his own chance of the WRC2 title, he was in position to support team-mate Lappi in his title race by reducing the points that rival Suninen could achieve. Team tactics! Standings in the series now saw Evans and Suninen equal not only on points but also on the number of wins, second, third and fourth places gained during the season. Lappi became Champion in Australia, the final round without the need to consider the rule book further. Kevin Abbring (Hyundai i20 R5) stopped on all three days, finally off the road avoiding a rock.

Four drivers were still able to win the WRC3 series, Simone Tempestini overtaking Yohan Rossel into second place where he finished, securing the WRC3 title at this event. The winner of the associated Junior World Rally Championship series, for which Wales was the final qualifying round, was also decided in favour of Tempestini. Best WRC3 at Shakedown was Martin Koči and he led the category from start to finish.

Volkswagen stopped WRC competition at the end of the 2016 season, a self-inflicted retribution for the company's production car diesel crisis.

END OF A WARRIOR

The incredible career of the World Rally Championship's most successful car (DS3 WRC chassis 317, registration number BN-404-MV) ended ignominiously when Craig Breen rolled off the road on the second pass of the celebrated Myherin stage. Since its debut at Monte Carlo in 2012, this car started 31 WRC events, won 11 (far more than any other car, nine times with Loeb and twice with Meeke), it only retired four times, always after an accident (Loeb France 2013, Meeke Germany and Mexico 2014, and now Breen GB 2016), never for mechanical reasons, and is reported to have won 80 stages in the WRC.

RESULTS

Event held: 28-30 October 2016. 12th round of 13 of Manufacturers' and Drivers' championships.
Start/Finish: Deeside/Llandudno. Overnight halts: Deeside.

58 starters, 49 finishers.
22 special stages – 330 kilometres (total 1296 kilometres).

General classification		Group	Penalties (h:m:s)
1 Ogier/Ingrassia	Volkswagen Polo R	WRC	3:14:30.2
2 Tänak/Mölder	Ford Fiesta RS	WRC	3:14:40.4
3 Neuville/Gilsoul	Hyundai NG i20	WRC	3:16:05.6
4 Paddon/Kennard	Hyundai NG i20	WRC	3:16:25.1
5 Meeke/Nagle	Citroën DS3	WRC	3:17:05.4
6 Sordo/Martí	Hyundai NG i20	WRC	3:18:32.8
7 Latvala/Anttila	Volkswagen Polo R	WRC	3:18:58.5
8 Østberg/Fløene	Ford Fiesta RS	WRC	3:19:08.5
9 Lefebvre/de Turckheim	Citroën DS3	WRC	3:21:42.4
10 Camilli/Veillas	Ford Fiesta RS	WRC	3:22:49.5
11 Lappi/Ferm	Škoda Fabia R5	WRC2	3:24:00.3
28 Koči/Kostka	Citroën DS3 R3T	WRC3/ JWRC	3:47:47.4

Leader: Ogier stages 1-22.

2017: Welshman Elfyn Evans wins with DMack tyres

This was a satisfying revenge for Elfyn Evans, whose entry on this event had been sensationally cancelled the year before by M-Sport. It was also revenge for Evans' heartbreak last stage defeat in Argentina earlier in the year, and for the British tyre supplier DMack, the first full WRC event not won by Pirelli or a Michelin company for 35 years. What a final day to remember! In the space of an hour three major WRC titles were secured, with first M-Sport winning the Manufacturers' title, followed shortly by Sébastien Ogier gaining his fifth successive Drivers' title. And a little later Jourdan Serderidis, the first Greek driver to win an FIA World or regional rally title, took the FIA's new one-off WRC Trophy. In the midst of all this, Wales Rally GB became the first WRC victory for the 28-year-old M-Sport Welsh driver Evans, earning a hard earned first WRC win for tyre supplier DMack, who provided a new design specially aimed for success on this wet and cold forest event with Evans in mind. The Hyundai team pushed M-Sport hard, but finally Thierry Neuville suffered small problems, and Ott Tänak's championship challenge petered out on Day 2.

A superspecial stage was run at a trotting track in North Wales on the Thursday evening, and on the Saturday evening there was again a return to Central Wales for two stages in darkness after visiting Cholmondeley Castle. It was the first appearance in Britain of the new higher performance World Rally Cars with their aerodynamic enhancements and more powerful engines. It was also the first time Toyota had been officially entered the event since 1999. Shakedown was held again in Clocaenog Forest, 50km away from the service park. Friday was spent in the area west of Newtown with 115km of stages

Yazeed Al-Rajhi from Saudi Arabia discovers a new view of the Welsh scenery.

Anticipating cold and wet conditions was exactly the reason for DMack's specially homologated 'joker' tyres. It was a ploy which Elfyn Evans worked spectacularly well!

After participating in Touring Cars and Cross Country activities, nine times World Rally Champion Sébastien Loeb dropped in at Rally GB to size up the current WRC scene. Here he is talking with Sébastien Ogier (left).

without service, the highlight being the 35km Hafren stage done twice. The Saturday stages were largely run close to Machynlleth, again run over 110km without service, before two stages in darkness. Sunday morning saw stages to the west of Deeside and south of Colwyn Bay, with the Finish held over 70km from Deeside at Llandudno.

It was hard to exaggerate the significance of Evans' victory, the number three driver in the M-Sport team, the only driver supplied with the same car all year. With his team-mates Ogier and Tänak eyeing the opportunities to win the World Championship for Drivers, and an awareness of the importance of a good back-up result, should the rivalry of his team-mates have a bad ending, Evans did not have an open book about what M-Sport team expected from him. As he continued to lead the event he became Ogier's ally, knowing that while Evans headed the rally he reduced the potential points score of both drivers, standing to hurt Tänak's championship chances more than Ogier's. The traditionally wet and cold rally started off unexpectedly mild with conditions completely different to the wet conditions experienced by the teams during pre-event tests. The weather, however, changed when the rally reached the two night-time stages on Saturday evening, run with inconsistent fog patches. The stage was very tricky. On the

After losing time in foggy conditions, Ott Tänak finally managed to finish sixth. In this picture he has the Llyn Brenig reservoir as a backdrop.

first of these stages Ogier was fourth quickest, jumping up to second – albeit at the cost of a puncture which broke his front left brake disc and which he and co-driver Julien Ingrassia had to repair before the final stage. Tänak was fazed by the fog and dropped from third to sixth. As Tänak's efforts faded away, Ogier found he had a different championship challenger in Neuville. This threw a new emphasis on the supplemental points from the final PowerStage. Could Ogier settle the series in Wales without waiting for Australia? In the end Ogier won his fifth World Drivers' title in Wales.

Citroën suffered another unconvincing event with Kris Meeke as inconsistent as ever, while Craig Breen missed a stage when he slid off the road on Day 1. By now M-Sport no longer had a 1-2-3 domination on the event, and attention now focussed on Hyundai where Neuville had an unsettled event, caused firstly by a Ten Second penalty incurred before the start of stage 1, because his car would not immediately start, then by the imposition of a jump start penalty, but the subsequent removal of that penalty restored Neuville's championship chances. His team-mate Andreas Mikkelsen gradually gained confidence with the car, and on the final day scored two scratch times, eventually climbing back up to fourth place, passing the Toyota of an unhappy Jari-Matti Latvala. Finally Hayden Paddon had a steady run into eighth place.

Over at Toyota it was to be the final rally with the team for Juho Hänninen who was lying tenth before impacting a heavy straw bale at the Cholmondeley Castle superspecial on Saturday while Esapekka Lappi was uncomfortable but finished ninth, splitting the Hyundais of Paddon and Dani Sordo. Elsewhere in World Rally Cars, Mads

Østberg entered his non-championship 2017 Fiesta, but suffered many problems trying to trace electrical issues which seriously affected the car's handling, while Yazeed Al-Rajhi brought his 2016 version Fiesta only to have a spectacular roll on the Sweet Lamb spectator stage. The only running WRC Trophy car was now Jourdan Serderidis' Citroën, which carried on and finally took the Trophy, with one available qualifying entry still left.

With both the WRC2 and the WRC3 titles already settled in Spain, WRGB was the chance for new drivers, but the Škoda factory entry for the WRC2 champion Pontus Tidemand sounded like a certainty for success, and he walked away from the opposition. His team-mate this time was Ole Christian Veiby who this year had been sent to Asia-Pacific to gain experience. He was lying second when he lost time off the road. A battle developed for second place between the Fiestas of Eric Camilli who was chased by the Welsh driver Tom Cave before Cave lost time on the final morning with a spin, and dropped back to third. Eyvind Brynildsen held fourth position before suffering engine problems, letting the Scottish driver David Bogie rise to fourth in front of the new trainee Škoda driver Juuso Nordgren. Teemu Suninen had electrical trouble, Matthew Wilson (on his first WRC event for two years) missed stages when he had a double puncture, Simone Tempestini had steering problems, while Kalle Rovanperä broke the radiator. WRC3 was poorly supported with just two entries in Peugeot 208 R2s, with Frenchman Raphael Astier leading throughout from the Italian Enrico Brazzoli.

2017 saw Juho Hänninen's career retirement.

RESULTS

Event held: 26-29 October 2017. 12th and penultimate round of Manufacturers' and Drivers' championships.
Start/Finish: Conwy/Llandudno. Overnight halts: Deeside.

75 starters, 65 finishers.
21 special stages – 304 kilometres (total 1488 kilometres).

General classification		Group	Penalties (h:m:s)
1 Evans/Barritt	Ford Fiesta	WRC	2:57:00.6
2 Neuville/Gilsoul	Hyundai i20 Coupé	WRC	2:57:37.9
3 Ogier/Ingrassia	Ford Fiesta	WRC	2:57:45.8
4 Mikkelsen/Jaeger	Hyundai i20 Coupé	WRC	2:57:50.4
5 Latvala/Anttila	Toyota Yaris	WRC	2:57:50.9
6 Tänak/Jarveoja	Ford Fiesta	WRC	2:58:02.9
7 Meeke/Nagle	Citroën C3	WRC	2:58:21.1
8 Paddon/Marshall	Hyundai i20 Coupé	WRC	2:59:16.9
9 Lappi/Ferm	Toyota Yaris	WRC	2:59:47.1
10 Sordo/Martí	Hyundai i20 Coupé	WRC	3:00:51.1
42 Serderidis/Miclotte	Citroën DS3	WRCT	3:41:44.5
44 Astier/Vauclare	Peugeot 208 R2	WRC3	3:45:26.7

Leaders: Ogier stage 1, Evans 2-21.

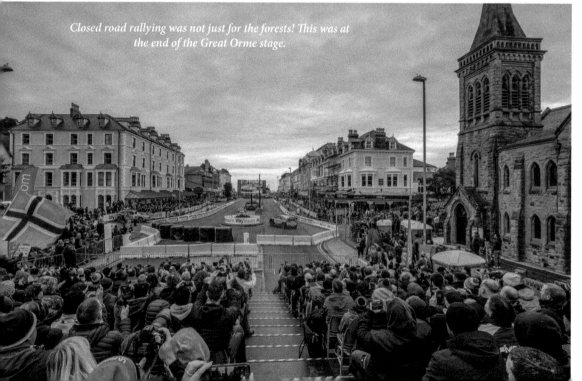

Closed road rallying was not just for the forests! This was at the end of the Great Orme stage.

2018: Finally closed public roads in Britain!

The three-way battle for the 2018 World Drivers' championship between Sébastien Ogier, Thierry Neuville and Ott Tänak continued in full force at the Wales Rally GB. In a car repaired after his earlier crash in Shakedown, Tänak led convincingly until the Saturday afternoon when his car stopped. He had done nothing wrong to cause his sumpshield to be wrenched off his Toyota Yaris WRC and damage the radiator, but it severely dented his World Championship hopes. This opened up a fight for victory on the event between Ogier and Jari-Matti Latvala. Neuville lost time when he slid off the road and dropped to eighth, Ogier had gearbox trouble on the first full day, but fought back from eighth place, and one day later was in the lead which he then held until the finish.

Main novelty was the use made of recent UK legislation which allowed the closure of public roads, an option which was cautiously trialled. Friday and Sunday were spent in North Wales and Saturday in mid Wales, each region offering stages of different character. This year the rally was held very early in October, three weeks earlier than in 2017, but wet and slippery roads still presented the traditional Rally GB challenge, while a distinct drop in temperature on the final day supplied the typical colder temperatures. Midday service on Friday was at Deeside, but on Saturday there was only a midday tyre and light fitting zone at Newtown. The Finish was at the northern coastal town of Llandudno, famous for its stage round the adjacent Great Orme promontory, which was now extended to finish actually inside the town and used twice, including the final stage. This stage was entirely on asphalt which prevented it being used as the PowerStage. Unusually the PowerStage was held on the Sunday morning instead of the final stage.

In the closing stages the battle for the Drivers' title was intense, and each team had to react to the changing conditions and the way they favoured either the medium or the softer tyre compound. As the rally drew close to the finish the battle for the lead on the event between Latvala and Ogier was unresolved, and Ogier pulled out all his hidden resources, demoralised the Finn, and gained victory. It was Ogier's turn to show why he was such a formidable driver. Ogier said, "It was a big push. I wanted this victory, so I was going to fight for it!" Tänak's speed had earlier dazzled his

Hardly the most attractive area of Elfyn Evans' native Wales, the Slate Mountain stage near Blenau Ffestiniog was publicised as "the perfect spot to watch your rally heroes," but the weather had other ideas!

More waterproof testing for Hyundai! Andreas Mikkelsen finished 1.5 second behind his team-mate Thierry Neuville.

Younger and younger come the rally drivers. Ninth-placed Kalle Rovanperä won his class.
The event ran the weekend after he had his 18th birthday.

Toyota team-mates as much as M-Sport driver Ogier. His team-mates were unlucky. Elfyn Evans had held second place, but had injection trouble, and Teemu Suninen third, before he went off the road. Citroën completely struggled to match the pace of its opponents, with Mads Østberg's one stage win its only success. Both Østberg and Craig Breen lost time with spins, and eventually a wrong setup change of no great apparent significance actually dropped Østberg three places. This elevated all three Hyundais on the final morning, of which Neuville held the highest place. The event ended on a sad note with an accident in a supporting spectator attraction held on part of the Llandudno course between the rally stages. This led to a long delay before the finish ceremonies could be held.

Škoda Motorsport pursued its equal opportunities policy for its designated WRC2 championship contending drivers, entering Pontus Tidemand while leaving Jan Kopecky at home. This time Škoda also entered its young trainee driver Kalle Rovanperä, who had celebrated his 18th birthday just three days before the start, and whose performance was quite extraordinary to win the category. Third placed R5 car was the Fiesta driver Gus Greensmith (the highest placed British driver) ahead of Hyundai driver Jari Huttunen. Wales Rally GB ran a two-part round of the British national championship. At the end of the first part the British Rally Championship was decided in favour of Matt Edwards, who then also finished the best BRC driver at the end of the rally. Edwards' closest championship rival had been David Bogie who won the first part of the BRC event but retired on the second. Non-championship MRF tyre company's R5 driver Gaurav Gill finished 22nd overall. In the WRC3 category there were only four starters and every driver completed the full route. British driver Tom Williams led all the way in his Fiesta R2 after Taisko Lario led following the opening superspecial.

There was an anxious time for the organisers at the end of their contract with the Welsh government agency, but happily the title of the 2019 event would again include the name Wales.

MAKING THE MOST OF CLOSED ROADS

Only four forests in the region of North Wales – administered by Conwy Council, with stretches of closed asphalt public roads – were selected for inclusion in the route. The new legislation also allowed closure of roads within the town of Llandudno, which provided an extension to the stage which uses the asphalt tourist road around the Great Orme promontory. The legislation enabled the lengthening of stages where adjacent forest areas were individually small, as in North Wales. Drivers commented that these parts of the route, which used the sections of closed public roads, almost all on asphalt, simply increased the unpredictable nature of the grip, and as more cars passed, so the mud collected from the sides of the road, and increasingly made the surfaces slippery.

Aware of problems on other events there was only limited use of chicanes on the stages. For example, for the previous two years there was a chicane on the Sweet Lamb stage, to slow the cars down before the narrow bridge over the river. There were three chicanes on the Great Orme Llandudno stage; two designed to slow the cars down before corners with large drops to the sea below, the third was in the town section.

RESULTS

Event held: 4-7 October 2018. 11th round of 13 of Manufacturers' and Drivers' championships.
Start/Finish: Towyn/Llandudno. Overnight halts: Deeside.

57 starters, 48 finishers.
23 special stages – 318 kilometres (total 1401 kilometres).

General classification		Group	Penalties (h:m:s)
1 Ogier/Ingrassia	Ford Fiesta	WRC	3:06:12.5
2 Latvala/Anttila	Toyota Yaris	WRC	3:06:23.1
3 Lappi/Ferm	Toyota Yaris	WRC	3:06:47.6
4 Breen/Martin	Citroën C3	WRC	3:07:22.9
5 Neuville/Gilsoul	Hyundai i20 Coupé	WRC	3:07:26.9
6 Mikkelsen/Jaeger	Hyundai i20 Coupé	WRC	3:07:28.4
7 Paddon/Marshall	Hyundai i20 Coupé	WRC	3:07:30.9
8 Østberg/Eriksen	Citroën C3	WRC	3:07:34.1
9 Rovanperä/Halttunen	Škoda Fabia R5	WRC2	3:15:27.2
10 Tidemand/Andersson	Škoda Fabia R5	WRC2	3:17:01.4
28 Williams/Hall	Ford Fiesta R2	WRC3	3:49:44.9

Leaders: Lappi stage 1, Tänak 2-15, Ogier 16-19, Latvala 20+21, Ogier 22+23.

Bringing it all together (Andrew Kellitt)

Andrew Kellitt has been Rally GB's full time Route Co-ordinator since 1989. He started out working for the local council in his native Cumbria, competing as a hobby, then working as a Stage Commander, and later the Clerk of the Course of the event which became known as the Pirelli Rally. "I was a little unusual. Route Co-ordinators tended to be co-drivers. Before me Paul White did this work, earlier it was Dave Whittock, John Brown and Phil Short. Before them Jim Porter took over after the 1971 RAC Rally, when everyone got stuck in the snow and nobody knew what was going on for a day and a half!"

Route co-ordinating is an all-year-round job. "The couple of months after each event is time for a debrief. For an October event February/March is when it really gets serious. In 2018 we had to apply for a Motor Race Order for the closed roads six months beforehand, so we had to know exactly what we were doing several months before then! Since 1989 I've never run the same route two years in a row. The first decision is to decide the area where the rally will be held and therefore where the service park will be, somewhere within reach of the stages. Finding a big flat space in this crowded island of ours is difficult. Then you need the service area to be where there's going to be people. Sponsors want the service area to be where they can see people coming to it. We have only a limited number of places where this can be."

As to the requirements when it comes to selecting the stages: "We need a total of over 300km stages, which is usually 150km done twice, spread over Friday-Saturday-half Sunday, while we must plan a suitable place for a live TV stage on the Saturday, then the PowerStage on the Sunday. The order of running is mainly geographical. In 2018 there was the new opportunity to merge nearby stages through the road closing system. That is how we could have a 29km stage on the final day, using a combination of the previous year's Brenig and Alwen stages plus bits of adjoining closed road and bits of forest we haven't been in since the mid '90s. Most UK forests are made challenging if you join them together."

Some ideals are hard to achieve. "Its always difficult to bring the event back to service during the day, because the forests can be spread out. The service area at Deeside is at the furthest-most point from the stages. But there is also a commercial wish to bring the cars back midday. There is a huge opportunity for finding stages. I could almost double the distance in North Wales, but I just don't need to because of the 80km limit between tyre changes, another constraint as to what you can do. You can't just run the longest version of every stage because you would then have to trim the route back to 80km for complying with the tyre change limits, but that still provides 160km in a day".

Any danger of running out of ideas? "2018 was the fifth year based out of Deeside, and to be honest without the closed roads it could have been largely a repeat of what we had done already. After about four years you run out of the various permutations in which stages you can run, which is what happened to us when the rally was based down in Cardiff. The chance to use the closed roads to join the smaller forests in the north was a welcome chance to do something different."

What is the policy about long stages? "Anything over 30km starts to become difficult to manage, difficult to resource from marshals and a very high risk for losing more than 10% of the event's total mileage, just because something might happen or some incident might block the roads. And the weather might prohibit it. So 25-30km is still a significant challenge, and the closed roads gives us that option."

Finally do you personally prefer the rally to be run as the last slot in the championship, when the weather can inflict misery on your spectators? "Inflicting misery? I think they quite enjoy it! The event's history is about the challenge of mud, fog, rain, snow, everything else. I lived through plenty of those with the snow in the '90s, not that I really want to go back to that again. It is very hard work running in snow. But that's the character for Rally GB. Finland has jumps and Turkey is rough, we're a story of unpredictable grip and slippery tracks. That is our unique selling point these days!"

www.veloce.co.uk / www.velocebooks.com
All current books • New book news • Special offers • Gift vouchers

Chapter 10

THE WINNERS – 1932 TO DATE

During the 1930s there were no official winners for this event, so none is listed below. After that:

Year	Car	Driver/co-driver
1951	Jaguar XK120	Ian Appleyard/Mrs Pat Appleyard
1952	Allard J2X	Godfrey Imhof/Mrs Barbara Frayling
1953	Jaguar XK120	Ian Appleyard/Mrs Pat Appleyard
1954	Triumph TR2	Johnny Wallwork/Harold Brookes
1955	Standard Ten	Jimmy Ray/Brian Harrocks
1956	Aston Martin DB2	Lyndon Sims/Tony Ambrose/Roger Jones
1957	– Event not held –	
1958	Sunbeam Rapier II	Peter Harper/Dr Bill Deane
1959	Ford Zephyr II	Gerry Burgess/Sam Croft-Pearson
1960	Saab 96	Erik Carlsson/Stuart Turner
1961	Saab 96	Erik Carlsson/John Brown
1962	Saab 96	Erik Carlsson/David Stone
1963	Volvo PV544	Tom Trana/Sven Lindström
1964	Volvo PV544	Tom Trana/Gunnar Thermanius
1965	BMC Mini-Cooper 1275S	Rauno Aaltonen/Tony Ambrose
1966	Ford Lotus-Cortina	Bengt Söderström/Gunnar Palm
1967	– Event not held –	

Year	Car	Driver/co-driver
1968	Saab V4	Simo Lampinen/John Davenport
1969	Lancia Fulvia Coupé 1.6HF	Harry Källström/Gunnar Häggbom
1970	Lancia Fulvia Coupé 1.6HF	Harry Källström/Gunnar Häggbom
1971	Saab V4	Stig Blomqvist/Arne Hertz
1972	Ford Escort RS1600	Roger Clark/Tony Mason
1973	Ford Escort RS1600	Timo Mäkinen/Henry Liddon
1974	Ford Escort RS1600	Timo Mäkinen/Henry Liddon
1975	Ford Escort RS1800	Timo Mäkinen/Henry Liddon
1976	Ford Escort RS1800	Roger Clark/Stuart Pegg
1977	Ford Escort RS	Björn Waldegård/Hans Thorszelius
1978	Ford Escort RS	Hannu Mikkola/Arne Hertz
1979	Ford Escort RS	Hannu Mikkola/Arne Hertz
1980	Talbot Sunbeam-Lotus	Henri Toivonen/Paul White
1981	Audi Quattro	Hannu Mikkola/Arne Hertz
1982	Audi Quattro	Hannu Mikkola/Arne Hertz
1983	Audi Quattro	Stig Blomqvist/Björn Cederberg
1984	Peugeot 205 T16	Ari Vatanen/Terry Harryman
1985	Lancia Delta S4	Henri Toivonen/Neil Wilson

1986	Peugeot 205 T16 E2	Timo Salonen/Seppo Harjanne
1987	Lancia Delta HF 4WD	Juha Kankkunen/Juha Piironen
1988	Lancia Delta Integrale	Markku Alén/Ilkka Kivimäki
1989	Mitsubishi Galant VR-4	Pentti Airikkala/Ronan McNamee
1990	Toyota Celica GT4 ST165	Carlos Sainz/Luis Moya
1991	Lancia Delta Integrale 16v	Juha Kankkunen/Juha Piironen
1992	Toyota Celica ST185	Carlos Sainz/Luis Moya
1993	Toyota Celica ST185	Juha Kankkunen/Nicky Grist
1994	Subaru Impreza 555	Colin McRae/Derek Ringer
1995	Subaru Impreza 555	Colin McRae/Derek Ringer
1996	Toyota Celica GT-Four ST205	Armin Schwarz/Denis Giraudet
1997	Subaru Impreza WRC	Colin McRae/Nicky Grist
1998	Mitsubishi Lancer Evolution	Richard Burns/Robert Reid
1999	Subaru Impreza WRC	Richard Burns/Robert Reid
2000	Subaru Impreza WRC	Richard Burns/Robert Reid
2001	Peugeot 206 WRC	Marcus Grönholm/Timo Rautiainen
2002	Subaru Impreza WRC	Petter Solberg/Phil Mills
2003	Subaru Impreza WRC	Petter Solberg/Phil Mills
2004	Subaru Impreza WRC	Petter Solberg/Phil Mills
2005	Subaru Impreza WRC	Petter Solberg/Phil Mills
2006	Ford Focus RS WRC	Marcus Grönholm/Timo Rautiainen
2007	Ford Focus RS WRC	Mikko Hirvonen/Jarmo Lehtinen
2008	Citroën C4 WRC	Sébastien Loeb/Daniel Elena
2009	Citroën C4 WRC	Sébastien Loeb/Daniel Elena
2010	Citroën C4 WRC	Sébastien Loeb/Daniel Elena
2011	Ford Fiesta RS WRC	Jari-Matti Latvala/Miikka Anttila
2012	Ford Fiesta RS WRC	Jari-Matti Latvala/Miikka Anttila
2013	VW Polo R WRC	Sébastien Ogier/Julien Ingrassia
2014	VW Polo R WRC	Sébastien Ogier/Julien Ingrassia
2015	VW Polo R WRC	Sébastien Ogier/Julien Ingrassia
2016	VW Polo R WRC	Sébastien Ogier/Julien Ingrassia
2017	Ford Fiesta WRC	Elfyn Evans/Daniel Barritt
2018	Ford Fiesta WRC	Sébastien Ogier/Julien Ingrassia

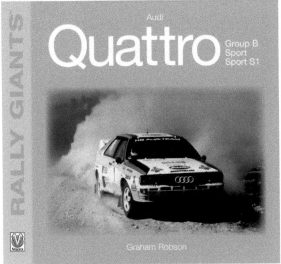

ISBN: 978-1-787111-10-3

ISBN: 978-1-787113-22-0

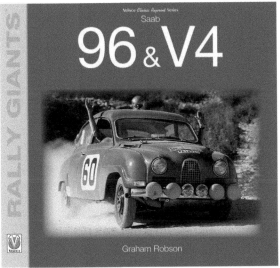

ISBN: 978-1-787113-32-9

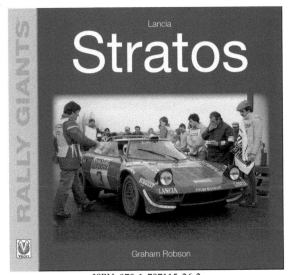

ISBN: 978-1-787115-26-2

Great value for money and packed with pictures, facts and feats from the annals of international rallying, this series tells the story of the cars and people that have made a big impression in the record books and the minds of rally enthusiasts the world over.

Paperback • 19.5x21cm • 128 pages

For more information and price details, visit our website at www.veloce.co.uk • email: info@veloce.co.uk
Tel: +44(0)1305 260068

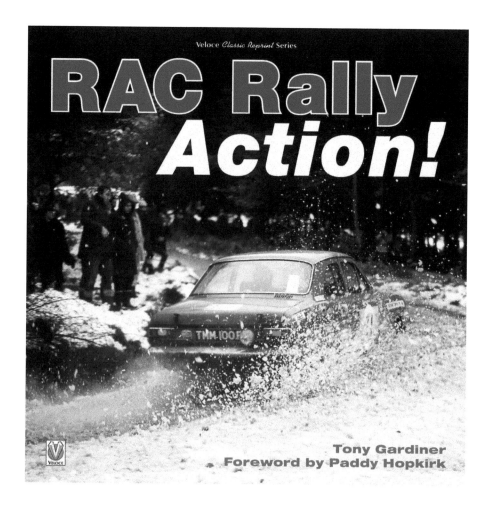

The next best thing to being there! Covering the pre-WRC 'Rally of the Forests' period. An incredibly detailed and highly illustrated review of a great era of rallying. Over 250 original photographs, and reproductions of rally documents, including regulations, programmes, road books, and crew notes.

ISBN: 978-1-787112-29-2
Paperback • 22.5x22.5cm • 208 pages • 335 pictures

For more information and price details, visit our website at www.veloce.co.uk • email: info@veloce.co.uk
Tel: +44(0)1305 260068

Lasting six weeks and covering 16,000 miles from London to Mexico City via some of the most varying, tortuous and difficult terrain on three continents, the 1970 World Cup Rally was a unique high-speed event. Attracting many serious works teams such as Ford and British Leyland, it was, and remains, the toughest rally of all time.

ISBN: 978-1-787112-28-5
Paperback • 22.5x22.5cm • 208 pages • 237 pictures

For more information and price details, visit our website at www.veloce.co.uk • email: info@veloce.co.uk
Tel: +44(0)1305 260068

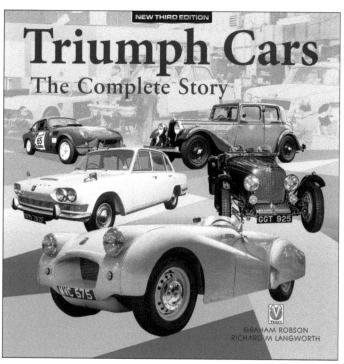
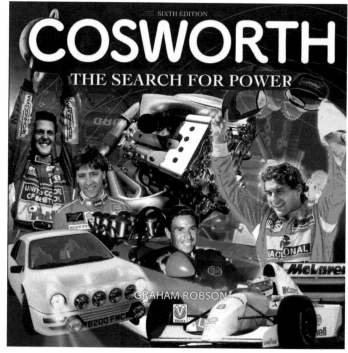

INDEX